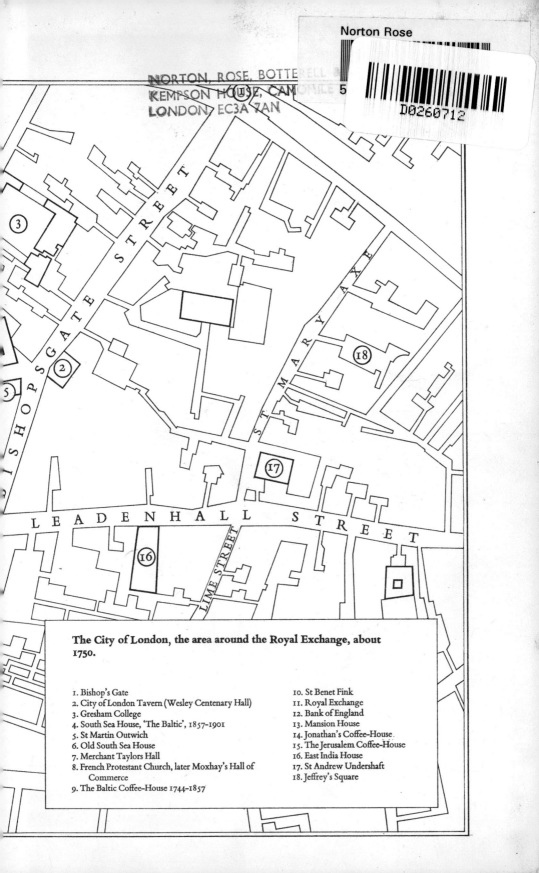

The City of London, the area around the Royal Exchange, about 1750.

1. Bishop's Gate
2. City of London Tavern (Wesley Centenary Hall)
3. Gresham College
4. South Sea House, 'The Baltic', 1857-1901
5. St Martin Outwich
6. Old South Sea House
7. Merchant Taylors Hall
8. French Protestant Church, later Moxhay's Hall of Commerce
9. The Baltic Coffee-House 1744-1857
10. St Benet Fink
11. Royal Exchange
12. Bank of England
13. Mansion House
14. Jonathan's Coffee-House
15. The Jerusalem Coffee-House
16. East India House
17. St Andrew Undershaft
18. Jeffrey's Square

THE BALTIC EXCHANGE

THE HISTORY OF A
UNIQUE MARKET

The Coat of Arms of the Baltic Mercantile and Shipping Exchange

HUGH BARTY-KING

The Baltic Exchange

THE HISTORY OF A
UNIQUE MARKET

HUTCHINSON BENHAM
LONDON

Hutchinson Benham Ltd
3 Fitzroy Square, London W1

An imprint of the Hutchinson Group

London Melbourne Sydney Auckland
Wellington Johannesburg and agencies
throughout the world

First published 1977
© The Baltic Exchange 1977

Set in Monotype Bembo

Printed in Great Britain by
The Anchor Press Ltd, and bound by
Wm Brendon & Son Ltd, both of
Tiptree, Essex

ISBN 0 09 128050 8

For truth and straightforward dealing – except perhaps in the sale of horses – the English had unusual respect. A liar or one afraid to avow his beliefs was despised; there was no place in their public life for a coward. Attempts to introduce a secret ballot into the electoral system were resisted as un-English on the ground that the franchise was a trust which an elector was bound to exercise publicly. 'Whatever he did', Bewick wrote of a neighbour, 'was done in open day, for, as he feared no man, he scorned to sulk or to do anything by stealth.' This insistence on frank dealing had a profound influence on Britain's overseas empire and trade. It caused peoples on whom the expansion of the English impinged, if not to like, to trust them. 'I would rather sacrifice Gwalior and every other portion of India ten times over' Wellington wrote, 'to preserve our credit for scrupulous good faith.'

ARTHUR BRYANT, *The Age of Elegance 1812–1822*, 1950

Contents

II. BALTIC, MOXHAY'S, JERUSALEM AND
SHIPPING EXCHANGE

III. THE BALTIC EXCHANGE

List of Illustrations

COLOUR PLATES

BLACK AND WHITE PLATES

Author's Preface

The central feature of any exchange is its Floor. For the succeeding generations of London merchants, shipowners and shipbrokers who are the subject of this study, the Floor was at the Royal Exchange, Paul's Walk, Moxhay's Hall of Commerce, the Baltic Coffee-House subscription room, the Jerusalem, the London Shipping Exchange, the Baltic Exchange – 'commercial resorts' all.

The centrepiece of the story is the Baltic Coffee-House and the Baltic committee which transformed its regulars first into subscribers and then into members of the Baltic Exchange. It is a bewildering title for a world chartering centre, and I have been at pains to account for it in the early chapters by pinpointing the importance of the Baltic Sea to British shipping since Henry IV gave royal letters of privilege to the Baltic Adventurers in 1404, and tracing the rise of the genus 'Baltic Merchant' to whom the Exchange owes its name.

I found nothing new to say about the Royal Exchange, but I am privileged to be the first person to whom the directors of the Baltic have given access to two sources of information not used by Mr J. A. Findlay for his *Short History* of 1927, and for this I am very grateful. These are the contents of the wooden chest in the vaults of St Mary Axe which have lain untouched for seventy years, being the incoming correspondence to the Baltic committee over their forty-five years' occupation of South Sea House from 1857, and the minutes of the Baltic committee for the same period and for the two years after vacating South Sea House. I am indebted to Mr Derek Walker, Secretary of the Baltic, for his help and co-operation, and to the late Mr Geoffrey Broughton of the Exchange staff who was in charge of the archives for his services as pilot along the shelves deep below the well-named Bury Street.

The correspondence from 1823 to 1857 while the Baltic was at 58 Threadneedle Street has not survived, nor have the board minutes of the Baltic Company, only the first visitors' book and several manuscript and printed documents, many inherited from the Jerusalem. James Findlay took several years assembling his material and what he did not use he put into a folder, the contents of which have been largely drawn on in the present book – articles from magazines now defunct like *Chambers Journal* and the *Ludgate Illustrated Magazine*, and cuttings and notes of great interest including the long memorandum from Sir Theo Angier. My thanks are due to a Baltic member, Mr Tom Dodd, for his valuable paper on life on the Exchange between the wars.

There is little published material on the London Corn Trade Association (now part of the Grain and Feed Trade Association), and I am grateful to GAFTA for making available to me the minutes of the LCTA from 1884, and the London Cattle Food Trade Association minute book 1906 to 1912.

It was decided to apply the Thirty Year Rule, so I had access only to the first eight volumes of the board minutes of the Baltic Mercantile and Shipping Exchange Ltd, up to September 1943, and the story ends with the Baltic, which had to suspend its activities to all intents and purposes during World War II, returning to business in 1946. I am grateful to those directors of the Baltic who took time to study the manuscript, in particular Mr M. T. Turnbull, chairman 1973–5, and give it their blessing.

Research has involved listening as well as reading, and I am indebted to all those who took the trouble to talk to me about the particular aspect of the story of which they had special knowledge: Professor Ralph Davis of Leicester University, author of *The Rise of the English Shipping Industry in the 17th and 18th Centuries*; Mr Robert Craig of the Department of History, University College, London, editor of the journal *Maritime History*; Mr Richard Storey, Chief Assistant Registrar, the National Register of

Archives; the late Mr Bryant Lillywhite, author of *London Coffee Houses;* Mr C. A. Howard, secretary of the London Average Market Letter Committee; Mr Albert Morris of the Institute of Chartered Shipbrokers; the late Mr Jack Logan, secretary of the Airbrokers Association; and his successor Mr John L. Jones; Mr J. C. S. Mackie, director general, and Mr W. J. Englebright, secretary, of the Grain and Feed Trade Association; Mr Derek Reffold, secretary of the Federation of Oils, Seeds and Fats Associations; Mr J. D. Hollis, Public Relations Officer, the Stock Exchange; Mr David Larner, Chief Information Officer, Lloyd's; Sir Leslie Phillips, c.b.e.; Mr Cyril Warwick; Mr Geoffrey Cook; the late Mr Alfred Bunker; Mr Morley Barnes; Mr Richard Hyde; Mr Allan Reid; Mr Peter Harding; Mr Geoffrey Playford; Mr Gilbert Findlay, o.b.e.; Mr Jack Walker; Mr A. A. Hooker; the late Mr Hal Saich; the late Mr William Frame; Mr Herbert Warrington; Mr Arthur Kirby; Mr Desmond Harper, and others.

I am particularly grateful for assistance given me by Dr A. E. J. Hollaender, in 1970 Keeper of Manuscripts, Guildhall Library, and the staff of the library, and by the editor and editorial staff of *Fairplay* in providing access to their back numbers; and for information and co-operation in a variety of ways from: Mr Basil Fehr of Frank Fehr & Co Ltd; Mr H. J. Blott of Glover Brothers (London) Ltd who sent their centenary booklet, 1853–1953; Mr R. G. Pendered of Bunge & Co Ltd; Dr E. W. Ferrier, Group Historian, BP; Mr G. A. Hone of C. W. Kellock & Co Ltd who sent their centenary booklet, 1820–1920; the late Mr Charles Edmonds, of Harris & Dixon; Mr R. Badrock, secretary of J. Henry Schroder Wagg & Co Ltd; Mr J. W. Whitwell of Price's Patent Candle Co Ltd; Mr P. A. Metaxa, RHM Flour Mills Ltd; Mr R. Griffiths of Spillers Ltd; Mr C. D. W. Souter of W. A. Souter & Co Ltd; Mr Randall Monier-Williams and Miss Gough of the Tallow Chandlers Company; Mr Paul Clifton-Ivall. editor of *The Agricultural Merchant;* Miss Ruth Samuels, Assistant Public Relations Officer, Timber Trade Federation of UK; Mr Richard Brown, Librarian, Port of London Authority; Mrs Joan Varley, Lincolnshire Archives Office; Mr David Bull, Librarian, Lloyd's; Miss Betty Masters, Deputy Keeper of Records, Corporation of

London; Miss Maureen Staniforth, Information Library, Unilever Ltd; Miss F. Coates, Post Office Records, St Martins-le-Grand; Mr Rodney Crouch, Public Relations Officer, British Transport Hotels, and Mr Allen Short, manager of the Charing Cross Hotel; Mr A. D. Campbell, Deputy General Manager, Reuters; Mr Caston Levi-Tilley, Instone Air Transport; Mr Norman Bidgood who lent the BAODS jubilee production programme of 1957 with the potted history since 1907; Mr Piero Sraffa, of the Marshall Library, Cambridge; Mr R. F. Sturges, of the Institute of Historical Research, London University; and the staffs of the Public Record Office, HM Customs and Excise Library, the National Maritime Museum Library, the Ministry of Agriculture Library, the Historical MSS Commission, the London Topographical Society, the British Museum Newspaper Library at Colindale, Companies Registration Office, the Business Archives Council Library, Bishopsgate Institute Library, the Baltic Exchange Library, the Bank of Scotland, 38 Threadneedle Street (once South Sea House), and the Secretary of the City of London Club (once Old South Sea House).

I am grateful to the Trustees of the National Maritime Museum for permission to reproduce material from the log of the *Benjamin* (John Lidgett, master) in their library; to the Keeper of Manuscripts, Guildhall Library, for permission to transcribe and reproduce extracts from the papers of Lane Hankey & Co and John Hubbard & Co in the department's custody; to Ward Lock Ltd for permission to print extracts from *Life on the 'Baltic'* by 'Baltico'; to the editor of *Punch* for *A Ballad of the 'Baltic'* from the issue of 11 December, 1918; to the editor of *Fairplay International Shipping Journal* for numerous quotations and the drawing of the proposed new exchange in St Mary Axe from the issue of November 23, 1899; to the editor of *Lloyd's List* for extracts; to David & Charles Ltd for extracts from the article by Susan Fairlie 'Shipping in the Anglo-Russian Grain Trade to 1870 – Part I' in vol. 1, No. 2 of *Maritime History*, September 1971.

The quotations from C. B. A. Behrens's *Merchant Shipping and the Demands of War*, and transcripts of Crown-copyright records in the Public Record Office, appear with permission of the Controller of Her Majesty's Stationery Office. I am grateful to HM Commissioners of Customs & Excise for kindly allowing me access to the copy of *Tables of the Revenue* etc. Part III, 1820–1833 in their library, but of course the responsibility for the use I have made of it is mine.

I would like to thank Mr John Long for his assistance in the writing of the Postscript.

I am grateful to Professor Ralph Davis, Professor of Economic History in the University of Leicester and to Mr Alan Pearsall, Historian, National Maritime Museum, for reading drafts of the first part of the book leading to the formation of the Baltic Exchange, and for their helpful comments.

H. B-K.

Foreword

by Sir Charles Trinder, G.B.E., M.A., D.SC, F.I.C.S.
Lord Mayor of London, 1968–9

The many people who have never seen the Floor of the Baltic Exchange or even heard of it, will not only be enlightened by this book, but also rewarded.

The high principles of conduct that have made the Baltic and its members a universally trusted institution, though central to the historian's theme, are but the background to his wide sweeping view. The life of this institution is a part of history, and more specifically a part of London.

London is very old; very competent; very jealous of her reputation; steeped in tradition, yet ever willing to learn. All this, save very great age, is true also of the Baltic.

When the Livery Companies were taking form (and we should not forget that they were religiously based foundations) the shipmasters and merchants who congregated in Lombard Street, and later in the Royal Exchange, were guided by, and believed in, the good custom of London. That good custom is still ours today.

In the 1720s the 'unacceptable face of capitalism' swindled thousands. The merchants and brokers, who were the forerunners of the Exchange, met to draw up rules of good conduct.

Through devastating wars, through booms and slumps, ever affected by national or commercial crises occurring in any part of the world at any time, the Baltic has retained its world importance, its efficiency and its reputation.

The institutions to which we belong are the children of history. They also make it, and in doing so profoundly affect all those who come after. For this and for many other reasons Mr Barty-King's wide-ranging work will be of great value to all who love London.

22 Southampton Place,   C.T.
London, WC1

I

WHERE MERCHANT MEETS CARRIER

For the increase of the shipping and the encouragement of the navigation of this nation, which under the good providence and protection of God is so great a means of the welfare and safety of this commonwealth; be it enacted . . .

Preamble to the Navigation Act of 1651

That the letting Ships to Freight to other Nations is profitable.

Charles King, *The British Merchant*, 'General Maxims in Trade', 1721

1. Mercantile Adventurers

Though the telephone is generally regarded as advancing the process of civilization, to many the conduct of business across a wire, when the voice is the sole medium, the inflections are distorted and the accompanying grimaces absent, is a poor substitute for the face-to-face confrontation in which the word which is to be the bond must be given openly, where mental reservations, exaggerations and downright lies can be detected in the twitch of the eyes, the pursing of the lips, the shrug of the shoulders, the false note of insincerity which no telephone line will ever convey.

Apart from that, if the buying and selling of commodities and services was done every day entirely between couples at either end of a telephone or teleprinter, or either side of a desk in an office for that matter, no one would know what everyone else was paying, no rate could be established against which everyone else could notch up a loss or a gain. The answer to the question, What is everyone paying? is never available when single transactions are carried out in isolation, only when they take place openly in a pool with a level which can rise and fall. The coming into existence of a market protected the lone operator from the seller who sought to gain from the bidder's ignorance of what others were bidding. A market created a floating rate, known to all, which remained when the market place was deserted, constituted the starting point of the activities of those who were to gather there the following morning and, in the case of the market for settling the rate for the carrying trade, which involved ships tramping the oceans, was taken as its regulator by *the world* whose office hours covered the clock.

This continuing role of market and market place gave buyers and sellers a relationship, lacking in conditions of isolated transactions, akin to that of members of a club. Interdependence, breeding a cogent *esprit de corps*, bound them by obligations at first unwritten and later embodied in a written code of behaviour. It was a code however that many saw as applying not purely to their activities in the market place. For these commerce was something which should be governed by the same moral code as any other activity; business was not a compartment of life which for some reason had ethics of its own looser than those which conditioned behaviour between men and men, men and women, in their homes, in their social relationships. The practice of such a creed was made easier by the inescapable interlacing of commercial and social life. Meeting daily not only in the market place but also over drinks at the bar, at lunch, rowing in an eight together, in a football team and devising practical jokes for New Year's Eve, it was difficult for one *socius* to tell another a lie to his face – twice.

The service provided by the carrying trade had its market price like any commodity. It was known as the freight, a word which confusingly has three meanings: the cost of hiring a vessel, the activity of hiring and the goods which constitute the cargo. In the City of London the place where the freight (in the sense of the freight rate) was established, along with the information of a necessarily more complicated nature than that required for the comparatively simple transaction of buying and selling wool or corn, was first of all a street.

In the days when a merchant lived as well as worked in the City, all he had to do was to take a short walk into Lombard Street and there he could find standing, talking, gesticulating, laughing, sneezing, scratching their heads, rubbing their hands, all the people he would want to meet in a day's business and most of those he was particularly anxious to avoid.

Lumbard Strete dates from the reign of Edward III (1327–77) who farmed out the sources of royal revenue to Italian merchants and bankers from Florence who set up shop in the king of

England's capital to be near the client. Their descendants became financiers to anyone able to buy their services or hire their capital. The name and activities of the Lombardi stuck to the short street which ran (and still runs) from Poultry to Gracechurch Street – the market place which provided a resort for the open-air exchange of pleasantries, information and contracts. It was the setting the Italians preferred. They made no effort to come to terms with the climate, but suffered the cold and the wet because they knew the value of maintaining the tradition which had given this particular stretch of cobble stones an aura almost mystical in character which shone on whatever was said or done there. The making of an agreement in London invested it with a trustworthiness which perhaps it did not always merit, but more and more came to acknowledge that the word of an Englishman given on Lombard Street was his bond.

London clung to its open street tradition longer than other capital cities. In 1537, when Henry VIII was on the throne, the business of Richard Gresham, a leading London merchant, took him to Antwerp in the Netherlands, the then financial centre of the world. There he saw what amounted to a continuous fair being held in a big building called the Bourse. When he returned to London he wrote to Thomas Cromwell, Henry's Chancellor, and suggested that a similar building be erected in the City of London, preferably in the Lombard Street where merchants and bankers were already in the habit of congregating. But the Mayor and Corporation, to whom the matter was referred, turned the idea down. The merchants of London, they said, preferred to meet as they had always done, in the street. And that, for the time being, was that.

It was convenient to have a meeting place 'on your doorstep'. A large area was unnecessary as the number of merchants – the word denoted *overseas* traders – who operated on their own account in London was small. In 1537 little overseas trade was undertaken further afield than what was called Nearby Europe – towns on the coastline from Hamburg just south of the Danish peninsula which bars the entrance to the belts of water which form the Baltic Sea, Mediterranean of the North, to the Spanish town of Seville. It was the legacy of the inertia of ancestors who left the hazardous business of foreign trade to foreigners. Moreover, small merchant ships of light tonnage and draught had no special attachment to the deep water of the Thames, though London was always the largest port and handled wool exporting and wine importing which constituted the greater part of England's medieval trade. Most of the rest was carried on from east coast ports and from Southampton, favoured by the Italians.

Merchants' risks were reduced by banding together. They formed gilds and companies and fellowships. In 1404 Royal Letters of Privilege were issued to a group of English merchants calling themselves the Baltic Adventurers. But they soon ran foul of the biggest monopoly of them all, the German merchants of Cologne, Hamburg and Brunswick who, with those of the Baltic cities of Lubeck and Danzig, were mounting a sophisticated exercise in collective bargaining known as the Hanseatic League. Within seventy years the English Baltic Adventurers had disbanded. By 1470 the Hanseatic League had regained full control of all traffic between England and the Baltic Sea.

That the cobbles of Lombard Street sufficed for the City's merchanting business in 1537 was due more than anything else to the unique position in world trade held by the Hanseatic League. Initially, for want of native claimants to the job, the League were invited to establish an organization in London to handle on an exclusive basis the export of English wool and other raw materials, and the import of the more valuable finished products. They were known as the Easterlings and their headquarters and warehouse were on the north bank of the Thames. This building they called their Stapelhof or Staelhof, and their English hosts turned the word into Stilliard or Stillyard or the more confusing 'Steelyard' (which never had anything to do with steel).

The Stillyard was the great store for the whole of England. In it were kept raw products for exports – tin, hides, wool – and the range of imports handled by the Easterlings such as wheat, rye, wax and tar. The Easterlings organized themselves on the lines of a religious order with a yearly elected Master and committee, communal meals, and a commercial brotherhood vowed to celibacy. The gates of the fortified walls of this grave monastic organization dedicated to Mammon were closed every evening at an early hour. Their discipline and methods, though daunting, were, not surprisingly, highly successful – the word 'sterling' derives from them – and long before 1537 they had made themselves an indispensable part of England's commercial life – well, almost.

One part of that life over which they never had any control was the buying and selling of what used to be called corn (as in Corn Laws and Corn Exchange), but to avoid confusion with modern sweet corn is nowadays called grain (but until that time is reached in this book the product will continue to be referred to as corn).

So long as enough corn was grown to feed the whole of England everyone obtained the bread he needed by dealing direct with the producer. It was 'enough' only when harvests were good, and was yearly becoming less than enough as the rising population widened the gap between supply and demand even in normal years. To feed the poor at prices they could afford irrespective of good or bad harvests was regarded by the Corporation of London as their special responsibility. They ordered City livery companies and chartered guilds to maintain a supply of corn in their livery halls and to sell it at the prices and at the times they told them to. If a company had no room in its livery hall, it had to rent space in the huge granary on London Bridge known as the Bridge House.

The public granary system of London was born out of a high sense of social responsibility and was maintained for two centuries in the face of cynical opposition from those who chose to black-guard the authorities for denying them what they considered a legitimate field of private enterprise. The City livery companies jibbed at their enforced 'public duty', and in 1546 the Corporation appointed two aldermen in weekly rotation to ensure that the markets were always well supplied and prices kept down. In their view the interests of the consumer were paramount. The un-reliability of the weather was bad enough. They could not allow the additional uncertainty of how and when the private dealer would respond to scarcity to stand in the way of a mission which they regarded as one of honour and trust.

It was a short step to Lombard Street, up Thames Street, Fish Street Hill and Gracechurch Street from Billingsgate Dock and the Custom House just below London Bridge, London's only bridge across the Thames. Ships' commanders home from a voyage would go there to join the merchants on whom their voyaging depended, and report the transactions they had carried out at their various destinations, the cargoes they had found for the return, the ships they had passed, the storms and pirates they had encountered. The captains would be eager to hear from the merchants what was in the offing for the next voyage, to learn of the death of the respected Mr Barclay, the sudden bankruptcy of Mr Arnold, the arrest of Mr Furlong and all the other news since they had been away. Information was what people came to Lombard Street for, whether by word of mouth or from the letters which the captains brought in their ships and delivered to those who stood and complained, as they did in 1545, about the latest piece of state interference, the establishment of a Navy Board for the civil administration of the navy which was responsible for the building and repair of ships and the buying of naval stores.

The Navy Board became the sole customer for pitch and tar (for coating and preserving decks and hulls), hemp (for rope-making), timber (for planking) and spars (for masts). Throughout the era of wooden ships English oak was used only for hull timber, particularly for framing. All the wood for planking – the decks – was best quality timber imported from Poland and Prussia through Dantzick (as it was then spelt) and Königsberg, the Prussian towns on the East Sea (the Baltic), from Riga, the Livonian town further north at the top of the Gulf of Livonia, and from inland Bohemia (which had Prague as its capital and is now Czechoslovakia) taken via the river Elbe to the port of Hamburg in the German Ocean (North Sea). The other naval stores were likewise 'outlandish' and 'East Country goods' from 'Eastland'.

The establishment of the Navy Office was welcomed by many as regularizing the Baltic trade and emphasizing its importance, but there was little enthusiasm among the merchants on Lombard Street eight years later when they read the Prospectus and Testimonie of Richard Eden for a joint stock company for 'the newe navigation and discoverie of the Kingdom of Muscovia by the Northeast' which he issued in 1553. Apart from exposing their conservative attachment to Nearby Europe (albeit modified around 1400 by certain of the more enterprising merchants opening up a trade with Turkey), Eden's plan threatened competition in the naval stores trade. Worse, it was what every self-respecting merchant despised and feared, a monopoly.

It was not to be a 'regulated' company however, with a royal charter, but, because of the hazard of voyaging into an undeveloped and unknown region, the risks were to be shared. Subscribers were invited for a single voyage or a series of voyages, or to the 'Common Stocke'. The Muscovy Company was England's first joint stock company for trade and, prompted by the breakdown of trade with Turkey, attempted to find more lasting overseas markets for English goods beyond the English Channel, the British Sea, the East Sea and the Bay of Biscay.

The prospectus said:

Those merchandises which strangers in the memories of their ancestors used to seek and desire were now neglected and not sought after, and the prices fetched for them very low, yet foreign merchandise was highly valued and big prices paid for them. So certain grave citizens of London and men of greater wisdom and careful for the good of their country began to think with themselves how this mischiefe might be remedied.

For many years part of this charter hung on the walls of the offices of John Hubbard & Company at 17 St Helens Place where there was also the chair in which John Cabot sat when he was Governor of the Muscovy Company.

An expedition left Radclife with Richard Chanceler in command on May 20, 1553. After some weeks news came to the merchants on Lombard Street that two of the ships had been lost in the snows of Lapland, but that the third under Richard Chancellor (to give him his modern spelling) had gone on to 'discover' Russia by penetrating the Arctic Circle, rounding North Cape in the Frozen Sea or Northern Ocean, coming south again into the White Sea and landing at Archangel in the Bay of St Nicholas.

From Archangel Chancellor was escorted inland to Moscow where he was received by the Tsar, Ivan the Terrible, who gave him a letter for King Edward. It was all going to plan. Richard Chancellor returned to London in the *Edward Bonaventure*, presented Ivan's letter to his sovereign and set about organizing the Muscovy Company as the sole importer and exporter of commodities to and from Russia – furs, felt, cordage, masts, wax, tallow. Hemp, another of the naval requisites, was at first sent in rough state, but soon the company established a rope works on the Russian side. The company's intention was to trade fairly and generously and establish a monopoly. The 'Russia merchant', who plays so large a part in this story, had arrived.

The merchants on Lombard Street watched the successful building up of the Muscovy Company's exclusive trade with Russia with some misgiving, and the chance of finding a loophole through which they could themselves legally participate in this obviously lucrative trade seemed further reduced when in 1555 Mary I granted the company a royal charter with the wider title 'The Mysterie and Companie of the Merchant Adventurers for the discoverie of Regions Dominions Islands and places unknown', though defining quite clearly what was meant by Muscovy. But when, three years later, the Russians took the port of Narva in Esthonia, which was outside the Muscovy Company's trading area as given in the charter, merchants who were not members of the company saw their chance and took it. They sent expeditions to Narva and started trading with the Russians. The company complained to Parliament, but there was little they could do about it. There was further rejoicing on Lombard Street when Queen Elizabeth, who came to the throne the year the Russians took Narva, at once abolished the law which restricted English merchants to shipping goods in English vessels or ships belonging to the country of the goods' origin.

For years the rulers of England had placed value on the existence of a native merchant marine for its own sake and for the prestige it brought, though to be fair to the Plantagenets and Tudors their merchant ships were also the basis of their navies. Queen Elizabeth broke new ground by being persuaded that there might be value in something called 'shipping', in the carrying trade as such, from which profit could be derived – albeit 'invisible' and incalculable in terms of wood and canvas – which was independent of ship ownership.

As Rupert Jarvis has pointed out,

the matter of the precise circumstances in the foreign port in which English-owned merchandise of foreign origin might or might not be lawfully shipped to an English port in foreign bottoms, was one to be nicely weighed between the interests of the English shipowner, interested in the greatest quantity of freighting, and the interests of the English merchant concerned about the lowest freight rate . . . The Eastland merchants protested that by these restraints 'the strangers themselves will easily import the commodities of those countries at better rates'.

('Ship Registry – 1707', *Maritime History*, Vol. 1, No 1, April 1971)

Queen Elizabeth's repeal of the Act of 1381 (and Henry VII's of 1488) was to mollify the jealousy of England's commercial rivals and anticipate retaliation. But it was only temporary. The following year (1559) an Act 'for the maintenance of the Navy' restored the restrictions and the brief spell of free trade was over.

Queen Mary had dismissed Thomas Gresham, Sir Richard's son, from the post of Royal Agent or King's Merchant at Antwerp, to which he had been appointed by Edward VI, but Elizabeth re-appointed him. In 1561 Thomas's factor in Antwerp, Richard Clough, wrote to him expressing surprise that 'considering what a City London is . . . that in so many years the same found not the means to make a Burse, but merchants must be contented to stand and walk in the rain, more like pedlars than merchants'. Many however took cover at this time in Paul's Walk, as the nave of the old St Paul's Cathedral was known. Services were held behind the rood screen and the 300-foot nave became the resort of souvenir sellers, letter writers, lawyers, soldiers of fortune, servants and merchants, soliciting business and doing deals. But it was all rather undignified and inadequate. So Thomas Gresham, mindful of his father's plea of twenty-six years before, re-submitted the idea to the Court of Aldermen in 1563, and this time they accepted his 'very gentle and fryndely offer'. They were even persuaded to provide a site between Thread Needle Street and Corn Hill, and Gresham engaged a Flemish architect and had the place built at his own expense. The Queen laid the foundation stone on June 7, 1566 (the year she confirmed the Muscovy Company's charter) and by Christmas 1568 work was far enough advanced to allow such merchants as felt able to do so to leave the thin line of Lombard Street and saunter through Exchange Alley to sample the rectangular advantages of a more formal commercial resort of the kind many of them had already used in Antwerp. On January 23, 1571, Gloriana rode into the City in full state to declare Sir Thomas's 'comely Burse' open, and put the royal seal of approval upon it by allowing it to be called the Royal Exchange. The magnificence and scale of this brick building can be judged from the print opposite page 60. It was, after all, the Renaissance.

Little is known about how this first Royal Exchange was run, but it was certainly spacious. According to Walter Besant, the high spirits of the young apprentices whose homes were in the City got the better of them once the merchants had finished, and they used the floor as a football field. But in 1576 all games of football were banned from the Royal Exchange. There seems to have been little sacred about Paul's Walk however at any hour. As L. W. Cowie has written, 'At the end of the 16th century it was said that more deals were still made in the cathedral than in the whole of the Royal Exchange which by then had been established for nearly thirty years.'

The departure of the merchants from the Royal Exchange which signified the all-clear for football was not the end of their business day. When their legs began to ache they took themselves for relief and refreshment – the Royal Exchange had neither urinals nor bars – to the taverns where the talk continued at benches over glasses of wine and there was always the chance of meeting a new acquaintance anxious to do business, or picking up a useful piece of information from a tired captain just back from Memel or Riga, from the latest broadsheet or from a letter telling them their ship had come in.

The establishment of an exchange in the centre of London gave the City's merchants not only a new meeting place out of the rain – though in fact it was only semi-covered on the lines of a cloister – but new heart. For to their even greater delight the Queen, at the instigation of Sir Thomas Gresham, followed up her opening of the Royal Exchange by putting an end to the 500-year domination of the detested Easterlings and their sinister Stillyard. 'At a stroke' the Queen boldly declared all the privileges of the Stillyard merchants null and void for ever, and forbade them ever again to handle the export of English wool. The Easterlings had to be quit of England by February 28, 1597. The Stillyard was handed over to the Admiralty who used it as a store till the South Eastern Railway Company tore down its hefty walls in 1863 to make room for Cannon Street Station.

London merchants read the Queen's proclamation at Royal Exchange with considerable relish and set about taking over where the Easterlings had left off. They were soon forming groups of staplers (to operate from a fixed overseas station) and companies of merchant adventurers, to try their fortunes at marketing English manufactures wherever they could, in Northern Europe as well as Nearby Europe.

Inspired by the enterprise of the Muscovy Company, a group of Baltic merchants of London formed themselves into the Eastland Company. It was incorporated by royal charter for trading to 'Eastland' – Norway, Sweden and countries bordering the Baltic Sea except Narva which had now been made part of the Muscovy Company's territory. A big part of the trade of its sixty-five members was the importation of the ever-needed naval stores.

Other events had helped to shift the axis of European trade. The sack of Antwerp by Spanish mutineers in 1576 and the Dutch cutting the city off from the sea in 1585 had put paid to her long reign as the financial centre of the world. Hamburg and Amsterdam were the main beneficiaries – and eventually London.

If the year 1587 can be said to have been the climax of English penetration of the Baltic, it was also the year in which the merchants on the Royal Exchange first began to realize that successful though the Queen and Gresham had been in handling the Hanseatics, their real commercial rivals were going to be not the Germans but the Dutch.

The Dutch were penetrating further north than the English – into Finland even. By 1600 they were doing more trade than the

B

English in Archangel. The grain, hemp and flax ports on the south coasts of the Baltic – Danzig, Königsberg and Riga – became dependent on Dutch middlemen for contacts with the West. They operated at lower levels of cost and with more advanced commercial methods. They were more flexible than the top-heavy state-regulated English company.

The impetus to go into Russia fell away. In 1602 the Muscovy Company mounted only two voyages, and three years later there was an attack in Parliament on the way it was being managed. It was accused of being a monopoly within a monopoly; fifteen of its eighty shareholders were directors; they acted 'as one man', the very opposite of the opening up of commerce by the free exchange of information and bargaining on the floor of the Royal Exchange. They had created a corner in cordage. Worse, even their own members were not honest with one another. The Muscovy Company was having a crisis of trust, and soon underwent yet another reorganization.

With the opening of the seventeenth century, 'overseas' began to mean very much more than just North and Nearby Europe. In 1600 an East India Company was formed to trade with India and the no longer legendary Cathay; in 1606 another company was formed for the colonization of the land which Sir Walter Raleigh discovered on the other side of the once feared Atlantic and named after the Virgin Queen he served.

A merchant did his business on the floor of the Royal Exchange with roughly the same people every day – those who dealt in the kind of commodities in which he dealt, who traded with the part of the world with which he was connected. They walked and talked in the same corner, round the same pillar, up and down the same stretches of floor, every day; and when they decided to break off, they went together to the nearby tavern which they chose to patronize because of the friendliness of its proprietor, the quality and price of his wine, and the relevance of the news-sheets and pamphlets he kept to the kind of business they were interested in. Taverns soon came to identify themselves with regular customers from one or other of the 'walks' at the Royal Exchange, and gave themselves signs and names accordingly.

In 1603, or earlier, a forward-looking vintner opened a tavern on the north side of Thread Needle Street behind the Royal Exchange, to which he gave the name the Virginia Wine House. This may have been in Sun Court or further east in the house which, when street numbering was introduced in the seventeen-sixties, became No 61. At least by 1610, the date of its first known listing, another vintner opened a tavern a few houses westward, at what was to become No. 58, and called it the Antwerp Tavern. In taverns such as these raged the great controversies of merchant versus shipowner, the high cost of shipbuilding, the high cost of shipping. Fostered by the 'clubiness' of habitually meeting in the same part of the Royal Exchange and in the same taverns, common attitudes on matters of concern, informally expressed in closed circuit as it were 'within these four walls', came to be formulated and then directed at 'the authorities'. In 1615 Baltic merchants at the Virginia and the Antwerp could have been heard complaining to their shipowner friends about the high freights of English ships in the Baltic trade which were compelling them to charter foreign ships. There was no yielding by either side in the taverns or on 'Change, but the Privy Council brought both sides together with the result that an Act was passed which 'accommodated all those differences and at so easy rates as the merchants are well contented withal'. But the differences were more deep seated, and to resolve them James I ordered a commission of inquiry into 'how England's merchant shipping might be enlarged and how foreign shipping may not be employed while English want employment'. The commissioners' remedy was an ordinance by which all northern traders importing any commodity other than corn from Danzig were ordered to use English ships. This move in 1624 anticipated the wider and more famous application of the same principle by the Lord Protector. In 1618 only ninety English ships as against 1794 Dutch entered the Baltic; but with the Dutch involvement in the Thirty Years War up to 1647 forcing them to charge freights fifty per cent above their peacetime levels, English shipping acquired a more balanced share of the business.

But as soon as they disengaged themselves from the war the Dutch returned to their mercantile activities with such vigour that Cromwell decided to meet the challenge with force. But where to get the ships? Revival of the royal bounty of five shillings a ton for building ships of more than 200 tons, which had been dropped by the impecunious James I, had done little to give England either a mercantile marine capable of maintaining the country's trade or a navy fit to fight the Dutch. Dutch and French privateers were fast driving the English from the Baltic.

War hardened the conflicting interests of shipowner and merchant. To shipowners war brought opportunities for increasing profits. Risk of capture from enemy men-of-war or privateers was a legitimate excuse for them to raise freight charges. War opened up additional ways of putting their ships to use. They could hire them by the month to the Admiralty as water carriers, fire ships, hospital ships, transports; they could take out letters of marque by which captain and crew took their share of the prizes and the Lord High Admiral and the Crown took a sixth. But for the merchant, wartime convoys, which were liable to bring in, say, a whole season's supply of sugar in a single voyage, played havoc with market prices, to say nothing of presenting storage problems. For him war meant high freight rates and, perhaps worse, Government interference.

In 1650 Cromwell set up a Council of Trade and the following year introduced the Commonwealth Navigation Ordinance by which goods bought from any country in the world had to be carried to England either in English ships or in vessels belonging to the country which produced the goods. The penalty was confiscation of both goods and vessel. The resentment of the merchants on Royal Exchange, from whose steps the ordinance was published with great pomp and ceremony as an act which favoured one section of the community, the shipowners, at the expense of another, themselves, was to go on rumbling for a couple of centuries.

What price the Commonweal now? What made the minority – the shipowners – more privileged than the majority – the consumers whom the merchants served? It was patently directed by Cromwell against the hated Dutch who had made a treaty with the Danes assuring them free passage into the Baltic and sheltered and befriended the pretended Prince of Wales in his exile. It could not exclude the Dutch from the plantations but it dealt them a severe blow. It greatly curtailed, though did not end, their activities.

W. S. Lindsay wrote:

It is undeniable that from the date of these [Navigation] laws the merchant navy of England steadily increased; and that soon afterwards the power over the seas previously claimed by the Dutch was permanently transferred to the English. Whatever may have been the cause of these changes, whether the Navigation Acts or 'the stoppage of trade, insecurity of capital, inherited debts and taxes on ships' sustained by the Dutch during the war, England's maritime resources increased while those of Holland declined; and London became what Amsterdam once was, the chief emporium of the commercial world.

(*History of Merchant Shipping*, Vol. II, 1874)

While the Navigation Act of 1651 certainly revolutionized English shipping, a change of no less import to London society was introduced a year later by Daniel Edwards, an English merchant who had lived for a long time in Smyrna and who, on his return home, brought with him the habit he had acquired in Turkey of drinking the hot beverage made from crushed berries, the Turkish name for which was best written phonetically as kahveh or coffee.

The servant whom he brought with him, with a name anglicized as Pasqua Rosee, made the drink every morning for his master's breakfast, and when Edwards' friends came to visit him he invited them to try a cup. Making coffee for his master's friends took up so much of Pasqua Rosee's time that Edwards was persuaded to allow him to set up in St Michael's churchyard, off Cornhill, and devote his full time to selling cups of coffee to all and sundry. Edwards' father-in-law seems to have been behind this scheme, and he seconded his coachman, Kitt Bowman by name, to assist Rosee in his enterprise. When past misdemeanours caught up with him and Pasqua was obliged to flee the country, Bowman took over. London's first coffee-house was born, and there was no lack of imitators. The tavern keeper started serving coffee as well as wine, and many a tavern became a Tavern and Coffee-House. The drink was an antidote to alcoholic excess and was good for custom. The separate houses which sprang up, first in the City and then in fashionable Westminster, were mostly on the first floor and had one big table. A visitor climbed the stairs, paid a penny to the woman at the door, then entered and took his seat where he gave his order. No intoxicants were served, but cold soft drinks were available such as saloop or a sassafras-and-sugar drink called bocket.

With the taverns, the coffee-houses became the commercial resorts of merchants and shipping men both before and after attendance at the Royal Exchange, and in between visits to their counting houses (the first 'offices'). They multiplied throughout the rule of the Lord Protector and by the time he was in the grave, and his son had been replaced by the exiled Prince of Wales who returned from the continent as Charles II, they were an established part of the social scene. In them the merchants heard the good news of the lapsing of all Commonwealth ordinances, the un-popular Navigation Law among them, only to re-double their grumbles on learning that the king had introduced the new and more comprehensive Act for the Encouragement of Shipping and Navigation. This included a clause naming a wide range of goods which could only be imported in English ships with masters and three-quarters of their crews English, or in ships of the producing country or of the place of first shipment. These enumerated goods covered the principal products of the Baltic including masts, timber, boards, salt, pitch, tar, resin, hemp, flax – the 'naval stores' of such importance. It also covered all the products of the Russian and Turkish empires. This meant the Dutch could no longer bring the main products of Norway or the Baltic to England but the Danes, Norwegians and Swedes could. It meant the role of the Dutch as the general carriers for England was ended – a situation they were unlikely to accept. In 1665 war broke out with them once again.

But, war or peacetime competition with the Dutch notwith-standing, the purchase of naval stores had to go on. In 1660 the Navy Board was reconstituted and the victualling of the fleet was farmed out to a series of contractors who one after another ran into debt as the Treasury's lack of funds prevented it from ever being able to pay them.

The Navy Board reckoned the cost of fitting out the fleet at this time was £180 000 and of this £72 800 was for hemp (1300 tons).

It was the most costly indirect item. The best quality hemp from Riga and Königsberg came through the Baltic, and in 1661 was costing £55 a ton. In November 1665, Samuel Pepys, Clerk of the Acts at the Navy Board, purchased 300 tons through a broker, half of which was from Riga and Königsberg at £55, the rest from Flanders at £50. The following year he had to pay a merchant £57. Pepys told him he had heard that a private trader had paid £49, and was told that if the Government was prepared to pay ready money it would be charged the same.

Government policy was to buy forward and stockpile tar against an emergency, for the price was always rising. Pepys regretted the Stuarts' lack of ready money 'to tempt merchants to sell, which I perceive everybody now desires to avoid at any price almost, in confidence of gaining by keeping their goods in their hands'.

The procedure was to place a notice in the Royal Exchange and the Custom House and an advertisement in the *London Gazette* inviting bids for naval stores. For small orders the lowest offer was generally accepted. For a big contract a merchant would have to furnish sureties of people of good repute binding themselves in a fixed money bond that he would execute the order.

But to quote Ralph Davis 'by the middle of the 17th century regular demand for Norwegian and Baltic products in England was so great that the Northern trades had come to be leading users of English shipping'. The bigger ships of 200 to 300 tons came to London; only the smaller ones to such outports as Hull and Bristol. The role of the London Baltic merchant in the economy of England was a major one, and he was to maintain it for many years to come. But sea warfare cut the country off from East Country goods, so that when the first Dutch War broke out in 1652 the Navy Commissioners looked to America for masts, to the pine forests of Maine and New Hampshire.

When in 1666 the Great Fire of London destroyed Gresham's Royal Exchange along with the greater part of the buildings between it and the Thames, including the public granaries which were never revived and the wharfs and warehouses on the north bank of the river, temporary quarters were offered to merchants and shipping men at Gresham House, but most of the work which had been done at the Royal Exchange was transferred to those taverns and coffee-houses which had escaped the flames and to the establishments which rose on the old sites and on many new ones.

Plans for a second Royal Exchange were made immediately, and the new building of Portland stone was opened by Charles II in 1669. But as a commercial resort it never had the popularity of the old building. In the three-year intermission many had lost the habit, and yielded to the less formal attractions of the coffee-house.

> Now being enter'd, there's no needing
> Of complements or gentile breeding,
> For you may seat you anywhere,
> There's no respect of persons there;
> Then comes the Coffee-man to greet you,
> With welcome Sir, let me entreat you
> To tell you what you'll please to have,
> For I'm your humble humble slave.
> (*The Character of a Coffee House by an
> Eye and Ear Witness*, 1665)

Coffee-houses survived a petition from women who called coffee ninny-broth and turkey-gruel, and complained that it 'made men as unfruitful as the deserts whence the unhappy berry is said to be brought'. They survived a petition of vintners and ale-house keepers who prayed that tea, coffee and brandy should be prohibited as interfering with consumption of native barley, malt and wheat. They survived because, in days of unorganized delivery of newspapers and letters, they became useful centres for the dissemination of information and for the gathering of it by writers and traders and shipowners and shipbrokers. Moreover they were cheap, as the author of *Coffee Houses Vindicated* pointed out:

First in regard of easy expense being to wait for, or meet, a friend, a tavern-reckoning soon breeds a purse-consumption; in an ale-house you must gorge yourself with pot after pot . . . But here for a penny or two you may spend two or three hours, have the shelter of a house, the warmth of a fire, the diversion of company.

King Charles suspected they were hotbeds of conspiracy and issued a proclamation suppressing them as places 'where the disaffected meet and spread scandalous reports concerning the conduct of His Majesty and his Ministers'. The uproar which followed this cavalier treatment of a much loved institution led to the order's quick withdrawal. But his Secretaries of State had a monopoly over the news, and between 1675 and 1678 prosecuted all who infringed it.

Big Baltic importers like Edward Callender, Samuel Clark, Theodor Jacobson, Peter Joy, John Mitford, Martin Taylor, whose main client was the Admiralty, seized every opportunity to attack the established trade companies, advocate free trade, expose the illusion of the sole market theory, and the belief that commercial allegiance could be guaranteed by political allegiance or military conquest. Though not yet institutionalized, their ability to present a common front on such issues as these was sustained in large part by their daily use of the same City coffee-houses and taverns, and daily meetings at the Royal Exchange.

Proud of the sneering sobriquet of Whig, they looked down on the overdressed Tories, who patronized the fops' coffee-houses in Westminster and Whitehall, and performed the rituals of the Mother Church more from a sense of loyalty to their kind and social conformity than religious conviction. They revolted from the scandalous and economically wasteful behaviour of a merry monarch out of touch with the new spirit of the age and the growing social consciousness. In the words of J. H. Plumb, 'aggressive, suspicious, hard-fisted, relentless in the pursuit of wealth, they [the City merchants] were the sinews of England's trade'.

The middling class could not claim the unity of the landed aristocracy, but they found common ground in their reaction to the profligacy of the Restoration court and welcomed the temperance of the coffee-houses, as opposed to the drunkenness of the taverns, for sober debate and discussion on the issues of the day. The paying of a penny at the 'bar' before entry tokened agreement to abide by certain rules of conduct and behaviour, and whoever entered became 'members', as it were, of a 'club' for that day. The coffee-houses brought the social classes together.

> First, Gentry, Tradesmen, all are welcome hither
> And may without Affront sit down together.

A lively topic of conversation in the 1670s was the pamphlet of one of the wealthiest merchants of the day, Sir Josiah Child, whose son was able to build Wanstead House, the largest residence in England before it was topped by Vanbrugh's Castle Howard. The Navigation Act had been in operation eighteen years, he wrote in *A New Discourse of Trade* (written between 1670 and 1680?), but in this time not one English ship had been built fit for the Eastland trade. It was cheaper to freight a Danish or Easterling ship 'and it being so, and all men naturally led by their profit, it seems to me in vain to expect that even this Law will procure the building of one English ship fit for that employment'.

He saw beyond the immediate profit which such trade could bring, beyond the visible 'balance of trade'. He called attention to

The Trade of Denmark and Norway, the Imports from whence are certainly many times the value of our native Commodities exported thither; and yet it cannot be denied but that Trade is advantageous to the Kingdom, not only because it gives or would give employment to two hundred or three hundred sail and English shipping, if we did a little mend our Act of Navigation, but principally because the Commodities imported from thence as Timber, Pitch, Deals and Tar are of such necessary use in order to the building and supplying our Shipping that without them other Trades could not be carried on.

In his preface he gave a list 'Of Trades Lost', headed by the Russia trade where the Dutch, he said, had last year twenty-two sail of great ships and the English but one. The Navigation Act, however, had come to the rescue –

a very beneficial Act for this Kingdome especially by the Masters and Owners of Shipping and by all Seamen; yet some they are, both wise and honest Gentlemen and Merchants, that doubt whether the inconveniences it has brought with it be not greater than the conveniences. For my own part I am of the opinion that in relation to Trade, Shipping, Profit and Power it is one of the choicest and most prudent Acts that ever was made by England, and without which we had not now been Owners of half of the Shipping nor Trade nor employed half of the Seamen which we do at present.

All this made for lively reading and keen discussion in John's Coffee-House in Birchin Lane which, according to H. B. Wheatley, was 'the principal place of resort of merchants, shipbrokers or

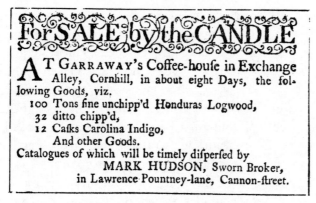

For SALE by the CANDLE

AT GARRAWAY'S Coffee-houſe in Exchange
    Alley, Cornhill, in about eight Days, the fol-
lowing Goods, viz.
    100 Tons fine unchipp'd Honduras Logwood,
    32 ditto chipp'd,
    12 Caſks Carolina Indigo,
    And other Goods.
Catalogues of which will be timely diſperſed by
            MARK HUDSON, Sworn Broker,
        in Lawrence Pountney-lane, Cannon-ſtreet.

Advertisement for a sale at Garraway's Coffee-House, 1751

ships captains for the transaction of shipping business' at this time;
at the Jamaica Coffee-House in St Michael's Alley; at Hain's
Coffee-House in Castle Court, Birchin Lane which changed its
name in 1676 to the Marine Coffee-House; in Robin's Coffee-
House in Old Jewry; at Edward Lloyd's Coffee-House in Tower
Street, where for a consideration the proprietor would arrange
protection of merchant seamen from impressment into the navy,
and had a special arrangement with the Post Office for the supply
of ships' news which attracted those concerned with the business of
indemnity and insurance; at the fashionable Garraway's Coffee-
House in Exchange Alley where wine was sold at candle auctions;
in the Virginia Wine House, the Antwerp Tavern and the Sun
Tavern, all in Thread Needle Street (and the latter maybe in Sun
Court), where coffee and chocolate were also being served in an
upstairs room. After and before hearing what news was to be had
on Royal Exchange, the active merchant went from one coffee-
house to another, to find a buyer in the first, a seller in the second,
space in a ship in a third, insurance at a fourth. For information
about the latest stock prices he went to Jonathan's Coffee-House
in Exchange Alley. In each he found a wide selection of newspapers,
custom entry forms, auction notices, price lists, announcements
giving the walk on which shipowners and commanders were to be
found at the Royal Exchange for arranging charters and passages.
In each he found a copy of Josiah Child's pamphlet and in each he

expounded his views on it anew, and on the new Act for the Regulation of Brokers upon the Royal Exchange to prevent 'all usurious Contracts and Bargains, false Chevance [acquisition of wealth] and other corrupt Devices and crafty Deceits'; on the fire which destroyed the Navy Office in Seething Lane; the resignation of the king's brother, James, Duke of York, as Lord High Admiral; the appointment of young Mr Pepys as Secretary of the Admiralty – all news stories of importance to Baltic and Russia merchants and shipbrokers, shipowners and ships' captains in 1673.

The biggest news of the year, however, was the report of the Committee of Inquiry under Sir George Downing into the decay of the Muscovy Greenland and Eastland Trade which led to the first break in the Eastland Company's monopoly. The Act for the Encouragement of the Eastland Trade, which followed the report, allowed every person, native or foreigner, to have free liberty to trade into and from Sweden, Denmark or Norway, *anything in the charter of the Eastland Company notwithstanding*. Half of the Eastland Company's exclusive trading area was taken away from it and given to private enterprise.

In 1685, according to Sven-Erik Aström who has made a study of seventeenth-century Anglo-Baltic trade, there were 108 merchants in England who imported typical Baltic products of greater value than £500. Most influential of these was Gilbert Heathcote, who began as a factor in Stockholm and by 1685 was importing a wide range of goods from Stockholm, Riga, Danzig and Königsberg, including iron, hemp, flax, potash, tar, pitch, canvas, oaken plank, linen, bristles, wainscots, pipestaves, clapboards, oaken timber and glass bottles. 'The richest commoner in England', he was the leader of the group of Whig magnates and free traders who helped to destroy the established trade companies, and not content with mere lobbying entered Parliament and ended up Lord Mayor of London.

Sir Gilbert Heathcote was one of the committee under the chairmanship of William Patterson which in 1694 set up a Bank of England in an attempt to bring order to the country's budget and prevent a recurrence of the financial shambles of the Stuarts. Two years later a permanent Board of Trade took over from the

Privy Council all matters relating to trade and the plantations, with an 'Inspector General of Imports and Exports'. The commissioners were enjoined *inter alia* 'to inform yourselves what naval stores may be furnished from our plantations'.

Dealers in stocks and shares had for long had a walk on the Royal Exchange, but when in 1697 other users of the Exchange accused them of loitering and gambling, the majority of stockbrokers took their business to nearby Jonathan's Coffee-House in Exchange Alley. Worse followed. Parliament passed an Act 'to restrain the number and ill practice of Brokers and Stock jobbers' which disallowed broking in produce unless brokers were admitted, licensed, approved and allowed by the Lord Mayor and Court of Aldermen. 'For the conveniency of Trade' ran the preamble, 'Sworn Brokers have been anciently admitted and allowed of within the City of London, and liberties for making bargains and contracts between merchant and merchant and other tradesmen were given their Goods Wares and Merchandizes and Moneys', but they had overstepped the mark. As a penalty only a hundred were given licences and their names had to be posted for all to see at the Royal Exchange. They were identified by their official silver medals and certificates of registration. They were not allowed to carry on any other trade. The provisions of this Act were perpetuated by Queen Anne and George III, but they were never very strictly regarded.

Merchants of the old school used to making their deals man to man resented the loitering and gambling of middlemen, though as business grew in volume the value of intermediaries grew more evident. In 1707 many merchants were petitioning for the Act to be repealed.

Questions of the day which were to become subjects for petitions were first debated round the tables of the coffee-houses and taverns; the first signatures were those of the regulars at the Virginia and the Antwerp, Jonathan's and Hain's. On the floor of the House of Commons the Whig cause could be pressed more directly. In 1698 Whig members were attacking the Muscovy Company 'as a kind of Government Department', protected and controlled once by privilege and now by statute. The Navigation Act, they pointed

out, had in any case made a greater part of the company's privilege
redundant, why should it be allowed to continue? And within a
year the monopoly of the Muscovy Company was ended. Trade
with Russia was thrown open to any merchant able to pay a £5
'membership' fee. Dissolution of the old East India Company
followed and in spite of opposition from Bristol and Liverpool
merchants and London financiers who complained the profits
were too big, a new 'United' company rose in its place. An English
commercial treaty with Danzig in 1706 made further inroads on
the monopoly of the Eastland Company, though the Naval Stores
Act of two years earlier had had less effect than anticipated.
Queen Anne was persuaded to introduce an Act for encouraging
the importation of naval stores from Her Majesty's Plantations in
America. Four pounds a ton was to be paid for pitch and tar; £1
a ton for 40-foot masts and bowsprits. The Navy Board was to
have first refusal with the option open for twenty days. But in
spite of a subsidy the plantations found it difficult to compete with
the Baltic trade, and were soon admitting they could not offer
pitch and tar at as low prices as the Swedes. It put the Commissioners of Trade and Plantations in a quandary. In their journal
entry for December 18, 1706, Messrs Sergison, Lydell and Tollett
of the Navy Board let it be known that they wished to distinguish
between the interest of the Navy and the interest of England. 'They
were bound by their instruction to "buy naval stores wherever
they find them cheapest without enquiring whence they come"!'
Thus they often bought pitch and tar from Sweden; but to import
naval stores from the plantations was in the national interest and
would lower the prices from other places. Tar from North America
was good but dear. The introduction of 3000 German Protestant
refugees from the Palatinate to the Hudson River in 1710 to develop
naval stores for the English regrettably ended in failure.

The Muscovy Company was kept in being as 'The Russia
Company' throughout the eighteenth century with the dying
Eastland Company as satellite – its last member was enrolled in
1711. But the Russia Company lived mainly on past glories. It was
relegated to a consultative role and doubtless helped with the
difficult decisions of protocol presented by workmen at Deptford

Dockyard having to be told that the Peter Michaeloff who worked beside them on the bench was in fact Peter the Great, Tsar of All the Russias, who had taken it into his head to learn shipbuilding the hard way and visit the shipyards of Holland and England to assimilate at first hand the details of the arts involved.

A potentially delicate situation was obviously handled to the great man's satisfaction, for he returned to his capital determined to encourage trade in every way he could. He developed Petersburg as his principal Baltic port, and business with the East Baltic began to expand more rapidly than that with any other trading area. Peter died in 1725 but in 1734 the Empress Anne made a commercial treaty with Britain after which Russian iron became available in large quantities.

The Baltic merchant's trading season was necessarily a short one. All ships had to be clear of the Gulf of Finland and Riga by October because of the ice. They could not return till May. A ship would make two round voyages in this brief summer, sailing early in April to fetch a cargo for delivery in London in July, then speeding north to 'Eastland' to be home again by November. The ships were small – between 80 and 150 tons – and easily manoeuvrable in harbour. There was a quick turn-round in London and at the Baltic ports where English merchants were well served by regular factors.

In the winter the same ships sailed to the Bay of Biscay to lade French wine. Few merchants could supply full cargoes and were rarely able to charter a whole ship. Many took out mixed cargoes in small vessels and returned with parcels of Baltic goods laded by a number of different factors.

The carrying trade was now an industry in itself. One of the General Maxims of Trade pronounced by Charles King in *The British Merchant* in 1721 was 'That the letting Ships to Freight to other Nations is profitable'. Ralph Davis has shown that between 1560 and 1689 shipping multiplied seven-fold. To this growth the Baltic trade was a major contributor. Confidence in Britain's ability to pay her way rose with the departure of James II, but his welcome by His Most Christian Majesty across the Channel and the existence of a Prince of Wales harbouring pretensions to a throne he was undoubtedly heir to, were not conducive to the even further growth for which regulars at the Virginia hoped.

If public credit was imperilled by the triumph of a Tory-supported Jacobite cause which in 1715 showed itself to be a very live one, the scheme for a South Sea Company to deal in African slaves to absorb England's floating debt of ten million pounds which Robert Harley propounded in 1711 was an even greater threat to the economy. Mindless investment in the South Sea Company and the other 'enterprises' which it inspired around 1720 was an alarming example of the snowballing hysteria which could result from large-scale trading on credulity. Many were led to believe there were fortunes to be made even in naval stores. Citizens with money to lose were invited to Waghorn's Coffee-House to invest in a £4 000 000 scheme 'for a trade to Norway and Sweden to procure pitch, tar, deals and oak'; to the Castle Tavern to speculate in a £2 000 000 company 'for the purchase of pitch tar and turpentine'; to the Ship Tavern to share in the proceeds of 'importing masts, spars, oak &C for the Navy'. At the Marine Coffee-House stock could be bought in a £2 000 000 enterprise 'for insuring ships and merchandise'; at the Virginia Coffee-House customers could share in the undoubted profits from the £1 200 000 it was hoped to invest in 'carrying on a trade to Germany'. When the bubble burst the credulous went bankrupt, the 'old school' said 'I told you so' and welcomed a return to plain methods.

The Royal Exchange was still London's only exchange, though since 1700 Essex farmers had been in the habit of meeting buyers at an inn in Whitechapel. Those who had not taken orders left samples with the landlord who received a commission on the amount he sold to those who came on a later day – the first 'corn factor', using his inn as an embryo corn exchange. But this apart, there were no specialist exchanges in the City as such. *Every* kind of business was done on the floor of the Royal Exchange. And, as an up-dated edition of John Stowe's *Survey of London* published in 1732 stated, 'for the more easy expediting of their work the merchants dealing in the same Commodities have by Custom fixed on these different Parts of the Exchange to meet one another, called Walks'. His floor diagram named each of the walks and their positions, which of course were frequently changing. There was no 'Baltic Walk', but there was an 'East Country Walk' in the north-west corner along the Threadneedle Street side; a 'Hambrough [Hamburg] Walk' opposite the north entrance, and a 'Norway Walk' just below the 'East Country Walk'. In the centre beside the statue of Charles II was 'Brokers, &c. of Stocks Walk'. On the south side there was a 'Virginia Walk', a 'Jamaica Walk', a 'Spanish Walk' and a 'Jews Walk'.

This second Royal Exchange occupied the site of Gresham's building, as today's building does. The two front doors opened north on to Threadneedle Street and south on to Cornhill, though 'behind the Royal Exchange' always indicated Threadneedle Street. There were houses in the open space in front of today's portico, separated by Castle Alley; on the east was Swithin's Alley which had no association with the rain-bringing saint but was named after a Dutch merchant Henry Swieten (it later became known as Sweeting's Alley and Sweeting's Rents). Inside the Exchange were two open piazzas.

In 1724 Daniel Defoe wrote in his *Tour Through the Whole Island of Great Britain*:

The Royal Exchange, the greatest and finest of the kind in the world, is the next public work of the citizens, the beauty of which answers for itself, and needs no description here; 'tis observable that though this Exchange cost the citizens an immense sum of money re-building, some authors say eighty thousand pounds, being finished and embellished in so exquisite a manner, yet it was so appropriated to the grand affair of business that the rent or income of it for many years, fully answered the interest of the money laid out in building it. Whether it does so still or not, I will not say, but those shops of which there are eight double rows above, and the shops and offices round it below, with the vaults under the whole, did at first yield a very great sum.

More than half the ships belonging to those who met on the East Country Walk of the Royal Exchange, and to owners in Hull and Newcastle, sailed from England to the Baltic in 1738 in ballast. Many of them, however, took corn to Portugal and then returned to England via Riga and St Petersburg where they discharged salt and loaded hemp, flax and iron for England. The export of corn was stimulated by an export bounty of five shillings a quarter for wheat and a smaller amount for other types of grain if shipped in a British vessel. This three-cornered trade flourished for half a century, but very few English ships exported Baltic corn to the Mediterranean at this time – a trade handled almost entirely by the Dutch. But, to quote Ralph Davis, 'gradually, through growth of an English trade with the Baltic which was kept out of Dutch hands, and through the development of a modest share in the North–South carrying trade, England grew towards equality with the Dutch in the Baltic, the original and final stronghold of Dutch maritime supremacy'.

This growth was due to a large extent to the persistence of the masters in building up personal friendships and goodwill with the Swedish and Baltic factors. Once the voyage was under way the master, out of touch with owner and merchant, was in complete control. For this reason, in the days of sailing ships, of crude charts and not too reliable navigational aids, when the quickest and most profitable voyage was made by the commander familiar with the weather, the tides and the geography through plying the same route year after year, shipping was more akin to today's liner operation than tramping. Though, as has been seen, when the Baltic was inaccessible in the winter, the ships' masters who ran timber, hemp, corn and iron from Stettin, Danzig, Königsberg, Memel, Riga, Narva and St Petersburg, would sail south.

But in 1738 Great Britain's free tramping of the seas was challenged by her other great commercial rival, Spain. A convention was on the point of being signed by the king of Spain who, according to George II, had agreed to make reparation for 'all those grievances and abuses which had hitherto interrupted the commerce of Great Britain in the American seas by their searching of British ships'. But customers in the Virginia Coffee-House, in the Antwerp Tavern, in the New England and North & South American Coffee-House (newly opened next door at 60 and 61 Threadneedle Street), and those who paced the Virginia Walk and the Spanish Walk at the Royal Exchange, objected to the leniency of the proposed convention. In the words of Tobias Smollett:

Divers merchants, planters, and other trading to America, the cities of London and Bristol, the merchants of Liverpool, and owners of sundry ships which had been seized by the Spaniards, offered petitions against the convention by which the subjects of Spain were so far from giving up their groundless and unjustifiable practice of visiting and searching British ships sailing to and from the British plantations, that they appeared to have claimed the power of doing it as a right; for they insisted that the differences which had arisen concerning it should be referred to plenipotentiaries . . . They therefore prayed that they might have an opportunity of being heard, and allowed to represent the great importance of the British trade to and from the plantations in America; the clear indisputable right which they had to enjoy it, without being stopped visited or searched by the Spaniards on any pretence whatsoever; and the certain inevitable destruction of all the riches and strength derived to Great Britain from that trade.

Here once again was political action by merchants and ship-owners in unmistakable terms. And it worked. King and Parliament were moved to action. An English squadron in the Mediterranean made prize of two Caracas ships, and declaration of war against Spain followed 'amidst the acclamations of the people', the merchants and shipping community in particular. The latter, however, weighed up the advantages of being able to charge double freights against the halving of their crews by the operations of the Press Gang. But it was their war; a war for commerce.

Within four years the French king's continual violation of the treaties by which the plotting Stuarts were excluded from France led to a confrontation with that country too. There were nodding heads of agreement at the Virginia when customers read the uncompromising speech of George II in their *Gentleman's Magazine* for April 1744.

The preparations which were so long carried on in France to invade this kingdom in favour of a popish pretender have at last been followed with a declaration of war by that Crown against me. The duty, affection and zeal for me and my family ought to have convinced our enemies how ill-grounded any hopes of success were.

He could appeal to the whole world for the rectitude and equity of his conduct as regards the maintenance of commerce and essential interests of his kingdoms without invading the rights of any other power. He had, therefore, declared war against the French king but 'you may depend upon my endeavours to make this war as little burthensome as possible' (hear hears and grunts of approval from the coffee-drinkers and pipe-smokers). There had indeed been an attempt at a French invasion with Bonnie Prince Charlie at the head in February 1743, which was 'disconcerted', to use Smollett's word, only by a strong north-easter blowing the French fleet in the wrong direction down channel to ignominious destruction.

With the outbreak of war with France the price of naval stores from the Baltic rose. Russian hemp fetched £23 a ton, Riga hemp £26. In March the price had risen to £31. When the Navy Office complained merchants pleaded war conditions and the difficulty of quoting firm prices on a rising market. For Norwegian masts the Navy Office was willing to pay 15 per cent above previous prices.

Though a Committee of Trade report had shown in 1721 that North America could supply all Britain's naval stores and make her independent of the Northern Crowns, the Navy Office was reluctant to place orders with the plantations – except for masts. Huge prices were demanded to compensate for the hazards of shipping from North America in war. A contractor called Henniker asked for a 60 per cent increase on 1740 prices for masts, yards and bowsprits from New England – and got it. A 38-yard mast costing £172 in peace became £230 in war.

It was a state of affairs which must have strained official relationships between merchants, shipowners, shipbrokers and ships' commanders on the Virginia Walk at the Royal Exchange with their counterparts on the Baltic Walk (as the East Country Walk became). But when they met afterwards on the other side of Threadneedle Street in their favourite tavern, now named Virginia and Maryland Coffee-House, the rival contenders for naval stores contracts would have common ground in complaining of the Navy Office's handling of the matter and they drowned their differences in coffee and liquor and lighting their pipes at the same candle. By 1744 certainly Virginia merchants and Baltic merchants constituted the majority of the regulars, and to reflect this the proprietor of the Virginia and Maryland Coffee-House took 'Maryland' out of his title (according to Bryant Lillywhite it had been in use for a very short period after March 26, 1743) and put 'Baltick' in its place. He spent two shillings on an advertisement in *The Daily Post*, No 7713 of Thursday, May 24, 1744, which carried the news item that 'Yesterday died, after a tedious Indisposition, at his House at Twickenham, that celebrated Poet Mr Alexander Pope'. It read:

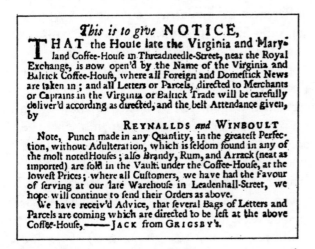

This is to give NOTICE,

THAT the House late the Virginia and Maryland Coffee-House in Threadneedle-Street, near the Royal Exchange, is now open'd by the Name of the Virginia and Baltick Coffee-House, where all Foreign and Domestick News are taken in ; and all Letters or Parcels, directed to Merchants or Captains in the Virginia or Baltick Trade will be carefully deliver'd according as directed, and the best Attendance given, by

REYNALLDS *and* WINBOULT

Note, Punch made in any Quantity, in the greatest Perfection, without Adulteration, which is seldom found in any of the most noted Houses ; also Brandy, Rum, and Arrack (neat as imported) are sold in the Vault under the Coffee-House, at the lowest Prices; where all Customers, we have had the Favour of serving at our late Warehouse in Leadenhall-Street, we hope will continue to send their Orders as above.

We have receiv'd Advice, that several Bags of Letters and Parcels are coming which are directed to be left at the above Coffee-House,——JACK from GRIGSBY's.

Advertisement placed in the Daily Post, *24 May 1744 by the proprietor of the Virginia and Maryland Coffee-House*

Reynallds and Winboult, a firm of wine merchants who used to have cellars in Leadenhall Street, had taken over the vault under 61 Threadneedle Street to which they moved their stock of brandy, rum, arrack and punch and were purveying it from there to customers of hot chocolate and coffee visiting the Virginia and Maryland Coffee-House on the ground floor above. Jack, who had been head waiter at Grigsby's which owned this vault and ran the ground-floor coffee-house above it up to 1732 or 1735, had been retained by the proprietor of the Virginia and Maryland, now the Virginia and Baltick, and took this opportunity of telling his customers that the change of name meant no change in his appointment. There are doubtless many interpretations of this much quoted advertisement, but this is a reasonable one.

Bryant Lillywhite, whose detailed research made him the

leading authority on the subject, states in his *London Coffee Houses*, 'Between 1735 and 1743 it seems that Grigsby's went out of business.' He quotes an indenture dated March 26, 1743, shown to him by the North British Mercantile and Insurance Company relating to the easterly portion of the building later known as No 61 Threadneedle Street which describes the house as 'The Dutch or Grigsby's Coffee House, and now the Virginia Coffee House'. References in directories continued to refer to Grigsby's in Threadneedle Street, however, right up to 1833. Dr Kennet Rogers, says Lillywhite, also located Grigsby's as being the easterly portion of No 61 Threadneedle Street, giving a date 1708–1732. Grigsby's and the Virginia may have been side by side in Sun Court which was entered by a narrow alley off Threadneedle Street, according to Roque's map of 1746, just where No 61 would have been. The Sun Fire office held meetings at the Virginia between 1709 and 1721. The Virginia may have been at 62 and Grigsby's at 61, which was also occupied, according to Lillywhite, between 1702 and 1824 by coffee-houses calling themselves Dutch New England, West India and Antigallican; and from 1720 to 1848 was the third house (most easterly portion) of the New England (sometimes New England and North & South American) which occupied Nos 59 and 60 Threadneedle Street. Adjoining these three houses on the west side, as has been seen, was the Antwerp Tavern at No 58.

The story hovers over this short stretch of eighteenth-century Threadneedle Street, as here it must descend. In the Virginia and Baltick Coffee-House, wherever it was, the story must take up residence for a time.

2. Free Traders

The Virginia and Baltick Coffee-House of 1744 was an open house, a public house. It had no members, only regulars. Nothing occurred in it which would call for any records or minutes. Anyone could come in from the street for a drink and a meal but there was a nucleus of regulars with common interests – the Virginia and Baltic trade – a trend cultivated by the proprietor in providing the kind of newspapers, pamphlets and commercial information they wanted. A merchant would be a regular at more than one coffeehouse. In the course of a day he would move from the Virginia and Baltick, to his counting house, to the Royal Exchange, to Lloyd's, to the New England, and when this closed, along with most other coffee-houses at five, he moved to a tavern or inn for supper.

There was a dearth of coffee-houses in the immediate vicinity of the Royal Exchange following the fire which began in a wigmaker's shop in Exchange Alley one afternoon in 1748. This destroyed many which had been rebuilt after the greater fire of 1666, including Garraway's, Jonathan's and the Marine, and many newer post-Great Fire coffee-houses, of which the most important for this story was the Jerusalem Coffee-House in Fleece Passage, Cornhill, later known as Cowper's Court.

Bryant Lillywhite found no contemporary mention in support of the Jerusalem being in existence before the 1730s, but he was unable to pin any definite date on it. He quotes an advertisement

---

OVER Europe divided into its several states according to their modern extent, 1794

in the *London Evening Post* of May 29, 1735, which describes the
position of a shop for sale in Exchange Alley by reference to the
Jerusalem Coffee-House – the first contemporary reference. It was
certainly in existence at the time of the fire of 1748, was destroyed
by it and quickly rebuilt. To it were attracted, according to
William Hickey writing in 1776, 'all those who had anything to
do with India' and particularly with East India Company ships'
commanders. A 'Society of East India Commanders', which was a
kind of Friendly Society in which the commanders made regular
deposits to ensure themselves a pension on retirement, met, and
was probably formed, in 1773 at the Queens Arms Tavern in St
Paul's Church Yard. In 1775 it moved its regular meeting place
to the Antwerp Tavern at 58 Threadneedle Street, and in January
1780, to the Jerusalem. A directory of 1798 described the Jerusalem
as

Frequented by gentlemen who are, or have been, in the service of the
honourable East India Company, and by the managing owners of ships
employed in their service; also by the merchants, policy and insurance
brokers concerned with the East India trade, and to this coffee-house and
Lloyds are transmitted the earliest accounts of the departure, arrival and loss
of ships in the company's service and of all important events that happen.

Neither the Royal Exchange nor the Virginia and Baltick
suffered from the fire of 1748; indeed, the rooms of the latter
became more crowded than ever from having to cater for those
who waited for the rebuilding of regular haunts. Apart from this,
coffee-houses were becoming generally busier as the population of
London, indeed of England, steadily rose – a circumstance which
affected not only coffee-house keepers but farmers. Not only was
more coffee being consumed, but also more bread.

England's farmers had for long been flourishing, though not to
the extent they would have liked, under the protection of the Corn
Laws by which the Government of the Restoration had imposed
heavy duties in the importation of corn from abroad, and virtually
prohibited it until wheat stood at famine prices. This, in fact,
happened in 1662 when the price rose from 41s. to 62s. 9d. a
quarter, but this was a rare occurrence in the seventeenth century.
Indeed, William III encouraged farmers to ship as much of their

crops as they could out of the country by offering a bounty of 5s. for every quarter they exported, by which he hoped to reduce the amount of corn available at home and raise its price. But the succession of good harvests which followed 1688 provided plenty of corn for both home consumption and export without the incentive of a bounty. To the satisfaction of the people of England, particularly the poor of London who no longer had a benevolent Corporation to protect them, and the annoyance of farmer and landlord who raised the familiar cry of 'agricultural distress', food was cheap. In such circumstances an export bounty designed to raise the home price of corn became a premium on production which led farmers to sow larger acreages of wheat than ever before and make supplies more abundant – and cheaper. For as long as the rise in population was gradual – it rose from $5\frac{1}{2}$ million to $6\frac{1}{2}$ million between 1700 and 1750 – competition between farmers kept prices low, and, so far as the consumer was concerned, the Corn Laws and the bounty had little effect. To ease the distribution of corn in London in 1746 Essex farmers and Aldgate dealers founded the Corn Exchange of London – 'the Old Corn Exchange' – in Mark Lane.

But the picture changed when in the second half of the eighteenth century the population shot up from $6\frac{1}{2}$ million to 9 million, an increase of 52 per cent, and home demand for corn soon outstripped supply. The dormant Corn Laws at last made themselves felt and under their protection farmers grew rich by charging increasingly exorbitant prices as crops annually grew more inadequate. The average price of wheat between 1791 and 1801 was nearly 76s. a quarter and famine years brought it up to 128s. 6d. Shipowners were not the only people who welcomed a war. One writer called Napoleon the patron saint of farmers and landlords.

But before the war broke out there had been one chink in the armour of protection. In 1773 the Parliament of George III passed an Act allowing the importation of foreign wheat at a nominal duty of 6d. a quarter so long as English wheat was not more than 48s. In 1791 a duty of 24s. 3d. was imposed as long as English wheat was less than 50s; if it was more than 50s. the duty was 2s. 6d. But the farmers considered their legitimate gains were

being unfairly reduced, and were not content until the level before
which importation was allowed was raised to 63s. and then 80s.

All this was a talking point at the Virginia and Baltic (the 'k' had
by now been dropped), not only because much of imported corn
came from Danzig, but for the reason that the Act of 1773 revealed a welcome willingness on the part of the Government,
albeit in extreme circumstances, to modify its protection policy.
It was the nearest approach which Britain was to make to free
trade before 1846.

The debate was stimulated by the publication in 1776 of Adam
Smith's *The Wealth of Nations*. It reinforced the farmers' scorn for
that persistent survivor from the bad old days of commercial
monopoly, the East India Company, which they were glad to see
in 1772 was in financial difficulties and had asked for a government
loan. The independent merchants of the Royal Exchange heard
of Parliament's decision to set up a Committee of Inquiry into the
company's management with considerable satisfaction. Its terms of
reference included substantiations that the company could build
and navigate ships at less cost than they could be chartered. Sir
Richard Hotham, a leading shipowner, told the committee that
the company's existing methods of freighting were absurd. Liverpool and Bristol shipowners wanted participation in the East India
trade, but in spite of their protests the company secured a renewed
lease of exclusive commercial power in 1784, though with a
Board of Control as overseer. In 1796 the company's charter was
again renewed with a clause stating that neither Indian nor English
merchants were allowed to export or import except in ships belonging to or chartered by the East India Company, appropriating
3000 tons of space for use of private traders at the reduced rate in
peacetime of £5 outward and £15 homewards per ton of cargo.
As W. S. Lindsay says, 'Few British merchants availed themselves
of this, fettered by the jealousy of powerful monopolists.'

That these cracks appeared in the once hide-bound constitution
of the 200-year-old East India Company was due in no small
measure to the 'philosophic apology for individual initiative', to
use S. G. Checkland's phrase, promulgated by Adam Smith. He
preached resistance to the claims of authority, yet implied that

society in spite of any disruption this caused was nevertheless stable, and the system as such would never start to slide beneath their feet.

Becoming discredited too, along with the sole market and chartered company theories, was the belief that trade followed the flag, that commerce was only possible with the countries acquired by military conquest or loyal to the mother country through colonial ties.

By virtue of the Navigation Act, up to the moment when the united colonies became the United States, the whole trade of the plantations was carried in British ships only; their produce was exported only to Britain or another plantation; European goods were imported into them only in British ships. But overnight, in 1783, the USA became just another foreign country.

One of the 'repeated injuries and usurpations' of the king of Great Britain listed as causes of the Declaration of Independence and included in that document was 'cutting off our trade with all parts of the world'. When they got their independence the Americans contended that commercial relations should not be dropped between two countries even if one of them sided with the enemy of the other, so long as it did not actually become a co-belligerent. One of the gambits of the American colonists was to get Benjamin Franklin, their agent in Paris, to make an alliance with Britain's enemy, France. But one of the clauses of their treaty of alliance was that free ships should be able to make free ports – American ships, in other words, were free to carry the goods of the enemies of France.

From 1793 when Britain, with the acquisition of French Canada and French India and the loss of America behind her, was committed to a final struggle with France to determine which of them was to be the world's carrier and colonizer, the minds of merchants and shipping men at the Virginia and Baltic were constantly occupied by the meaning of the word 'neutrality'. True to their undertaking of 1778 the National Convention of France, in ordering their ships of war not to respect British property in neutral vessels, excepted American ships. Those not drawn into the conflict opted to abide by the principles first enunciated by

Catherine the Great of Russia in 1780, that other people's wars should not be allowed to interfere with their normal trading activities. Furthermore they considered they had every right to take over whatever trade the belligerents had had to give up. Neutrals, they claimed, should be free to sail the seas under their own flag, visit any country they wished, pick up any cargoes they were offered and deliver them to the port of consignment without fear of molestation on the way. If the flag on the mast was neutral so were the goods in the hold, and subject to exemption from search and seizure – always excepting arms, universally recognized as contraband.

The 'principles' of the 'confederacy' of France, Russia, Prussia, Denmark, Sweden and the USA, which had combined to under-mine Britain's maritime supremacy, were dismissed by William Pitt as a rag-bag of maritime expedients concocted to suit their book in the special circumstances obtaining and contrary to the traditional code of international law in wartime sanctioned by time and usage. *He* would be guided by the principle of seizing enemy merchandise wherever he found it. He would declare as contra-band *any* cargo which could give succour to the enemy no matter in whose ship it was being carried. 'Rather than thus sacrifice our naval greatness at the shrine of Russia,' he said in reference to the theory's origin, 'it were better to envelop ourselves in our own flag and proudly find our grave in the deep than admit the validity of such principles in the maritime code of civilized nations.'

'Naval greatness' meant no mere showing the flag or arrogant patrolling of the oceans, but a vast fleet of merchant ships protected if need be by armed escorts, should any power take it into its head to challenge Britain's supreme position in the carrying trade of the world. In spite of Napoleon's victories on land and his attempted blockade at sea, this great mercantile navy went about its business virtually unhindered, while the merchant fleets of France, in the words of Nelson, 'were shut up in her ports and could not send a cockle boat to sea without fear of capture'. But, of course, it was not all plain sailing.

As always, when peace conditions gave way to a war economy, the interests of merchant and shipowner diverged. Commercial houses began to collapse and Parliament made £5 000 000 available in exchequer bills as a loan to merchants, of which some £3 850 000 was applied for. But true to form shipping at first prospered. The bad winter of 1794–5 made food scarce and the price of wheat rose. The dread of famine created a big demand for ships. With the sea infested with privateers and enemy men-of-war, voyages designed to evade them were riskier and longer – and dearer.

But when, after the short interval following the Peace of Amiens, war was resumed, British tonnage had been reduced by 173 900 tons, though this was compensated by the capture of 112 819 tons of foreign shipping. This second phase of the war went harder for the British shipowner. The value of cargoes exported, which came to £41 411 966 in 1802, fell to £31 438 985 in 1803. Neutrals could obtain their naval stores from a Baltic sea virtually closed to the British who could only obtain them elsewhere at very much greater costs. The British Government levied a tax on timber, hemp and canvas, and made shipowners take out licences from Customs for the construction of new ships.

At the Royal Exchange and at Hain's, the Jerusalem and the Virginia and Baltic there was grumbling against a government which refused to allow its hard-used traders to trade on equal terms with other nations. Some of them wrote a letter to the *Morning Chronicle* in February 1804, pointing out that 'so long as they continued to be burthened with tonnage convoy, port-duties, extra insurance, heavy taxes for docks, canals, tunnels and a thousand other water-brain schemes, they will continue to drag on a miserable existence till even the profitable concerns of shipbreaking shall be seen no more'. Others formed an association to maintain the Navigation Act as originally conceived, but Pitt's administration would not listen. 'However wise and salutary the navigation laws might have been in the infancy of our commerce,' declared a member of the Government, 'I do not perceive the efficacy of them at present or the necessity of strictly adhering to their original provisions.'

The interests of the nation as a whole were once more clashing with those of a section of it. To raise funds to wage and win the war British shipowners were charged with duties on every item of

naval stores up to seven per cent of a ship's value and a double
duty was levied on gross tonnage as a 'War Tax'. British shipowners remembered the palmy days of the first phase of the war
and were quick to compare their lot with the lucky neutrals who
could build and navigate so much more cheaply and charge the
low freights which won over so much of the business. Though the
British Mercantile Marine, escorted by ships of the Royal Navy
under Admiral Saumarez, Commander-in-Chief, Baltic, 1801-12,
sailed in convoy to Baltic ports in 1808 and 1809 and did their
business in spite of the Danish gunboats, commercial intercourse
was severely curtailed after Nelson's bombardment of Copenhagen
in 1801.

It was all very deplorable, but the more constructive shipowners
saw the problem more as enlarging the cake than crying over the
shrinking size of their slice, and urged the Government to expand
the amount of foreign trade available, particularly in the West
Indies. They asked for commercial agents to be appointed in the
Mediterranean. Yet another effort was made to open up the
timber trade in Upper and Lower Canada for masts, and to plant
pitch-pine trees to make Britain free of her dependence on Russia
and the Baltic for pitch, tar, resin and turpentine.

There was scope, too, for making sure that the fullest use was
being made of what wood there was at home. The Committee for
Improving the Navigation of the River Thames and for Preventing Encroachment Thereon, the precursor of the Port of London
Authority, considered a report in April 1796 on the drift timber
which had accumulated at Nine Elms – a 51-foot length of Riga,
'8 Pieces of Memel' (239 feet) and '3 Pieces of Brewick' (49 feet).
Mr Waterbailiff was directed to keep a Journal of all Estrayer and
Drift on the River Thames.

In the last bitter years of the war, when Napoleon's Berlin
Decrees imposed a blockade of Britain, all warehouses belonging
to the English on the continent were declared to be 'good prize',
and all post services ceased between the two countries. By March
1807 there was a virtual suspension of all shipping to the continent.
Insurance from England to Holland went up to 30 guineas per
cent. Many merchants, reading about the fighting in the comfort

and warmth of their coffee-houses, felt the war was the concern of King George with the Emperor of France, but no business of theirs. 'Those merchants who were not ship-owners', wrote W. S. Lindsay, 'cared little in what vessels their goods reached the continent so long as the insurance effected secured them from loss and they could carry on the trade to a profit.' From 1808 they were denied the use of even American vessels. Napoleon ordered all US ships in French ports to be seized. Freight on wheat from the Baltic rose to 50s. a quarter from 1807 to 1808 and the price of linseed from 43s. to 150s., hemp from £58 to £108 a ton, flax from £58 to £118 a ton; Russian tallow from 53s. to 112s. a hundredweight. Timber was charted for freight at £10 a load, tallow at £20 and hemp at £30 a ton. (These prices, Lindsay pointed out, were ten to twenty times higher than in 1874 when he was writing.)

Though British ships were excluded from the Baltic, the whole of which froze over in 1809, shipowners were given the monopoly of the East and West Indies carrying trade which happily from 1807 excluded the legal supplying of slaves. The successful shipping of colonial produce to Britain and the continent in defiance of Napoleon's blockade employed the huge merchant navy to the full. The pessimistic mood of the beginning of the second phase of the war disappeared. Britain's shipping was busier and more profitably employed than ever before; and there were signs of future developments which augured even greater prosperity. Gossip round Charles II's statue in the Royal Exchange where shipbrokers now gathered – according to the plan in Grose's Antiquities of 1798 – was of a steam paddle boat called *Clermont*, modelled on Symington's *Charlotte Dundas* by an American called Robert Fulton, which was plying the River Hudson, and of another called *Comet*, developed by Scots Henry Bell, which was carrying passengers between Glasgow and Greenock – the first steamboat built in Europe.

But in 1807, the year Fulton showed, as Lindsay puts it, that the steamboat could be made not only 'an instrument of vast importance to mankind but a source of profit', unheeding East Indiamen continued to demonstrate the romance, and practicality, of sail. In wartime, as it was now, they sailed to India and China in convoy

C

guarded by the Royal Navy. Salvaged from the Jerusalem Coffee House which, as mentioned, had special ties with the East India Company, and kept in the archives of the Baltic Exchange, is a large leather book inscribed 'Samuel Holbrow, HC Ship *Walmer Castle*, 6th voyage St Helena, Bencoolen and China'. It is a log which opens on October 29, 1807, and records a round voyage from London starting on December 5 and ending back again in the Downs on September 14, 1809. 'Luke Dodds Esq, age 40, Commander' headed the list of 120 officers and crew. It took 35 passengers, including 8 women, plus 100 Chinese working their passage to China. The Rev. Atwill Lake was returning to his flock in Penang. Miss Luisa Green and Miss Eliza Cox were described in the column headed 'Qualities' as 'Going to get married'. Mr John Pringle, Agent, travelled with his wife, Mary, his Adjutant, Josiah Luson, and five servants.

The *Walmer Castle* sailed in company with HMS *Isis* and four other East Indiamen, the *Elphinstone*, *Winchelsea*, *Phoenix* and *Essex*. They were at St Helena on April 17, 1808, punished Michael Torrenson, seaman, for mutinous and disorderly conduct on April 28, dropped anchor in False Bay off the Cape of Good Hope on May 31, hove to at Penang on September 18, and arrived off China on November 5, staying there till March 1809. Within six months Commander Luke Dodds was back in the Jerusalem with the commanders of the other ships in the convoy to exchange stories of high adventure and leave his log.

He might even have been persuaded to look in to the Royal Exchange – though he would not have been particularly welcome. If he had ventured in he would have seen, in the words of Robert Hawker, D.D., vicar of Charles, Plymouth, a place which, though spacious, was full of persons. Of his visit in 1808 he wrote:

Earnestness was strongly pictured upon every countenance. The clamour of voices, to an ear unaccustomed as mine was to such confused sounds was almost deafening; and though no doubt perfectly intelligible to one another, yet seemed to remind me of what I had read of Babel. But what at first view made the greatest impression upon my mind was that one general feature marked every character, whether buyer or seller: – I mean the unwearied perseverance, uniformly distinguishing all, to accomplish the object of their distinct pursuits. Here were no vacant countenances. Nothing like the show of indifferency. Everyone appeared alive, zealous and indefatigable.

Some of the clamour of voices was doubtless discussing the building of the East Country Dock to accommodate the Baltic trade which had started in 1807, and the meeting held a few months earlier at the London Tavern in Bishopsgate Street at which Alderman Sir Charles Price, Bt MP, had announced the formation of the Commercial Dock Company to buy the Greenland Dock and the adjoining Norway Dock for £35 000. The object, he said, was to attract the expanding Baltic trade. The Act of Parliament which incorporated the company in 1810 stated that the object was to relieve the river of ships laden with timber, hemp, flax, pitch and tar, and secure for the cargoes the benefits of lower insurance rates against loss and pillage which occurred in the northern docks. In 1809 Joseph Moore and others had formed the Baltic Dock Company to acquire an estate of forty-five acres at Rotherhithe with the idea of converting the estate into pounds for storing and bonding timber, an enterprise in which many customers of the Virginia and Baltic were probably shareholders.

These dock enterprises in London, promoted in anticipation of an expansion of the Baltic trade, showed remarkable faith in a quick and favourable end to the biggest war in Britain's history; for in 1810 the trial of strength was far from resolved, particularly in the Baltic where news of naval engagements, sinkings and shipping movements came daily to John Bennett, secretary of Lloyd's in the Royal Exchange, who was corresponding with Samuel Champion, secretary of the Admiral on the Baltic Station. Bennett considered this correspondence to be private in every sense of the word; he did not publish it in full but posted extracts on the notice boards at Lloyd's to help underwriters form judgements on Baltic risks. However, he was taken to task for not revealing all the information he received in this way when very heavy claims were made on Lloyd's underwriters for the seizure of a large number of ships in Swedish, Prussian and other Baltic ports. Underwriters rose to the occasion, but it was their biggest blow of the war. The claims were difficult to prove, so a meeting was called of both sides to investigate them.

Any concern which regulars of the Virginia and Baltic Coffee-House might have shown at these disasters, which should have brought home to them the realities of war at sea, would have been displayed in new surroundings. For according to James Findlay (who wrote a book about the Baltic Exchange in 1927) the Virginia and Baltic Coffee-House in the easterly portion of No 61 Threadneedle Street closed in 1810, and reopened three houses westward at No 58, which for 200 years had housed the Antwerp Tavern. This move occasioned the dropping of 'Virginia' from the title, and the resort became known as the Baltic Coffee-House to which the custom of the Virginia and Baltic, a name which now disappears, was transferred.

From October 1775 to January 1780 the Antwerp Tavern, to which the number 58 has never been attached in a directory, was, as noted, the meeting place of the Society of East India Commanders which later moved to the Jerusalem. The Glass-Sellers Company met here in 1783. Bryant Lillywhite reports that on December 18, 1794 John Durham, landlord of the Antwerp Tavern, signed for some goods belonging to the Glass-Sellers Company deposited at the Antwerp, and that on March 21, 1799 he told the company he was quitting the tavern as the building was about to be repaired. In 1801 the Antwerp is known to have accommodated a meeting of the proprietors of the proposed new Stock Exchange in Capel Court. In the year 1810 when Findlay alleges the tavern became the Baltic Coffee-House, Holden's Directory gives Thomas Butler as its proprietor.

'Antwerp Tavern' continues to be mentioned in directories of 1814, and indeed as late as 1833, but the inaccuracy of these publications is well known. Bryant Lillywhite states that on December 10, 1819, the Clerk to the Glass-Sellers Company reported that the glass, plate chest, tables and other effects deposited at the Antwerp had been removed to the King's Head Tavern in the Poultry, but if the rest of this story has any foundation in fact the threat of demolition must have been a false alarm.

There is no mention of a Baltic Coffee-House in directories before 1825, but when it does appear its number is given as 58. Perhaps it was there all the time – on top of the Antwerp. To complicate matters, Dr Kenneth Rogers, who put in considerable research in the Guildhall Library on these matters, apparently came to the conclusion that the Antwerp Tavern was further west than No 58. Mr White, tax collector for the Broad Street ward, told James Findlay on December 14, 1905: 'The whole of the coffee house (i.e. the Baltic) was in Hercules Passage.'

Be that as it may, Thomas Butler seems to have retired, and the Baltic Coffee-House* opened under the management of a man called William Melton, a wine merchant who lived over the premises – another reason for believing that the Virginia and Baltic had been there all the time.

That the proprietor of the Baltic Coffee-House, wherever it was, decided to drop the 'Virginia' and not the 'Baltic' indicates a confidence in a present and future role for a Baltic trade which was fully justified, though at the time the war made it a trade of considerable danger as has already been seen.

A shipowner not only had to put guns on board to defend his ship from attack by French privateers, but had to go to the additional expense of insuring against 'Enemy Risks' over and above the normal hazards of the sea. One of the many vessels insured against enemy risks in 1811 was the 213-ton brigantine *Janes* valued at £4000. In July 1813, it was chartered from the three owners, John Scott, Robert Knox and Thomas Tindall of Scarborough, by a firm of Russia merchants called Busk, Ord & Company of Old Broad Street to carry from Archangel to London a load of the coarse fat of sheep and cattle used in candle and soap-making known as tallow. The paper deed or charter (*carta*) on which were written the conditions of hire, terms of carriage, date of delivery, etc. was divided into two parts and for this reason was known in medieval Latin as a *charta partita*, and in French as a *charte partie*. It was similar to an indenture, a mutual covenant of which there

*There was another Baltic Coffee-House. A directory of 1765 gives a Baltic Coffee-House in what it calls Sweetings Rents (the Swithins Rents, of Roque's map of 1746), which ran along the east wall of the Royal Exchange up to Threadneedle Street at the corner of St Benet Fink, a church long demolished. Today the site is an open space with the Peabody statue on one side. It was immediately opposite the alley leading to Sun Court and the 58-59-60-61 row of houses in part of which were the Virginia and Baltic and the Antwerp. Its number in Swithins Rents was given as No 6. There is no reference to it after 1783.

were two copies, one for the merchant, one for the shipowner. The English version of this word is a corruption of the French, and entered the language as 'charter-party'. At the top of the document (reproduced in the illustrated section between pages 60 and 61) dated July 26, 1813, for the voyage of the *Janes* to and from Archangel, it was printed all in one word, 'Charterparty'. This is claimed by the firm of Harris & Dixon Ltd, who own it, as the oldest existing charter-party on the Baltic Exchange. (There are of course older ones in the Public Record Office.) Their copy is signed by John Ord and by James Bentley, who in 1810 became a partner with his uncle, Goland Burton, who had set up in Leman Street, Wapping, in 1797 as a coal factor, ship and insurance broker. John Ord was signing for Busk, Ord & Company, Russia merchants; James Bentley for Burton & Bentley, shipbrokers acting for John Scott, the owner. In 1841 Burton & Bentley became Bentley, Harris & Dixon and when James Bentley died in 1846 the firm adopted the name of Harris & Dixon which it still carries today.

Claiming foundation in 1797, Harris & Dixon are the oldest firm of shipbrokers on the Baltic Exchange. The simple wording of their 1813 charter-party, beginning 'It is this Day mutually agreed', has been the basis of many subsequent documents and, as the late Charles Edmonds pointed out, can be found in many coal and ore charter-parties of modern times. Part of it was printed with gaps for the details to be filled in by hand. After the printed words 'That the ship being tight, staunch and strong and every way fitted for the Voyage' were written particulars of the sailing date and of the 490 casks of tallow which were to be the cargo, which (in printed text) 'the said Merchants bind themselves to Ship not exceeding what she can reasonably stow and carry over and above her Tackle, Apparel, Provisions and Furniture.' Freight was to be £7 a ton; twenty days were allowed for loading at Archangel and fifteen days for unloading in London. Above the printed sentence 'Restraint of Princes and Rulers during the said Voyage always excepted' was written by hand 'The Acts of God, King's enemies'. The final sentence read 'And *Ten* Days on Demurrage over and above the said laying Days at *Seven* Pounds per Day. Penalty for

London Average Market Letter Committee. The first page of the 1813 minute book

Non-Performance of this Agreement £2000.' The figures in italics were inserted by hand.'

The tallow which was the *Janes*'s cargo has a special significance for this story. It played a sufficiently important role in Britain's commercial life for merchants to specialize in it and form a group with a title which gave no hint of the product they were dealing in, the London Average Market Letter Committee. At about the

London, October 14th, 1795.

A TABLE OF THE
Prices of TALLOW,
regulated from the Rough Markets.

℔ Stone.		₱ ⊕	₱ Stone.		₱ ⊕
2 : 0	7 - 0	34 : 6	3 : 6½	9 - 8	60 : 6
2 : 0¾		35 : 6	3 : 7		61 : 0
2 : 1		36 : 0	3 : 7½		62 : 0
2 : 1½		37 : 0	3 : 8	10 - 0	62 : 6
2 : 2	7 - 4	37 : 6	3 : 8½		63 : 6
2 : 2½		38 : 0	3 : 9		64 : 0
2 : 3		39 : 0	3 : 9½		65 : 0
2 : 3½		39 : 6	3 : 10	10 - 4	65 : 6
2 : 4		40 : 0	3 : 10½		66 : 0
2 : 4½	7 - 8	41 : 0	3 : 11		67 : 0
2 : 5		41 : 6	3 : 11½		67 : 6
2 : 5½		42 : 6	4 : 0	10 - 8	68 : 0
2 : 6		43 : 0	4 : 0½		69 : 0
2 : 6½	8 - 0	43 : 6	4 : 1		69 : 6
2 : 7		44 : 6	4 : 1½		70 : 6
2 : 7½		45 : 0	4 : 2		71 : 0
2 : 8		45 : 6	4 : 2½	11 - 0	71 : 6
2 : 8½		46 : 6	4 : 3		72 : 6
2 : 9	8 - 4	47 : 0	4 : 3½		73 : 0
2 : 9½		48 : 0	4 : 4		73 : 6
2 : 10		48 : 6	4 : 4½		74 : 6
2 : 10½		49 : 0	4 : 5	11 - 4	75 : 0
2 : 11	8 - 8	50 : 0	4 : 5½		76 : 0
2 : 11½		50 : 6	4 : 6		76 : 6
3 : 0		51 : 6	4 : 6½		77 : 0
3 : 0½		52 : 6	4 : 7	11 - 8	78 : 0
3 : 1	9 - 0	53 : 0	4 : 7½		78 : 6
3 : 1½		54 : 0	4 : 8		79 : 0
3 : 2		54 : 6	4 : 8½		80 : 0
3 : 2½		55 : 0	4 : 9		80 : 6
3 : 3		56 : 0	4 : 9½	12 - 0	81 : 6
3 : 3½	9 - 4	56 : 6	4 : 10		82 : 0
3 : 4		57 : 0	4 : 10½		82 : 6
3 : 4½		58 : 0	4 : 11		83 : 6
3 : 5		59 : 0	4 : 11½	12 - 4	84 : 0
3 : 5½	9 - 8	59 : 6	5 : 0		84 : 6
3 : 6		60 : 0			

London Average Market Letter Committee. A price list of 1795

time the *Janes* set sail for Archangel, which was the principal
source of tallow during the Napoleonic wars, these merchants
divided themselves into two, a West Committee, which met in
the Grecian Coffee-House in Devereux Court off the Strand, and

an East Committee, which met at the New England & North and South American Coffee-House at 59, 60 and 61 Threadneedle Street. The East Committee became so closely associated with their meeting place that they were often known as the New England Society, which indicates more a 'club' than a business committee. None of the records of the West Committee have survived but, apart from a gap between 1846 and 1851, the present Committee have all of those of the East group since 1813. How long it had been meeting before 1813 is not known, though the New England is first heard of in Threadneedle Street in 1720.

The purpose of the London Average Market Letter Committees was to publish a weekly letter for the guidance of merchants in the tallow trade giving a table of average prices fetched by tallow of various qualities during the previous week. A letter dated 'London October 14, 1795' (illustrated opposite) is headed 'A Table of the Prices of Tallow regulated from the Rough Markets' and shows prices ranging from 7s. a stone to 12s. 4d. But a meeting for this simple undertaking, which cannot have taken more than fifteen minutes, was hardly worth the candle, and the occasion became prolonged by the kind of horse-play and gambling which were features of the age. As the stakes were bottles of wine, the consumption of the winnings by winners and losers made a social and convivial event out of what otherwise would have been excessively tedious. The very first entry for January 1, in the earliest extant Minute Book of 1813, after noting that Town Tallow stood at 9s. reads: 'Mr Skipper betts Mr Harriss 1 BW [i.e. one bottle of wine] that Mr Treacher is more than 57 Years of Age.' The second reads: 'Mr Skipper betts Mr Brooks 6 Bots of wine that France will not Invade Russia again before the 31 July 1813 – In the event of Peace taking place between the 2 Powers this Bett to become Void.' Later Mr Barton bet Mr Skipper one bottle of wine that the French army 'now at Wilna' would be able to maintain itself during the winter. He lost. For even while he made his bet Napoleon's troops were quitting Russia. When there were no other events of importance to inspire members of the New England Society to speculation, they turned to such dull subjects as next month's price of tallow. Not all the wine won by members was drunk the same evening; much of it was consigned to the cellars below – or never taken out but labelled with the winner's name – to accumulate for the annual dinner. It was all very jolly.

There may have been times when the jollification got the better of them. A meeting of butchers, according to an announcement in *The Courier* of May 8, 1817, was convened on May 6 to consider the way in which melters and tallow chandlers published the average price of fat, with a Mr John Warmington in the chair. They resolved 'it is notorious that the price of fat has not been given on a fair average of the public sale thereof in Whitechapel market for some time past . . . materially affecting the property of the major part of the butchers throughout the Kingdom'. To prevent a return to this state of affairs a committee of twenty-one was appointed to consider measures for making and publishing, just and fair average market price of fat. No doubt Messrs Barton Skipper and the rest bet five to one against the butchers coming up with any better way of settling the matter.

The tallow merchants were not the only people issuing circular 'letters'. In the Baltic Exchange archives is a printed sheet issued by Robert & John Hewetson of Catherine-Court Tower-Hill dated May 26, 1817, which runs, 'Sir, In the course of last week the arrivals of Foreign Wheat was tolerable large, but this morning having rather a moderate supply of English, the sales were again brisk for fine, at a further advance of full 4s. per qr. though can scarcely note any amendment in prices of inferior, or yet in the sales.' Good bright barleys were 4s. dearer; oats were getting scarce. Prices were quoted of wheat from Dantzic, Mecklenburg and Pomerania, Riga and Liebau, Petersburgh and Archangel, of oats from Poland and crushing linseed. Between May 12 and 17, 1817, 6578 quarters of foreign wheat were imported and 6878 of English.

For a long time tallow had been the only source of lubricant and a main source of light – tallow dips with their smelly, smoky flame made by dipping a hank of cotton yarn in melted fat. Making tallow candles was an old trade. A Guild of Tallow Chandlers had been formed in the fourteenth century. In 1456 the Worshipful Company of Tallow Chandlers was granted a coat of arms which it still possesses. The quickly expendable products of the tallow chandler were always in demand, and not only for interior illumination. Queen Elizabeth's privy council insisted that 'every householder in the City from the 1st October to the 1st March in every year for ever should cause a substantial lanthorn and a Candle of Eight in the Pound to be hanged without their Doors'. The practice of 'illuminating' – putting lighted candles in windows – to support a demonstration or national celebration, kept up sales, as did the auction sales of ships and wine by an inch of candle, described by Samuel Pepys. 'In our office where we met for the sale of two ships by an inch of candle, I observed how they did invite one another and how at last they all did cry and we had much to do to tell who did cry last.' (*Diary*, November 6, 1660.) Self-extinction of the flame on the wick was a more decisive moment for determining the bid to be accepted than a man-administered hammer blow. Lighthouses needed a ready supply – the Eddystone, built in 1698, was still being lit by candles in 1801, though most of them would have been the superior kind made of beeswax. Tallow also went into soap.

Tallow's position as a leading commodity at the beginning of the nineteenth century is shown in the list of eleven commodities and produce given by the *Gentleman's Magazine*, of which tallow was one. The editor only gave one page to market prices each month and presumably chose what he considered the most important. The eleven were corn, flour, oatmeal, sugar, hops, hay and straw, meat, coals and 'tallow, soap and candles'. A typical entry was: 'Tallow, per stone, 8 lb St James's, 4s. 10d.; Clare Market, 0s. 0d.; Whitechapel 4s. 9d. Soap, Yellow 104s.; Mottled 116s.; Curd, 120s. Candles, 13s. 6d. per doz. Moulds 15s.'

A table of unknown origin in Unilever's archives headed 'Quantity of Tallow exported from St Petersburg, Riga and Archangel – Prices of Tallow in London' from 1753 to 1815 indicates a trade from St Petersburg in British ships which grew, albeit in fits and starts, from nil in 1753, 664 casks in 1754, 2 casks in 1755 to 66 525 in 1815. By 1774 the figure was 11 473; in 1781 it was up to 16 303. In 1788 it was 43 592, a high spot not exceeded until 1799 with 57 644. The word 'war' takes the place of figures in the years

1808 to 1811, but the trade started again with 2971 casks in 1812 and by 1814 it was back to 61995 and the following year 66525.

The amount of tallow exported to Britain from Archangel and Riga was comparatively small – 7754 casks from Archangel in 1815 and 870 from Riga. The average price of a stone of tallow in London in the first quarter of 1807 was between 52s. and 57s., in 1809 95s. to 113s., in 1812 73s. to 78s., in 1814 104s. to 111s. 'Ton Tallow' became the standard unit for measuring all types of freight and remained so into the twenteth century.

These fluctuations in price tempted many to speculation of a kind frowned on by others. Those who have read William Thackeray's novel *Vanity Fair* will remember the horror for that kind of thing held by George Osborne's father, 'a plain, simple humble British merchant – an honest one', who lived in his humble mansion in Russell Square and would certainly have been a regular at the Baltic Coffee-House. George, who was to fall at Waterloo, was seeking the hand of Amelia, daughter of Joseph Sedley, 'the coarse man from the Stock Exchange where they love all sorts of practical jokes'.

'You shan't want, sir. The British merchant's son shan't want, sir. My guineas are as good as theirs, George, my boy; and I don't grudge 'em. Call on Mr Chopper as you go through the City to-morrow; he'll have something for you. I don't grudge money when I know you're in good society, because I know that good society can never go wrong. There's no pride in me. I was a humbly born man – but you have had advantages. Make a good use of 'em. Mix with the young nobility. There's many of 'em who can't spend a dollar to your guinea, my boy. And as for the pink bonnets' (here from under the heavy eyebrows there came a knowing and not very pleasing leer) – 'why, boys will be boys. Only there's one thing I order you to avoid, which, if you do not I'll cut you off with a shilling, by Jove; and that's gambling, sir.'

'Of, of course, sir,' said George.

'But to return to the other business about Amelia; why shouldn't you marry higher than a stockbroker's daughter, George – that's what I want to know?'

'It's a family business, sir,' says George, cracking filberts. 'You and Mr Sedley made the match a hundred years ago.'

'I don't deny it; but people's positions alter, sir. I don't deny that Sedley made my fortune, or rather put me in the way of acquiring, by my own

talents and genius, that proud position which, I may say, I occupy in the
tallow trade and the City of London. I've shown my gratitude to Sedley;
and he's tried it of late, sir, as my cheque-book can show. George! I tell you
in confidence I don't like the looks of Mr Sedley's affairs. My chief clerk,
Mr Chopper, does not like the looks of 'em, and he's an old file, and knows
'Change as well as any man in London. Hulker & Bullock are looking shy
at him. He's been dabbling on his own account I fear. They say the *Jeune
Amelie* was his, which was taken by the Yankee privateer *Molasses* [America
had declared war against England in 1812]. And that's flat – unless I see
Amelia's ten thousand down you don't marry her. I'll have no lame duck's
daughter in my family. Pass the wine, sir – or ring for coffee.'

A real-life character who would have earned the scorn of the
fictitious John Osborne, Russia merchant, was Jeremiah Harman;
another was Richard ('Dicky') Thornton who sailed and fought
his own ship to Memel for a cargo of hemp, bet a Greek merchant
£10000 to £1000 Consols would not go below £85 in five years,
offered all newly married members of Lloyd's 100 to 1 against
their having twins, and when he died aged ninety in 1865 left a
fortune variously stated as being between £2 million and £4
million. The anonymous author* of *The City, or the Physiology of
London Business* (1845) described him as 'one of the "greatest of the
great" of our city men . . . who next to the Rothschilds and the
Barings, stands A1 in point of wealth and connection with foreign
countries' and reported he was said to have accumulated a considerable part of his property by his successful operations in tallow.

This gentleman appears to be one of the most adventurous speculators, and,
though ranked as one of the 'old school', so great a success has attended his
pursuits, that something more than mere fortune must have directed his
plans, or else, in the various grades of his speculations, from the export of
old clothes for the service of the Miguelite troops in Portugal, to his subsequent loan contracts, he could not have been so completely triumphant.
   Mr Thornton, who is now [1845] upwards of seventy, has a much younger
appearance. His activity is very great; and he is as early and punctual in his
attendance at business as most of the leading City men. He is a member of
Lloyd's, the North and South American, the Jerusalem, and all the other
coffee-houses of note and standing; and this is nothing extraordinary,
considering that he will take a 'risk' at Lloyd's for £7000 or £10000 with
a good premium, as readily as he would a few casks of tallow at the Baltic.

*In fact D. Morier Evans (1819–74).

The description of him in *The City* adds 'there is only one weak point about Mr Thornton, which is perhaps excusable considering the station he occupies, viz., his boast of his wealth, and his acquaintance with foreign ministers, which is always sure to creep out when he makes his appearance in public'. A not very articulate cockney, he offset his bombast with donations to charity which doubtless he saw that all his friends and enemies knew about. He was the leader of a flash set who aimed to make big profits by taking advantage of cheap money and the fluctuations in the price of a commodity like tallow which they had no interest in buying. Business ethics had changed from the days when those who indulged in engrossing and forestalling were regarded as social outcasts.

Thomas Tooke wrote in *High and Low Prices,*

By the end of 1816 exporters were acting with great forbearance and prudence because almost every class of merchant was at that time suffering from the effects of the too eagerness of adventure of the two preceding years; this great forbearance was of course attended by a large profit to those who adventured; and the consequence of the favourable result of shipments on a small scale was as usual on such occasions, not only that the houses regularly in the trade extended their shipments but that fresh adventurers embarked in them to a considerable extent. Under these circumstances all indicating revived confidence, there arose inevitably a tendency to speculation.

Richard Thornton was one who adventured again and again. He bought all the tallow he could lay hands on at as cheap a price as he could find, and kept it in store until the price rose and gave him a big profit. In 1816 20858 tons of tallow and 18473 tons of hemp were imported into Britain; in 1818 27149 tons and 33020 tons. 'Importers, speculators and manufacturers were successively ruined by having embarked too largely upon the anticipation of the maintenance of the former range of high prices' (Tooke). Figures in the *London Gazette* showed that bankruptcies rose from 1012 in 1818 to 1582 in 1819. Stocks had fallen low by 1816 when the war ended and a boom of imported commodities followed.

One of those who kept his feet on the ground in this tempting period of tallow speculation was a Scotsman called William Wilson who had come south in 1812 at the age of forty with £100 in his pocket following the failure of his fathers' ironworks at Clench in Lanarkshire. He had had business experience in Russia, so he took a man called Benjamin Lancaster into partnership and together they set up as Russia merchants importing tallow from St Petersburg and Riga. Within ten years William Wilson, a regular at the Baltic Coffee-House, was making £4000 a year.

Another regular was a fellow Russia merchant, John Hubbard, who formed John Hubbard & Company in London in 1820. His nephew went to Russia and set up Egerton Hubbard & Co in St Petersburg which did a trade in tallow from Siberia, wheat from the Volga basin, and timber from Archangel. Later, when German competition became severe, Hubbard's went into manufacturing and acquired two large spinning and weaving mills outside St Petersburg.

Within a circle of Russia and Baltic merchants who regularly attended the Baltic Coffee-House, of the type of William Wilson, Benjamin Lancaster and John Hubbard, there was a growing resentment against the Thornton clique, and the suspicion that successful speculation depended on sharp practice and far from straightforward dealing.

A Richard Dighton cartoon of the time obviously refers to Dicky Thornton's unscrupulous dealings in tallow. Captioned 'A Scene on the Baltic Walk, Royal Exchange in November 1822' – the East Country Walk had changed its name as has been noted – the coloured drawing shows ten men in billycock hats, tail coats and breeches advancing menacingly towards a man in a gown and tricorn standing on two casks of tallow with others kneeling and standing beside him. Over them flies a winged 'Old Nick' saying 'I have mark'd you down as my Game, Oh ye Hypocrites'. From the mouths of the others issue 'balloons' carrying cryptic remarks like 'I never was ashamed of John Bull before' and 'Here I stand with as honest a Face as any Man on 'Change, and I must say this is a rascally trick, although it does not proceed from the Trade.'

One spouts a verse:

> What is Friendship but a name,
> A Charm that lulls to sleep,
> A Shade that follows Wealth or Fame
> But leaves poor Herman Gerrard to weep.

One of the men facing the angry mob is saying 'Well, what are you all staring at? A man has a right to make money as he pleases – I don't care who gains the day so long as I get my 2/- turn of the market.' A man on his knees with his hands clasped in prayer says 'O Richard look down on my Hypocritical Face and receive the grateful thanks of an unworthy Character, for this Act of thy Mercy towards my Old Master.'

What act of Dicky Thornton the cartoon is referring to is not clear, but it would seem not to have met with the approval of Richard Dighton who drew it, and he was probably reflecting the view of the majority of his readers.

In his book James Findlay wrote:

Large speculations in tallow took place at the Baltic, and at one time there was as much gambling in that commodity as in Consols – proper settling days were fixed, when sales for purchase and delivery were arranged much in the same way as business is conducted by the stockbrokers; large sums of money changed hands and, while there were heavy losses, it is known that several capitalists in the City secured vast sums through their speculations in tallow.

It was a reputation that lingered. Twenty years later the anonymous writer of *The City, or the Physiology of London Business* described the Baltic Coffee-House as

an establishment of considerable notoriety from the large speculations which at different periods have been carried on among the subscribers who, representing the trade in so important an article as tallow, have followed under a certain position of affairs that course of dealing that, like transactions on the Stock Exchange, frequently terminated in the ruin of the parties concerned.

When the speculations exploded, he said, they brought much loss to the unfortunates who happened not to be in the secret of the proper time to sell.

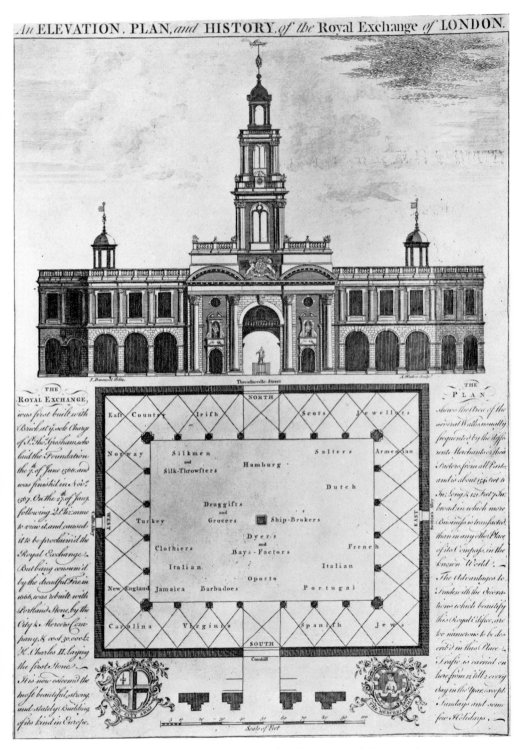

Front elevation of the first Royal Exchange, completed in 1567, and diagram of the various 'Walks' with shipbrokers in the centre

Opposite: Charter-party dated 1813, perhaps the oldest still existing on the Baltic Exchange

The interior of the second Royal Exchange

To the Right Honourable WILLIAM PITT, first Lord Commissioner of the TREASURY, Principal Secretary of STATE, and CHANCELLOR of the EXCHEQUER, this humble Perspective VIEW of the Inside of the Royal Exchange in LONDON, is by Permission humbly Dedicated, by his most Grateful, Obedient, and most Obliged humble Servant — J. Chapman.

Charterparty.

LONDON, *26 July 1813.*

IT is this Day mutually agreed between *Mr John Scott*
Owner, of the good Ship or Vessel, called the *Jaines*
of the Burthen of *212* Tons, or thereabouts, now *in the River Thames*
behalf of himself & Partners under the firm of Brook,
and *John Ord Esqr for on*
Ord & of London Merchant. **Merchants**;

That the said Ship being tight, staunch and strong, and every way fitted for the Voyage.
shall *& will set sail on or before the second day*
of August next ensuing, & proceed to Archangel
or so near thereunto as she may safely get
and there receive on board from the Agents
of the said Freighters a full and complete
Cargo of Tallow, and other Goods, but not
less than Four hundred and ninety Casks
of Tallow

which the said Merchants bind themselves to Ship not exceeding what she can
reasonably stow and carry over and above her Tackle, Apparel, Provisions and
Furniture; and being so loaded; shall therewith proceed to *London.*

——————————— or so near thereunto as she may safely get, and deliver the same on
being paid Freight *at & after the rate of Seven Pounds*
& Ton Gross Weight for Tallow and for other
Goods in the Customary proportion thereto
with Five Pounds & cent on the Amount
of the Freight in lieu of Primage & Port
charges *(The Acts of God, Kingsenemies, Fire,*
Restraint of Princes and Rulers during the said Voyage always excepted.) The Freight to
be paid on unloading, and right Delivery of the Cargo, *One half in Cash & the other*
by Bills at Three months. Twenty *running* Days are to be allowed the
said Merchant (if the Ship is not sooner dispatched) for loading the said Ship, at *Arch-*
angel and Fifteen days for unloading
London.

And *Ten* Days on Demurrage, over and above the said laying Days, at *Seven* Pounds
per Day. Penalty for Non-Performance of this Agreement *£2000:*

John Ord

Witness James Bentley
Broker

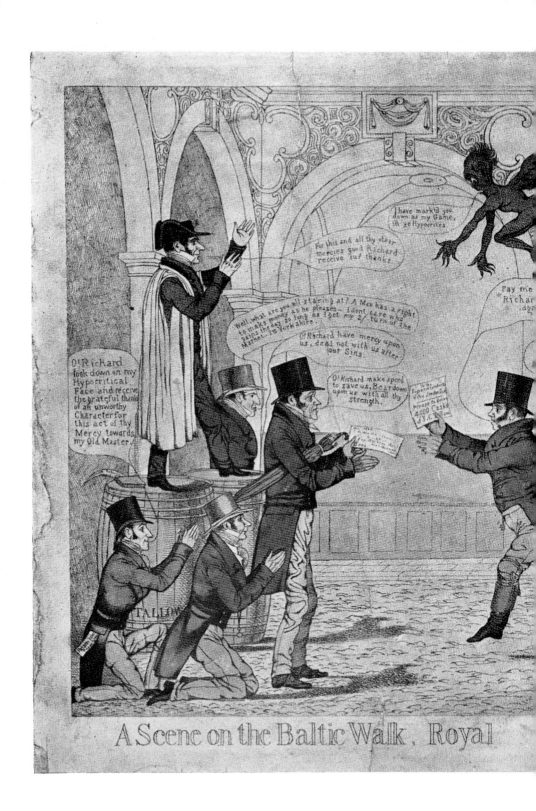

A Scene on the Baltic Walk, Royal

A Richard Dighton cartoon referring to Richard Thornton's unscrupulous dealings in tallow. What act of Thornton's Dighton depicts is not clear but it would not seem to have met with his approval, and he was probably reflecting the view of the majority of his readers

Richard Thornton, a
prominent member of the
Baltic, drawn by Richard
Dighton, 1823

Thomas Tooke, author of *Thoughts and Details
on the High and Low Prices of the Past Thirty
Years* (1823), and the subject of this punning
cartoon by Dighton, 1822

Opposite above: 'The destruction of the Royal
Exchange by fire on Jan. 10th 1838', drawn
on stone by William Heath

Opposite below: Queen Victoria opens the fourth
Royal Exchange, in 1844

The Destruction of the Royal Exchange by Fire on Jan.ʳ 10ᵗ 1838.

Drawn on Stone by Mr WILLIAM HEATH from a sketch made by him on the spot.
This Print is by permission most respectfully Dedicated to Richard Lambert Jones Esq.ʳ

The brig, a two-masted vessel square rigged on both masts – the most common form of small British merchant sailing ship until the middle of the nineteenth century. This vessel was built in 1858

'An outward bound East Indiaman sailing from the Downs'

The Russians who were the great movers of these schemes were chary in giving too large a supply to the English market, and being in the habit of keeping to themselves the true state of stock at home, were enabled to play with the London dealers just as they pleased, because from St Petersburg came nearly the whole of what was imported.

It was a reputation which more and more regulars at the Baltic Coffee-House deplored, and none more than forty-two-year-old Thomas Tooke, who in 1823 published *Thoughts and Details on the High and Low Prices of the Past Thirty Years*, already quoted. He was born in Cronstadt (the port of St Petersburg) where his father had been chaplain to the British factory. At the age of fifteen he entered a business house in St Petersburg and later came to London and joined the firm of Stephen Thornton & Co as a partner. Later still he was a partner of Astell, Tooke & Thornton. He was the subject of a Dighton cartoon with the punning caption 'I TOOKE thee for thy betters'. Robert Craig calls him 'a failed Russia merchant'. His national fame certainly rests elsewhere. In 1821 he founded the Political Economy Club with David Ricardo, Robert Malthus and James Mill, and was elected a Fellow of the Royal Society. But he earns his place in this story through being one of the group – and that the most distinguished – who in the spring of 1823 decided to stop talking about the undesirable amount of speculation in their midst and act.

3. Coffee-House Subscribers

How many regulars of the Baltic Coffee-House attended a general meeting called for April 22, 1823, at 58 Threadneedle Street to discuss ways of closing ranks against the unwanted speculators is not known, but twenty-three of them volunteered to serve on the committee elected to put the establishment on the new footing and carry out the plans of reform they had in mind.

Two of them were William Wilson, of Wilson & Lancaster,* and Thomas Tooke, the economist. Others were Thomas Wilson, senior partner of Thos. Wilson & Co. of 6 Warnford Court and a Member of Parliament; Thomas Forster, head of T. F. Forster & Co., merchants, of 6 St Helen's Passage, Bishopsgate; Nicholas Garry, son (?) of Joseph Garry, a tallow chandler, of 70 Grays Inn Lane; John Harvey, a timber dealer, of 44 Brick Lane, Spitalfields; John Cattley of Cattley & Carr, Russia merchants; Benjamin Hawes, a partner of Thomas & Benjamin Hawes, soapmakers, of Commercial Road, Lambeth; S. C. Holland, a partner in Holland & Elborough, tallow chandlers, of 52 South Audley Street; William Levin, a partner in William & James Levin, merchants, of 36 Great Winchester Street; Alexander Macdonald, attached (or perhaps son of) John Macdonald, Russia and oil broker, 16 George Street; J. L. T. Melville (who also appears as Miéville), perhaps of Miéville & de la Chaumette, stockbrokers, of 11 Angel Court; John Mitchell of John Mitchell & Co., merchants, of 52 Old Broad Street; Benjamin Pead, merchant, of 6 Broad Street Buildings; Richard Raikes of W. & T. Raikes, merchants, of 79 London Wall; William May Simonds, merchant, of 80 Old Broad

* Benjamin Lancaster was master of the Tallow Chandlers Company in 1823.

Street; Charles Soames, partner in H. A. & C. Soames, commercial and general brokers, of 1 Pope's Head Alley; Samuel Thornton of Samuel Thornton & Co, Russia brokers, of 57 Old Broad Street; C. G. Thornton, probably of Steven Thornton & Co, Russia brokers, of 54 Old Broad Street; and A. H. Thomson, probably of Thomson & Mildred, Turkey merchants, of 3 Howford's Building, Fenchurch Street, who presided at the meeting.

Of the three others there was no mention in Pigot's Directory of 1823–4. Their names were Henry A. Douglas, Edward Parsons and John Schneider.

The meeting of April 22 drew up a list of thirteen 'Rules and Regulations'. Number one was that the establishment should have the name of the Baltic Coffee-House. Those who were to use it, or rather part of it, were 'subscribers' not members. It was not a subscription house, the heading under which Pigot listed Boodle's and White's, but the establishment had one room in it to which only subscribers were admitted – the subscribers' room or subscription room.

As Bryant Lillywhite puts it,

The growing population and need of living space; disruption caused by fires, demolition, rebuilding and improvements ever present in a city such as London; the development of communications and travel facilities; the more efficient administration of public services such as the Post Office and the organised distribution of the press &c, made it inevitable that the early type of coffee-house would one day outlive its usefulness . . . by the early years of the nineteenth century the coffee-houses were mostly in the hands of vintners, and coffee drinking but a minor attraction. Although many maintained the description of coffee-house, their character varied with the ebb and flow of custom, the mode of the time or perhaps the licensing laws. Changes are noted from inn to tavern, tavern to coffee-house, thence to coffee-house tavern and hotel, and lastly to hotel. Others changed from coffee-house to subscription house, paving the way for clubs.

The meeting of April 22 decided to restrict the number of subscribers to 300, a firm being reckoned as a single subscriber. They wanted only six subscribers (individuals or firms) who were stockbrokers, a decision which points to the anti-gambling and speculating purpose of the exercise – not too many of those coarse men from the Stock Exchange who delighted in practical jokes. If more than 300 subscribers were to be admitted the change would have to be approved by a general meeting. No longer could anyone walk over from the Royal Exchange, pay their penny and become a member of the 'club' for the day; the door of the Baltic Coffee-House, or at least its heart, the subscribers' room, which kept the papers and commercial information, was now closed to all but the chosen 300. The names of candidates for admission to the ranks had to be recommended by six existing subscribers and such recommendations approved by the committee of twenty-three.

Individual subscribers were to pay four guineas (£4 4s.) a year and firms of two partners six guineas. If there were more than two partners, a firm paid eight guineas. Each subscriber had also to give an 'allowance for the waiter' – a guinea a year for individuals, a guinea and a half for two-partner firms, two guineas for larger firms. They made it a rule 'that no additional remuneration be given to the waiters in the room' and added that at least four waiters be provided.

In addition to the inner sanctum to which only subscribers would be admitted – the 'subscription room' – they decided that 'a dining room and a sale room be provided for the accommodation of the subscribers *and the public* [our italics], and that wine, tea, coffee, chocolate and sandwiches be furnished in the coffee room'. 'The establishment' therefore consisted of 'the room', 'a dining room', 'a sale room' and 'the coffee room'; and anyone could walk in from the street and use any of these except 'the room'. It thus retained to a large extent its former public coffee-house role. James Findlay adds that the sale room was in the upper part of the establishment, the entrance to which was by Hercules Passage, and measured 69 feet by 30 feet. Subscribers could bring a visitor to the Room, but he had to be introduced by a member of the committee who had to write his name and place of abode in a book kept for the purpose. An entry gave right of admission for seven days. Visitors were confined to retired gentlemen living more than twenty miles from London and those still in business who lived fifty miles out or more. To prevent gate-crashers rule 8 stated that 'there be only one door for admission' – this was presumably to the subscription room and probably fronted Threadneedle Street, while entrance to the public rooms was through Hercules Passage and into Sun Court.

The establishment was to be run by the committee of twenty-three meeting twice a month on the first and third Tuesday at two o'clock in the afternoon, five members of the committee forming a quorum. If subscribers had anything to say about the management of the coffee-house, they had to persuade fifty of their number to sign a requisition asking the committee to call a general meeting and state the reason for the meeting. Apart from this, the committee had the power to call a general meeting at any time.

'The room', they declared, was to open on the first day of May 1823, and subscriptions were to be paid for one year in advance within a month of when it was due.

The ninth rule gave the names of the papers and publications to be provided for subscribers' reading. There were thirteen English papers: *The Times, New Times, Morning Herald, Morning Chronicle, Morning Post, Morning Advertiser, Public Ledger, British Press, Courier, Sun, Globe, Star, Traveller*; two French papers: *Journal de Débats* and *Le Moniteur Universel*; two German papers: *Hamburg Correspondence* and *Börsen Haller Liste*; *Amsterdam Courant*; *New York Paper*; and the following: *London Gazettes, Farmers Journal, London Price Currant*, Liverpool Papers, Bills of Entry A & B, Trade List, Lloyd's List, Sound and St Petersburg Lists, Parliamentary Papers, Tarifs (*sic*) of Russia, France, Holland, Germany, America, Popes Custom & Excise Laws, Robsons Directory, Brooke's Gazetteer, Court Calendar, Almanack.

A note beneath the list stated

that the whole of the Lists and Foreign Publications be filed; together with *The Times, New Times, Ledger, London Gazettes* and *Farmers Journal*. That there be a complete collection of Maps and that there be a sufficient number of each publication to answer the demand of the room; the number of the above, and of any other publications, to be determined by the Committee.

The tenth rule was 'That Ship Bills connected with the Russian and Baltic Trades only be allowed to be displayed in the room' –

confirmation that the regulars of the Baltic Coffee-House were almost entirely confined to Russia and Baltic merchants, and dealers and manufacturers concerned with the old East Country goods of hemp, oil seeds, timber, tallow etc., and that the Virginia element had dropped out.

The meeting would have been held with the concurrence and co-operation of the proprietor of the Baltic Coffee-House, William Melton, the wine merchant, who is listed as such in directories of 1825. He will also have taken part in the meetings before April 22, at which the rules and regulations were drafted, and his approval given to the final thirteen. He probably acted as head waiter.

The thirteenth rule was 'That a book is to be kept by the Secretary in which is to be entered the rules and regulations of the establishment – together with the names of the Committee and subscribers.' The honorary secretary, who entered in the rules and kept the book of visitors, was William Wilson Junr of whom nothing is known apart from the fact that he was not the son of William Wilson of Wilson & Lancaster.

The Room duly opened on May 1, 1823, and six visitors were welcomed; two men from Tipton in Staffordshire called Stevenson and Cochrane, introduced by Benjamin Hawes and William Wilson; a Mr Cross from Hull, introduced by John Cattley; a Mr Lashmar from Brighton, introduced by William Wilson; Mr Penford from Riga and Mr Kausler from Havannah, introduced by William Wilson and a subscriber called Scheer. Over the next few weeks there were to be visitors from Dudley, Leith, Ipswich, Newcastle, Hull, Hemel Hempstead, Paris, Leeds, Stockholm, Londonderry, St Petersburg, Marseilles, Amsterdam, the Canaries, Sydney, Antwerp, Gibraltar, Madrid, Hamburg, Madeira and Jamaica. The 'Baltic' was off to a good international start.

Subscribers' names in the visitors book for that first month included J. Rodwell, J. Walker, Thos Anderson, H. Nelson, C. Greenwood, G. Bond, Wm Paton, H. Nevill, W. W. Simpson, H. Seymour, J. B. Rayner, J. Houghton, Geo Burworth. Sixty-seven visitors were introduced that May, twenty of them from overseas.

In forming the committee, setting up a Subscribers' Room within the coffee-house, and inviting approved subscribers to pay for the privilege of using it, Arthur Thomson and his friends had done nothing original or exclusive. In 1769 certain insurance under-writers who, as already noted, used Lloyd's Coffee-House in Lombard Street were, like the first committee-men of the Baltic Coffee-House, shocked by the gambling of certain of their fellow regulars. They hesitated to change the routine or clientele of the Lombard Street establishment, and opted for removing themselves to other premises, inviting those who felt as they did to join them. After two years at what they called New Lloyd's Coffee-House in Pope's Head Alley, they decided to move as a working group to a building which would be less of a coffee-house and more suited to their specific business of marine insurance. In order to raise money for building or renting such a place, certain of their number immediately became distinguished from the rest as those who subscribed to such a project. Seventy-nine of them volunteered to put up £100 each and chose nine of their number to act as a committee to make the necessary arrangements. Three years later Julius Angerstein organized three rooms for them on the upper floors of the Royal Exchange, to which they moved in 1774. The rooms formed a separate suite which became the new Lloyd's Coffee-House, with all the services which had been avail-able to the public at Pope's Head Alley but were now only open to subscribers in a Subscribers' Room. For a time the coffee-house part was open to the public but in 1778 entrance to any part of 'Lloyd's' – the Subscribers' Room and the Captains' Room – was restricted to subscribers and their guests. The pattern, therefore, is very similar to that of the Baltic Coffee-House after 1823.

For most of the eighteenth-century City coffee-houses which had managed to survive into 1823 – and they were not many – the terms of entrance instead of being a penny each day were 'a certain sum per annum'. An exception was Garraways, which remained a public house until it closed in the middle of the nineteenth century. But the Jamaica Coffee-House in St Michael's Alley had 300 sub-scribers or so, mostly traders to Madeira and the West Indies. It had an 'exceedingly commodious' subscription room to which admis-

sion was three guineas a year. John's Coffee-House at 86 Cornhill
had a small subscription room for merchants and brokers in the
Gibraltar, Portugal and Turkey trades. The Jerusalem Coffee-
House had 400 East India and Sydney merchants and captains as
subscribers. Its subscription room had all the Chinese, Malayan,
Indian and Australian papers, prices current and shipping lists. It
was thronged with subscribers from two to three every afternoon.

But the largest and most important was the North and South
American Coffee-House in Threadneedle Street, whose subscription room was patronized by subscribers interested in trade with
the United States ('South' America) and British North America,
(Canada). They paid an annual subscription of three or four
guineas. In their room they read all the arrival and departure dates
of steamers, packets and traders to and from America.

The author of *The City* says,

[In] affording a complete circuit of information necessary for mercantile life
the North and South American Coffee-House will scarcely yield the palm
to any place of public business resort, not even Lloyds . . . The North and
South American Coffee-House has assumed the character of a general news
emporium and, unlike the Jerusalem, the Baltic and the Jamaica, has departed
from the rules which seem to guide these establishments in the regulation of
their proceedings by closely confining themselves to the particular interest
with which their names are identified and keeping connection only with
that interest and catering for its support.

Many, if not most of the subscribers of the Baltic Coffee-House,
however, also subscribed to the North and South American,
Jerusalem, Jamaica and Lloyd's.

No contemporary description of the Baltic Coffee-House of
1823 has survived, but it cannot have changed to any great extent
when in 1845 the author of *The City* called it

a very snug little place managed under the superintendence of a committee
of management in a highly creditable manner . . .

The whole arrangements of the place show a nice taste for economy and
comfort, and there is no lack of one or the other. The attendants are obliging
and civil, having an eye to the committee of management who are sure to
take notice of any irregularity in this respect. In the upper part of the house
is the public sale-room, where tallows, oils etc. are offered at auction by the
selling-brokers. It is a long narrow apartment, having no peculiar charac-

teristic beyond a slight effluvia from the samples exhibited, and the dingy appearance of the place, besmeared with ink from the pens of the juveniles, or clerks in attendance for principals who are not buyers, and who, from the age of twelve upwards, may be seen either marking the prices paid in their catalogues, or designing figures, after the antique, upon the deal tables appropriated to their use. The sales occupy about a couple of hours, beginning two and three, often not concluding till four or five o'clock p.m.

The first of these sales under the new organization took place on Friday, May 9, 1823, at two in the afternoon. It was announced in an advertisement in the *Public Ledger* of May 4 under the heading 'Sales By The Candle' which listed the following goods:

30 CASKS PETERSBURGH PEARL ASHES
300 BARRELS STOCKHOLM TAR, JUST ARRIVED
9 CASKS ITALIAN TALLOW
27 TUNS GREENLAND WHALE OIL, BANKRUPT'S EFFECTS
AND OTHER GOODS
Catalogues and further particulars in time by
J. B. RAYNER, BROKER, CORNHILL

Sales by candle were a common feature of all City coffee-houses. The same day sandal wood, elephants' teeth, sea horse teeth and East India sealing wax were being offered at Garraways; claret and sherry at Hambros; tobacco at the London Commercial Sale Rooms; skins at Gill's; a fast sailing brig, a fine yacht, a steam packet at Lloyd's Coffee-House, Cornhill.

When the Baltic advertisement was repeated on May 6 three additional items were listed:

70 tons fine Sicily Barilla.
36 Ditto Palm Oil.
20 casks Riga Pearl Ashes.

J. B. Rayner, as shown in the visitors book, was a member. On July 8 Wilson & Lancaster, Russia brokers, of 80 Old Broad Street, held an auction of Petersburgh Yellow Candle Tallow; and on July 20 of 120 tons of Sound East India hemp just landed ex *Moira*, Captain Hornblow, from Calcutta, lying at the East India Docks under the care of Captain Eastfield, to be sold in small lots for the convenience of the trade.

In 1830 William Wilson bought the patent of a man called James Soames for a method of separating the solid and liquid constituents of coconut oil by hydraulic pressure and formed a company to exploit it. The process yielded a fat which could be used as a substitute for tallow in candle manufacture. He acquired 1000 acres of coconut plantation in Ceylon and set up a pressing factory in Vauxhall. His partner in his Russia broker business, Benjamin Lancaster, became a fellow director. Neither of them wished to use their names in this separate manufacturing venture, so borrowing the name of an aunt of Benjamin Lancaster, they launched out as 'E. Price & Company'. This had a distinguished career as Price's Patent Candle Company, re-formed under that title in 1847 with James P. Wilson and George F. Wilson, William's sons, as joint managing directors. In 1854 they set up another factory at Bromborough, on Merseyside, to make candles and cloth oils. In 1937 Price's (Bromborough) Ltd became part of Unilever as a unit for the manufacture of fatty acids. Both this, and the part of Price's which continued independently at Battersea, still operate.

From 1823 the demand for tallow for candles began to fall away. In that year a Frenchman called Chevreul discovered that the fatty acid could be resolved into a liquid and hard white non-odorous crystals called stearine, which made much better candles than smelly soft tallow. William Wilson and Benjamin Lancaster developed this in England.

How far the action of forming a committee and drawing up rules and regulations for the Baltic Coffee-House was the result of righteous indignation at the wilder aspects of speculation in Russian tallow, and how far they were motivated by the desire to create a 'closed shop' to ensure fair shares all round, is difficult to say. There was, it seems, an element of sour grapes in their action, an anxiety to keep outsiders from spoiling the market, a move to preserve the *status quo* for the less adventurous, 'humble' John Osbornes. But it would be interesting to know how many, if any, of the regulars of the Baltic Coffee-House found themselves excluded from their favourite haunt on May 1, 1823, as a result of not having been able to find six friends willing to recommend them as one of the select 300. It was a situation which the pressure group of Lloyd's underwriters obviated by moving out of the Lombard Street house and leaving those whose behaviour they resented in the place of their choice, and setting up elsewhere. Arthur Thomson's group, who would have been the majority, made the revolution from within, occupied the place and, at least by implication, invited all those who disagreed with their reforms to leave the premises and then shut the doors against their re-entry. Whether, in fact, this happened and to what extent is not known. The committee which drew up the rules and regulations and directed with business-like precision that they be written into a book, would have kept some kind of minutes of their fortnightly meetings, even if they were as hilarious as those of the Average Market Letter Committee, but sadly they have not survived.

But, for the outbreak of speculation at this time which is said to have driven them to do what they did there is ample evidence, notably from the most articulate of the committee's founding fathers, Thomas Tooke. In the second volume of his *History of Prices* he wrote:

In the early part of 1823 the entrance of the armies of France into Spain giving rise to the apprehension of a general war in Europe caused a speculative advance in the prices of colonial produce and of some other commodities of which the cost of production was likely to be raised or the supplies obstructed by such an event.

But the speculation of this time had deeper roots. During the ten years which followed the end of hostilities with France commodities had poured into Britain in ever increasing quantities to replenish empty stock rooms and give industry the raw materials to get factories and factory hands fully employed again. Merchants embarked on a buying bonanza and inevitably bought on a much greater scale than the immediate situation justified, for supplies were plentiful and cheap. They could be hoarded and sold later – at a profit. It was too easy, and plenty of amateurs were unable to resist 'having a go'. Mushroom companies were recklessly formed to exploit the peace and benefit from Britain being the only country in the world on the gold standard. A mini-South Sea Bubble ensued. In 1824 some 624 company prospectuses were issued. One of them was for the drainage of the Red Sea to recover the treasure left by the Jews when, according to the Old Testament, the waters divided to let them pass. The Bank of England began to refuse to discount bills of exchange and many country banks went bankrupt. Many merchants overdid the importing and held on to their stocks for too long. As H. Macleod has described, when the obligations of the speculators became due, the sale of the commodities they had bought had to be forced to meet them.

Universal discredit now succeeded, goods became unsaleable so that stocks which are usually held in anticipation of demand were wholly unavailable to meet the pecuniary engagements of the holders. Merchants who had accepted bills of exchange for only half the value of the goods consigned to them were unable to realise even that half, or even obtain advances or security on the bills of lading. The usury laws which limited interest to 5 per cent greatly aggravated distress.

Though it was demonstrably the purpose of the Baltic 300 to dissociate themselves from such activities, the fact remains that a large part of the commodities for which there was now a big demand came from Russia and the Baltic Sea, open once again to English traders after so many years. Prominent among them were the familiar 'naval stores'. Treaties of Reciprocity were made with Prussia, Denmark and the Hanseatic Republics by which British ports were opened to their ships – a first step in the penetration of what Lord John Russell called the Deep Forest of Protection.

By far the largest amount of tallow came from Russia. But there is mention of imports of tallow from the States of the Rio de la Plata in 1829 – 62 hundredweight. This had become 27983 in 1834, the year in which 357 hundredweight were first imported from Brazil, 2163 from the United States and 565 from the British North American Colonies.

The opening up of new sources of tallow in South America, and later Australia, severely curtailed the operations of the Richard

Thornton school of Russian tallow speculators who depended on a single producer for the fluctuations in price and supply which enabled them to buy cheap and sell dear. It was a change of circumstances which impressed the author of *The City*, writing in 1845.

The increasing quantity brought yearly from Buenos Ayres and Monte Video, and the new source of supply derived from the successful manufacture of the staple in Sydney, has quite changed the aspect of business in tallow. Stocks regularly coming forward from St Petersburgh, aided by the South American and Australian imports, the market is kept in a proper condition, with a fair equilibrium in prices; and hence, less chance than ever is presented for our northern friends to take advantage of our extended use of the article which originally they almost exclusively supplied.

It has certainly been a fortunate thing that the excess of agricultural stock, both in South America and Australia has had the effect of turning the attention of parties there to the manufacture and of causing competition, to the benefit of our own country. South American tallow has all along maintained a fair and remunerating price in the market, and though perhaps not equal in point of quality to P.Y.C. [Petersburgh Yellow Candle – one of the technicalities of the trade], still it is found useful by the chandlers; while recent imports of Sydney tallow promise to become a strong rival, late sales having brought high rates.

Large sums of money have been made and lost in the article, but anterior to the date of import of foreign and colonial tallow. A few years ago, the three or four failures that then took place gave, apparently, the finishing stroke to extended speculation; and, notwithstanding the amount of money involved was little less than £300000 or £400000, it was found that the business had been transacted on such an unstable basis as to warrant great precaution in future transactions with several of the persons who figured in them. The danger that some of the wealthy houses escaped by the early closing of the speculation was very evident when certain facts were disclosed; and such was their effect, that ever since, making due allowance for other causes, little or no speculation has occurred in this market.

Speculation in tallow for the last few years has existed but in name. Numbers of the brokers would be found, even now (1845), willing enough to conduct such business provided principals intimated an inclination to enter into it. But as no such disposition is shown they are obliged to confine themselves to what are termed transactions 'on the spot' instead of 'delivery'; the latter being the description of contract that would allow of a rise or fall in price, it usually embracing a period of two or three months forward, while the former is the dealing that settles the business at once, without a margin for fluctuation being given.

But the South American and Australian tallow trade did not fully develop till later. In the 1830s British shipping's principal playground was still the North Sea. More British ships were sailing to Hamburg, through the Skager Rack, the Categat, the Sound, the Baltic Sea and the Gulf of Finland, than those of any other nation. Of the 2180 vessels (213 044 tons) entering Hamburg in 1829, 754 were British (115 076 tons), 353 were Danish, 205 Dutch. In 1830 1009 were British out of a total of 2530. Out of the 1510 ships (267 054 tons) entering the Port of Cronstadt for St Petersburg in 1832, 773 were British (165 348 tons). The average freight rates for articles carried from St Petersburg to London in that year were 50s. a ton for hemp, 25s. a ton for tallow, 4s. an imperial quarter of wheat, and 50s. for a standard hundred of deals.

The figures come to life in the logs of John Lidgett, master of the brig *Benjamin*, who spent a large part of his life sailing from London to Cronstadt and back. One of these accounts started on May 5, 1831, with the *Benjamin* in dock stowing away cargo. A pilot came on board on the 10th and they dropped down river, and when they anchored at Blackwall at seven that evening they found that James Thompson, the cook, had had enough and run away. At Holyhaven (Holehaven) on the 12th, they secured another cook from London, and by the 17th they were free of the river, sent 'Main Royall' yard up and 'set sail, the *Union* of London in company, Bound for St Petersburg'. They sighted Ostergarnsholm on June 12, passed the Koskar and Summers lighthouses and came to at 1 a.m. on June 18 in six fathoms one mile below the Mould head. Lidgett handed over 21 dogs in wooden crates to the harbour master. On July 1, just under two months after he had left London, he was in Cronstadt where he took on 480 bags of oats, 27 casks of tallow, four 21 foot deals 4 inch, five 21 foot deals 2 inch, 94 pieces of beef for ship's use, and coils of cordage. The next day he loaded a further 424 bags of oats, 30 single mats (?), 12 bags of bread. During the next three days he stowed another 50 bags of oats, 267 bags of linseed, and a final 50 bags of oats. By July 10 they were at sea again.

They had only been sailing for a couple of days when at 1.30 a.m. one of the crew, Miles Bremer, felt unwell and thirsty, and drank a great quantity of cold water.

Second Mate said he was doing wrong and stopped him. Captain called at 3.30 a.m. and found him sitting on deck without shoes and stockings. On previous day it being a very hot day he lift off his flannels, shirt and other warm clothing that he had been in the habit of wearing for years and put on a damp frock alone, after which time he was never well as he complained of pain in his stomack and Captain thought it was inflammation in his bowels and gave him Ruebor & Jollop and put his feet in warm water.

The next day Miles had blisters on his chest, and the captain put a mustard plaster on his feet; on the 15th he developed hiccups and drank only barley water. The next afternoon he died, and 'at ½ past 4 p.m. committed his body to the sea all hands being present'.

Two days later there was a similar but worse crisis. John Apps reported feeling unwell and was given an emetic. He was given Ruebor and Jollop with a little laudanum but it did not stay in his stomach. On July 18 Apps

changed for Death, matter coming from his nose and mouth of a green colour; at 2 p.m. he died having had the venereal diseases upon him all the voyage and every day getting worse. The men in the forecastle supposed him to have killed himself by taking part of lotion of Bluestone & Water & Mercury which lotion was pretended to apply outwardly, saying he would either kill or cure this with the emetic in his then emaciated state.

Passing the Trindlers Light on July 25 they spoke to the brig *Roselinda* from Samtaming Bound to St Petersburg out ten weeks which 'desired to be reported at Loyds'. On August 4 they were off Lowestoft and two days later moored at Stangate Creek. It had been a three-month trip. They unloaded their cargo. 'The tallow still continues melten in the hold with heat of the grain; middle part hard' noted Captain Lidgett. Before rounding the Nore Light and sailing into the Medway and anchoring a mile below Graves-end he received orders 'to go to the Guard Ship for Pratticque', which the Oxford Dictionary spells 'Pratique' and defines as 'the permission granted to a ship to hold intercourse with a port after quarantine or on showing a clean bill of health'.

On that voyage of the *Benjamin* John Lidgett had had fine weather, including at least one 'very hot day' when Miles Bremer sat on deck wearing only a damp frock.

Lloyd's List of March 4, 1823, reported 'navigation of the Weser has been impeded by frost and all Vessels hauled into Brake and other small harbours. The intensity of the frost has exceeded the utmost degree of cold experienced in these parts in the memory of the oldest inhabitants.'

At the other end of the year it was equally stormy. Even in July *Lloyd's List* was reporting how the *Ocean* of Shields, laden with deals, was seen 'driving about in the East Sea full of water and abandoned by the Crew'. On August 31 came the message from St Petersburg 'the night before last the Lighter no 156 having on board 55 chests indigo and 36 barrels of cochineal from the *Rapid*, Warren, – also sugars, logwood & C from sundry vessels, – was in a sinking state near the floating light at the Bar.' No sweeter, bluer sea can there have been for many a year.

The Russia and Baltic trade in the year the committee of the Baltic Coffee-House was established was being won by manly determination and nautical expertise of a high order, with no small element of heroism.

Few merchants sitting in the snug little room of the Baltic Coffee-House can have had much idea of the hardship and endurance which these voyages entailed. They had their own problems, however, different in kind from the dramas of the sea but eventful and stimulating in their own way. The correspondence of Baltic member James Sharp, of Sharp & Whitbourn, corn dealers, with his nephew Henry in Danzig shows the sheer hard work of it all.

On May 18, 1830, he wrote in his scrawly hand:

Mr Catt wishes to have his 90 Lasts Ship'd by two Vessells. I wrote to him last Night advising the improbability of getting Vessells of that description and recommending it to be ship'd by one (& that British if to be had). You need not hurry in purchasing unless tempted by quality or price. And should any superior parcel offer we should like a [illegible] – but are not driven to buy, but some of that description are desirable should you not find the 40 Lasts good. Wheat dull yesterday and am fearfull the Duty will advance a Shill^g this week but expect it down again before our Wheat can arrive from Dantzick.

On June 8 Uncle James wrote to say

the distant Country Markets are scantily supplied with Wheat and prices full as high as London, so that the last Weekly Average for 28th May and

London average are the same. Duty now 21/8d probably may be 1/- lower in three weeks. We wish the wheat purchased for us to be shipp'd as soon as good Vessells can be obtain'd. We hope the 60 Lasts bo^t by Messrs Soermans are in condition to bear the voyage without old, but if you find it absolutely necessary to mix a few old with it, let it be in small proportion and such as are sweet as we have no wish to import old wheat ... We think you might prepare part of your letters on leisure days and write more fully what is going forward so to shipments, Vessells etc.

Poor Henry! He was rushed off his feet as it was. On March 15 the following year (1831) he received a letter from James telling him wheat was dull at Danzig and giving way at Hamburg

where supplies are increasing and where I think it may be advisable for you to go after staying at Rotterdam a week or ten days ... If you find you cannot purchase to your mind at Rotterdam and learn that the Hambro Market is more tempting you have our consent to repair thither immediately, leaving instructions for letters &C to be forwarded ... There will be no risk to purchasing a cargo or two at Rotterdam at or under the price we talk of and then go on to Hambro, but should you purchase any at Rotterdam dispatch part or all by first good Vessell you can obtain and order the Capt to report as soon as possible after his arrival here.

Exhausting. And no fast motor cars or aeroplanes, nor railways even, to move about in.

Engaged in the same kind of exercise were Thomas Usborne & Son of 5 New London Street, who, unlike Sharp & Whitbourn, still operate with an office at St Mary Axe, as Usborne & Son. They possess a copy of a printed circular dated December 14, 1840, on the lines of that of the Hewetsons of 1817, listing the prices of British and Foreign corn – the latter being wheat from Danzig and Königsberg, Rostock and Stettin, Hamburg, Odessa, Taganrog and Marianople, Riga and Petersburg, the United States and Spain; barley, rye and oats from most of these places too.

In their determination to check increases in these duties, indeed to abolish them altogether, by every means of extra-parliamentary agitation at their disposal, competitors like James Sharp and Thomas Usborne were at one, as were all subscribers of the Baltic Coffee-House – and none more than Thomas Tooke. In 1820 he had drawn up his famous Petition of the Merchants of London,

D

and persuaded all the leading men in the City to sign it, headed by
Samuel Thornton, a disgruntled Russia merchant prejudiced by the
duties favouring Canadian timber. Lord Ashburton (Alexander
Baring) presented it to Parliament. On presentation, as was customary, the petition was debated. In it Tooke had set out all the
principles of the Free Trade theory. Lord Liverpool, the Prime
Minister, could not dispute their truth and cogency, but could
hold out no hope that the petition would be conceded. In a
memorable passage of his speech the Prime Minister declared that
the hindrance to it was vested interests which had grown up under
the existing system, interests which would be imperilled if the
petition became the test for practical politics. Thomas Tooke's
petition inspired a similar document from the merchants of
Edinburgh. Both demanded the removal of all duties not required
purely for revenue. As a result, a committee of the House of
Commons was appointed to inquire and report. It was a beginning.
With the reorganization of Lord Liverpool's administration under
which Robert Huskisson, 'a politician of manly sense and a liberality
of opinion, acceptable to the commercial part of the community',
became President of the Board of Trade in 1823, the advancing
duties began to retreat.

The outgoing President of the Board of Trade, Thomas Wallace,
replied to an address presented to him by bankers, merchants,
shipowners and others connected with the Port of London in
terms which every subscriber of the Baltic Coffee-House would
have approved. The objects to which his life had been devoted,
he said on February 26, 1823, were

to relieve the shipping of the country from every vexatious and unnecessary
burden, to simplify the laws of navigation, to recommend a system of trade
more adapted to the age in which we live and the enlightened and liberal
principles that characterize it, freed from the antiquated prejudices that made
us view with jealous apprehension the industry and progress of other nations
and unincumbered by the shackles and restrictions those prejudices have
imposed . . . to render this island the universal emporium of trade and to see
the city of London the metropolis not only of the first commercial kingdom
but of the commercial world itself.

The Government's liberal principles soon had their effect. The *Annual Register 1823* declared:

The country in the beginning and throughout the whole of the present year exhibited the most unequivocal marks of a steady and progressive prosperity. Every branch of manufacturing industry was in a flourishing state . . . The shipping interest too, which had experienced more than a proportional share of the late depression and embarrassments, participated in the general improvement. Not only was there employment for the good vessels that were in the docks but the shipbuilders' yards began again to present a scene of busy industry.

Some 723 new vessels had been built (62534 tons), and 25642 vessels registered (2519044 tons), at September 30, 1822.

Import of undressed hemp rose from 426163 hundredweight in 1820 to 667141 in 1823. Hemp from Russia and the Baltic carried a duty of 9s. 2d. a hundredweight and 8s. if it came from the plantations. But from 1825 hemp from the plantations was relieved of any duty and that from elsewhere was reduced to 4s. 8d.

The efforts of the Government to divert trade in what for so long had been dubbed East Country Goods, to the new British commercial settlements in the west, led the 'Baltic' merchant of the ilk of Samuel Thornton to an awareness that in the modern nineteenth century, with its expanding horizons and improving means of communication, the activity called 'trade' on which their livelihood depended was no longer a matter of dealing merely with Nearby Europe, the countries bordering the Baltic Sea, or indeed any single geographical area, but with the world at large. Yet the tag 'Baltic' died hard. As the synonym of overseas trade its roots were deep, and, to the bewilderment of foreigners and others unacquainted with the nomenclature of the City of London, the title remained.

The general improvement of the 1820s did not immediately extend to the starving poor, who were driven to rioting, nor to the farmers and their labourers still crushed by direct and indirect taxes and the chaotic state of the currency, who considered their lot with growing despondency. They met in country inns to pass resolutions and devise petitions which they already felt in their bones the new climate of opinion spread by the Anti-Corn Law agitators had made out of date and irrelevant. Why should the farmers, any more than the shipowners, be made a privileged class protected from the risks of commercial competition? Why now? Of laws to prevent the importation of human food our ancestors knew nothing, William Cobbett told farmers at Battle in Sussex on one of his Rural Rides in 1822. If there was not enough corn grown to feed the people in the valley of the Rother, it would have to be fetched from the Danube.

But large-scale buying of foreign corn meant a merchant had to trust his money with foreigners whose commercial honesty and standards of conduct, he feared, might be far removed from those of subscribers of the Baltic Coffee-House. The day after the new-style Baltic opened, one of the most distinguished members of its committee, Thomas Wilson, MP, addressed a meeting of merchants and bankers in the City of London Tavern on this very question. The meeting was called 'to adopt measures for greater security of the money they advanced on the deposit of merchandise and goods, for more adequate protection against fraudulent conduct of foreign merchants'.

'The English capitalist advanced his money at his peril,' proclaimed John Smith, MP who chaired the meeting, 'and to his loss, if goods were not after all the property of the person borrowing.' Thomas Wilson said he had sympathy for the foreign merchants; care should be taken to protect them too from abuse of trust. Heads would have nodded in approval as the new subscribers of the Baltic Coffee-House read reports of this meeting in their papers of May 2, 1823, over their chocolate and sandwiches. The commercial community to whom Huskisson was acceptable felt it their responsibility to let him know why his policies met with their approval and to make sure he was aware whenever his popularity was in danger of waning – and why. The concentraton of 'interests' which the 300 subscribers of the Baltic Coffee-House represented, which made for the easy formulation of a corporate view, facilitated the self-appointed task of keeping a direct line of communication to the Government. When one of their subscribers was also a Member of the Commons, their task became that amount easier.

A matter of considerable importance was still the postal service, the reliability and speed of which was an important factor in the forecasting of markets now playing an increasingly big part in the commercial life of London. The cost, too, had become prohibitively high, In 1823 inland postage was 4d. up to fifteen miles, 1s. 2d. to France, 1s. 8d. to Russia, Sweden and Germany and 2s. 2d. to America. A society was formed to which many Baltic members belonged to collect evidence of the evils of the high rate of postage. Lord Ashburton was once more the presenter of a petition from leading merchants and bankers. A select committee was appointed and reported on the injurious effects of the existing postal system not only on commerce and industry but 'on the social habits and moral condition of the people'. Apart from this, changes were needed in view of the 'rapid extension of the railroads'. But by 1837, the year in which George IV's nineteen-year-old niece ascended the throne, a more revolutionary means of communication than the railway had made an appearance – the electric telegraph.

Either from a consciousness that the inauguration of the Victorian era marked a world so entirely different from that of George IV in which the committee and rules of the Baltic Coffee-House had been brought into existence, or out of a desire to gain from the experience of the first fifteen years to update the subscription room's administration, on May 5, 1837, a general meeting of subscribers was called to re-draft the thirteen rules and regulations under which the coffee-house had been run since 1823. They were not prepared to admit more subscribers – a word which in the rules had significantly been changed to 'members', though the heading still referred to a general meeting of 'Subscribers'. The new first rule read: 'That the number of Members, reckoning Firms as Individuals, shall not exceed Three Hundred.'

They decided to increase the size of the committee from twenty-three to thirty. In fact, though there were twenty-three places, only fourteen of them were filled. When committee members had died or retired, people had not always been elected to take their place. Ten of the original committee of 1823 remained: John Cattley, Benjamin Hawes, Alexander Macdonald, Edward Parsons, Benjamin Pead, John Schneider, W. M. Simonds, Charles Soames, A. H. Thomson and William Wilson. Three had been elected to take the place of the ten who had dropped out: Henry Cayley, John Hubbard and Thomas Stephenson. There also appeared the name of William Wilson Junr, both in the committee list and at the foot as Hon. Secretary. To these fourteen were now added another sixteen of which two had been on the 1823 committee, must have resigned and were being re-elected: John Harvey and John Mitchell. The other fourteen were: Joshua Bates, William Hawes, James Hill, James Holford, Benjamin Lancaster (William Wilson's partner), John D. Lewis, J. W. Lubbock, John Mollett, John Ord, John Smith (the MP?), Thomas Tooke Junr (son of Thomas Tooke?), John Walker, T. M. Weguelin and Benjamin Woolner. The main reason for calling the meeting was probably to bring the committee up to its new full strength, but there was also a fairly drastic re-drafting of the rules.

The need for six members to recommend the candidature of a new member was modified to a requirement for each individual or firm having to be proposed by one member and seconded by another 'to both of whom he or they must be personally known'. The candidate's name, firm, residence, profession or trade had to be inserted in a 'Book of Candidates' with the signature of the proposer and seconder. The book had to lie open for the inspection of members for at least a fortnight. The vague stipulation that the candidate also had to be approved by the committee gave way to a formal ballot.

As the number of individuals and firms who constituted 'members' of the Coffee-House could not exceed 300, they wanted to avoid having to give individual membership to anyone who already had that right by virtue of their being partners in a member firm. This would seem to be the meaning of the fourth rule which stated 'Individuals belonging to a Firm not to be eligible without subscribing for the Firm'. A 'Firm' meant the partners in that firm, all of whom were entitled to use the subscription room by virtue of their firm's membership. The rule made the exception that if, in fact, a firm with an address in London, or forty miles round it, consisted of only one partner, then it was better if the membership should be in the name of that partner.

The fortnightly committee meetings gave way to monthly ones – the first Tuesday at three o'clock. A quorum of five could ballot for any candidate proposed, one black ball in five to exclude. To guard against any mistake, if ten members signed a requisition asking for it, there could be a second ballot.

An innovation was that a member who left town for more than a month could introduce his clerk as a substitute, who had, however, to be balloted for as if he were a new member. The clerk, if elected, would not have to pay a subscription, but no brokers' clerks were to be admitted except in this way.

Presumably some members had got into the habit of showing samples in the room. It was *not* a sample room, and a rule was introduced prohibiting the exhibition of samples. They still did not want more than six members of the Stock Exchange to join, either firms or individuals, and they made the further stipulation that any Baltic member who became a stockbroker must retire and be re-balloted for as one of the six Stock Exchange members when a vacancy occurred. The new ruling was not, however, to be retrospective. They also drew the line at having more than two solicitors as members, firms or individuals. The old seventh rule was retained by which retired gentlemen no longer in business and living twenty miles out of London could be admitted by members as 'strangers' on signing their names in the Strangers' Book; and the same went for any gentleman in business who lived forty miles from London – it had been fifty miles in 1823. Strangers could not be admitted for more than a month at a time. 'If he continue his visits to the room after that time, he must pay to the Proprietor, at the rate of ten shillings a month from the time he was first entered on the book as a Visitor.' If his visits to the Room went on longer than six months his status as Visitor ceased and he must be balloted for as a candidate.

In 1823 they gave themselves no way of getting rid of a subscriber who for any reason became 'undesirable'. In fifteen years there would have been occasions when they wished they had, so in 1837 they introduced the thirteenth rule: 'Members having the misfortune to fail, or who compound with their creditors, after the adoption of these Rules, to be by that act excluded from the Society, but to be re-eligible on the same footing as new Members, after they have obtained their discharge, or settled with their creditors.' The use of the word 'society' was significant.

After fifteen years the annual subscriptions remained the same, but included the allowances for waiters and attendance – so in effect they were reduced. The name of any member or firm who, after written notice, neglected to pay his subscription during May and June would have his name placed over the mantelpiece of the coffee room on July 5 following. If it was not paid by August 1 the defaulter ceased to be a member.

To these two reasons for ridding the subscription room of a member was added, in the sixteenth rule, a third.

In case the conduct of any Member, either in or out of the room, shall have been, or shall in future be, in the opinion of the Committee, or of any Twenty-five Members, who shall certify the same to the Committee in writing, derogatory to his character as a man of business, he shall be subject to expulsion (without appeal) by the Committee, which shall be specially summoned for the purpose of considering the same; and provided a majority of at least two-thirds of the *whole* Committee at that time in London shall concur therein, such Member shall thereupon cease to be a Member, and the portion of his Subscription from the time of his expulsion to the close of the year ending 30th April shall be returned to him.

Wisely without attempting to define what they meant by conduct derogatory to a man of business, the committee bravely declared themselves on the side of the angels and set themselves up as arbiters of business ethics independent of the law and the judiciary, as most professions had already done, in the hope of establishing an élite with standards few could ignore and all would emulate. They risked having the ground cut from under their feet and being left on their high horse for all to mock, but the calibre of those who declared themselves ready to stick their necks out assured their mission a more than reasonable chance of success. The courage of their convictions had spurred them to raise the

^Standard; if they started marching with it, they believed the majority would fall in behind.

A key figure in the commercial chain of trust was the broker. His trustworthiness, however, was still vouched for by the Corporation of London. Under an order made by the Court of Mayor and Aldermen in September 1818, they were still issuing certificates to brokers which stated that they had entered

into two Bonds or Obligations, the one in the penalty of One Thousand pounds for his honest and good behaviour in the office and employment of a Broker, and the other with security in the penalty of Fifty pounds conditioned for the yearly payment of five pounds upon every Twenty-ninth day of September, having provided further security in two persons of this Court in the penalty of Two hundred and fifty pounds each for his honest and good behaviour in the said office.

The Court then admitted him as a broker within the City of London 'during the pleasure of this Court and no longer'. Finally he was sworn in.

There were brokers for every branch of commerce imaginable. In *Robson's London Directory* of 1838 there were thirty-two categories of broker, from 'Dry Saltery & Spice' and 'Ivory & Tortoiseshell' to 'Ship & Insurance' and 'Russia'. Of the eleven 'Brokers, General and Commercial' eight gave their address as the Baltic Coffee-House; the others as the North and South American. All the eleven 'Brokers, Russia' gave their address as the Baltic Coffee-House: Thos. Blandford, Wm. Girdler, Geo. Gull, John Macdonald, Thos. Macdonald, Jos. North, Francis Perry, Henry Schaaf, W. Simons, W. W. Simpson, Wm. Stobart. The four tallow merchants in the directory under this heading gave only their counting house addresses: F. O. Berger, Thos. & Benj. Hawes, John Oulds and Jos. Ezra Tibbs. In the street directory section seventy traders were listed as using the Baltic Coffee-House as their address, of which fifty-two were described as merchants, eight as general and commercial brokers, seven as Russia brokers, one insurance broker, one shipbroker and an agent for tin.

The proprietor to whom visitors to the Baltic Coffee-House paid their ten shillings for staying more than a month was now John

Monger, by whose name many came to know the place. A Mr
Callow wrote in his book on London Taverns: 'In Hercules Passage
[which led to Sun Court] down a few steps, were some small wine-
rooms known as the Baltic Coffee House or "Mongers".' As head
waiter John Monger had bought the coffee-house and the goodwill
of the business for £2000 in 1832 when his employer William
Melton, the then proprietor, had died of cholera after returning
from a dinner celebrating the passing of the Reform Bill. Melton
had a son, but in 1832 the boy was only ten. John Monger claimed
he had been a waiter at 58 Threadneedle Street since 1821; when
he became head waiter is not known. (He may have been a
descendant of the James Monger who started a brewhouse early in
the seventeenth century on the site of the burnt-out Globe Theatre
on Bankside, which became the Anchor Brewery which Mrs
Thrale sold in 1781, with the aid of Dr Johnson, to David and
Robert Barclay and John Perkins.)

When William Melton junr grew up he became a small
shipowner/merchant, went bankrupt, studied law, moved abroad
and for a time before his death in 1880 was Acting Chief Justice of
the Gold Coast – details given by his son Ernest Melton who in the
1920s made a gift to the Baltic Exchange of the Visitors and Rule
Book of 1823.

Henry Cayley was chairman at the meeting which in 1837
unanimously agreed to the new set of rules, and chairman of the
committee. 'The Baltic Coffee-House' was now a coffee-house
only in name. It had successfully re-structured itself to face the
demands of the new world of the telegraph, steamships and railways, but remained only too aware that human nature rarely
changed.

II

BALTIC, MOXHAYS, JERUSALEM AND SHIPPING EXCHANGE

This night is to decide between the policy of continued relaxation of restriction or the return to restraint and prohibition. This night you will select the motto which is to indicate the commercial policy of England. Shall it be 'advance' or 'recede'? Which is the fitter motto for this great Empire? Survey our position, consider the advantage which God and nature have given us, and the destiny for which we are intended. We stand on the confines of Western Europe, the chief connecting link between the old world and the new. The discoveries of science, the improvement of navigation, have brought us within ten days of St Petersburg, and will soon bring us within ten days of New York. We have an extent of coast greater in proportion to our population and the area of our land than any other great nation, securing to us maritime strength and superiority. Iron and coal, the sinews of manufacture, give us advantages over every rival in the great competition of industry. Our capital far exceeds that which they can command. In ingenuity – in skill – in energy – we are inferior to none. Our national character, the free institutions under which we live, the liberty of thought and action, an unshackled press, spreading knowledge of every discovery and of every advance in science – combined with natural and physical advantages to place us at the head of those nations which profit by the free interchange of their products. And is this the country to shrink from competition? Is this the country to adopt a retrograde policy? Is this the country which can only flourish in the sickly artificial atmosphere of prohibition? Is this the country to stand shivering on the brink of exposure to the healthful breezes of competition?

SIR ROBERT PEEL on the Repeal of the Corn Laws, House of Commons, February 16, 1846.

4. *South Sea House*

When Henry Cayley, Ben Pead, John Mitchell and others went as usual to the Royal Exchange on the morning of January 11, 1838, they found the building in ruins. The previous night a fire had broken out in the Captains' Room of Lloyd's and spread to the entire building which was gutted. Those who lived nearby had seen the flames; members who had lingered in the subscription room of the Baltic Coffee-House had watched the conflagration from the windows. Next morning they kept their appointments at Guildhall and in the quadrangle of the Excise Office in Broad Street, the building erected in 1768 on the site of Gresham College which had become the temporary bourse after the fire of 1666. By January 17 Lloyd's had found temporary accommodation in South Sea House at 39–41 Threadneedle Street.

Plans were at once put in hand for the building of a third Royal Exchange. The Corporation of London and the Mercers Company contributed £150 000 and Parliament £40 000. The Prince Consort laid the foundation stone in 1842. Two years later another Italianate building with an open central courtyard opened its doors for business. This time the pillared portico and steps faced towards the Mansion House, and the buildings on the west side were cleared away to form an open space. Queen Victoria rode in to give her blessing to the third emporium of trade as Queen Elizabeth had done for the first 300 years before. She opened the building which still stands today. Lloyd's returned to a new suite of rooms on the upper floor and remained there till 1928. The new building also housed a Metal Exchange.

During the four years the Gresham Committee took to plan and build the new Exchange, there was no floor where merchants and shipbrokers could meet. Subscription rooms of coffee-houses became busier than ever. To fill the gap an idealistic amateur architect and wealthy biscuit-maker, called Edward Moxhay, took it into his head to build a 'general commercial room' on the lines of such establishments in Liverpool and Manchester. He acquired the disused French Protestant Church at 52 Threadneedle Street, pulled it down and built in its place a massive building of his own design at a cost of £70 000 which he called the Hall of Commerce. He opened it with a grand banquet two years before the new Royal Exchange was ready. Subscribers were invited at five guineas a year which was soon reduced to £1 10s. The main hall was the Reading Room in which subscribers and their visitors met and did their business. He had their names called by 'callers' when they were wanted, after the manner of Lloyd's in the Great Hall of South Sea House. There was another large room on the ground floor for meetings and sales, and upstairs were smaller rooms for private conferences and arbitrations. A coffee room was open to the public.

Writing a year after Moxhay's Hall of Commerce had opened, the author of *The City* feared for its chances of survival. Moxhay's hunch was not working out. He

appears to have imagined that, by creating such a centre of attraction, he would have depopulated those separate and secluded haunts of the different interests and brought them together in one focus. This was the mistake. The members of Lloyd's, the merchants who attend 'Change, the subscribers of the North and South American, the Jerusalem, the Jamaica, and the Baltic, never can be persuaded to leave their old resorts where they find everything ready to their hand, for the chance of being, in one incongruous mass, served better elsewhere. The members of the North and South American, the Jerusalem, the Jamaica and the Baltic were already well provided in their respective establishments.

But the Hall of Commerce never really got into its stride. It never attracted the revenue needed to run it, in spite of the over-crowding of the coffee-houses due to the absence of a Royal

Exchange. When Moxhay died in 1849 the Hall, according to Bryant Lillywhite, was sold for £44 900 and used for banquets and meetings, but its days as a subscription house ended. It became a temporary headquarters for stockbrokers during the rebuilding of the Stock Exchange in 1853, and on reconstruction in 1855 became Parr's Bank. It was demolished in 1921.

More durable were the London Commercial Sale Rooms in Mincing Lane which had started life in 1811 as the Commercial Hall designed for the sale of colonial produce. The London Commercial Coffee-House was next door. In 1844 the London Commercial Sale Rooms had a subscription room on the ground floor with the usual selection of newspapers, catalogues and produce lists, and sale rooms and office upstairs.

None of these were substitutes for the Royal Exchange whose re-opening was particularly welcomed by subscribers of the Baltic Coffee-House. Some of them had no doubt been attracted by Moxhay's innovation with a central 'hall' acting as the floor of the Royal Exchange, under the same roof as coffee-house facilities. Many would have pigeon-holed the idea in their minds for future reference; some would have become subscribers to see how it worked and learnt from its mistakes. All would have quickly returned to the habits of the dual system of the commercial resort/exchange, physically separated from the social coffee-house/subscription room. But in 1845 it was not only a matter of returning to a former routine, but also welcoming the arrival of circumstances long awaited in which a 'floor situation' came into its own.

As Queen Elizabeth's opening of the first exchange in 1571 had signalled the end of the 500-year-old regime of the Easterlings and the Stillyard, so Queen Victoria's ride to the City for a similar purpose in 1845 marked the beginning of the end of the 200-year-old domination of the Protectionists. A great part of the energies of those in the Baltic and other coffee-houses had been devoted in the years leading up to the re-opening of the Royal Exchange to devising ruses for evading the Navigation Act, which by 1845 had become a tangle of anomalies. Minds which would have been more fruitfully engaged in solving the problems of steam's effect on the freight market sought new interpretations of phrases like 'British ships' and 'landing in Europe' to outwit the Customs officers. A merchant with a contract to deliver Dutch coffee chartered a British ship to pick up the beans in Amsterdam, sailed with them to the Cape, landed them, took out fresh papers consigning them to England and brought them back to London. Coming 'direct' from a British colony they were admissible for home consumption as a 'naturalized' product. Such absurdities only rewarded members of the Society of Shipowners.

An easing of the Navigation Act came in 1840, prompted by the greater use of ships propelled by steam, 'that mighty instrument of civilization' in Lindsay's sonorous prose, which 'drove itself through numerous acts of Parliament and showed how vain were legislative measures when opposed to the progress of science'. Clauses in the treaty with Austria relating to the use of non-British ships were modified accordingly. New prospects of commercial adventure had opened up for inland nations without seaports with the application of steam power to navigation on canals.

In 1847 John Lewis Ricardo called for a select committee to inquire into the operation of the Navigation Act. The representative of the Board of Trade, John Lefevre, advocated its total abolition.

William Richmond, representing the shipowners of Tynemouth, told the committee that for the last twenty-five years the shipping trade had been a losing one. Those employed in the Baltic during the whole of that time had made no money whatever. A distinct class of men now existed, he said, who were shipowners not merchants, whose fathers had been shipowners for successive generations and had left them ships as their only inheritance. The business of chartering a ship belonged to the shipbroker not the captain, who was now only the coach driver. He saw Russia, Sweden and the northern powers as formidable rivals. The law of Charles II should be fully implemented: 'no goods from Africa Asia or America should be imported into England in any ships but in such as do truly and without fraud belong only to the people of England'.

The free traders pointed out that the vast proportion of Russian trade was carried on by British ships, as there was not a large enough Russian merchant navy. But American cotton, once landed at Le Havre, could not be brought over to British manufacturers whatever the demand might be. Parliament was dissolved before the committee had finished its hearings; but in the general election the free traders, now coming to be called the Liberals, topped the poll. The Queen, in her speech at the opening of the new Parliament, said the houses would be asked to consider the adoption of changes in the Navigation Act 'without danger to our maritime strength'. The conflicting interests of consumers, merchants, shipbuilders, shipowners, merchant seamen and naval seamen were expressed and re-expressed in sitting after sitting. None were incontrovertible. The advantages of free trade were unprovable. But in spite of compelling points about the manning of the Royal Navy and the maintenance of the British fleet, the Government were convinced they were right in principle. Without the Navigation Act, they were told, shipowners would be free to build ships in cheap foreign countries and the shipwrights of Britain on whom the safety of Britain's shores depended would be diminished. Maybe. British shipbuilders would have to compete in the open market along with everyone else. Admiral Sir George Byam Martin showed how far-thinking a seaman he was by insisting that 'in addition to our usual fleets there must be an immense number of steamers in a great measure as an addition *though not as a substitute for* sailing ships'. That would never do. Mr Gladstone recommended a gradual dismantlement of the Navigation Act. England should set an example to the world of free navigation. 'We should live to see the ocean that great highway of the nations as free of ships that traverse its bosom or the wind that blows over it.' Mr Disraeli, from the opposition benches, reminded Members that it was 1848, the year of revolutions. 'This is not an age of commerce, peace and international improvement but an age of no trade, intended war and communists tearing up railways; Naples in a state of siege, Paris in insurrection, Vienna in revolt, Berlin barricaded, the Baltic and Adriatic blockaded.' He would not by his vote endanger that empire gained by so much valour – the empire of the seas. On and on went the arguments, to and fro. For her speech from the throne for the opening of Parliament in

1849 Queen Victoria's opinion about the Navigation Laws was now that they were unnecessary for the maintenance of the country's maritime power, while they fettered trade and industry. When Labouchere, the President of the Board of Trade, introduced a Bill for the Abrogation of the Navigation Laws, Ricardo appealed to Englishmen to depend on themselves and their energies and not put their trust in Acts of Parliament. 'It would be better to send forth our ships free as the winds which filled their sails with liberty to go where they would and come from where it suited them, than to start them from our ports encumbered with 8 & 9 Victoria cap 88 and ballasted with 12 volumes of Hertslet's *Commercial Treaties*.' (Hear, hear.) At the second reading on March 9, 1849, James Wilson, the framework knitter's son from Hawick who was to found *The Economist*, pertinently asked why the shipping interest should be exempted from rivalry which other interests had successfully encountered. His question was answered by a majority of sixty-one for the Bill which after going to the Lords received the royal assent on June 26. After twenty-nine years the free trade movement, officially launched by Thomas Tooke's Petition of London Merchants of 1820, had triumphed. In the subscription room at the Baltic Coffee-House that summer evening call was made on Mr Monger's stocks of rum and arrack to celebrate the Act's removal, as on few other occasions. It equalled the rejoicing in the mid-1830s when private shipowners had been allowed to trade to all parts of the East, including China, on the same conditions as East India Company vessels, and when the company had eventually given up trading altogether and sold their ships on the grounds that they could not compete without protection.

Only three years before, they had celebrated the triumph of the Anti-Corn Law League campaign when in 1846 the Corn Laws had been repealed, resulting in wholesale importation of corn. The cheap loaf (at last) was the toast in the ale-houses and gin shops patronized by the mere consumers; in the subscription rooms of the Baltic Coffee-House they drank to the huge new area of trade which now lay at their feet and was to give the establishment its special character for the next hundred years.

The economics of buying corn from the various wheat-growing countries of the world to feed Great Britain were complicated and became more so as the population grew. To stabilize prices it was necessary to be able to some extent to forecast the market. The invention of Charles Wheatstone and Fothergill Cooke had brought this possibility very much nearer. In 1845 the Electric Telegraph Company had been formed to exploit their patents. But their lengths of wire and ticking needles were only a means. Their principal application so far was on the railways – by 1848 2000 miles of line were equipped with telegraph. The purposes to which they could be put for helping subscribers of the Baltic Coffee-House in supplementing the printed commercial information received daily and weekly in their subscription room in Threadneedle Street were being thought out in a room in Royal Exchange Buildings by a thirty-five-year-old German Jew by the name of Israel Beer Josaphat, who, on becoming a Christian in 1844, had changed his name to Paul Julius Reuter.

A provider of the kind of commercial information which Julius Reuter was seeking to make his business was Samuel Bartholomew Gaze, Clerk of what was now described as the City Average Market Letter Committee, which, as has already been noted, had been publishing tallow prices at least since 1813. The records of the committee between 1824 and 1851 are missing, but in the latter year Market Letters appeared with Gaze's name at the foot with the address 26 Princes Street, Spitalfields and the advice 'Attendances given at the Office, "Baltic Coffee House" Threadneedle Street on Fridays from Half Past Four to Five o'clock'. A letter of October 24, 1851, gave prices on that date for town tallow, yellow Russian tallow, melted stuff, rough stuff – tallow graves, good dregs, and the number of casks imported that week from Petersburg (the highest with 3213), Italy, South America, Australia, East Indies. On the same sheet was a 'Comparative Account of Stock and Delivery For Five Years' – 1847 to 1851. The stock of foreign tallow for the corresponding week in 1847 was 25288, and in 1851 38387. Samuel Gaze, who began his duties in 1820, had five sons and coupled his work for the committee with a watch-repair and clock-making business.

The prospects of unending material prosperity which free enterprise and *laissez-faire* seemed to offer swelled the ranks of the middle-class mercantile community in London and brought, initially at any rate, great riches to many a princely merchant in his counting house, to use Palmerston's phrase.

They raced to jump on the wagon to which new momentum had been given by the repeal in quick succession of Corn and Navigation Laws. The number of would-be subscribers to the Baltic Coffee-House swelled. New blood entered, not only from London but from the outports, attracted to the metropolis as the great centre of world trade.

In 1847 eighteen-year-old John Glover left South Shields, the north-east coast town of which his father had three times been mayor, and came to London to seek his fortune. He obtained a job with a firm of shipbrokers and shipping agents, first as office boy then as chartering clerk. When his contract was about to expire, he wrote to say he would be prepared to accept a partnership on condition that his employer paid more attention to the business and stopped withdrawing capital which it badly needed! 'The mistake', he told the man he hoped would make him a partner, 'consists simply in your having placed the importance of attendance in your own counting-house last instead of first.' It was a lecture not entirely lost on the recipient who, so far from giving the cheeky writer the sack, offered to increase his salary but declined to make him his partner. John Glover took the hint and early in 1853 set up a shipbroking business at 9 Eastcheap with his elder brother, Robert, who came down from Hartlepool to join him as junior partner. They both joined the Baltic Coffee-House subscription room.

Glover Brothers flourished from the start, as many others did in this great period of expansion and development. That October he wrote to his father on Tyneside, who had lent him the £500 with which to start the firm,

I remember that a new business could not be tested for many months after it was commenced and that this year in freights, and consequently in our commissions, everything was so expanding that to infer from it what other years would be, without making great allowance, might be very fallacious.

Two months ago, however, I found that the character of our business was such that if in other years we did only half of what we have done in this our first year all would be well.

The third brother, Septimus, who plays an important part in this story, was not to come south to join John and Robert until 1874.

The opening up of trade with America brought activity, too, to the outports on the west coast. London had its 'Baltic'; in 1853 Liverpool acquired its 'Atlantic' – the Association of the Liverpool Corn Trade which was formed in that year and rented accommodation in Atlantic Buildings, Brunswick Street, where the original Corn Exchange Company, with which they amalgamated, had been founded in 1808. (The Hull Exchange was similarly dubbed 'the Pacific'.)

In London the time had come for another review of the Baltic Coffee-House rules and regulations. A general meeting of subscribers was called for February 23, 1854, with John Cattley, a member of the original committee, in the chair. They now had more applications than vacancies, and the first decision of the meeting was to raise the limit of their membership from 300 to 325. At the same time they reduced the committee from thirty to twenty. The new committee consisted of three members of the original body, John Cattley, John Harvey, and William Simonds; eight members elected in 1837, Joshua Bates, John Mollett, John Ord, John Smith, Thomas Tooke Junr, John Walker, T. M. Weguelin and Benjamin Lancaster; and six new members, Pantia Ralli, J. H. W. Schroder, Richard Smith, H. A. Soames Junr, John Todd and Edward Wilson. Benjamin Lancaster, now a director of Price's Patent Candle Company, had succeeded William Wilson Junr as Hon. Secretary.

Monthly committee meetings were changed from three o'clock on the first Tuesday to one o'clock on the first Thursday. It was no longer considered necessary to ballot for the clerk who became a member's substitute for more than a month; five members of the committee could sanction him instead. Subscriptions remained the same – four guineas for an individual, six for a two-partner firm, eight for a bigger firm. All the rules of 1837 remained the same except for a slight modification of the sixteenth. In 1837 expulsion was only possible 'provided a majority of at least two-thirds of the *whole* Committee [their italics] at that time in London shall concur therein'. The new rule, in effect, said a two-thirds decision of the *quorum* could lead to expulsion.

Of the new members of the committee nothing is known except of Pantia Ralli, the first of a family of Greek corn merchants and bankers who played a central role in the development of the Baltic, and J. H. W. Schroder, the banker – both names now linked with organizations of international repute. John Henry William Schroder was son of the John Henry Schroder who came to London in 1804 and formed J. Henry Schroder & Co in 1818. In 1854 J. H. W. Schroder was twenty-nine and had been a partner in his father's firm since 1849. John Walker, who attended the meeting of February 23, was only destined to live another three months. He was a Russia merchant, and later a Russia broker, who had been a subscriber since 1830. The inscription on his bust reads:

To perpetuate the memory of one who during a long commercial life was distinguished by the universality of his benevolence. This bust of the late John Walker who died suddenly May 6, 1854, in his 70th year, was sub-scribed for by the members of the Baltic Coffee House, London, May 31, 1854.

When, in 1923, this bust was found in the Post Office in Threadneedle Street, which was built* on the site of the coffee house at 58 Threadneedle Street and given to the Baltic Exchange, no one knew who John Walker was. When the *Daily Express* ran a story headed, 'Do you know anything about John Walker?', the editor received a letter from a Miss Mary Rogerson Searle, living in a vicarage in Portsmouth, who volunteered the information that he was the eldest son of John and Mary Walker, whose maiden name was Rogerson, both of whom came from Yorkshire. He was a man, she said, whose judgement and integrity were much esteemed. (*Text continues on page 102.*)

*According to *The Financier* of January 18, 1910, the coffee-house was not demolished but converted into a post office, and was still standing in that year (1910).

FACING PAGE AND FOLLOWING TWO PAGES *Baltic Coffee-House rules & regulations, 1854*

BALTIC COFFEE-HOUSE.

COMMITTEE.

Messrs. JOSHUA BATES
EDMUND BRANDT
JOHN CATTLEY
JOHN COOK
JOHN HARVEY
JOHN HODGSON
BENJAMIN LANCASTER
JOHN MOLLETT
JOHN ORD
PANTIA RALLI

Messrs. J. W. H. SCHRÖDER
W. M. SIMONDS
JOHN SMITH
RICHARD SMITH
H. A. SOAMES, Jun.
THOMAS TOOKE, Jun.
JOHN TODD
JOHN WALKER
T. M. WEGUELIN
EDWARD WILSON

(BENJAMIN LANCASTER, Hon. Sec.)

RULES AND REGULATIONS,

AGREED TO

AT A GENERAL MEETING OF SUBSCRIBERS, HELD 23rd FEBRUARY, 1854,

JOHN CATTLEY, Esq. in the Chair.

First.—That the number of Members, reckoning Firms as Individuals, shall not exceed Three Hundred and Twenty-five.

Second.—That the Committee do consist of the following Gentlemen:—viz. Messrs. J. Bates, E. Brandt, J. Cattley, J. Cook, J. Harvey, J. Hodgson, B. Lancaster, J. Mollett, J. Ord, P. Ralli, J. W. H. Schröder, W. M. Simonds, J. Smith, R. Smith, H. A. Soames, Jun., T. Tooke, Jun., J. Todd, J. Walker, T. M. Weguelin, E. Wilson.

Third.—That each Individual, or Firm, being Candidates for Admission, must be proposed by one Member and seconded by another, to both of whom he or they must be personally known. The Candidates name, or Firm, Residence, Profession or Trade, to be inserted in the "Book of Candidates," with the signature of the proposer and seconder, (which book is to lie open for the inspection of the Members) at least a fortnight before the day of election.

Fourth.—Individuals belonging to a Firm not to be eligible without subscribing for the Firm, unless in the case of a House having only one partner resident in London, or within forty miles of it.

Fifth.—The Committee shall meet on the first Thursday of every month, at one o'Clock, when they shall ballot for any Candidate proposed, five to be a quorum, and one black ball in five to exclude; and with a view to guard against any mistake which may have occurred at a first ballot, a Candidate may be balloted for a second time, on the next balloting-day, provided his proposer or seconder produces to the Committee a requisition to that effect, signed by Ten Members. If not admitted on this second balloting, his exclusion to be final.

Sixth.—A Member leaving town for more than one month may introduce his clerk as a substitute, subject, however, to the sanction of five members of the Committee, only without payment.

Seventh.—No Brokers' clerks to be admitted, except under the provision of Article Six.

Eighth.—No samples of goods to be exhibited in the room.

Ninth.—Only Six Members of the Stock Exchange admissible, reckoning Firms as Individuals. Any Member of the room becoming a Member thereof after his admission, must retire to be re-balloted for when a vacancy occurs.

Tenth.—Only Two Solicitors (Firms or Individuals), to be admitted.

Eleventh.—Gentlemen *not* in business, and residing twenty miles from London, and Gentlemen *in* business, residing forty miles from London, are admissible as Strangers, on their Names and Residences being entered in the Strangers' Book, and signed by the Member admitting them.

Twelfth.—A Stranger not to be admitted free as a Visitor for more than one month. If he continue his visits to the room after that time, he must pay to the Proprietor, at the rate of ten shillings ⅌ month, from the time he was first entered on the book as a Visitor; and if his visit is prolonged beyond six months, he will be no longer admissible as a Visitor, but must be balloted for as a Candidate.

Thirteenth.—Members having the misfortune to fail, or who compound with their creditors, to be by that act excluded from the Society, but to be re-eligible, on the same footing as new Members, after they have obtained their discharge, or settled with their creditors.

Fourteenth.—The year to commence, as at present, on 1st May, and the Subscription to be

For an Individual £4. 4 0

For a Firm of two 6 6 0

For a Firm of three or more 8 8 0

which Subscription is to include all charges for waiters and attendance.

Fifteenth.—The name of each Member or Firm neglecting, after due written notice, to pay his or their Annual Subscription during the months of May and June in each year, shall be placed over the mantel-piece of the Coffee Room on the 5th of July following; and if the Subscription be not paid on the 1st August following, the defaulter shall cease to be a Member, and his name shall be erased from the List of the Members accordingly.

Sixteenth.—In case the conduct of any Member, either in or out of the room, shall have been, or shall in future be, in the opinion of the Committee, or of any Twenty-five Members, who shall certify the same to the Committee in writing, derogatory to his character as a man of business, he shall be subject to expulsion (without appeal) by the Committee, which shall be summoned specially to consider the case; and if they consider the complaint proved, the Member complained of shall thereupon cease to be a Member; and the portion of his Subscription, from the time of his expulsion to the close of the year ending 30th April, shall be returned to him. The decision shall not be considered valid, unless (at least) two-thirds of the Committee shall concur therein.

He was called on at times to decide in questions of business, and his aid was greatly valued as evidenced by the presentations of a large silver salver and of a fine embossed silver mug. On his death at the age of 65 years (not 70 as inscribed on the marble bracket) some merchants of London to the number of 60 subscribed £2 2s. each and asked his sister, Miss Mary Walker, to allow a famous sculptor of the day to take a bust of her brother; it was considered an admirable likeness and was intended for the Baltic Coffee House. I was then 6½ years old and I remember accompanying my parents to the studio, with my sister; my mother had been brought up by her uncle, as her father died when she was a very young child; her suggestions at the studio were considered valuable. I am now, I believe, the only member of the family in England but there are relatives in Australia and Tasmania who correspond with me.

It is not clear from this letter what relation Miss Searle was to John Walker, but it seems that her mother was his niece, so John Walker would have been her great uncle.

A few weeks following the meeting of February 23, 1854, after forty years of peace, Britain joined with her late enemy, France, in declaring war on Russia. The Tsar Nicholas had claimed the right of protecting members of the Greek Orthodox Church in Turkey, and when this demand was refused he invaded Moldavia, a high-handed action which caused indignation throughout Europe, and embarrassment to every Russia merchant and broker on 'Change. When the English and French arrived on the scene they decided to attack the Russian stronghold of Sebastopol on the promontory on the north of the Black Sea known as Crimea, a siege which lasted a year. The English conducted their part of the operation from Balaclava Bay.

In the archives of the Baltic Exchange is a charter-party of affreightment headed 'Hired Store Ships' and dated March 17, 1855, made between William Shanly of Old Broad Street, ship-broker, trading under the name of Geo. & A. Herring & Co, acting for the owners of a 693-ton, fast sailing clipper the *Gauntlet*, William Inglis master, and the Commissioners for Executing the Office of the Lord High Admiral, for carrying Ordnance Stores to Balaclava. The shipbroker covenanted that the ship 'shall be tight strong and substantial both above Water and beneath' and provided with sufficient men to navigate her according to the practice

of the merchant service, the crew consisting of one half able seamen before the mast, the remaining half of the officers and of the
ordinary seamen who must have been to sea. The masts, yards,
sails, anchors, cables, cordage and boats had to be supplied by the
agent of Sir Snow Harris (the Admiralty commissioner?) 'or by
other persons upon an equally safe principle', and provided with
guns, small arms, powder and shot. Apart from the crew the ship
was not to carry more officers, soldiers or other persons than four
to every 100 ton of stores. Payment for these passengers would be
made at a rate of two tons freight for the passage of each man or
woman, and half for a child, plus one shilling a day for victualling
each man, eightpence for each woman and five pence for each
child. Twenty working days were allowed for putting the lading
on board in the Thames, and twenty days for unloading the other
end. Demurrage was at the rate of ten shillings a ton a month.

The eventual evacuation of Sebastopol by the Russians brought
an end to the fighting and peace came formally with the Treaty of
Paris in 1856, which neutralized the Black Sea and recognized the
independence of the Ottoman Empire. The Powers also agreed to
abolish privateering and made enemy's merchandise (except arms.
safe from search on the high seas when carried by neutral ships)
England had at last to abandon the 'right', which Pitt had insisted
on, to search a vessel flying a neutral flag and seize goods considered to be of succour to her enemies.

Above all, peace in the Crimea meant a renewal of the Russian
grain trade. The buying and selling of home-grown corn had
been conducted at the Corn Exchange, but the bigger scale trade
in foreign grain was handled, mainly by Greeks, at the Royal
Exchange and in the subscription room, dining room and coffee
room of the Baltic Coffee-House.

Before the Crimean War Russian grain was normally exceeded
in value by tallow, flax, linseed and timber, but after the war it
was regularly the largest single item – wheat, barley, oats, rye,
maize. As has been seen, tallow was now coming in large quantities from South America and Australia, and at this time there
was added the tallow business of Switzerland – in 1857 H. Fehr
moved from Zürich to London and laid the foundations

of the great trading house of which his grandson is still head.

Britain's exports to Russia were comparatively small and the balance of trade in Russia's favour rose from £1 million between 1826 and 1835 to £5½ million in 1860.

When the Corn Laws were in operation Britain only bought heavily in foreign grain markets when crops in Kent and Essex failed, and only from the Russian ports in the Baltic. From 1838, when she could not obtain enough from nearer north-west ports like Danzig and Königsberg, she bought also from the Black Sea. Of the northern Russian ports, most grain was imported from St Petersburg; of the southern ports, from Odessa. Of the 123 ships bringing wheat to Britain from the Russian Black Sea in 1842, 99 were from Odessa, 13 from Kerch, 5 from Taganrog and 1 from Berdiansk. Of these more than half – 63 – put in to London. Ten years later London was still the largest single importer of Russian grain – it was the port of entry for 77 of the 290 ships, though there was a swing to Ireland (103 of the 290), Gloucester, Bristol and Liverpool. The latter, however, only took 15.

Susan Fairlie, from whose studies these figures are taken, points out the difficulties which the Russian ports presented. Apart from being closed by ice for four to five months every year, St Petersburg and Riga were shallow. 'Ships drawing more than 8 ft were not allowed up to St Petersburg at all, having to dock at the island of Cronstadt 20 miles down river [which was what Captain Lidgett had to do with the brig *Benjamin*]. Odessa was virtually ice free (though in January 1854 loading was held up a fortnight by ice) and had a deep harbour with a hard bottom.'

The sailing ships would congregate at Gibraltar waiting for a favourable wind to take them through the straits. The weather also affected arrivals at ports of call, many ships from Gibraltar reaching Queenstown, Falmouth or Plymouth about the same time. As a result, the brokers were busily occupied in disposing of the cargoes; samples were taken in boxes and sent to merchants' offices, the cargoes sold, and final orders given for ports of discharge. Some ships would occasionally have pigs and poultry on deck, and the question would arise – Who had fed them on the voyage, the captain or cargo?

The journey to England from the Baltic by sail took a few weeks. In 1824 a 200-ton ship did the return journey three times in eighteen months, though by 1847 three times a year was more normal. From the Black Sea and Azov a fast one-way journey could be a month or less, but the average was seventy-five days. The round trip took from eight to twelve months.

Susan Fairlie assumes there were no steamers in the Russian grain trade until about 1856,

in spite of G. S. Graham's assertion that by 1852 almost all British trade in the Mediterranean and the Levant was carried in iron screw steamers assisted by sails. There were steamers in Russian waters before 1856 of course – the Russian government was experimenting with them in the Black Sea from the 1820s and in the Baltic and White Sea from about 1830. By 1844 there were 25 in the Russian Black Sea including two steam freighters in the Azov, and by 1853, 64. But there is nothing to link any of these to the British grain trade . . . The first evidence of British steamers in Odessa dates from 1857 when there were already 44 of them in addition to 218 British sailing vessels.

Shipbrokers and merchants who used the Baltic Coffee-House watched the move away from sail with mixed feelings. A steamer the *Savannah*, had first crossed the Atlantic in 1819, putting into the Mersey after twenty-seven days. By 1824 only seventeen steam vessels had been built in Britain. In every corner of the coffee-house different views were expressed on the *commercial* advantages of the new steamships. What was in it for them?

The biggest controversy of all would have been over the plan of Mr Brunel to build an iron leviathan of steam and sail, six times the size of any ship then in existence. It would carry 5000 tons measurement of cargo and 500 passengers, he said. The first plates of the *Great Eastern* were laid at Millwall on the Thames on May 1, 1854, and the final launch took place in April 1858. The Atlantic cable to link the United States with Europe was completed in the summer of 1858, and the Government were urged to use the ship for laying it. Many doubted its commercial potential; none more vehemently than W. S. Lindsay. He told his constituents at Tynemouth at the end of 1857,

If such a ship as the *Great Eastern* be found to answer commercially most of our property will go to the wall, for in a short time our small vessels will be of very little use to us. The course of commerce is this: if a Manchester merchant has 1000 bales of a particular description of goods to send to Calcutta, he does not send the whole of them in one bottom, because he might thus overstock the market. On the contrary, he sends them in from four to six different vessels, and he does this for two reasons: first, that by so doing he feeds the market; and secondly, that he gets thereby quicker returns. The principle of commerce is to send out supplies in relays.

(*History of Merchant Shipping*, vol. 4, p. 539)

Was the course of commerce to be re-directed by an *engineer*? However that might be, it would never be more than half the story. A Baltic member who knew that ships might change, but those with whom he had to do business never, was W. Stuart Lane. Among the Lane Hankey Papers in the Guildhall Library in London is a small green leather notebook with a metal clasp dated 1856 which Stuart Lane carried in his pocket wherever he went, taking it out after a first encounter to jot down impressions and information about his new acquaintance. The pages are unlined and the spidery handwriting is barely legible.

> D. Carnegie & Co: He is evidently disinclined to do business with us, and indeed seems to dislike any change in the old way of going on. He is losing his popularity and a great deal of his business, and seems sulky about it.

> B. C. Dahlgren: *Nasty*. He will soon lose the large agency he has. Said to be getting rich.

> C. J. Dymling: Said to be quite safe for all he does and to be an agreeable man to do business with.

> Francke & Braune: Francke is said to have come into money and Rohss says they are quite safe. They are forming a company for their sugar works and keep ½ the shares.
> Proposed blank credit £2000 – and trans. purchases to the amount of £5000 at one time. [trans = transatlantic]

> Ullberg & Cramer, Hamburg: credit now £3000 & old £1000. Agreed to extend the credit to £4000 and wrote them a letter arranging this, also remitted ½% coms on last *trans*. business as it was entered into by mistake about £10 in their favour. Arranged that this is no precedent.

> Rosendalls Fabrikers AB: They want no credit but insist on low coms, same as offered by Hambros . . . They wanted their bills

discounted at current rates and Hambro offers to do this, but I declined urging this was bankers business. I proposed 5% pro and con. In case our buying sugar we are to receive remittances as soon as we can inform the Co, even by wire. If not we charge for cash advance ½% or 1%. Probable business 300/500 tons sugar monthly.

A. Fry Kinan: Very civil. E I & Co say he is likely to come into some money thro' his wife; but at present only has a few agencies who may be worth 4 to 500. [added later] Failed some time ago and lost his wife's money.

L. J. Furst: A Jew not very generally liked, but doing a large import business and really thought to be rich. Some call him *sharp*. [added later] Insecci says he was unlucky at first, but for some years has been doing well and on enquiry thinks he must have 7000 to 10000.

H. J. Gerhardt: Saw him 31 May. Very friendly, and expects to do some business shortly if coffee prices are not too high. Only speaks German. Has raised himself by his own exertions and may therefore be better than he looks.

H. Rumerstrom, Malmo: apparently a good man of business, has sent peas to Leith but with bad success and even intends bringing the peas back to Malmo. Seems friendly and promises business in the autumn. Should be kept well advised.

In another part of the booklet he noted procedures and current charges. On a page headed 'Proforma a/c Sales of Wheat on Consignment to London Sold ex Ship' he gave a list of charges:

Trimming on board (3/6 a day at present where one trimmer employed . . . *Trimming* loosens the Cargo and makes it turn out greater bulk, of much importance should the article not be sold by bulk).

Freight. a good way to get at this is supposing Gothenburg Oats freight (always well known) be 2/- Stockholm & Noorkoping will be about 3/- - the 'Baltic Rates' tell you the proportion.

Brokerage. 6d. a quarter (The factor charge is 1/- and 1% delivered. He gives us back 6d.).

Supposing the wheat to be landed
add
Lighterage & landing. 9d. p gr

Rent & Insurance.   4s. 6d. p 100 gr p week
   (These always go together in granaries. Granary keepers wont
   separate them so that in landing we need never insure)
Turning and trimming in granary. (to keep the wheat in condition)
   about 4/6 a 100
Screening where necessary. (to free it from foreign seed, dirt and
   fresh) a third of the turning and trimming charge

Wheat is frequently (indeed most generally) sold by weight –
62 lbs p basket being the most usual standard tho' some kinds are
sold by 60 lbs such as Danubian and by 63 lbs such as Calcutta, but
when wheats are light as the wheats of this year give all on 60 lbs –
more frequently this standard.
   The charge for weighing on board ship is about 2d. a gr.

Sometimes a buyer will have landed wheat reweighed and re-
rented [?] whether landed in sack or in bulk, and this landed but
the day before, but this is rare. If the stuff has been landed several
weeks, and even tho' in sacks, the buyer will always have it re-
rented [?] and re-weighed which will have a consideration in the
price.

The granary keeper's charge for re-renting and re-weighing is
about 4/2 but as some of them have a wonderful knack of bringing
out the quantity, buyer will in the case of some granaries always
have it recounted [?] by the City Meter in which case the charge
is a little more.

The charges for barley and oats were about the same as wheat.
There followed notes on something called 'Blandiad'.

   The same as barley. Should anyone argue that this Commission
   should be the same as oats point out that this article being new to
   London is more difficult to sell well than either barley or oats. I
   arranged on the market that the Barley Commissions should be
   charged on blandiad, and you will take good note who, if anybody,
   is undercharging.

A cryptic note on a blank page read: 'Power of foreigners to
hold estates in case of bad debt. Mortgages & P.N.' A point to
raise in the subscription room. He was also a romantic. On another
blank page he had copied the couplet 'Il tempo fa passare l'amore/
L'amor fa passar il tempo' and beneath the translation 'If time can
make love's passion die/'Tis love that makes those moments fly'.

Then followed:

Iron – April 1856
Value of good E.S. assortments to ship London £14 10/ @ £15.

Charges
Insurance according to season
Freight from 5/– as ballast to 15/ @ 20/ whole ship
Sound dues 2/0 @ 2/1
Discount 2½% ⎤ 6 per cent
Brokerage 1% ⎬ on the
Commission 2½ ⎦ gross amount

Broad sizes are different if sale above £13 10/–
3 × ½ will however command £14 present moment.
Steel in Kegs & Faggots

  £19 10/ £21 10/
Sold on same conditions as Iron and charges the same.

Steel Iron is always sold 9 months in Sheffield – present value for good Lancashire marks from £13 10/ to £15 p ton

S/Iron is shipped to London at ballast freights; the transhipping charges are: lighterage from 1/6d
     Freight to Hull 5/– @ 6/–
     Insurance do

Blooms are sold either on same terms as Iron in London or pr 6 months when 4% is charged for Com. & Guarantee, together with 1% Brokerage.

One of the most useful functions of the subscription room of the Baltic Coffee-House was to provide the facility for the exchange of confidences, the giving and taking of hints, the updating of information which contributed to the building up of a dossier of the kind Stuart Lane and countless others kept in their heads or private notebooks with metal clasps, as the reference point for the risk-taking and trust-placing on which commercial success or failure depended.

But in 1857 the Room had one major drawback. It was nowhere near large enough. The snuggery in what had been the Antwerp Tavern in Sun Court had served its purpose for forty-seven years.

E

But now not only the waiting list but the prestige of the Baltic Coffee-House called for a move to larger premises, capable moreover of allowing for even further expansion. The committee appointed a sub-committee of volunteers to examine the problem and make recommendations.

What other buildings they considered is not known – the Hall of Commerce perhaps – but considering the terms of reference, which will have included proximity to the Royal Exchange, Corn Exchange and the shipping companies, their choice was limited.

In 1855 the City had been shocked by the failure of the Royal British Bank whose major asset was the building it owned, and partly occupied, at the junction of Threadneedle Street (north side) and Bishopsgate Street – the South Sea House. This was not the building used by the South Sea Company when it was formed in 1711. The company's first officers did their business in Merchant Taylors' Hall, further west on the south side of Threadneedle Street. In 1715 they transferred to the large Excise House facing Broad Street, where they rented a suite of rooms from 1715 to 1720, the year of the Bubble which ignominiously brought the company crashing down with discredit and dishonour. The company was reconstituted, however, and turned its hand to whaling. In 1725 the rector and churchwardens of St Martin Outwich, on the south side of Threadneedle Street at the point where it joined Bishopsgate Street, leased to the South Sea Company the premises in Hammonds Alley immediately opposite the church. The company occupied these houses for another five years and in 1730 they pulled them all down except one, 'the Flower Pot' coaching inn (which remained in business till its demolition in 1863). On the rest of the big site, which stretched right back to within a few yards of the Excise House behind, the company erected a building to their own design which was completed in 1732 and named 'the South Sea House'.

The company's association with the Excise House in the days of its notoriety caused this building to be known as 'Old South Sea House' – it is so named on Rocque's map of 1746. It was badly damaged by fire in 1826 and in 1832 the City of London Club was built on the site.

To what extent the building owned by the Royal British Bank in 1855 was that built by the South Sea Company in 1732 it is difficult to say. It is said to have been sold in 1750 ('for a few thousand pounds' says James Findlay) and may have been re-built then. A writer in *John O'London's Weekly* in 1920 said it was only erected in 1772–3. Two engravings in the Crace Collection show the house in 1754 and the same building in 1830, so it seems the front at least remained the same in that eighty-year period. In his *History of London*, written in 1773, John Noorthouck describes the 'new' building as

a magnificent structure of brick and stone about a quadrangle supported by stone pillars of the Tuscan order which form a fine piazza. The front in Threadneedle Street is large, plain and of the Doric order; but the decoration about the door and the central window over it are remarked as much too elegant to correspond with the style of the rest of the building. The walls are of a great thickness; the several offices are admirably disposed; and the great hall for sales, the dining room, galleries and chambers are hardly to be equalled. Under all are arched vaults to preserve everything that is valuable from accidental fires.

The writer Charles Lamb got his first job as a clerk at South Sea House on leaving school in 1792. In the August 1820 issue of the *London Magazine* there appeared an essay by Charles Lamb entitled 'Recollections of the South Sea House'. A fellow clerk had the odd name of Elia and he took it as a pseudonym.

This was once a house of trade, a centre of busy interests. The throng of merchants was here – the quick pulse of gain – and here some forms of business are still kept up, though the soul be long fled. There are still to be seen stately porticos; imposing staircases, offices roomy as the state apartments in palaces – deserted or thinly peopled with a few struggling clerks; the still more sacred interiors of court and committee rooms, with venerable faces of beadles and storekeepers – directors seated in form on solemn days (to proclaim a dead dividend) at long worm-eaten tables that have been mahogany, with tarnished gilt-leather coverings supporting massive inkstands long since dry; the oaken wainscots hung with pictures of deceased governors and sub-governors of Queen Anne and the two first monarchs of the Brunswick dynasty, huge charts which subsequent discoveries have antiquated; dusty maps of Mexico, dim as dreams, and soundings of the Bay of Panama! The long passages hung with buckets, appended in idle row to walls whose substance might defy any, short of the last, conflagration; with vast ranges of collarage under all where dollars and pieces of eight once lay, an 'unsunned heap', for Mammon to have solaced his solitary heart withal – long since dissipated or scattered into air at the blast of that famous BUBBLE.

Eighteen years after this was written, Lloyd's took temporary offices in the building during the reconstruction of the Royal Exchange, as we have already seen. Lloyd's vacated South Sea House in 1844, after which the Royal British Bank took over.

From its position, its elegance and antiquity, South Sea House seemed ideal for a new 'Baltic', and the sub-committee reported accordingly. There is no record of their report or how it was received, what opposition was shown and for what reasons, what discussion took place on how they intended to raise the money, what they should do about giving up 58 Threadneedle Street, or how they ought to compensate its proprietor, John Monger. What is known is that on April 8, 1857, the leasehold of South Sea House was put up for auction by direction of the assignees of the Royal British Bank in bankruptcy. The particulars of sale said it had an estimated annual value of £4000. The building was commanding and noble in appearance, substantial in construction, and for the most part in excellent repair.

The admirable arrangement of the interior, its extent and adaptability for business and professional purposes, combined with its immediate proximity to the Bank of England, Royal Exchange and other important Public Offices, render the property worthy of the attention of Bankers, Merchants, Shipping, Insurance and other Companies requiring accommodation of a superior character.

The ground floor contained 'the finest Banking Room in the Metropolis, its admirably constucted Glass Roof supplying it abundantly with light'. It had a handsome stone entrance at the east end of the building leading to the upper three floors where sitting tenants included the Public Works Loan Commissioners, the New British Iron Company, the Mid-Kent Railway Company and, appropriately enough, the Russia Company. A suite of three rooms at the eastern end of the second floor was occupied by – the South Sea Company.

In 1855, when the Royal British Bank went bankrupt, the building was sold by Beadel & Sons to William Tite, presumably acting as liquidator, for £55 750. At the auction there must have been someone representing the Baltic Coffee-House with authority to bid on behalf of the subscribers. Who else put in bids for the building is not known, but the leasehold of the property was sold to the bidder from the coffee-house. No less suitable headquarters could have been found for businessmen pledged to maintain high standards of trust and plain dealing than the building connected in the public mind with a criminal confidence trick deliberately devised and executed for their own personal gain by trusted leaders of the commercial and political community headed by the Chancellor of the Exchequer.

A month after the auction, on May 8, 1857, a company was registered with the name 'The Baltic Company Limited'. Its objects were

to purchase the property known as The South Sea House in Threadneedle Street as lately in the occupation of the Royal British Bank and their tenants, to let to the Subscribers to The Baltic Coffee House the two lower floors and such other parts of the building as may be required by the said subscribers to the Baltic Coffee House and to let such parts as may not be required from time to time to other persons and generally to hold and manage the same as owners thereof.

The nominal capital was £20000, divided into 200 shares of £100 each. It was registered without articles of association and was incorporated under the Joint Stock Companies Act of 1856. Its registered office was at 5 Church Passage, Guildhall Yard, and John Hunt Junr was its secretary. On August 18 it moved its registered office to 39, 40 & 41 Threadneedle Street, commonly called the South Sea House. Its first shareholders were all members of the Baltic Coffee-House committee: John Mollett, merchant: John Henry William Schroder, merchant, of 145 Leadenhall Street; Richard Brandt, merchant, of 3 Crosby Square; Henry Adwin Soames; Thomas Prehn, merchant, of 57 Old Broad Street; John Todd of All Hallows Chambers; George Goss, Russia broker, of 80 Old Broad Street, who sometime between 1854 and 1857 had succeeded Benjamin Lancaster as hon. secretary. An eighth name seems to be 'Henry Elder'.

The twelve directors were: John Mollett, chairman, J. H. W. Schroder, M. E. Rodocanachi, Richard Brandt, George Goss, John Todd, Thomas Prehn, Edward Wilson, Antonio Ralli, Richard Wilson, Charles B. Colchester and F. G. Goodliffe.

The subscribers of the Baltic Coffee-House formed the Baltic Company of their own free will. They were the first shareholders named in the Memorandum of Association; from their ranks came the first directors. It was a ploy contrived to enable them to buy the leasehold of South Sea House and to share in its ownership without individual liability in the event of the scheme failing to work out – Moxhay's experience was still within the living memory of many of them.

There is no record of a general meeting of subscribers which passed a unanimous or majority resolution to move out of 58 Threadneedle Street and form a limited company to purchase no 39. Something of the kind must have occurred, however, for it was entirely a domestic affair. It was not imposed on them from outside. The committee had doubtless been under pressure from a minority of active subscribers, as always happens, more concerned than the rest that action should not be further delayed. Some of these would have joined the official sub-committee charged with finding a solution; others would have elected to remain outside, free to criticize whatever schemes were put up. One faction apparently favoured staying where they were and persuading John Monger to enlarge his house and make other improvements – see his letter below.

All this is conjecture. The fact remains that four subscribers elected to the Baltic committee in 1854, John Mollett, J. H. W. Schroder, John Todd and George Goss, were among the company's founder directors. Thus a third of the board also served on the committee. A leader in all this seems to have been Henry Schroder, though John Mollett was chairman of the company and of the committee. The other eight directors were all coffee-house subscribers.

At the start, therefore, the Baltic committee and the Baltic Company were one, though they had separate secretaries. George Goss was honorary secretary of the committee, though within a few months he handed over to a full-time professional, William J. C. Oxley. John Hunt Junr, who appeared as secretary of the company in the Memorandum of Association, was probably the solicitor who conducted the legal formalities of the formation. But the administration of both company and committee took place in the same building – probably in the same room. The upper hand remained with the committee whose creature the company was.

The immediate task was to make arrangements for the move, to decide what to take and what to leave, and to plan the alterations required to change a bank into a subscription room, sale room coffee room and the rest. A sub-committee was appointed on April 16, 1857, a week after the auction, 'to make all the necessary arrangements for the removal of the Baltic'. Unfortunately they interpreted their brief as including the destruction of the com-mittee's correspondence and records for their thirty-four-year occupation of No 58. Part of the job would have been advising the committee on how to handle their late manager and proprietor, John Monger, who felt himself shabbily treated and wrote to the committee on July 23 to say so.

Gentlemen,
　　　　　Allow me to place before the Committee for their kind consideration a few facts in relation to my very long connection with the Baltic Coffee House, which may not be known to many of the present members of the Committee now appointed to arrange [on] removal of the business to the South Sea House. My services have extended over 36 years as servant and master. When I became proprietor I paid £2000 for the business. I then took all the furniture fixtures &c &c at a full valuation, but now unfortunately shall be obliged to sell off for what I may get. My leases have recently been renewed at a very much higher rental owing to my having a large body of Subscribers, and the difficulty of finding any other place suitable for their accommodation. The improvements and alterations I have carried out have been considerable and very expensive to meet their requirements. I am now upward of 60 years of age and consequently feel incompetent to commence a new business. I must therefore turn all I possess to the best advantage and make what provision I can for the future support of myself and family, much of which will depend upon the kindness and liberality of the Committee, as I find myself suddenly & unexpectedly deprived of the goodwill of my business

and all the benefits which it has been my hope to realize; it is true I have a Lease of the premises, but denuded of the business with an increased high rental it is a mere speculative property. I do therefore humbly and respectfully hope that in dealing with my case the Committee will take a liberal view and consider my length of service, my age and the due necessity for my future provision together with my entire inability to avoid what I cannot but consider my present calamity.

Neither James Findlay nor Bryant Lillywhite offer any information on the fate of the little coffee-house inside Sun Court at the end of Hercules Passage off Threadneedle Street which had been the Antwerp Tavern and then Mongers and the Baltic Coffee-House for all these years. It almost certainly did not continue as a straight coffee-house with another name without a subscription room – they had already gone out of fashion. The name 'Baltic Coffee-House' was transferred to South Sea House. Further research would be necessary to throw light on how No 58 Threadneedle Street spent its days until it became a post office at the end of the century.

The scheme at South Sea House was to be the same as at 58 Threadneedle Street – a central subscription room for members only, and a public sale room, coffee room and dining room. To adapt the bank for these purposes needed considerable structural alterations. According to James Watson the central entrance was closed and side doors opened. 'Internally great alterations have been made and one of the last relics is the partners' old dining room with its formal and plain oak. The subscription room itself is partly built upon the inner quadrangle which was contained in the Threadneedle portion of the building.' Building works were put in hand at once. They took five months.

News of the move from 58 Threadneedle Street soon spread to the City's catering fraternity. First off the mark was Robert Devar who wrote to John Mollett, chairman of the committee, on May 4. He would have much pleasure in negotiating to supply the refreshments at the new establishment. He had taken over the business of Angell & Son of Cornhill in 1834 and run it successfully for twenty-two years. He had just disposed of it. The next day Messrs Bland & Kelsey wrote from Garraways to 'The Committee of The

Baltic Exchange' – the first time the establishment was given the now familiar title (see illustration on p. 118). Reuben Hibberd wrote on May 20 offering his services 'having been informed by several members of The Baltic Coffee House that the Refreshment Department of your Institution is open to competition'. Many Baltic members, he said, already frequented his place in Finch Lane. He also purveyed for the Milton Club in Ludgate Hill and provided its 700 members with luncheons and dinners from the simplest to the most recherché character. He enclosed a copy of his agreement with the committee of the Milton to prove it. Alfred Nicholes, who had been cook at the London Tavern 'from Boyhood' for the last sixteen years, offered either to supply the refreshments or undertake the entire management of the department. 'I am young, but with great judgement in the selection of viands suited to the wants of any first class Establishment.' Edward Sewell craftily lobbied John Mollett before he formally told the committee that he had lost the appointment at Lloyd's by only one vote, and was now wine steward to the Salters' Company and Sadlers' Company.

Nicholes gave the name of W. R. Bathe, of the London Tavern, as a reference and Henry Schroder wrote to Bathe not for this purpose but for general advice. Bathe suggested selecting a competent manager

who would have to pay no rent but similar to the Steward of a club, and who would have to provide refreshments of the very best quality at the very lowest remunerative charge; in fact the Committee should provide their own tariff and stipulate that the Wines should be purchased at some first rate Merchants and be engaging the Manager for a year only subject to any alteration then the Committee will be at that time better enabled to judge and to make perhaps a more advantageous arrangement.

The refreshment department was to be a thorn in the side of the committee for the next hundred years. Changes of policy, indeterminate decisions, lack of appreciation of the problems involved, dogged the handling of this important aspect of the Baltic's role from the outset. None of the applicants who wrote between May and August was engaged. When the committee finally made an appointment, they ignored Bathe's advice and asked for rent.

Garraway's Coffee House.
Change Alley 5th May 1857.

To

The Committee of
The Baltic Exchange.
Gentlemen,
            We beg respectfully to inform
you that we are desirous of supplying the Refreshmen
at your Exchange.

            Having been many years
engaged in the Luncheon and Wine Trades, we
feel assured, that should you confide this busines
                                                        "to

Letter from Bland & Kelsey, caterers, to the Baltic committee, 1857

to our hands, we shall give you every satisfaction, in respect both to quality and price.

If you will favour us with the Terms which you propose to offer, we shall be happy to treat more particularly for the same.

We are,

Gentlemen,

Your obedient Servants,

Bland & Kelsey

On October 1 a deputation from the Baltic committee was received by the directors of the Baltic Company. This was less, however, of a confrontation between the two 'sides' than a general meeting, still at their old home, of leading subscribers to discuss the implications of their latest step and plan some kind of general policy for the future. Motions were put to, and voted on by, all those present whether members of the deputation or the board.

As already suggested, the Baltic committee are likely to have kept minutes of the meetings between 1823 and 1857 but they never survived the clear-out at No 58. They started a new minute book, however, in 1857, and the first entry in it was a report of this deputation of October 1. No minutes of the board meetings of the company have remained, however, to give their version of their relations with the committee.

As a basis for discussion the meeting had a memorandum prepared by George Goss, hon. secretary of the committee and a director of the company, which set out the terms on which he suggested the new rooms should be 'transferred' – there was no question of leasing at this stage – to the subscribers of the coffee-house. He read it out to the meeting.

The annual subscription for individuals, he suggested, should be five guineas and this should be paid by all existing members. New members should pay an annual subscription of five guineas plus an entrance fee of the same sum. The committee of subscribers alone should have the power of admitting new members. All subscription money would go to the company who would deduct a sum of not more than £500 and give it to the committee to pay for the wages of the waiters, the newspapers and the general upkeep of the Room.

If the company were going to get the subscriptions, Antonio Ralli and Thomas Prehn thought the five-guinea entrance fee was too little and should be raised to ten. But the others disagreed. Goss's first proposal was put to the meeting and passed. The board then proceeded to double the amount Goss had said the committee might need for running the Room and placed an annual sum not exceeding £1000 at their disposal.

The sub-committee appointed on April 16 reported the result

of their labours to John Mollett, chairman of the committee (and chairman of the company), on Thursday, October 15.

As you are already aware the Building in Threadneedle Street, lately belonging to the Royal British Bank, was secured by parties connected with this room, and principally by means of subscriptions raised among its members for the purpose of affording us the requisite accommodation. A portion of these premises has been fitted up with this object, and under the supervision of your committee in a manner worthy, we venture to believe, of the large and influential body it is intended to accommodate, and with a liberal regard to their increased requirements and comfort. Not only is the general accommodation very superior in every respect to that we have hitherto enjoyed, but luncheon and dining rooms have been added for the convenience of members and a very excellent sale room has been built in connection with the subscription room, but totally detached from it. Having alluded to the refreshment rooms, we may add, that a strong feeling having been expressed that the management of this department should be placed on a liberal and satisfactory footing, an arrangement for that purpose has been entered into with the Messrs Staples on such terms as leave no reasonable doubt of the desired object being effectually secured, and as at the same time to give full power of control to the committee of Subscribers without involving responsibility on their part. The necessary arrangements for your comfort are now sufficiently advanced to admit the rooms being opened for your reception on Thursday next [October 22]. Such being the case we have further only to give you an outline of the terms which the 'Baltic Company Limited' (the landlords of the building) are prepared to admit us and in the arrangement of which we have had the benefit of the counsel and sanction of your permanent committee. These terms are simply as regards all existing members of the Baltic Coffee House, whether partners or firms or not, an individual Subscription of £5 5s. per annum commencing from the 1st Inst; and as regards new members the payment of an entrance fee of £5 5s. in addition to the above annual subscription. It is further understood that all emolument arising from other sources whether country members, visitors &c, as may hereafter be arranged, shall belong to the Company who, on the other hand, place at the disposal of the Committee of Subscribers any sums not exceeding £1000 per annum, that the latter may find necessary for the general management of the room. Thus the full control of all matters connected with the admission of members and the internal regulations of the Subscription Room, is left in the hands of the Committee of Subscribers, while they are freed from the pecuniary risk and responsibility. As many points of detail cannot be conveniently arranged, until the rules and regulations of the New Room have been decided upon, these minor matters have been left for future arrangement between the Directors of the 'Baltic

Company' and your Committee on the basis of the above terms. At the same time, it is most important that this should be done as early as possible, and as we feel that we shall but inadequately have discharged the duties for which we were appointed, until we have submitted for your adoption a code of rules and regulations altered to suit our circumstances, we propose to call a General Meeting of the Subscribers to the New Room as soon as convenient after our arrival. On that meeting will devolve the duty of considering and adopting any amendments that may appear necessary in the existing rules, and of electing a new Committee of Management, as the duties for which we were appointed having been discharged, we shall then resign to you the temporary powers which you did us the honor of entrusting to us; and we believe we are authorised by your permanent committee to state that they consider their term of office expires with the existence of the present Coffee House. May we add that we trust our labours will meet with your approval; they have been somewhat more onerous than most of us at the outset had anticipated, but if the New Baltic keeps up and extends the high standing for general energy, ability and integrity of its members, so long maintained by the old, they will not have been in vain.

During the first week at South Sea House John Mollett and his old committee met to select those they would recommend members to elect as the new committee and consider amendments to the rules. Again George Goss came up with detailed suggestions, all of which the committee agreed with. They decided to post the draft of the new set of rules which they were proposing in the subscription room, together with the names they were proposing for a committee; and three days later to call a general meeting of all subscribers to discuss and adopt them in what form they wished.

This meeting was held in the sale room at South Sea House on November 4. Eight of the old members were re-elected to a new committee of twenty by whom the 'general concerns' of the Room were to be managed and referred to as the house committee – George Goss, John Mollett, John Ord, Pantia Ralli, Henry Schroder, John Smith, John Todd and Edward Wilson. A new-comer was Edward Baring, of the famous banking family. Nine members of the new committee were also members of the board of the Baltic Company: Richard Brandt, Charles Colchester, George Goss, John Mollett, Thomas Prehn, Antonio Ralli, Henry Schroder, John Todd, Richard Wilson.

The first of the new rules and regulations adopted by this

meeting referred to the establishment as 'THE BALTIC' and put no limit on the number of members who could join. The number of members would be determined by the committee after the capabilities of the subscription room had been fairly ascertained. The procedure for proposing new members was unchanged. The new fees were as already mentioned, but retired members and anyone living outside London paid three guineas annual subscription and a one guinea entrance fee. A member elected when clerk to one firm who then became a partner in that firm or left to become a clerk in another, ceased to be a member and would have to seek re-election. The report of the meeting in the Baltic committee minute book stated that the committee were asked to consider the establishment of a court of reference for the settlement of disputes but no mention of this is ever made again. The meeting added a further formality to the process of expulsion by laying down that the committee's decision to expel a member was not valid until it had been confirmed at a subsequent special meeting of the committee attended by at least twelve, of whom three-quarters must vote in favour. The meeting agreed to compensate John Monger with 'one year's subscription' (rent?) but he was writing two months later reminding them that he had not yet had the promised remuneration in consideration of past services 'and the sacrifice which your unexpected removal has entailed upon me'.

The sale room was well patronized from the start. Tallow sales were held every Tuesday, and Churchill & Sim, timber merchant of Lambeth, held sales every first Friday of the month. It was up to the landlords, the Baltic Company, however, to solicit hirings of the public rooms, and any request which came to the house committee they passed on to the board.

The new house committee met for the first time the day following the general meeting which had elected them. They elected sixty-eight new members, the first of which was a firm called E. Rainford. The election of ten candidates was deferred, and three were blackballed.

John Hunt Junr sent a circular to all those who had been proposed for membership over the previous six months and were still waiting election to discover whether they still wished to join under the

Sir, I am favored with your note of the 10 inst.

I am desirous of being a Member under the new regulations.

I shall therefore be glad if you will kindly forward this object.

Very Ob'd'ly

Henry Vallance

20 Essex St. Strand
14 Nov: 1857

To The Secretary
Baltic Coffee House

Letter requesting membership of the Baltic, 1857

new circumstances and were willing to abide by the new regulations. 'In that case it will be desirable that you have your name put again on the Books – proposed and seconded as before.' Many returned the letter with a note scribbled on it giving agreement; others took umbrage at being kept waiting so long and not having been told of the move, let alone any new regulations. Old George Parton wrote from Rotherhithe on November 19,

The first day of the opening of the New Rooms the Clerk said I fear, Mr Parton they will want to make you a new Subscriber as you were not formally admitted by the Committee the last time you were proposed. I replied, what had I to do with their blunder? I was told I had no more to do. The receipt from May 57 to May 58 was sent to me and I paid it; my friend Mr Bunning was by me at the time and said he could not see that I could be anything but an old Subscriber. You have attempted to smuggle me in, but you will not succeed.

He went on to complain that he had been asked to agree to the new rules but had heard nothing of them. Worse, he had received a second circular letter, before he had replied to the first, saying he had been elected – without his consent. He asked Hunt to remove his name. By being a 'new' member he would have to pay the entrance fee. John Hunt's desire to please his masters by drumming up as many members as he could and swell the revenue, and thus the dividends, was getting the better of him.

The house committee elected another fifty-six new members when they met on November 17 and blackballed another three. One of the latter was a Greek, called Uzielli, who before the Baltic Company had been formed had been asked by Michel Rodocanachi, who became one of the directors, to make a contribution towards the new Room on the understanding that he would have the same rights as other subscribers. He thereupon made a gift of £100 towards the committee's funds and got a receipt for it on April 18. He wrote to John Mollett on November 23,

I am now informed with astonishment that there is an opposition to my admission as a subscriber. I have heard it stated that the cause of this opposition is that I said something disrespectful regarding the committee. Now I beg most emphatically to deny having made use of the expressions which have been imputed to me . . . I feel persuaded that Gentlemen in your position never intended to take my money for the purpose of furnishing the Rooms and then refuse my admission, neither am I sure would any Gentleman of the Committee wish to cast upon me a personal insult by such conduct.

He was right. No gentleman of the committee had any such idea. His letter was considered by the house committee at their next meeting, together with a requisition from ten members for a second ballot. Theodosius Uzielli, stockbroker, was elected and thereafter kept his opinion of this touchy committee of merchants to himself.

On April 29, 1858, the committee put on their other hats for the Baltic Company's first ordinary general meeting of shareholders with John Mollett in the chair. The Report of Directors stated,

The capital was originally fixed at £20000 in 200 shares of £100 each, and your directors hoped that there would have been no difficulty whatever in obtaining subscriptions for that sum from the members of the Baltic, and other parties who might take an interest in this undertaking, which your directors believe will afford commercial facilities of a very superior character. The result however to the present time is that 180 shares only have been subscribed for, and consequently the expenditure has been in excess of the capital. There is another reason which your directors regret to state has operated unfavourably to your interests viz, – that the expenditure in the necessary improvements and adaptation of the building to the purposes for which it is required has exceeded the original estimates. To some extent this is owing to the desire of your directors to afford the very best accommodation to the subscribers to the Baltic from whom, as you must be aware, the Company expects to derive a very large portion of its income, and this has led to a liberal expenditure in the Refreshment department; and your directors would also observe that the character of the alterations and improvements was such as to render it almost impossible to obtain accurate estimates previously to the commencement of the works.

A balance of £1330 remained which, however, would not be available for dividend as it should be held in suspense to cope with the building's future arrangements. Some items of expenditure, said the directors, would doubtless surprise shareholders. They alluded

with a feeling almost of shame to the large amount which has been paid to the rector for tithes, it being notorious that the duties performed in a parish possessing a very few resident inhabitants do not bear any proportion to the income of the living provided by persons who, as in your case, become owners of property, without being aware of the existence of such a fearful burthen.

That God should filch a mite or two from Mammon setting up a palace in his parish was really a bit much.

On the other hand, the directors could offer shareholders their congratulations on having obtained possession of the whole of the offices except two small rooms on the third floor (the South Sea Company's?) and having let them all on fair terms. When some of the existing agreements expired a large revenue might safely be anticipated. A further cause of congratulation was the steady increase in the number of subscribers to the rooms which boded well for the income of future years.

The Report ended,

In conclusion your directors would observe that they have every confidence in the ultimate success of the company, and although they regret that the novelty of the undertaking has led to an underestimate of the outlay required to adapt the building to the wants of a mercantile community, they are satisfied that by a judicious conduct of its affairs, the company will after it has acquired the freehold of the building be in receipt of an income sufficient to return a fair dividend on the capital embarked.

An extraordinary meeting followed 'to consider whether new provisions in addition to the existing regulations of the company, should be made in order to effect the purchase of the freehold of the building and to raise the necessary funds for that and other purposes'. A number of resolutions were passed.

It was stated that South Sea House was demised to the company by an indenture of lease dated May 25, 1857, and for the purpose of purchasing the fee simple and inheritance of the property the directors were given powers to borrow any sum not exceeding £45775 (the reckoned purchase price) and to mortgage the building as a security for its repayment. They could raise any part of the £45775 by the issue of debentures or creation of new shares at a preferential rate of not more than £5 per cent instead of borrowing. The capital of the company was increased by £5000 to be raised by the issue of further preference shares to rank *pari passu* with the others. Both lots were to be offered in the first instance to existing shareholders.

All went very nearly according to plan. The freehold was purchased for £46821 6s. 10d., a sum which included stamp duties and counsel's fees – an indication of trouble. A loan of £35000 was raised on mortgage from the Alliance Assurance Company for seven years at 4½ per cent, and £12000 by the issue of preferential 7 per cent shares redeemable in ten years. The annual charge, they reckoned, would be £2437.

South Sea House became 'the Baltic'.

5. *Investment or Club?*

By the middle of May 1858, the attractions of the Baltic Company as an investment had become fully established, and there were 15 shareholders, many of whom were not members of the coffee-house. They included eighty-seven merchants, thirteen Russia brokers, two Russia merchants, four gentlemen and three ship-brokers. A few held two £100 shares and these included Richard Brandt, Thomas Prehn and Ambrose Theodore Ralli. Thirty-seven Greeks were shareholders and they included Pandia Theodore Ralli, Pandia Alexander Ralli, Eustrato Ralli, Michel Emanuel Rodocanachi, Leone Rodocanachi, Eustratius Ionides, insurance agent, who held three shares; and Theodosius Uzielli, of the Stock Exchange. Shareholders included indigo brokers, tar distillers, seed brushers, oil brokers, hide brokers, colonial brokers, corn factors, tallow dealers, ships agents, linen manufacturers, wharfingers, clerks and at least one shipowner (Anthony G. Robinson).

One of the shareholders, and a member, was George Dornbusch, who described himself as a merchant but was better known as a purveyor of commercial information. In 1858 he launched a publication called *George Dornbusch's Floating Cargoes Evening List* to give information to speculators in produce like grain about consignments on the way by sea to Britain (and elsewhere) which dealers could purchase before they arrived. He also seemed to be acting with someone who might have been considered a rival. On June 29 (1858) he wrote to the committee of the Baltic Company (he was not the only one confused by two bodies):

I am desired by Mr Reuter of the Royal Exchange to inform you that he offers to supply the Baltic with telegraphic news as follows

Daily – the Liverpool Cotton market

Twice weekly, the cornmarkets of Liverpool, Dublin, Belfast & Wakefield also daily

the Continental Exchanges at Paris, Amsterdam, Frankfurt, Madrid, Hamburg, Berlin, Vienna

The whole of the above stated news he offers to the Baltic for the very moderate sum of One Guinea per week.

A trial might be made for a month.

In addition to the above named informations Mr Reuter can supply the Baltic daily with the quotations of public funds of all the principal Stock Exchanges of Europe, and for supplying this important information he would charge only £10 10/ extra in addition to the above charge of one Guinea weekly.

Mr Reuter is desirous to receive your decision at your earliest convenience in order that he may make his arrangements accordingly. If you should wish to see Mr Reuter he will call upon you any time that should be appointed.

At their meeting of July 1, at which William Oxley appeared for the first time as secretary, the committee declined Dornbusch's offer of Mr Reuter's telegraphic services. So the great man wrote to the committee himself.

> Continental Telegraph
> under the direction of Mr Julius Reuter
> Offices: 1, Royal Exchange Buildings

Gentlemen,

Since the 1st of Octr. I have established a telegraph service for receiving news from all parts of the Continent which I send to all the London papers.

I also receive from Liverpool and Southampton *by telegraph* the arrivals of the American, Brazil and West Indian steamers, the amount of specie brought and all interesting political and commercial news. These messages (which would be of great interest to your members) I am able to give you several hours before they are published in the papers.

This letter was read to the committee, who deferred the matter 'to make enquiries'. At the same meeting they accepted the resignation of Messrs Staples who had the concession for the refreshment department. Staples said they had made a loss of £80

Letter from Julius Reuter to William Oxley, Secretary of the Baltic committee,
1859

Continental Telegraph,
under the direction of Mr. Julius Reuter.
Offices 1. Royal Exchange Buildings.
London June 28th 1859

Wm. C. Oxley Esq.
Baltic

Sir,

In reply to your letter of the 26th May last I beg to inform you that I am ready to supply the Baltic Coffee house with the following information for One hundred guineas per annum. ——

Liverpool Cotton Report twice a day
Liverpool Corn „ twice a week
Paris Bourse daily Opening prices & away——
The arrival of the Brazil mail in Lisbon & Southampton
The „ „ „ West Indian mail in Southampton
and all extra commercial intelligence I may receive——

Requesting the favor of a reply,
I am, Sir,
Yours obediently
Julius Reuter.

during the first three months of their tenancy and since then had only cleared expenses. Refusing to learn a lesson from this, or to take Mr Bathe's advice, the committee appointed another caterer called J. D. Hebert, and charged him a rental of £50. A new member admitted at this meeting was twenty-eight-year-old Horace Clarkson, who had founded the firm which bore his name with Leon Benham in 1852. An old member whose name disappeared from the list this same year was Thomas Tooke, who died in 1858 at the age of eighty-four. He had been a prime mover in the formation of the committee which was now finding its feet in its new environment and learning to manage a membership which rose from 627 in March 1858, to 737 in March 1859, and to provide for them with the £1200 granted by the company out of the £4400 subscription income. The company's total income was £7000, and in addition to subscriptions and entrance fees included £1860 from the rent of the other rooms at South Sea House and £650 from letting the sale room. Outgoings included £353 on rates and the £250 tithe. They paid a dividend of £6 a share, which was at a rate of 3 per cent. They broke down the £100 shares into five of £20 each, and ruled that a director must hold at least £100 worth of qualifying shares.

Managing the membership and providing the facilities of a commercial resort was the passive function of these amateur committee-men – professionals in their jobs as Russia merchants and shipbrokers but amateurs in the art of running what to all intents and purposes was now a club. It was the official and principal role of the 'house committee'. But the lengthy association of its members with trade and shipping gave it another, more active, role. The Baltic had become an institution.

There was two-way consultation. British and foreign governments and organizations looked to it for advice and guidance; and within it was generated a body of opinion which men like John Mollett and George Goss, Edward Baring and Charles Colchester saw fit to communicate to 'the authorities' – be it Thames Navigation Committee, the Shipwrights Company, the Shipowners Society, the General Post Office or the Board of Trade – using as their medium the house committee, which on these occasions became the mouthpiece for all that the Baltic had come to represent in the national life.

In 1858 trade with Russia was still the main preoccupation of the majority of the members of the Baltic. A firm called Leach & Neal of Mark Brown's Wharf were allowed to place a box in the hall of South Sea House for the convenience of merchants, brokers and buyers in the Russia trade 'where letters orders &c can be deposited and which will be conveyed to the Wharf by our Messenger at 11, 1 & 3 o'clock daily'. They had similar boxes in the Commercial Sale Rooms. Delay in delivering letters was a constant cause of complaint and William Oxley's letter to the General Post Office produced a detailed explanation.

The Letter Carrier of the Crosby Square district commences his delivery at Crosby Square, whereas the Baltic Coffee-House is situated about the middle of the walk of the Letter Carrier who is employed in Threadneedle Street, and I am assured that owing to the great number of unpaid letters upon which the postage had to be collected your letters could not be delivered earlier than they were.

When the French mail arrived, said the writer, letters were delivered to the Baltic Coffee-House about twenty minutes after delivery began.

When members complained that letters they were expecting from the continent had not been delivered, Oxley telegraphed to Dover to find out whether they had at least arrived there. Some time between May 1858 and January 1859, the Magnetic Telegraph Company established a telegraph office at South Sea House at a rental of £50 a year. A window of communication was made between the office and the library. The office was staffed by women and was open to the public as well as members. It was styled 'Baltic Coffee-House' and the impression of its date stamp is reproduced here. The female staff were continued after the transfer of the tele-

Post Office stamp of the
Baltic Telegraph Office

graphs to the Post Office in February 1870, but were replaced by men in October 1877.

Postal communications with Scandinavia were of no less importance to members of the Baltic, a large number of whom were heavily engaged in the timber trade with Sweden, which in the 1850s gathered considerable momentum. Two English brothers called Dickson, both members of the Baltic Coffee-House, pioneered the timber export trade when they emigrated to Sweden in the first decade of the nineteenth century. They bought forests and water mills, and received the fullest support from leading agents like Churchill & Sim, and Foy, Morgan & Co.

Between 1846 and 1850 Swedish exports of timber had amounted to only six million rix dollars (£1 sterling equals 18 rix dollars). But by the end of the 1860s this had increased 1000 per cent – the average annual value of exported Swedish timber had become 64 million rix dollars, of which Britain took half (some £1½ million worth).

The increased activity of the early 1850s stemmed mainly from Gothenburg, where merchants set up their own mills and financed others assisted by credits from importing firms in England, France and Holland. Gothenburg discouraged all forms of speculation and its reputation for commercial probity earned it the name of 'Little London'.

One who contributed to Gothenburg's reputation was W. Stuart Lane, from whose notebook quotation has already been made. In the spring of 1858 he took into partnership twenty-seven-year-old Henry Alers Hankey, son of banker John Alers Hankey of Fenchurch Street.

Lane's contact in Gothenburg, Ernest de Bunsen, wrote to congratulate him (June 8, 1858):

My dear Lane,
          Your letter received to-day caused us much, though not unexpected pleasure. You are turning a new leaf, and so I take as new and good a one as I can find to express what you know to be not only our hope but our belief that the turning of this leaf of Lane Hankey & Co was and will be for the best. I certainly do believe that for the next years we must expect great changes and convulsions. How this may affect

England or Sweden no man can tell. But of this I am pretty sure; if there
is a great future for any of the Northern States of Europe it is for
Skandinavia. And this I say independently of the expectation I
communicated to you that Gold will be found there one day in great
abundance.

Whether he meant this literally or figuratively is not clear.

Stuart Lane was upholding all that the Baltic stood for when on
August 9, 1858, he wrote to a customer, William Austrim, in
Stockholm:

My dear sir,

      I am obliged for yours of the 30th ult. As regards the supervision
of shipping it is most unusual for it to be necessary for *respectable* shippers
to have their goods inspected during shipment; they always consider that
they may be trusted to ship according to contract and hold themselves
liable to make good any *fair* claims should they [indecipherable] do so.
The remarks about impatience were merely called for by your own as
regards terms. We could not afford to pay 4% for this, and would decline
any transaction which involved such a cost. I can only say that shipping
goods of any kind is done by anyone at 2% in London – of course
however this is only done when they have people who can either attend
to it themselves and do business with those they can themselves trust. I
think Mr Wilkinson would ship properly.

                                  Yours very truly,
                                  W. Stuart Lane

In his notebook Stuart Lane mentioned the City Meter by which
grain was measured at London docks, and the cost of trimming
when he sold wheat by bulk. Selling grain in this way was felt by
an increasing number at this time to be a far from satisfactory
method, and corn dealers at the Baltic Coffee-House, disturbed
by the 'great inconvenience with delay, and increase of cost which
arises from the present inaccurate method of selling Grain by
various weights and measures throughout the kingdom', drew up
a memorial to the Secretary of the Board of Trade headed 'SALE
OF GRAIN BY WEIGHT WITH UNIFORMITY'. They circulated
copies to importers, shipowners, corn factors and merchants of
Tralee, Dublin, Glasgow, Cork and elsewhere and invited
signatures. It read:

The system of selling Grain by Measure is universally admitted as inaccurate, and in many Markets selling by Weight (*in some form*) has been substituted.

The object now desired is to establish the sale of Grain by WEIGHT with UNIFORMITY.

In making the change, injury and inconvenience should be avoided to Shipowners as carriers; the Customs, as Collectors of Duty; and to Importers as Contractors for purchase and sale; also, to create as little disturbance as possible in the present forms of contracts in which great advantages will arise in preserving the name of the IMPERIAL QUARTER so universally known abroad and at home as the British Standard.

To gain these objects it is proposed to form a Deputation to wait on the Secretary of the Board of Trade requesting that a short Act of Parliament may be passed establishing hereafter the Imperial Bushel of Grain as

40 LBS OF OATS
50 LBS OF BARLEY
60 LBS OF WHEAT

Other Grain, in proportion, to be arranged with equitable care.

If adopted, the Customs would then collect Duty by *weight*. Freight would be paid by *weight*; and considering that Twelve Millions of Quarters are annually imported into the various Markets of the Kingdom, *Uniformity* in the sale by *weight* promises success, and the honest Trader would be better protected from frauds and disputes, at present of daily occurrence.

Statistic Returns of Agricultural Produce and of Foreign Imports would be more accurate and more easily collected.

If approved, when signed, please forward this to

> The Secretary,
> Committee of Merchants,
> Baltic Coffee-House,
> LONDON.

At their April meeting the committee set up a sub-committee to consider the matter, which approved the general views of the memorialists but suggested a more practicable means of obtaining the desired end would be to ask the Board of Trade to levy Customs Duties on grain by weight instead of per imperial bushel or quarter. The quarters should be calculated as 480 lbs to wheat, 400 to barley and 320 to oats.

In September 1860 the Baltic had 760 members, of whom thirty-three were country subscribers. The limit of 325 set in 1857 had been doubled. So had the chance of their admitting a black sheep. When someone told the house committee they considered a member's conduct was derogatory to his character as a man of business, a special meeting was called to decide whether their interpretation of the allegations justified action under their rule.

A broker member called John Tibbs, it was alleged in January 1860, had refused to pay a bill, claiming by affidavit before a judge that it was not legally recoverable as it was incurred on a time bargain. As a result of this accusation the committee expelled him and then wrote and asked him to give them a reason why they should change their minds. In the course of a long letter he showed them there was very good reason. He had sold some tallow for Messrs Chope to a man called Flockton, and then sold the same quantity for Flockton to Chope. No tallow changed hands but during both transactions the price rose. Certain differences accrued which ended in Tibbs owing Flockton, though in fact it was Chope's debt. Chope eventually paid Tibbs with a bill which was dishonoured, but to please Flockton Tibbs covered this up and carried the amount himself. But when a second bill of Chope's was also dishonoured, Flockton issued Tibbs with a writ. Flockton stated that he would not proceed against Chope, the acceptor of the bill, but only against Tibbs. The question of liability was left to the judge who decided in Tibbs' favour. It was Flockton, Tibbs pointed out, who had instituted legal proceedings. It was Flockton, not he, who had made liability the matter of a decision in a court of law – this is what apparently piqued the Baltic committee. It was Flockton, who, by doing this, had removed it from the jurisdiction and cognizance of the committee of the Baltic.

Tibbs ended his letter:

I have little more to say except that if I have erred against the Rules which have been framed for the regulation of the conduct of the members of the Room, it has been done in ignorance of their true meaning. I could not apprehend that any defence to an action at law could be considered derogatory unless it were untrue. The defence I made was in strict accordance with the simple facts of the case, but had I known that by so doing I was committing a breach of the 15th rule I beg to assure the committee that I would have adopted some other mode of settlement.

What was alleged to be in the affidavit, that the bill was irrecoverable because it was a time bargain, was not so. He had said nothing of the sort.

It was difficult to see how John Tibbs could have known what constituted derogatory conduct seeing that this was never defined in the rules. They obviously disbelieved his version of what had occurred and refused to reverse their decision to expel him.

If they thought they had heard the last of John Evan Tibbs they were mistaken. Twelve months later they received a letter from him as follows:

Gentlemen

An event of a painful description has occurred within the last few days. I only allude to it with a view of referring to other matters; amongst them to a resolution passed by the committee in January 1860 which affected myself.

It has come to my knowledge within the last few months by information derived from various sources that there are several gentlemen in the Baltic who have been at various periods unable to pay differences on settlements, that the inability of such persons to pay such differences in full has been kept secret and that such parties have continued to be members of the Room. The last circumstance of the kind is that which is now the subject of investigation in another place.

In regard to my own matter it was entirely a question of disputed liability under very peculiar circumstances, but for goods delivered. I of course paid in full. The committee will probably remember that a portion of those contracts was settled by the buyer and seller, my principals, one day during my absence from Town and, in the opinion of myself and many other Gentlemen, this arrangement being made without my knowledge, intervention or concurrence, clearly exonerated me from all liability. It was simply a question of disputed liability which should have been settled by legal arbitration, and I should have been quite willing to waive any plea of 'time bargain' and to let the case rest on its merits.

My object in drawing the attention of the Committee to these facts is respectfully to enquire on what grounds I have been compelled to absent myself from the room, while *others* for *years past* have been permitted to continue members, and to ask as a matter of justice to myself that the resolution passed by the Committee in January 1860 be rescinded.

The Tibbs affair, if nothing else, confirmed the stand taken by the John Molletts and Charles Colchesters in establishing an élite, and their belief that others would come to regard association with them and their standards as something worth acquiring and keeping. From his letter John Tibbs showed the value he placed on being a member of the Baltic, and on being known to be one; even more the cost of being known to be an involuntary ex-member.

The matter of how best to settle such disputes was exercising not only the Baltic but the Judicature Commission, who told the committee that they had been instructed to ascertain the views of the commercial community with respect to the expediency of establishing tribunals of commerce on the lines of those already operating abroad. They sent them a questionnaire to answer. Had they found the tribunals of commerce (in these foreign countries) expeditious and inexpensive? Did the commercial community in such countries prefer the tribunals to ordinary civil courts? Should they be introduced to this country? Why? Should they be composed wholly of mercantile men or partly of lawyers? All very relevant questions which the Baltic were well placed to answer. It is likely they opted for businessmen like John Tibbs continuing to be judged by fellow traders according to standards, probably higher than those exacted by statute, to which they could refuse to subscribe by the simple device of resigning from the body which operated them, a course of action not open to a citizen under the law.

While buyers and sellers of tallow had plenty of money with which to speculate, those who relied on a more regular income were less buoyant. For the first twelve months after the repeal of the Navigation Act the falling off of business forecast by shipowners caused considerable gloom and many disposed of their vessels, or at least threatened to do so. With shipyards empty, the shipbuilders, too, were despondent. The Americans were building big iron steam ships propelled by screws. But, though fast, these treated their cargoes roughly. By 1852 optimism had returned; the shipowners of Britain had learnt to live, like other industries, without protection, and business boomed. The rise in exports brought a demand for more shipping space than existed. Freight rates doubled. The freight from Odessa rose from £15 to £22 a ton. Shipbuilders and shipowners shared in a new prosperity which the Crimean War at first enhanced. But when the import of Russian grain stopped altogether in 1855, to be followed by the Indian Mutiny in 1857, the General Shipowners Society went running to the Government again to plead for protection and for committees of inquiry to show the people of Britain how severely the removal of the tariffs had affected them. As a result of the repeal of the Navigation Act, British shipping had indeed increased, they told the electors at the 1859 General Election, but the level of foreign shipping had risen even more.

It was no concern of theirs that consumers – the people of Britain – had benefited by being able to obtain all they required from foreign nations at considerably reduced rates; that the general wealth of the country had increased beyond the hopes of the most optimistic free traders.

The shipowners held a public meeting in the City of London Tavern to demand the return of the colonial trade to British ships. *The Times* described them as 'the largest collection of political and commercial fossils which could be got together in these adverse days for political antiquarianism'. The role of the Government was not to ensure profits for shipowners. Once again they were told that there was no reason for making shipowners a protected class with advantages from which other members of the community were excluded.

Not only the shipowners, but the shipbrokers, who formed a large section of the Baltic membership, were worried. Each year Glover Brothers' annual circular carried a review of the current state of shipping affairs. The writer of the circular dated January 2, 1860, asked,

Is it a hopeless depression? Will freights be better in 1860 than in 1858 and 1859? May we look for improvement? These questions are of vital importance, for there is a limit to the capacity of the British shipowner to sustain loss . . . There is the never suspended law of reaction, whose operation is as certain as that of the law of gravitation. We cannot predict what agencies it will bring under tribute to vindicate its presence and continued power; it may be war as in 1854, or famine as in 1847, or gold discoveries as in 1852, or Guano deposits as in 1844, or better than all, it may be such a complete settling down of the European nations to industrial pursuits after the approaching Paris Congress as shall open up an era of commercial greatness such as Europe has not yet seen, such as our past has only indicated, for which our increasing facilities of communications have been organised before hand, and the beneficial results of which shall exempt us from the wars, and never ceasing rumours of wars, with which Europe has been troubled for the last ten years.

But first things first. Glover Brothers wrote to the committee of the Baltic in December 1860 from 34 Great St Helens:

We take the liberty of suggesting to you whether it is not desirable to make a representation to the Police authorities on the great public inconvenience and danger which result from the omnibus traffic through Threadneedle Street to the Bank, with a view to its prohibition. Both the inconvenience and danger have recently been aggravated by the introduction of three-horse omnibuses, part of the iron fittings of which project considerably over the pathway, which is so narrow as not to admit of two persons passing when one of these large vehicles is in the way.

No doubt having to cope with problems of this kind was responsible for Oxley's inability to take action on matters of greater import, such as the delay in supplying telegraphic information from Liverpool, but in 1862 William Oxley (at a salary of £180 a year), the secretary, clerk or manager of the Baltic, had time on his hands. For in that year he suggested he also took over from John Hunt as company secretary of the Baltic Company.

As secretary of the committee he would have consulted the chairman when the Gresham Committee asked for the Baltic's support for covering the open area of the Royal Exchange, and he would have been given firm instructions to place a notice in deference to repeated complaints which read 'Gentlemen are respectfully requested not to smoke or light any cigars in the passage of the Baltic'. But he would have used his own initiative in helping the Lloyd's Agent and Vice-Consul at Harwich, who had unknowingly fixed a Jewish holiday for a ship sale and wanted to change the date; and dealt summarily with the letter from the firm of auctioneers starting 'It has come to our knowledge that an order emanated from your Committee at their last meeting casting a slur upon us which we really cannot allow to pass unnoticed'. The 'slur' was being charged 10s. 6d. for posting a handbill advertising

F

a sale 'for the information and possible advantage of the several subscribers'.

And there was always the 'disagreeable circumstance' to bring to the committee's attention.

To the Committee
    of the Baltic Coffee House

April 1861

Gentlemen,
        I consider it due to myself to lay before you the particulars of a most disagreeable circumstance which took place last Saturday at your Coffee House. I was quietly conversing with a few friends when Mr M. E. Manogintati (the Insurance Broker against whom so far from having any ill will I have for some time entrusted part of my insurance to him) suddenly called me aside and not only began to insult me in the grossest manner but even to threaten me with personal violence.
        As such scenes ought not to take place in a Coffee House frequented by Merchants & Gentlemen, I lay the matter before you requesting you to make such use of my communication as you think proper.

I am Gentlemen,
Yrs truly,
J. S. Galatti

When Greek met Greek these things would happen. And merchants were not always gentlemen.

Sometimes the mere threat to bring a member's action to the attention of the committee as a possible basis for expulsion under rule 16 brought withdrawal of threatened action. In the autumn of 1862 W. R. Arbuthnot & Co thought it their duty to bring to the committee's notice the conduct of a Mr William Kern, a broker member of the Baltic, who left a parcel of linseed oil in their hands for acceptance by 11.20 a.m. at the commercial sale rooms. Their clerk was there on time and waited another five minutes without Mr Kern arriving. He went over to Kern's office to see if he was there, and when he returned he met Kern coming in by the back entrance. Kern told Arbuthnot's clerk he could no longer have the oil as he was too late. 'It is necessary to remark here that even at this moment only 10 minutes had elapsed beyond the limit, and that the market was improving.' The clerk told

Kern he had been on time and could not release him from his engagement. Kern retorted that he left the rooms at 11.21 so he was free. Arbuthnot's insisted on his ratifying the contract or submitting the question to arbitration, offering to abide by the decision of any respectable broker or merchant Kern might name. He at first refused. But when Arbuthnot's said in that case they would refer the matter to the Baltic, he agreed to accept arbitration by a Mr Hirsch, who heard both sides and declared that Kern was bound to deliver Arbuthnot's the oil. According to Arbuthnot's, on hearing the decision had gone against him, Kern declined to abide by it.

We have treated him as leniently as possible and given him every opportunity to escape from the false position in which he has placed himself but without avail. It is so important that a broker's word should be considered binding and trustworthy that we think you will excuse our claiming your attention to the transaction, the more so as many merchants and brokers in the oil trade express to us most strongly their opinion that he should not be allowed to escape with impunity for such a gross breach of faith.

Five days later Arbuthnot's wrote to say that on reconsideration Kern was now prepared to abide by Hirsch's award and fulfil the contract.

To be blackballed elicited surprise and regret from some; others kept their peace. On learning he had not been elected, B. Castello, stockbroker, challenged the strictest investigation into his character both private and commercial, for he was bound in honour to those who proposed and seconded him. 'I write this to induce you to reconsider your decision (which is naturally of some importance to me) as I am fully persuaded that no body of Gentlemen would willingly inflict a stigma upon any individual without having good grounds for so doing.'

Many activities which were not sponsored by the Baltic acquired a certain cachet by being launched in the Baltic sale room. In November 1862 the room was let to a number of merchants, shipowners and shipbrokers, many of whom were doubtless members of the Baltic, for the purpose of forming a Mediterranean and Black Sea freight committee. In March the following year they met again to receive the freight committee's report which stated:

As the standing circle for regulating charters, the Committee name Wheat as being of foremost importance in the trade of ports interested, and therefrom have attempted to arrange a scale of proportions for other grain, seed &c, as appears to them, after due inquiry, founded upon justice to the shipowner, and therefore deserving of acceptance by the merchant. It is as follows: –

Wheat to pay per Ton of 2240 lbs

Other products were then listed. Indian corn was to pay the same freight as wheat; dari and rye $2\frac{1}{2}$ per cent more; linseed 7 per cent more; barley 17 per cent more; oats 37 per cent more; tallow 39 per cent more. Merino wool was to pay 386 per cent more; other wool 282 per cent. Other articles were to be computed according to the London Baltic printed rates in proportion to tallow as fixed by that scale. The freight committee published Mediterranean and Black Sea freight tables computed by Albert Kahl, one of its hon. secretaries, which remained in force until 1890. The London Baltic printed rates referred to hemp, flax, tallow, ashes, bristles, hides, bees-wax, wool, horse hair, feathers, linens, pitch and tar, grain and wood.

A similar, but more general, exercise was launched by William Cooper in 1861 with *The Authenticated Freight List*. He also claimed to establish a central committee, or chamber, of commerce.

Fifty years after their earliest known meeting in 1813 the Average Market Letter Committee realized the value of association with the Baltic, and for a payment of £15 a year from 1863 they began holding their Friday afternoon meetings on tallow prices at South Sea House.

Like the tallow importers, members of the Baltic who imported linseed had also come to appreciate the value of co-operation – in 1848 they presented a common front to the seed growers of Taganrog and Kerch over adulteration. That had been an isolated meeting, and another had been convened by Henry Blundell, of Blundell Spence & Co of Hull, on November 17, 1857, when the seed crushers under the chairmanship of Hardman Earle, of Earle & Carter of Liverpool, decided 'the time had arrived for the trade of Seed Crushers to adopt measures of protection to ensure delivery of sound unmixed Linseed'; and a committee was appointed 'to confer with the trade and with the principal importer to provide a remedy for this evil'.

But the committee so appointed proved apathetic and little action was taken. Linseed from the Black Sea continued to be mixed with rape and other seeds and the practice was extended to Calcutta linseed. There was an unending series of arbitrations to settle disputes. The matter came to a head in the autumn of 1862 when three leading members of the trade, R. H. Page, J. M. Eastty and William Benecke, determined to call a public meeting to consider the subject – an idea which met with the concurrence of seed importers, crushers, exporters and brokers. On November 22, 1862, a letter of invitation was sent out as follows:

Sir,

The unsatisfactory conditions upon which business in the article of Linseed is carried on, render it advisable again to endeavour to frame rules for the better regulation of the Trade, so as to prevent the growing complaints of depreciation of quality, and also stop the incessant disputes which the present system engenders.

You are respectfully invited therefore to attend a Public Meeting of Merchants, Crushers and others as a preliminary to the formation of a Committee, having the above object in view.

The Meeting will be held in the Sale Room of the Baltic Coffee House, Threadneedle Street, London, at half-past twelve o'clock precisely on Wednesday 17th December 1862.

The letter was signed by five London firms – Bevan Cole & Harris, Edwards Eastty & Co, Laing & Merridew, Rose, Graham & Wilson and Soanes, Son & Page – and four Hull firms.

On November 26 a letter appeared in George Dornbusch's *Floating Cargoes Evening List* over the pseudonym 'Veritas' which turned out to be Stephen Ralli of Ralli Brothers. He urged the institution of a system of analysis for admixture under the care of an elected committee similar to that in operation at Marseilles. The promoters of the meeting took Ralli's recommendations as the basis for the resolutions which they put to the meeting which was attended by linseed traders from all over the country. George Soanes, of Soanes, Son & Page, was in the chair. Stephen Ralli moved the resolution 'That this Meeting is of the opinion that it is desirable to encourage the importation of Linseed free from any added admixture of extraneous substances, and as pure as harvested, and that a committee be nominated to promote this object.' It was carried unanimously and a committee was appointed 'to consider the present system at Marseilles with a view to its adaptation to the requirements of the English market'. The committee included Stephen Ralli, Antonio Ralli, M. E. Rodocanachi, J. S. Schilizzi. It met again at the Baltic on December 23, 1862, and resolved to call itself 'The Committee of the Linseed Association'. A sub-committee drew up proposed rules and by-laws and forms of contract for Black Sea, Azov and Danube linseed, East Indian linseed and linseed from St Petersburg and Archangel.

On March 9, 1863, a meeting of all the trade was held at Hull which recommended that the Marseilles system should be adopted in Britain for all qualities of linseed wherever it came from, but if it contained less admixture than was equal to 4 per cent of non-oleaginous seed, the difference should be added to the selling price.

Two weeks later the committee decided to widen its terms of reference and to set up 'the Linseed Association' to promote the importation of linseed as pure as possible, and nominated a committee of management to frame rules for the sampling and analysing of seed on arrival. A meeting of the whole trade endorsed this decision and the Linseed Association came into being on May 5, 1863. A. G. Kemp was its first secretary. The committee of management, which took an office, according to their announcement of October 19, at '8 Baltic Coffee House' (presumably one of the upstairs rooms of South Sea House), consisted of William Benecke, J. M. Eastty, A. (?) Floria, J. Garford Junr, F. Haggar, Dr Longstaff, R. H. Page, Stephen Ralli, John Todd and W. Yeames. They charged a fee of 3d. a ton with a minimum fee of a guinea and a maximum of six guineas for analysing samples of linseed and providing certificates of purity.

At South Sea House caterers came and went. The running of the refreshment department was in the hands of the committee but it was the company, or rather its directors, who, in July 1865, called attention to the nuisance caused to tenants and members by the activities of the kitchen. Books had been cooked in South Sea House without upsetting the occupiers of the upper floors, but fish and cabbage was another matter. Tenants and members had complained to the company, and the directors passed a resolution calling on the committee to do away with all cooking on the premises except chops, steaks and potatoes. Mabey, the caterer, was sent for and questioned by the committee on what they called 'extra cooking', by which it seems that they were accusing him of using his kitchen to make an extra pound or two on the side by selling hot meals to non-members and handing out hot dishes through the window to passers-by in the street. Mabey was instructed to place a watch on the kitchen entrance (perhaps he was pleading ignorance of the whole affair and implying it was being carried on under his nose by his kitchen hands) and to prohibit the passage of any articles other than those required for the members and for this purpose the window in the street was ordered to be closed. This was too much for Mabey and two months later he handed in his notice.

The fact that the board of the Baltic Company had had to pass a formal resolution on this comparatively trivial matter instead of sorting it out over the glasses of brandy in the coffee room was a pointer to the strained relations between 'board' and 'committee' which is difficult to understand in view of the two bodies, as already indicated, being largely the same individuals.

With only formal letters and resolutions to go on (the minutes of the Baltic Company board meetings being lost), it is difficult to build up a picture of what occurred, and there is a danger that their formality may give it a hard outline which, in fact, it never possessed; for it is easy to lose sight of the fact that they were largely writing memoranda and requests to themselves. William Oxley was the permanent link between the two, and, as both secretary of the committee and secretary of the company, should have had a stabilizing influence, for the business of both was conducted from his desk at South Sea House. But perhaps *because* of their overlapping he considered the lines of demarcation needed to be drawn particularly clearly, and in doing so left those who read his records after a hundred years' interval with an impression of antagonism which at the time was very much less marked, and had considerably less influence on events than it would appear. In basing a retrospective account of the relationships of committee and board on William Oxley's minutes, the only evidence available, it is necessary to remember that it was the differences which would demand minuting rather than the agreements, and that the absence of the latter tends to throw the former into a prominence they did not possess. Although finally the relationship reached a climax of incompatibility, there must have been a reasonably firm undercurrent of harmony and goodwill for the South Sea House era to have lasted as long as it did.

It cannot be said that the board were unaware of the pitfalls or of the need to take the initiative to forestall misunderstanding when it seemed that a clash of interests was threatening to obscure the common aim. It was best to know where everyone stood. On December 14, 1865, William Oxley, secretary of the company, wrote to William Oxley, secretary of the committee:

The Baltic Company Limited
London E.C.

December 14 1865

Gentlemen,

I beg to hand you the following Resolution passed at a meeting of the Board this day.

'That the Secretary of the Baltic Company request the Committee of the Room to appoint three Delegates to meet three Delegates of the Baltic Coy (Messrs Usborne, Rodocanachi and Goss) with a view to arrive at a clear definition of the position of the two parties.'

I am, Gentlemen,
Yours obediently,
Wm. C. Oxley
Secretary

For the Baltic Committee

Of their delegation Major Usborne was not a member of the committee, neither was Michel Rodocanachi; but George Goss was, and had been hon. secretary.

The committee, appointed four members, any three of which could make up the committee's delegation – William Muller,

Stephen Ralli, Peter Rodocanachi and Richard Wilson, none of whom were directors of the company.

It would seem that a faction within the committee, probably led by Stephen Ralli, were unhappy about the mounting income from subscriptions without any betterment of the service and amenities in the Room and other rooms.

To be fair to the company they had got off to a bad start, it will be remembered, by the absence of the expected rush to buy their shares when the company was first floated, and in 1860, though they had converted the £100 shares into five of £20 each, they still had only sold 180 of them (or 900 of them at £20), giving them a share capital of £18000. But in 1860 they did manage to sell the rest and at a premium of 10s. a £20 share. But the capital was still too small compared with their liabilities, and in 1860 they reduced the Alliance mortgage by £2000, and after paying their first dividend of £1 a share free of tax, they put the balance to reserve. Income from subscriptions amounted to £4474 and from rent £1972. The directors allotted themselves £100 as fees to be shared among the twelve of them. A peevish note in the 1860 directors' report stated that the revenue of the sale room was satisfactory, but they regretted that shareholders and members did not assist them in their endeavours to increase the sum received from this source.

Over the next three years the dividend remained at £1 a share and income from subscriptions rose from £4794 to £5230 in 1863. They built up the reserve fund to £7860, and in 1863, to remove the encumbrance on the property, they further reduced the mortgage by issuing debentures worth £30000. In 1862 the sum allocated for fees to the directors was raised to £300 'and annually for the future'. The amount allowed to the committee for running the Room was £1474.

In 1864 the directors announced that the mortgagees had refused payment and the idea of ridding themselves of it altogether had been abandoned. They also declared a change of policy as regards dividends. Their report stated:

Hitherto it has been the policy of your directors to pay only a small dividend and carry a large sum to Reserve Fund, but now, as the Reserve already amounts to a sum sufficient to pay off the preference shares the directors think the time is come when they may fairly give the shareholders the benefit of the increased value of the property and therefore propose a dividend at a rate of £3 a share (15 per cent).

This cost them £3000. They also invested money in the London North Western Railway, the Midland Railway and, of interest in view of later relations, had £2500 in the Great Eastern Railway Company. The allowance to the subscription room, however, remained the same – in fact at £1456 in 1864 it was £18 less than the £1474 of 1863.

Although in the following year subscriptions had risen to £5675 and rents to £2844, and although there was a reserve of £8593 and the directors felt able to raise the dividend to shareholders from 15 per cent to 20 per cent (£4 a share), the allowance to the Room was only raised some £60, to £1511. The wording of the director's report of 1865 hinted of defiance:

The directors see no reason to depart from the policy approved by the share-holders and adopted at the last annual general meeting, viz. that of dividing (as closely as possible) the profits of the past year and they therefore propose a dividend at a rate of £4 a share free of income tax.

Another special meeting of the house committee was held on February 15, 1866, 'to receive the Report of the Delegates appointed to consider the relations existing between this Committee and the Baltic Company'. Henry Schroder was in the chair. This meeting resolved to recommend 'that the Directors of the Baltic Company let and the Committee of the Baltic rent the Subscription Room under a yearly agreement terminable at six months' notice from October 1 [the company's financial year since 1864 had ended on September 30]'. This was a radical change in the relationship between the two bodies.

They further recommended that £3 10s. out of a town mem-ber's annual subscription of £5 5s., and £1 1s. out of a country member's subscription should be paid to the Baltic Company, and the balance retained by the committee 'for current expenses'. In other words, they were recommending that all the subscription

money went to the committee, who made the company an allowance, instead of vice versa. The company accepted the committee's
recommendations and the two bodies' relations hardened into
those of landlord and tenant. Since the committee had changed its
character, its current members decided to resign and give subscribers the opportunity of electing a new, more compact com-
mitte of twelve instead of twenty, the better able to shoulder the
new responsibilities.

The annual general meeting of subscribers of the Baltic (not of
shareholders of the company) took place on September 20, with
Stephen Ralli in the chair. The committee tendered their resignations and Stephen Ralli explained why they had done so. He then
moved that a new committee of twelve be elected by ballot. Three
members would retire annually. There would be a quorum of
four instead of five. As far as the election of new members was
concerned, one blackball in four would exclude instead of one in
five.

The following month the committee obtained a lease of the
subscription room from the company; they appointed themselves
a solicitor in the person of George (?) Edwards, of Sewell, Sewell
and Edwards; and withdrew £1000 of the £1810 balance in the
account they had opened at the Bank of England and placed it on
deposit at the London and Westminster Bank in the name of
Henry Schroder and others.

In the Baltic Company's balance sheet for the year ending
September 30, 1867, 'By Rent of "Baltic"' took the place of
'Subscriptions' as the main item under 'Income' and it came to
£4004 14s. Income from rent of offices was £3232, and from use
of sale room £1007. Their total income was £8470, and their outgoings consisted of £1929 plus £1865 for interest on their preference stock and shares, which gave them a credit balance of £4675.
They paid another dividend of 20 per cent. They begged to state
in their report 'that the arrangements made with the "Committee
of the Room" last year works satisfactorily in every respect and
that the number of Members has been steadily maintained'. At the
end of the year the committee lent the company £800 at 4 per cent,
the first of many such loans.

Far from the committee rooms and passages of South Sea House changes were taking place which were to alter the whole pattern of members' business. Twelve years after he had issued his prospectus, Ferdinand de Lesseps' £20 million Suez Canal was formally opened by the French Empress Eugenie on November 17, 1869. W. S. Lindsay called it that 'grand work, the greatest and grandest connected with maritime commerce either in ancient or modern times'. To say that it marked 'a new era' in shipping and commerce is no cliché. It gave impetus at last to the rapid and large growth of British steamship construction. Up to 1869 few British shipowners had the courage to abandon sails for steam propulsion. A few had led the way, notably Thomas Wilson of Hull, James Pyman of West Hartlepool, Edmund Watts of Newcastle, Pickernell Brothers of London, all of whom had early on built up fleets of steam ships for cargo carrying, and now new companies followed their lead. But most important for this story, as Archibald Hurd has it, 'It was not until after the opening of the Suez Canal that the great development of tramp steamers, in the modern sense of that term, came about.'

Londoners lagged far behind the north country ports in the race for steamship owning, mainly for want of the banking facilities which provincial banks afforded to local men whom they knew as neighbours and whose progress, or otherwise, they could watch. It was the provincial bankers who fostered shipbuilding on the Tyne and Wear and by doing so reaped large profits. For a long time London bankers were reluctant to invest in this kind of business. As steamers increased in size and cost, the old law limiting the ownership of steamers in shares of one thirty-second each was altered to one sixty-fourth. Most shipowners owned all or most of the sixty-four sixty-fourths of their ship – most tramps in the 1860s and 1870s were owned in this way.

But when bad times came the 'Sixty-fourthers', instead of receiving big dividends, found themselves liable for large calls. So they formed limited liability companies to safeguard their investments, of which the single ship company was a later refinement.

The development of tramp shipping coincided with the change from sail to steam, and this was given added commercial justification by the Suez Canal which opened up the carrying trade of the Far East and made world-wide voyages, picking up commissions on the way, practical and profitable. It brought new opportunities and an expansion of business to members of the Baltic and the Jerusalem as no other event had done since the repeal of the Navigation Act.

As the scale of shipping increased so did the network of communications and the need for fast and accurate commercial intelligence. In February 1859 Reuters Telegram Company offered to supply telegrams from New York, Havana, St Petersburg, Buenos Aires, Liverpool and Jamaica for £500 a year, which the committee's restricted resources could not afford.

A way of reducing the cost of commercial information was to share it with others. In January 1870, Charles Stephenson, the Secretary of Lloyd's, wrote to Oxley:

I am desired by the Committee for managing the Affairs of Lloyd's to inform you that they contemplate the extension of their telegraphic information, and amongst other arrangements they propose having telegrams at regular intervals, probably at least once a day, reporting the arrival and sailings of vessels in the Ports of the Baltic and the Black Sea, and the passing of vessels at Elsinore and the Dardanelles.

He invited the committee of the Baltic to contribute £500 towards the £2000 a year it was going to cost, and have a copy of the information sent across as soon as it was received at Lloyd's.

At their next meeting the committee ruled that the proposals 'be respectfully declined' – which was a pity as six months later they had members, including the Ralli Brothers, Glover Brothers and Barings, presenting them with a memorial in which they begged

to represent to you the inconvenience we experience from the want of a report of arrivals of vessels at the ports of call and telegraph stations, as posted at Lloyd's. A book, which is a transcript of Lloyd's arrival book, is kept regularly posted throughout the day at the Commercial Sale Rooms, and other Subscription Rooms, and to obtain such early information as is necessary for the proper conduct of our business we are obliged to send specially to other places. We trust therefore you will afford us the same facility in our room.

When forty members of the Baltic interested in the Australian trade petitioned the committee 'deeming it very desirable that reliable information should be obtained by telegraph from that colony, especially with regard to the shipments of produce' and asked for a monthly telegram giving particulars and statistics of the principal shipments, C. de Wolff wrote from the Commercial Sale Rooms in Mincing Lane, describing himself as agent to Reuters Telegram Company, offering to supply the subscription room daily 'with the tone of the tallow market, prices of beef and mutton and copper for £20 a month'.

The wide-ranging nature of the commercial information which reached the Baltic was the best indicator how the interests of members were no longer confined to the Baltic Sea, Northern Europe and Southern Russia – they were now global.

Julius Reuter had considerable competition. That early operator in this field, George Dornbusch, who had an office in South Sea House, in 1870 added to his service a '*Special Private New York Telegram,* Supplied ONLY to a Limited Number of Special Subscribers for their SOLE Use, on the Honourable Understanding that Non-subscribers shall not be allowed to have access to it'. It was a small printed sheet which gave stocks of wheat, maize and flour at Newyork (spelt as one word), 'Estimated Engagements of Ship-room at Newyork', freight rates per 60 lb wheat for steamer and for sail to Liverpool, and much else (see bulletin illustrated on pages 156–7). They took the service at £25 a year.

Also competing to supply the Baltic with commercial intelligence were the Anglo-Continental Telegram Company, the Oriental Telegram Agency Limited, the Press Association, the Lombard Telegraphic News Agency, the Exchange Telegraph Company, Robert Herbert & Sons City Correspondents and Market Reporters. Of these they patronized only the Press Association – from whom at long last they bought the telegraphic reports of Britain's corn markets – and the Anglo-Continental, whom they paid £16 16s. a month.

But the day of the private enterprise telegraph company now came to an end. The Government decided that the country's telegraph system should be run by the state – by the General Post

Registered No........................

In any further correspondence
on this subject, the above
Number should be quoted.

General Post Office, London

17th February, 1870

<u>Telegraphs.</u>

Sir,

I beg to acknowledge the receipt of your letter of yesterday's date, and to inform you that on re-publication of the Lists of Postal Telegraph Stations the "Baltic" shall be properly described, and orders have been given for all official letters addressed to that office to be addressed to the "Baltic" and not to the "Baltic Coffee House."

I am,

Sir,

Your obedient Servant,

H. du Plat Taylor

for Secretary

W.C. Oxley Esqr.
The "Baltic."

Letter from the General Post Office re the 'Baltic Coffee-House', 1870

[*No.* 80.] **GEORGE DO**

SPECIAL PRIVATE N

SUPPLIED ONLY TO A LIMITED NUMBER OF SPECIAL SUBSCRIBERS,
THAT NON-SUBSCRIBERS SHALL NOT BE

—o—

LONDON, SOUTH SEA HOUSE, THREADNE

NEWYORK: WEDNESDAY, 30 MARCH, 1870.

FORWARDED BY MESSRS. ARCHIBALD BAXTER & CO.

STOCKS AT NEWYORK.

1870	*WHEAT.* Imp. qrs.	*MAIZE.* Imp. qrs.	*FLOUR.* brls.
23 March	283,000	50,000	?
30 „	270,000	48,000	?

ESTIMATED ENGAGEMENTS OF SHIP-ROOM AT NEWYORK, specifying the qua ℘ steamer for Liverpool—and also, the total to all other ports, excepting Liverpool—also, the quantity ℘ sail to all ports in the U.K.

For SHIPMENT of In the week ending	*WHEAT.* ℘ steamr to L'pool only. qrs.	℘ steamer all ports U. K., excl. L'pool qrs.	℘ sail all ports U.K., incl. L'pool qrs.	Total. all ports U.K. Imp. qrs.	*MAIZE.* ℘ steamr to L'pool only. qrs.	℘ steamer all ports U.K., excl. L'pool qrs.	℘ sail all ports U. K., incl. L'pool qrs.	T al In
23 March 1870	10,000	5,000	11,000	26,000	nil.	nil.	nil.	
30 „	7,000	5,000	19,000	31,000	nil.	nil.	nil.	

PRICES AT NEWYORK, C. & F., INCLUDING 4 o/o COMMISSION.

1870	*Gold Premium* *closd*	*Bank Exch.* 60*d.*	Freight rates ℘ 60lb WHEAT. stmr. L'pl.	sail L'pl.	sail ordrs.	*WHEAT*, ℘ 480lb. Fair average No. 2 Spring free on board.	to Liverpool ℘ steamr	℘ sail.	for Orders‡ ℘ sail.	*MAIZE*, ℘ 480lb New Mixed. free on board.	to Liverpool. ℘ stmr.	℘ sail.
9 Feb.	$120\frac{1}{8}$	$109\frac{1}{8}$	3d.	3d.	$7\frac{1}{2}$d.	34/	36/	36/	39/	33/	35/	35/
16 „	$119\frac{5}{8}$	$108\frac{7}{8}$	3d.	3d.	$6\frac{3}{4}$d.	36/3	38/3	38/3	40/9	33/3	35/3	35/3
23 „	$117\frac{3}{4}$	$108\frac{7}{8}$	3d	3d.	$6\frac{3}{8}$d.	35/6	37/6	37/6	39/9	32/9	34/9	34/9
2 March	$117\frac{3}{4}$	$108\frac{7}{8}$	2d.	2d.	$6\frac{1}{8}$d.	36/2	37/6	37/6	40/3	34/2	35/6	35/9
9 „	$110\frac{1}{4}$	$108\frac{1}{4}$	4d.	4d.	$6\frac{1}{4}$d.	37/1	39/9	39/9	41/3	35/10	38/6	38/6
16 „	112	108	$4\frac{1}{2}$d.	$4\frac{1}{4}$d.	$6\frac{1}{8}$d.	36/8	39/6	39/6	40/9	35/5	38/3	38/3
23 „	$112\frac{3}{8}$	$108\frac{3}{8}$	4d.	$3\frac{1}{2}$d.	$6\frac{1}{4}$d.	35/10	38/6	38/	40/	35/1	37/9	37/3
30 „	$112\frac{1}{4}$	$108\frac{1}{4}$	$3\frac{1}{2}$d.	$3\frac{1}{2}$d.	$6\frac{1}{2}$d.	35/8	38/	38/	40/	35/11	38/3	38/3

The Market closing—for WHEAT steady, and for MAIZE active and upward.

‡ To call at Queenstown, Falmouth or Plymouth, and a U.K. port to discharge.

PRICE of CALIFORNIAN WHEAT at SAN FRANCISCO, per Sailing Ship to LIVERPOOL ℘ 500lb, C. & F.—including 4 o/o commission.

Wednesday,	9 February	44/	Wednesday,	9 March	44/
„	16 „	44/	„	16 „	44/
„	23 „	44/	„	23 „	44/
„	2 March	44/	„	30 „	44/

TELEGRAPHIC INFORMATION FROM ANOTHER SOURCE.

NEWYORK. DATE. 1870.	*Gold Premium.* *highest*	*lowest*	*closed*	*Sterling Exchange*	*MAIZE*, Old Mixed. ℘ bushel ℘ 480lb, f.o.b.	*FLOUR*—Extra State. ℘ barrel equal to ℘ 196lb, f.o.b.	Fre ℘ st t Live
Wednes., 23 Mar.	$112\frac{3}{4}$	$112\frac{1}{4}$	$112\frac{3}{8}$	$108\frac{3}{8}$	$1.03=35/1	$4.60-5.20=18/4 -20/8	4d
Thursday, 24 „	$112\frac{5}{8}$	$112\frac{3}{8}$	$112\frac{3}{8}$	$108\frac{1}{2}$	1·03=35/1	4.60-5.20=18/4 -20/8	
Friday, 25 „	$112\frac{3}{8}$	$111\frac{3}{4}$	$111\frac{3}{4}$	$108\frac{1}{2}$	1.03=35/1	4.50-5.10=17/11-20/3	
Saturday, 26 „	$111\frac{3}{4}$	$111\frac{3}{8}$	$111\frac{5}{8}$	$108\frac{1}{2}$	1.03=35/1	4.50-5.10=17/11-20/3	
Monday, 28 „	112	$111\frac{3}{8}$	$111\frac{3}{4}$	$108\frac{1}{2}$	1.03=35/1	4.50-5.10=17/11-20/3	
Tuesday, 29 „	112	$111\frac{5}{8}$	$111\frac{7}{8}$	$103\frac{1}{2}$	1.05=35/9	4.50-5.10=17/11-20/3	
Wednes., 30 „	$112\frac{1}{4}$	$111\frac{3}{4}$	$112\frac{1}{4}$	$108\frac{1}{2}$	1.07=36/3	4.50-5.10=17/11-20/3	3½

George Dornbusch's bulletin, 1870

SCH'S

RK TELEGRAM,

SOLE USE, ON THE HONOURABLE UNDERSTANDING,
HAVE ACCESS TO IT.

[*No.* 80.]

, THURSDAY, 31 MARCH, 1870.

STOCKS IN NEWYORK.

(Compiled from Messrs. Archibald Baxter & Co.'s printed circular.)

1869	WHEAT.	MAIZE.	OATS.	RYE.	BARLEY.
	qrs.	qrs.	qrs.	qrs.	qrs.
8 January, 1870	427,878	73,988	163,867	7,908	43,737
15 ,, ...	410,591	70,892	162,601	7,908	43,461
22 ,, ...	390,269	65,089	154,167	7,908	44,044
29 ,, ...	380,058	65,938	153,291	7,908	44,048
5 February	362,829	66,750	149,959	7,764	40,265
12 ,, ...	351,747	65,603	147,020	5,250	39,821
19 ,, ...	335,684	63,559	143,594	3,973	39,600
26 ,, ...	3x8,803	62,137	142,658	5,187	35,934
5 March	313,701	60,522	138,274	4,886	34,863
12 ,, ...	293,040	56,125	132,835	4,886	28,200

TOTAL EXPORTS FROM THE UNITED STATES (INCLUDING CALIFORNIA) TO GREAT BRITAIN AND IRELAND.

(Compiled from Messrs. Archibald Baxter & Co.'s printed circular.)

1870	WHEAT. qrs.	FLOUR. brls.	MAIZE. qrs.
the week ending 21 January	18,204	22,979	—
,, ,, 28 ,,	25,637	15,748	—
,, ,, 4 February	22,594	17,277	—
,, ,, 11 ,,	24,013	20,919	—
,, ,, 18 ,,	23,196	11,312	—
,, ,, 25 ,,	12,248	9,248	—
,, ,, 4 March	18,451	10,470	—
,, ,, 11 ,,	23,382	22,427	—
Total 8 weeks	167,725	130,380	—
rom 1 Sept.'69 to 14 Jan.'70....	1,373,791	392,333	—
Total from 1 Sept. '69 to 11 Mar. '70	1,541,516	522,713	—
Corresponding period 1868-69..	656,034	228,610	235,643

TAL EXPORTS FROM THE UNITED STATES TO THE U.K. & CONTINENT
From 1st September, 1869.

(Extracted from the "Newyork Shipping & Commercial List.")

	WHEAT			FLOUR			MAIZE		
	To U.K.	To the Cont.	Total.	To U.K.	To the Cont.	Total.	To U.K.	To the Cont.	Total.
n Mar.	qrs.	qrs.	qrs.	brls.	brls.	brls.	qrs.	qrs.	qrs.
YORK ...16	1030849	83,493	1114342	472,947	14,266	487,213	—	11,463	11,463
RL'NS .. 9	33,420	—	33,420	76,021	—	76,021			
'DELPHIA 12	88,665	—	88,665	18,976	—	18,976	—	—	—
'IMORE ..12	72,338	—	72,338	49,806	—	49,806	1,852	—.	1,852
'RANCISCO 4	584,526	—	584,526	5,775	—	5,775	—		
HER PORTS	1,507	6,514	7,571	2,118	2,212	4,330	—	895	895
atest dates.									
Total	1810855	90,007	1900862	625,643	16,478	642,121	1,852	12,358	14,210
,, 1868-69	1006095	18,288	1024382	230,513	21,680	252,193	276,455	5,677	282,132
,, 1867-68	1104676	45,748	1150424	365,228	51,127	416,355	613,706	4,150	617,856

Office, that is, who proceeded to take the operation of all the private networks under their wing. The gossip in the subscription room at Threadneedle Street was that their greatly prized telegraph office was going to be removed altogether. The usual collection of signatures was gathered for a memorial to the committee from members who

having heard that it is the intention of the Post Office Authorities to abolish the Telegraph Office attached to the Baltic, beg to draw the serious attention of your Committee to the very great inconvenience this would cause to the members of this Room.

They ventured to hope that the committee would without delay make representations to the Post Office to recall their decision 'which if carried through would be so detrimental to the interests of the Baltic'. But it was all a false alarm. The Post Office had no intention of closing down the Baltic telegraph office, but, run as a public service, it soon revealed shortcomings which made its principal users, those staunch upholders of private enterprise the members of the Baltic, soon yearn for the good old days of the Magnetic. Seventy-eight of them sent in a requisition requiring the committee to consider 'the apparent breakdown of the present Telegraph administration and take what measures be necessary to obtain redress'. Stephen Ralli called a special general meeting of members to discuss the matter (March 1870). They resolved

That since the transfer of the control of the Telegraphs to the Post Office the public has suffered much loss and inconvenience from delay and uncertainty in the transmission of messages which far outweigh any advantages derived from reduction of the rates; That the Public has a most unquestionable right to claim at the hands of the new Telegraph Administration speed and certainty in the despatch and delivery of messages at least equal to that which was obtained while the Telegraphs were in the hands of the old Companies; That this meeting requests 'The Baltic Committee' to communicate this resolution to the Members of the House of Commons who represent or are connected with the City and respectfully to request them to call the attention of Parliament to the urgency of the subject.

It was not the first time members of this persuasion had petitioned Parliament on the Post Office services, and it would not be the last.

This was a peak year in Britain's industrial history, a climax to a period of unparalleled prosperity. In 1870 there were only five industrialized countries in the world – the United States and the four European countries of Britain, France, Belgium and Germany, and together they accounted for four-fifths of the world's output of manufactures. In 1870 Britain had by far the largest share – 31 per cent of it, compared with the United States' 23 per cent and Germany's 13 per cent. In 1870 Britain's trade was worth £547 million, that of France, the next largest, only £227 million. The amount of shipping organized by members of the Baltic and the Jerusalem was proportionately enormous. That great British invention, the railway, which had been taken all over the world by contractors like Thomas Brassey, opened up prairies and the inland parts of continents hitherto exploited for commerce only on the coast where there were rivers – in America in particular. In Pitt's day a good sugar island with no transport problems was of greater value than a more potentially profitable but inaccessible mainland. In spite of all the forebodings of the Shipowners' Society, Britain's huge share of the world's carrying trade had come from a policy of free trade.

Shipbuilding left the Thames, but not shipping.

He who wants to study every form of ship, every kind of rigging, the thousand and one details of spars and ropes, the delightful play of light and colour which is a perpetual beauty about a clipper's deck; the sad human stories that crowd the emigrant vessel; the sailor of every clime and country; in short the immensity of commerce that counts warehouses by the mile and goods by the hundred thousand tons – can have no better field than these watery acres that give hospitable welcome to every flag.

The words are Blanchard Jerrold's which accompanied the rich drawings Gustave Doré made in 1870 for *London: A Pilgrimage.*

The light plays upon every known bunting. We thread our way round the busy basins, through bales and bundles and grass-bags, over skins and rags, and antlers, ores and dye-woods; now through pungent air, and now through a tallowy atmosphere – to the quay – and the great river where fleets are forever moored. The four thousand feet of river frontage of the St Katherine's Docks, only lead east, to where the London Docks take up the striking story of human skill and courage, centred from every navigable sea.

The owners of some of those ships were Glover Brothers, who in 1865, twelve years after setting up as shipbrokers, had laid the foundations of a merchant fleet with the 534-ton barque the *W. E. Gladstone*, built for them by Peverall of Sunderland, which sailed to India and China under their flag for thirteen unbroken years. Along with their fellow shipowners, John and Robert Glover had greatly feared the consequences of the repeal of the Navigation Act, but in 1870 John Glover was telling the Statistical Society:

After the repeal of the Navigation Act the new terms of competition were accepted, and instead of giving up the struggle for preponderance in our own carrying trade our shipowners took fresh steps to deserve it. We did not sell our ships and close our building yards; but we built them bigger and finer, and made them in every way more efficient and economical carrying machines, believing that the nation that possessed the best machines would win in the long run.

It was (almost) as simple as that. Prosperity came to Britain by her exertions, and only when she had established a lead was the rest of the world spurred to follow her example.

But, with all the prosperity, a porter at South Sea House was still only earning 17s. 6d. a week, a circumstance of the kind which appeared to affect, of all people, the Stock Exchange.

Committee Room, Stock Exchange

W. C. Oxley Esq,   London   Decr 14th 1871
Secretary, 'The Baltic'

Sir

Representations having been made by the waiters employed in the Stock Exchange with a view to the amelioration of their position, the Managers are desirous of considering the same in reference to the position of waiters or porters employed in establishments of a similar character. I am therefore directed to ask if you will have the kindness to inform me the wages paid to waiters and porters in your employ, the scale by which any increase in such wages is regulated, the hours of duty, and whether they are provided with liveries, have apartments on the premises, or have any emoluments in addition to or arising from the situations they hold under you.

I am sir,
yours obediently,
Walter C. Parker,
Secy.

And when the spring came those whom the waiters waited on demonstrated that the Stock Exchange was not the only harbourer of practical jokers.

57 Gracechurch Street, EC
London, 14th May 1872

To the Committee of the Baltic

Gentlemen,

I had occasion to introduce today at the Baltic as a visitor a gentleman of Patras named Mr Anino, and as is customary I wrote his name in the book of the Baltic.

This name has been impudently altered to *Asino* by Mr Caliero, a member of the Institution. This I consider is not only a great insult to myself, and also to the visitor, but an offence to the Institution itself. The visitor himself saw Mr Caliero altering his name, and to this he can positively assert. In putting the circumstances to your consideration I shall feel obliged by your dealing with the offender in accordance with the bylaws of the Institution.

Yours obediently,
D. Ancilotti

What by-laws? It seems that over and above the rules and regulations a number of so-called by-laws had become attached to the official rules and regulations which had never been submitted to, let alone approved by, members at a general meeting. Some were acted upon as if they had the full sanction of rules – such presumably as the one about not tampering with visitors' names in the visitors' book. The committee of the Room became aware of these unauthorized addenda to the rules at the beginning of 1872 and set up a sub-committee to recommend whether or not some or all of them should be incorporated into the rules to form one code. While they were about it, they were given the wider terms of reference of bringing the rules 'into accord with what experience and custom show to be convenient'.

The sub-committee made a very thorough job of it, re-numbering and regrouping the rules into twenty-three paragraphs. They recommended slightly easing the rule against the admission of anyone who had had financial difficulties. Anyone should be eligible who, though he had failed, had recovered to the extent of being able to pay his creditors 10s. in the pound. This, they said, should also apply to a member who had had to resign because of his failure. When he had paid his creditors 10s. in the pound he could seek re-election. Most important of all they recommended doubling the entrance fee from £5 5s. to £10 10s.

This of course now came to them not the company, and they needed all they could raise to pay for their rent which had gone up from £4298 in 1871 and £4663 in 1872 to £5416 in 1873 – in spite of the rates and tithes which the company had to pay coming *down* from £961 in 1871 to £806 in 1872 and £892 in 1873, and the rent they received from offices rising from £3065 in 1871 and £3280 in 1872 to £3341 in 1873. The directors made £17000 of the reserve fund, and a sum of £3000 spent on the building, part of the ordinary capital, and issued 20000 £1 shares for distribution *pro rata* as stock among the shareholders. This increased the capital of the company to £70000 – £40000 of ordinary stock and £30000 of 5 per cent preference stock, which, however, the directors considered much below the real value of the property but more properly representing what it had cost the shareholders.

They made no attempt, however, to find out the real value of South Sea House at this time. But confident in their new financial security, in 1873 the directors declared a dividend of 30 per cent free of tax – another 5 per cent up on 1871 and 1872.

As so many members were shareholders the committee might have considered they could have afforded to plough back some of their gains into the Room by raising the subscriptions, but they settled for the increased entrance fee and the other amended rules which for the first time they had printed in the form of a booklet with a pink cover bearing the words

THE BALTIC

RULES AND REGULATIONS

and

List of Members

1873

It was the first printed list of members. There were 1164 of them. They included seven with the name of Hill, five Ionides, six Mavrogordato, six Phillips, eleven Ralli, four Rodocanachi, six Schilizzi, five Ziffo, eight Smith, five Soames, ten Wilson. Country members came from Hull, Leeds, Leith, Bristol, Liverpool, Birmingham, Boston, Belfast, Exeter, Gloucester, Norwich, Manchester, Glasgow. Maurice Dalseme came from Paris. Joseph Crew gave his address as 4 Jeffrey Square; William Cotton as 47 St Mary Axe.

The 1873 committee consisted of Edward Baring, James Charles, John Glover, William Harris, William Muller, Stephen Ralli, Peter Rodocanachi, Richard Wilson, and Henry Yeames, plus the three who were also directors of the company, George Goss, J. H. W. Schroder and Edward Wilson.

It was a fitting publication for the jubilee of the formation of the committee in 1823 – of which no one took the slightest notice – and a succinct point of reference for the constitution of the Baltic of a hundred years ago.

But were they overreaching themselves? Richard Wilson, one of the old guard, felt that perhaps they were. Following his resignation he wrote to William Oxley on October 6, 1873, thanking him for the committee's kind message of goodwill. He continued,

I need hardly say that I experience much regret in withdrawing from the committee. I have served upon it for many years; and, during the whole time, my recollections in connexion with it afford me nothing but pleasure. I now retire because in my opinion – probably altogether a mistaken one – the committee undertakes functions which at a future time it may find it difficult and inconvenient to discharge.

6. Pressure Group at Work

The committee had no more important function than passing judgement on their fellow members' suitability to belong to the prized circle. By giving or withholding admission the committee could set the seal on a man's probity and creditworthiness which the community at large would take to be lacking if entry was refused. By their power to expel for financial failure or acts they considered derogatory to a man of business they could virtually deprive him of that business.

When it came to the notice of a Mr Bellamy that his name had been removed from the list of members he wrote to the committee to ask why. He was 'called in and questioned by the Committee' which resolved 'That Mr Bellamy's exclusion be confirmed'. That was the technique. Expel first, find out if it was justified afterwards. Being 'called in' must have been an unnerving experience. But the committee had no qualms. Their job was to apply the rules, and make *no* exceptions. If a member's principal failed, so that he no longer had a firm to represent, which was what had happened to Mr Bellamy, *he* ceased to be a member. At least that was their interpretation of rule 8 which stated 'A member elected whilst a clerk to a firm shall, if he withdraw from such a firm or become a partner in it, cease to be a member'. And there could be no going back and arguing.

Stephen Ralli gave a hint of the way the committee reached its conclusions when he wrote to Oxley in December 1876.

I beg to return you the letter written to the Committee by Mr Johnston.

I remember quite well that at the time of his examination by the Committee a favourable impression was gathered from his explanations, and we were inclined to re-elect him, but did not do so because afterwards the information which we gathered on the Corn Market was unfavourable to him. Now I see that he has been with his new firm for four years, and altho' his letter is certainly not a proper one, if during the said period it is ascertained that he has behaved himself honorably I think we ought to re-elect him.

John Johnston ceased to be a member of the Baltic on becoming insolvent, and in the letter which Stephen Ralli considered 'not a proper one' he said he had thought reference to the trustees of the insolvent estate of his late firm would have been sufficient to allow his re-admission as a member.

Had I not so believed I would probably never have raised the question of my re-admission, partly because I am coward enough to shrink from such an ordeal as a personal interview on such a subject, but mainly because such an interview would probably force me to make known certain facts which, grievously as I had been wronged, I was for the sake of others unwilling to divulge. But having once raised the question I was not the man to draw back, and I came before you prepared to demonstrate, if need were, my *right* to be a member of the Baltic.

This was a new concept of the role and status of the Baltic. To claim a right to be a member of it made as little sense as claiming a right to be a member of Boodles, but it was a pointer to its standing after fifty years. Thomas Tooke would have been flattered.

John Johnston went on to give a graphic description of inquisition by Baltic committee:

My interview with you took the form of questions put by you and answered by me. You went with some detail into the history of Johnston, Roos & Coy, and in the end Mr Harris said – 'Well, we shall take your case into consideration, but you must not have too much hope.' This surprised me after what had already passed. Some more questions were asked and answered, and I then said, – 'If you are not now satisfied, Gentlemen, of my *right* to be re-admitted, I have here in my pocket and am ready if necessary to produce – no statement of mine – but such evidence of facts as must demonstrate my right, and prove that I could no more have prevented the course and the causes which led to the collapse of Johnston, Roos & Coy than any one of you gentlemen could.' Mr Ralli, your chairman, replied, and I presume he spoke for your Committee, – 'No, it is not necessary – you have answered all our questions satisfactorily, and we need not trouble you further.'

I then left. From that day to this I have received no communication from you. I should have thought that the ordinary courtesy of life would have led you to acquaint me with your decision. That however is a mere matter of taste.

I look again at your Rule no. 12. It is vague – perhaps necessarily vague – but whatever case it be meant to refer to, it must be meant to refer to the case of a member who has failed from no fault or act of his own. Proof of this, it was, that I offered to submit to you.

He went into business as a corn factor, he said, determined that it should be solely one of commission, and he bound his partners to this course. But finally he was overpowered and his ruin brought about.

At least for 5 years I succeeded in so far controlling the recklessness of others, while within 9 months, under the Baltic Corn Association, all the efforts and precautions of four shrewd men of business (the Directors) for the prudent conduct of that Association were baffled and set at nought. And now for over 4 years the business of my present Firm has been conducted precisely as I sought to conduct the business of Johnston, Roos & Coy. Be this as it may, you were surely bound, sitting as a secret tribunal from which there is no appeal, to give a patient and unprejudiced hearing to all the evidence. It was this you failed to do in my case, and it is this which leaves, and will leave, with me, to the last day of my life, the conviction of a cruel and grievous wrong. For aught you knew your adverse decision might have blasted my career for life; and yet all you tell me is that I have answered your questions satisfactorily and that it is unnecessary I bring further evidence before you. And from what is it you exclude me? There are more in the Baltic who every day do things as a matter of course which I trust I may never stoop to do under any pressure of temptation; and it is with such as these you find me unworthy to associate. I did not seek re-admission to the Baltic for any gain or benefit. I sought only to have the slur on my character removed that exclusion from the room implied. You have decided that this slur shall remain. I do not for a moment believe – God forbid that I should – that any one of your number has done this wrong deliberately. But we all know the facility with which a body of men will concur in the first expressed opinion of one of themselves, and we also know how apt we are to judge hastily and lightly of others, especially when there is already a prejudice or a presumption against them.

You will not misunderstand me. I make no new appeal. I neither ask nor desire nor would have my case re-opened. I claimed to be re-admitted to the Baltic under one of its rules, and I have received your silent answer. I shall never again enter the Baltic – unless indeed it some day be at the solicitation, instead of by the sufferance, of those who rule it. Nor think that I write in anger. Any such feeling has long since passed away. All I ask – and I ask most earnestly – is that if ever you are called upon to judge a case at all similar to mine, you may have the wisdom to be more just, if not the heart to be more considerate.

This letter put its finger on many home truths which would have been unpalatable to Stephen Ralli. To have raised them, and in so emotional a manner, was hardly proper.

The purely commercial matter of interpreting a contract, or confirming a debt, the committee left to independent 'arbitration' by an umpire or referee. On occasion, if invited, they would act as a court of appeal to give a second opinion. Often the arbitration clause in a contract would state that any arbitrator should be a member of the Baltic committee, implying that anyone who belonged to it would be fair and impartial. But the committee as a body kept out of arbitration, though they frequently found themselves on the border line.

When Ruffle & Co appealed to the Baltic committee to help them recover £176 from H. N. Van Der Zee & Co, against whom they had started legal proceedings, the committee agreed to see Mr Van Der Zee and to examine the documents presented by Ruffles – a step which Richard Wilson might well have frowned on. But they refused to give their collective opinion on the matter and recommended Van Der Zee to submit the matter to arbitration. Ruffles consented and agreed to accept any arbitrator Van Der Zee chose to appoint, and whatever decision he came to. They dropped all legal proceedings. Van Der Zee chose a corn factor called Edward Majolier who began a long stint as a member of the Baltic committee in 1876. He, and not a judge, had to decide whether Henry Van Der Zee was justified in withholding the £176 from Ruffles, whom he accused of thoroughly ungentlemanly conduct at the quayside. In March 1876 he wrote to Ruffles:

We are greatly surprised you have not yet sold our 100 Tons Linseed ex 'Medea' as per instructions given you. You could have sold it at 49/– ex 'Warehouse' early last week, but you evidently preferred keeping our lot out of the Market in order to get rid of *your* own lots and about which your Mr Ruffle expressed so much anxiety. Sales have continued taking place [indecipherable] at 48/6 and then @ 48/– ex Warehouse and now we see that you sold 300 Tons on Saturday last at 47/3 ex ship still continuing to keep out of Buyers reach!

Under these circumstances we consider our 100 Tons above mentioned ex 'Medea' as good as sold at 49/– ex Warehouse early last week & of which please take note.

Worse than refusing to go to arbitration was agreeing to do so and then appointing a barrister as arbitrator. 'While distinctly disapproving of the refusal of Messrs Mesigh & Soule to appoint a Commercial Gentleman to act as their Arbitrator' pronounced John Glover, 'a majority of the Sub-Committee is of the opinion that the circumstance does not necessitate the Committee taking action under Rule 10' – the one about conduct derogatory to a man of business. But it was running close to the wind.

To Mesigh & Soule, as to others unconverted to the Baltic way of handling things, arbitration by a commercial gentleman was decidedly second best. They protested:

Such decision has been arrived at after due consultation with solicitors and counsel, and the respective solicitors have already been in conference. It will therefore be obvious to you that we cannot discuss matters which are 'sub-judice' without prejudice to ourselves or Messrs Raschen & Co, and we must consequently decline to attend [the Committee] at present and must further request you to be good enough to inform us in writing in what way we have infringed or are charged with infringing Rule X, and to let us have a copy of the letter accusing us of conduct that you consider authorises you to take so serious a step as to summon us under Rule X.

It was difficult to steer people away from the traditional reliance on documents and judgements which were 'legally binding', to the concept of binding themselves to others without the assistance of solicitors and counsel, by assertions declared voluntarily as one man of business and member of the Baltic to another. To substitute a 'mere' word for the written bond with legal sanction was assuming a climate of trust and openness whose existence cynics frankly disavowed, and many were not prepared to take the risk.

But the committee had only themselves to blame if the concept was taking time to be accepted, for they were doing very little positively to propagate it, which was why there were misunderstandings and, on occasion, unpleasant imputations.

When Watney & Keene complained about the behaviour of Forwood's in a dispute, Forwood's not only protested that anything the committee had to say would prejudice their case in court, but accused Samuel Keene, who happened to be a member of the committee, of making his complaint for the most disreputable of reasons.

Forwood's wrote to Oxley,

Mr Keene, occupying as he does the various positions above pointed to, threatened, and now has invoked, the 'influence' of his fellow Committee-men in regard to the personal interests of his firm, but I submit that he cannot properly be sustained in that course, and especially of as much of it as is conducted at the Baltic, that 'influence' should be brought to bear on an English merchant's freedom before the Public Tribunals in regard to interests committed by Colonial principals to his care.

His final paragraph contained a sinister threat.

In the event of your Committee entering upon all the questions of principle involved in the whole business, they will doubtless not overlook those which by Merchants at home and abroad may be considered to arise on the cir-cumstances that a member of your Committee, a London Corn Factor, and one very frequently acting as an Arbitrator, does not confine himself to business as a Factor, but enters as a principal into Baltic contracts for Corn; and further that in regard to technicalities (however untenable before the High Court or Arbitrator) raised by him as a principal he has invoked the 'influence' of your Committee, then – that is on *those* questions of principle – I as a merchant and member of the Baltic, may contribute further ideas.

Exposing themselves to insinuations of this kind indicated an overinvolvement which hinted at the 'inconvenience' of which Richard Wilson had warned.

In March 1884 the Corporation of London planned to establish a court of arbitration, 'having during many centuries provided for the trading community of London various means of settling dis-putes by Arbitration'. In a printed circular seeking the support of the Baltic committee, John Monckton, Town Clerk, said the court would be 'for the speedy and inexpensive settlement of disputes arising in the course of business between persons who voluntarily seek its adjudication'. Arbitrators would be nominated by the Corporation, certain livery companies, the London Chamber of Commerce, and the committees of the Stock Exchange, the Baltic and the Corn, Coal and Metal Exchanges. Either party could be represented by a counsel or a solicitor and the sittings would be in private.

A member of the Baltic who would have been happier with a more formal 'court' of this sort was Josias Alexander, who in October 1883 had been asked to attend before the committee to be questioned, he could only assume, about the award made against him in his arbitration with Messrs F. Lenders & Co. If this was the case, he told the committee, then he must respectfully decline their invitation. 'I have placed the matter fully before my solicitor Mr Hollams, and am advised by him that the award is not legally enforceable against me, and I consequently intend to have its validity tested by a legal tribunal.'

Lenders, naturally enough, took the opposite view. Alexander's repudiation of the arbitrator's ruling was based on his allegation that the papers which Lenders produced to prove his case were forged. Alexander asked the committee to state whether they agreed with him. Lenders asked them to say that anyone who voluntarily went to arbitration should abide by the award made. 'Every member of the Baltic, and in fact everyone in the trade, is honourably bound to respect the decision of the Arbitrators, and we think that the Committee ought to uphold this view and enforce it.' The assertion that his documents were forged was, of course, quite ridiculous.

If Messrs Alexander succeed in forcing us to a law suit on the award without the authorities of the Baltic interfering, it will have a most damaging effect against all London firms who have dealings with foreign countries, for hitherto the impression has existed, both here and abroad, that an Arbitrator's award was absolutely final, and could not be resisted; but if it once becomes known that such is not the case, awards will in many instances become practically valueless, and we hope not only in the interests of ourselves but of the trade generally, that your Committee will decide upon acting in this matter.

It seemed very difficult for people to understand that the point of *voluntary* arbitration was that it *was* unenforceable under the law, and that it depended on both parties' agreeing to stand by the arbitrator's decision *before they embarked on arbitration*; and that for this reason, as the City Corporation pointed out, it was swifter and cheaper.

In February 1885 the Baltic appointed a sub-committee, chaired by Henry Yeames, to report on complaints made to the committee of non-compliance by members of the Room with awards made under contracts. Their conclusion was 'that no complaint against a member of the Room arising out of an award shall be entertained by the Committee until the provisions of the arbitration clause of the contract under which the award was made are exhausted'.

Lawyers and stockbrokers were to be the committee's *bêtes noires* for many a day.

In March 1876 they called a special meeting 'to consider admission of candidates connected with Stock Exchange business'. They formulated three new by-laws which were later adopted as additional regulations at the annual general meeting in October. No stock or share broker or agent was to be eligible for election as a member if he was not a member of the Stock Exchange. A firm of stockbrokers might propose for election only one representative, who must be their *bona fide* clerk. From then on a new member who was not a member of the Stock Exchange, and subsequently decided to carry on the business of a stock and share broker or agent without becoming a member of the Stock Exchange, would cease to be a member of the Baltic.

Speculation on the share market was bad enough; gambling on horses was anathema. When Miss Bellamy, the clerk in the telegraph office, complained to the committee that she had been insulted by Smith, the hall porter, it was revealed that the incident had arisen out of Smith placing bets for members. Oxley was instructed to give Smith a month's notice. What, they then asked themselves, could they do to prevent members continuing the practice with his successor? Absolutely nothing, they decided.

The fact that the committee were unaware that members got the hall porter to place bets for them through the telegraph office shows a lamentable detachment from the general body of the membership which may have served them in the judicial aspect of their duties but proved their undoing as managers of the Room.

Knowing what was going on, what was being said and thought, was not considered part of the job. There was a big enough gap between the committee and the board; but it seems that between the committee and the members there was also a sizeable gulf. The grapevine had no connection to the office of the committee secretary/company secretary at whose door much of the blame may have to be laid. Fraternization with the Floor might have been *infra dig* for the committee, but for their paid employee it should have been a duty.

But the aloofness of the Barings and Schroders, the Rallis and Glovers was not studied. It was part of their way of life. As the writer of Glover Brothers' centenary booklet of 1853–1953 wrote,

The Glovers knew everyone of importance in shipping, and everyone knew them. After a long day in the City they lived in considerable comfort in large houses in Highbury, taking an active part in Nonconformist church affairs, and such other local activities as amateur choral societies. Septimus, who always wore an orchid from his hot-house in his buttonhole, rode to Highbury Station every morning where his attendant groom unbuttoned his gaiters and led his horse back home.

He was 'a toff' – and knew it.

Septimus Glover became a member of the Baltic when he came to London from South Shields to join his brothers, Robert and John, in 1874. He was honorary secretary of the committee of the Baltic which was formed in 1878 to draw up the standard form of charter-party for grain from the Black Sea, the Azov Sea and the Danube which constituted the most important tramp trade. Though these charters were for grain, the influence of tallow shipments from Russia still persisted, and the freight on these charter-parties took the Ton Tallow as their basis and assessed the grain or seed in proportion. The new form of charter-party drafted by the Baltic committee, of which Henry Yeames was chairman, used the Black Sea freight tables compiled by Albert Kahl for his independent committee in 1862.

Besides being a member of the Baltic committee John Glover was a member of the committee of Lloyd's Register of Shipping, an underwriting member of Lloyd's, and he chaired the initial meeting of the Chamber of Shipping, in the formation of which he was a prime mover. He was a member of the first committee of the Shipping Federation and was responsible for a readjustment of British representation on the Suez Canal which raised British membership from three to ten. He stood as Liberal parliamentary candidate for Scarborough and was only defeated by 124 votes by Osbert Sitwell's father, the eccentric Sir George.

It is against multifarious activity of this kind that the duties of members of the Baltic committee must be set, with all the trivia they involved. The amount of time and patience such people as John Glover would have been able to devote to sitting in the committee room at South Sea House and listening to the tortuous pleadings of recalcitrant tallow merchants and the unctuous excuses of insolent caterers must have been very limited.

They left the house-keeping to Oxley and saw their main function as enforcing a system of unequivocal identification of everyone who came on the Floor. To keep the pulse of gain at its desired rate, it was essential that there should be no doubt who was a principal, who was a broker, who was a clerk and whom the non-principal represented. The rules devised for this purpose were overhauled in February 1877. A member elected other than as a principal became liable to expulsion as soon as he tried to transact business on his own account, as did any member who did business for a member not elected as a principal. Any member who parted with his clerk had to notify the secretary. To the single penalty of expulsion was added censure and suspension.

'Strong censure' was expressed by the committee on the conduct of two members called Ellerby and Bernstein which prompted an anonymous letter from 'An Old Merchant' writing from the City Club at the back of South Sea House.

Gentlemen,
        I have been informed by several members of this club that a most brutal attack was made in the Baltic Club by an Englishman on a young Foreigner; that he kicked him in the back and legs in the most savage manner and threatened to murder him. I therefore call upon you at once to institute an enquiry into the facts and punish the offender in a public manner, or your Club will be a disgrace to the City. I can only say that had such an outrage been committed in this Club the offender

G

would have been turned out of it at once, and I doubt not that you will do the same.*

'Suspension' was threatened to the ringleaders if there was any recurrence of a disorderly scene in the Room when fireworks were let off on New Year's Day.

In July the committee turned its attention to visitors. 'No gentleman shall be eligible for admission to the Room as a Visitor who is not eligible for admission as a Member' they ruled. A member could then be certain that on any day *no one* in the Room had failed, whether a fellow member or an outsider. For seventy-six members this was going too far. 'It is unusual in any club or Subscription Room of this description to place Visitors in the same category as Members', they protested in a petition, 'and we think the rule would be practically very difficult to enforce, impossible in many cases, and certainly invidious to many if carried out.' The committee bowed to this criticism and resolved 'that an exception be made to this Rule if sanctioned by three members of the Committee'. But this was rejected at a subsequent annual general meeting, which showed the committee on this occasion to be more in touch with the general consensus than usual. But when Josias Alexander was reported for introducing a visitor who was entirely unknown to him, it was decided to play it down. He got away with an admonishment from Oxley to be more particular in future.

The committee's ignorance of what members were doing also led more seriously to clashes with parties outside the private world of the Threadneedle Street committee room. When member Julius Beerbohm started putting into his *Evening Corn Trade List* reports which Reuters Telegram Company were supplying exclusively to the Room, Frederick Griffiths, secretary of Reuters, wrote to point out that this was

an abuse which I must ask you to be good enough to move your Committee to prevent, as our reports are only supplied to the Baltic for the private use of members and not for publication by them in any shape. The unauthorised publication being very detrimental to the Company's interests, its continuance would compel us either to ask a higher rate of subscription or to stop the service, neither of which alternatives do we wish to adopt. We have arranged for the regular supply of the monthly tallow reports from Australia

*See page 186 for Christopher Ellerby's apology.

Reuter's Telegram Company Limited:
21, Old Jewry, London: E.C.

March 31 1874:

W. C. Oxley Esq
  Manager
  The Baltic

Dear Sir,

I find, as I have already mentioned to you verbally that the reports supplied by the Company to the Baltic are copied and printed every evening in the circular of Mr. Beerbohms who has no arrangement with us entitling him to do so. This I consider an abuse which I must ask you to be good enough to move your Committee to prevent, as our reports are only supplied to the Baltic for the private use of members and not for publication by them in any shape. — The unauthorised publication being very detrimental to the Company's interests, its continuance would compel us either to ask a higher rate of subscription or to stop the service, neither of which alternatives do we wish to adopt. — We have arranged for the regular supply of the monthly
Tallow

Part of the letter quoted opposite from the secretary of Reuters to William Oxley, Secretary of the Baltic committee, 1874

without additional charge and are always ready to make the service as efficient as possible. On the other hand, we must look to your Committee to adopt the necessary measures to protect us against practices which I am convinced beforehand have not been sanctioned by them.

Julius Ewald Beerbohm was a London grain merchant of mixed Dutch, German and Lithuanian extraction who became naturalized British. His second son, Herbert Beerbohm, was elected to the Baltic on July 2, 1874. Herbert was born in London, and while helping his father in his business at 28 Bishopsgate Street, devoted most of his spare time to amateur theatricals. He gained a considerable reputation as an amateur performer and in 1878, when he was twenty-five, he was offered a professional engagement. He took the stage name of Beerbohm Tree and became one of England's most distinguished actor-managers. He built Her Majesty's Theatre in the Haymarket, founded the Royal Academy of Dramatic Art, was knighted in 1909 and died in 1917.

The Market Letter committee had more serious cause of complaint.

Market Letter Committee (Tallow)
Committee Room, Baltic
January 7, 1876

To the Committee of the Baltic

Gentlemen,

By a resolution passed in the above Committee this day, I am requested to write to you on the subject of the very extraordinary discrepancy between the Stock Tallow, as published under your authority or by your sanction, and the real Stock as counted on the first of January.

It will not be necessary for me to point out to you the gravity of the circumstances whereby consumers and the public generally have had to pay a fictitious price for Tallow, raised above its legitimate value by the *apparent* smallness of the Stock; but this Committee, in the interest of the Subscribers to their letter, the character of which is depreciated by this erroneous publication, request me respectfully to express a hope that you will take some steps to ensure the correctness of figures posted in the Baltic by Brokers, or if unable or unwilling to do so, that you will prohibit altogether their publications in the Room, whereby an importance and authority is given to them which otherwise they would not possess.

I beg to remain,

Gentlemen
Your Obd: Servt.
B. Brecknell Turner
Chairman of the Committee

The Market Letter committee made their complaint with all the authority of sixty years as the Baltic's central activity. But tallow had given way to grain, and in 1878 the corn traders of the Baltic established the 'London Corn Trade Association' to

initiate any new form of contract which may appear requisite, to protect the interest of the corn trade generally, and to select from its members a limited number of gentlemen of matured judgement and honourable character, with practical knowledge of the Corn Trade to act as a final Court of Appeal in arbitrations.

Invitations to join were sent to every member of the trade, and though most of the principal firms in London gave it support, many were opposed to the idea. It had no headquarters and its committee met in the offices of members. Baltic member John Ross was its first president, and founder companies included William Adams & Co, S. W. Keene & Co, Ralli Bros, Raymond & Reid, Usborne & Son (still operating). Its first contract form was for East Indian wheat. This was followed by a Black Sea and an American form.

The American grain contract began:

A Cargo of . . . of fair average quality of the season's shipment at time and place of shipment. Shipment in good condition per . . . . a first-class vessel (Turks excepted) classed not lower than A 1 in red English, 5/6 1 1 French Veritas, or equal classification in Austrian, Norwegian or Italian, or other equal register from . . . . . . 10 per cent, more or less as per Bill or Bills of Lading dated . . . . . at the price of . . . . . say . . . . . per 480 lbs shipped including Freight and Insurance to any safe port in the United Kingdom of Great Britain and Ireland, calling at Queenstown, Falmouth, or Plymouth for Orders, as per Charter Party; vessel to discharge afloat, no charge for Dunnage.

On the back were ten rules. Sufficient days were given for sailing vessels and steamers. Rule 10 was the arbitration clause which said all disputes arising out of the contract should be referred to two arbitrators, one chosen by each party, and they had to be principals engaged in the corn trade as merchants, factors, or brokers and members of the London Corn Exchange or the Baltic.

LONDON CORN TRADE ASSOCIATION.

AMERICAN GRAIN CONTRACT.

No. 1. 1879.
Registered at Stationers' Hall.

LONDON, *9th February* 1880

Sold to Charles de Bruyn, Esq, London,
per Mess. Digan &Co,

on the printed rules endorsed on this contract.

A Cargo of *Mixed American Maize, new or old crop*

of fair average quality of the season's shipment at time and place of shipment.
Shipment in good condition.

per _____ A first-class vessel (Turks excepted) classed not
lower than A 1 in red English, 5/6 1 1 French Veritas, or equal classification in Austrian, Norwegian,
or Italian, or other equal register from *Baltimore, New York, Philadelphia or Boston*
say *Three thousand, five hundred units of 480lb each*

_____ 10 per cent. more or less
as per Bill or Bills of Lading dated *or to be dated February for March 1880.*
at the price of *25/1½* say *Twentyfive Shillings and*
three halfpence _____ per 480 lbs.
shipped, including Freight and Insurance, to any safe port in the United Kingdom of Great Britain
and Ireland, calling at Queenstown, Falmouth, or Plymouth, for Orders, as per Charter Party; vessel
to discharge afloat, no charge for Dunnage.
Buyer to have the right to send the vessel to the Continent between Havre and Hamburg, both
included, subject to the conditions of the Charter Party, on payment of the extra Freight and Insurance,
in which case the out-turn to be computed at 50½ kilos., equal to 112 lbs. English, in French, Belgian,
and Dutch Ports; 1016 kilos equal to 2240 lbs. English, in German Ports.
Sufficient days to be left for unloading and the usual time for waiting for orders.

3.   Payment by cash in London on or before arrival of vessel at destination, but in no case later
than the prompt, less discount for the unexpired term of 72 days from date of B/L at Bank rate on the
day of payment, in exchange for Bill or Bills of Lading and Policies and/or Certificates of Insurance. *or at*
Sellers option by the buyers acceptance of bill plus or Sellers draft
at 60 days from date of arrival of B/Lading in London
with Documents attached, as usual.
The unit of quantity under this contract shall be 480 lbs. English.
Any deficiency in outturn exceeding one per cent. of Bill of Lading quantity to be refunded by seller.
In case of sea accident (pumping up grain excepted) causing a deficiency Provisional Invoice to be final.
Seller to give Policies and/or Certificates of Insurance (free of war risk) for 2 per cent. over the Invoice
amount, and any amount over this to be for Seller's account, in case of total loss only.
Insurance to be effected with approved English and/or American Underwriters and/or Companies, but
for whose solvency seller is not responsible; if effected in America, losses to be payable in England.
Buyer to have the option of sending the vessel to a direct port in the United Kingdom @ *3 per cent*
reduction on above price if destination be given not later than 4 o'clock p.m. on
the first business day following the request for same. Should destination not be given within the time
specified, the vessel to be sent to Port of call for orders. If shipment be not completed within one
week from the day on which the demand for destination is made, seller to be bound to renew the said
demand, failing which buyer to have the option of rejecting the cargo.
In case of prohibition of export or blockade, preventing shipment, this contract, or any unfulfilled
part thereof is to be cancelled.
Seller to pay *Mess Digan &Co* Brokerage of *half* per cent., contract cancelled or not cancelled.
Should any dispute arise, this contract not to be void, but Buyer and Seller agree to have the same
settled according to the 10th printed rule endorsed on this contract, and this stipulation to be made a
Rule of any of the Divisions of the High Court of Justice on application of either contracting party.

(Signed) *Brown Milkey &Co*

For thirteen years the female clerks employed by the General Post Office in the telegraph office which formed an annexe to South Sea House had been suffering the insults of hall porters and the impatience of anxious speculators, and along its network of cables fast but limiting 'wires' had been tapped out in Morse code to every part of the world. (Glover Brothers dropped the 'e' when they named their new enterprise the Shakespear Shipping Company as a word of more than ten letters counted as two in cablegrams.)

But when in September 1877 the Engineer in Chief of the Post Office received an invitation to a demonstration of a new invention from a Colonel Reynolds, the London representative of Professor Graham Bell, he declined it on the score that his department already had all the details of the professor's claims and that in his view the possible use of the telephone was very limited. So private enterprise took over. In June 1878 the Telephone Company Ltd (Bell's Patents) was formed in London with an office at 36 Coleman Street. It laid private lines connecting one building with another and put instruments at either end imported from the Bell Telephone Company of America. One of the first private telephone lines to be erected in the London area was from the Chiselhurst house of Henry F. Tiarks, a leading member of the Baltic, and later a director of the company, to his stables.

But it was a rival company which first made contact with the Baltic.

The Edison Telephone Company of London Ltd
17 September, 1879

Sir,

I have the honour to request that you will lay before your committee the following application.

It is proposed to place the Baltic in direct telephonic connexion with those of the subscribers who may desire to communicate with their offices, or with one another without the necessity of writing or sending a messenger [the Exchange Telegraph Company ran a Messenger Service]. The instrument used is the sole invention of Mr T. A. Edison, its conspicuous superiority over telephones consisting in the great range of its power.

Your obedient servant,
Arnold White, Manager.

London Corn Trade Association American grain contract, 1880

MANAGER & SECRETARY.
ARNOLD WHITE.

The Edison Telephone Company of London, Limited,
Mansion House Chambers,
Rooms No. 113.   11, Queen Victoria Street, E.C.
London Oct 20th 1879

The Secretary
            Baltic &c

Sir,

            Edison's Telephone

I beg leave to request that pending a decision as to the question of telephonic communication with the Baltic, you will move your Committee to grant permission to this Company to run a wire from the Baltic in Threadneedle Street to the offices of one or more of the members of the Sub-committee appointed to investigate the question. My object in seeking this permission is that the Committee may judge for themselves, as to the general applicability of the Edison Telephone for practical purposes.

The instrument would be removed on the Committee signifying that the experiments should terminate.

            I am, Sir,
            Your obedient Servant,
                    Arnold White
                        Manager

Letter from Arnold White of the Edison Telephone Company to the Secretary of the Baltic committee, 1879

It was worth a sub-committee at least, and Edward Power, Septimus Glover and Edward Majolier were asked to look into it. Arnold White offered to run a wire from South Sea House to the offices of one or more of the sub-committee so they could judge for themselves. They decided it would be better to have a line to the Corn Exchange, and the Edison Company offered to do this free for a six months' trial.

A meeting was called with both Arnold White and J. B. Saunders, the general manager of the Telephone Company, who brought with him a printed prospectus (see illustration overleaf).

The committee decided to test both systems for six months simultaneously. The lines were to be from each 'exchange' to South Sea House and from South Sea House to the Corn Exchange.

Just how the committee organized the use of the new telephone in the subscription room of the Baltic in this trial six months is not known, but before Christmas they were complaining to Saunders of its inefficiency. Saunders died in January 1880, and the acting general manager wrote to Oxley to say 'it was not contemplated by our late Manager to throw open the use of the instrument to the Members generally, but simply for the convenience of those Members of the Baltic who might be subscribers to our system'. As for the poor results which were being obtained, would the committee allow them to place the instrument in the luncheon room or some other quiet place, as it was not getting a fair trial where it was, the noise was too great.

Subscribers had done without the telephone for over fifty years and they could afford to leave the magicians who had invented it to sort out the teething troubles – the rivals joined forces in 1880 as the United Telephone Company. A more positive attitude was needed, however, to solve the problem created by the mounting numbers of candidates which the committee, never noted for turning away good money, elected to membership at every monthly meeting. If the consequences of this open house policy had not been obvious from the start, they were dramatically brought to the committee's attention on August 5, 1880, when Oxley presented them with a ten-sheet, printed memorial signed by 380 members – 300 principals and 80 clerks, including W.

Licensed under Patents of ALEXANDER GRAHAM BELL, and other Patents
of THE TELEPHONE COMPANY, LIMITED.

THE TELEPHONE COMPANY, LIMITED.

City Office: 36, COLEMAN STREET, E.C.

Directors.

JAMES BRAND, Esq., 37, New Broad Street.

ALLAN MORRISON, Esq., of the Fore Street
  Warehouse Company, Limited.

J. W. BATTEN, Esq.

CHARLES SCHIFF, Esq., 43, Lothbury.

W. CUTHBERT QUILTER, Esq., 8A, Tokenhouse Yard.

W. H. REYNOLDS, Esq.

HON. G. G. HUBBARD.

TELEPHONE EXCHANGE FOR THE CITY.

A TELEPHONIC EXCHANGE has been established in the City.

Each Subscriber has a wire from his own residence or office, with the necessary instruments attached, to the Telephone Company's office. A signal from the Subscriber is answered by the clerk in the Central Office, who instantly makes a connection with the wire of any other person with whom communication is desired, and conversation can then be carried on with ease and privacy without the possibility of any third person hearing what is said. A signal to the attendant intimates when the conversation is finished, and the wires are then altered to communicate only with the Central Office. There are no complicated or delicate parts in the instrument requiring any previous knowledge or care; and the words are not only heard clearly, but the voices of speakers can be easily recognised.

For a fixed annual rental the Company fix and maintain in good order the wires and all apparatus required. For ease of communication between Merchants, Bankers, Brokers, and Business men generally, it will be found of great value. A number of Subscribers are using the system in the City. The only charge for Subscribers within a radius of a mile is a subscription of £20 per annum, payable in advance.

Should you wish for further information the Company's representative will be happy to wait upon you.

NOVEMBER 10TH, 1879.

Printed prospectus of the Telephone Company Limited, 1879

Bridges Webb, J. H. Wrenn, John Nisbet, Theo Angier, Seth Taylor and Henry Colchester. It read:

The Members of the 'Baltic', being impressed with the necessity of additional provision being made for the accommodation and convenience of the Subscribers to the Rooms, beg respectfully to submit the following for the consideration of the Committee:

The Income derived from the Subscription Room amounted last year, as we are informed, to £7999 19 0

viz.: 1239 Town Members at	£5	5	£6504 15	0
98 Country ,,	,,	3 3	308 14	0
113 Entrance Fees ,,		10 10	1186 10	0
			£7999 19	0

For this sum the 1337 members are provided with one large and two small Rooms, a Luncheon Room and Bar, Lavatory and Four Water Closets, Daily Newspapers, Stock Exchange and Trade Telegrams, and Telephone. The attendants comprise a Clerk to the Room, two Door Porters and Three inside Porters.

The above accommodation is, in our opinion, totally inadequate to the present large number of Subscribers and we therefore strongly urge the Committee not to renew the Lease [in May 1881] until some satisfactory arrangement for its extension is come to with the Baltic Company.

Such an arrangement would, we suggest, be brought about by throwing the Sale Room into the General Room, doing away with the present Luncheon Room, using the present Bar for the sale only of sandwiches, tea, coffee, sherry, etc., providing on the First Floor a good room for joints, chops, steaks, etc., also a Public Sale Room, utilizing for each of these objects about one-half of that Floor. Improved accommodation should also be provided in the Basement. We would also suggest that the Refreshment Department be conducted by a Sub-Committee elected by the Members, which Committee should superintend generally the management of the Rooms, supplying Provisions, engaging servants, etc., etc.

Amongst other improvements we would recommend an increase in the staff, the keeping of a Registry of the arrivals of Ships (taken from Lloyd's), and the posting in some suitable part of the Building all names called through the Telephone.

After twenty-three years the dual system of company and committee had patently broken down. What was the object of the exercise? To provide a commercial resort for members or an income for shareholders? The expiration of the lease in eight months called for an inquest.

The 30 per cent dividend of 1873 had not been repeated. It was reduced to 15 per cent the following year and remained at this level until 1877 when it was raised to 17½ per cent. In the eight years since 1873 rates, taxes and tithes had only risen £200 – from £802 to £1041 – while the rents received from offices had risen £500 – £3341 to £3824.

The share register of the Baltic Company of 1874, when the capital was £40000, gave 164 names as holders of ordinary stock. Michel Rodocanachi, one of the first directors in 1857 and head of Anglo-Greek corn dealers Rodocanachi Sons & Co of Odessa and London, held 1600 shares. John Prestage, a Manchester solicitor, held 1200; William Muggeridge, a Trinity Square merchant who was also a member, 1000; a Gloucester clergyman, 710. The largest number of ordinary shares were held by Robert Brandt who was a member of the Baltic but was described on the register as 'artist, St Petersburg'. He held 2600.

There were sixty-two preference shareholders. Henry and William Harris, both members, held 3200 and the Usborne family of Godden Green, near Sevenoaks, held 9075. Two more Usbornes, in Cork, held another 2800. These were the people who were reaping the rewards of the Baltic.

Job Ashton, James Charles and Edward Majolier discussed the possibility of turning the sale room into additional accommodation with Michel Rodocanachi, the chairman, and his fellow directors Richard Brandt, Henry Edwards MP, Antonio Ralli, Thomas Usborne, Edward Wilson and Baron J. Henry W. de Schroder, as he now styled himself,* and showed them the memorial from the 380 dissidents.

The board's reply of September 1 was formal and pithy. They were prepared to fix the rent at £5500 which, as there was no security of tenancy, they hoped the committee would not consider too much. Though income was £7999 the company only received £5532. Rent for the sale room would be £1500 (last year's income £1350).

---

*He became a baron of Prussia in 1868 on his father's appointment as one by King Frederick William IV of Prussia. The 'de' was not normally used.

The committee told Oxley to reply that this was 'totally inadmissible and to urge the directors to suggest some means to increase the existing accommodation'. The board said they were ready to make alterations if the committee handed over £1000 of their surplus funds and promised to renew the lease. When this was put to members at the annual general meeting in October they rejected the proposals for alterations as 'quite inadequate' and instructed the committee to make the directors submit a more comprehensive scheme. At the same time they turned down any suggestion of raising the subscription by a guinea.

Reviewing a remarkable lack of progress on any front, the committee at their next meeting contemplated asking the directors to take five shillings out of each subscription as 'rent' for the sale room. They also thought they might increase the entrance fee by another five guineas to make it £15 15s. They were not altogether sure they had the powers to do this and consulted Edwards, the solicitor, which was lucky. 'The Rules unfortunately contain no provision by which you as a Committee can carry out what is proposed, nor do they provide for calling any special extraordinary General Meeting' he told them. The committee might think they could make an 'additional regulation', he told them, and have it confirmed at the next AGM, but that was questionable. In the meantime, why not try and find out the subscribers' feelings? If the committee had the unanimous support of members, they would be more encouraged to act. He suggested circularizing them. They acted on this advice and members were sent a circular on December 11 (1880) which told them that one way of alleviating the overcrowding was by renting the sale room from the Baltic Company at £1300 a year and using it as additional club premises. To do this the subscription would have to be raised from five to six guineas. Only half of the members bothered to return the slip and there was a 272 to 220 majority against raising the subscription.

The dissatisfaction with the catering was a separate matter. The policy of charging a caterer rent and leaving him to run the refreshment department as best he could had been the subject of criticism from the very first, and resulted in one caterer after another having the concession for a few months, resigning or being dismissed, and

15 Leadenhall Street
20th Feb. 1877.

To the Committee
of the 'Baltic'

Gentlemen,

I beg to tender you my very earnest apologies for the circumstances which occurred in your Rooms on Friday Afternoon last:— If you will condescend to enquire into the details, you will find that the provocation I received was unjustifiable and excessive, but I quite admit that, out of deference to the Members of the **Baltic** and to the rules by which it is governed I ought to have restrained myself, and for my momentary infringement of the respect due to you and to the body whom you represent, I trust that you will kindly accept my very sincere and very humble excuses —

I have the honor to be
Gentlemen
Your very obedt Servt

Christr. Ellerby

Letter of apology to the Baltic committee, 1877

another being appointed in his place. Criticism came to a head in 1876 when the committee received the following letter:

Gentlemen,

I am directed to apply to you on behalf of a considerable number of the Members of this Room for the privilege of supplying the refreshments in the Bar and Dining Room.

They propose, should your sanction be obtained, to form themselves for that purpose into a limited Company with a capital of £1000 in £10 shares. . . .

These gentlemen feel that the interests of the members at large would be better cared for by a responsible Manager, with proper supervision, to whom at all times complaints could be made and at once remedied, – instead of having to rely on the caprice of an irresponsible contractor whose sole object is profit, without consulting the convenience and habits of those whose duties compel them to make use of the Bar and the food there provided.

I am, Gentlemen,
Your Obd. Servant,
Geo. Hall.

Sixty other members put their signatures to this. They included Septimus Glover and Thomas Usborne.

Nothing came of this sensible scheme, and in October 1880 the strained relations of members with Archibald Macdonald, the then concessionaire, came to a head. He was asked to explain his treatment of a member who had asked the committee for redress.

In reply to your favour of the 2nd inst [wrote Macdonald] I beg to say it is perfectly true that I have instructed my employees not to serve the member to whom you allude until such time as he may see fit to render me an apology for the libellous and untruthful remarks which he made in the presence of other members and who, I may add, corrected him. The member in question has (I am informed) repeatedly made offensive remarks as to the quality of the meat and other provisions supplied by me at the Baltic, and under such circumstances I have considered myself justified in declining his custom. I submit that all articles sold at the Baltic are of the best quality, but in the absence of a proper kitchen on the premises I am certainly not able to carry out the catering to my own satisfaction. I am ever ready to remedy any fault that may be pointed out to me, but in the present instance I do not admit of any. It is my earnest desire to please all my customers, and in pleasing them I make no doubt I further my own interests.

After that Macdonald had to go. They gave him £100 and told him the concession was terminated, and they reappointed Mabey who had done the catering twice before and twice been sacked for incompetency – and what is more, gave him a three-year agreement.

The committee's seven-year lease of their rooms at South Sea House which, as the company told shareholders, 'expired from efflux of time' in May 1881 was replaced by another.

Though they had had their telephone lines for another six months after the 'trial', the committee not very commendably tried to get out of paying. In September 1881 the United Telephone Company wrote to point out 'the desirability of coming to some arrangement with respect to the telephone lines which you now have from us, as up to the present time we have received no rent for them.' Oxley went to see them and suggested that the publicity which they had given the United Company was ample compensation. The company said they would remove their attendant the following week. They were willing to waive all payment up to July 1 but from then they would charge £40 a year. (There was no charge for calls, the annual subscription allowed use of the line as often as a subscriber pleased.) Members who were not subscribers to their system were constantly using their instruments. Calls from and to instruments in South Sea House numbered 200 a day.

The Post Office may have been outdone by the private companies in putting words along telephone lines but they outstripped them when it came to putting them on paper. The first typewritten letter in the South Sea House correspondence of 1857–1901 was from the General Post Office on the subject of weather reports and was dated August 26, 1881. Another did not appear until two years later – from the London & Globe Telephone Company and dated November 17, 1883.

The telephone brought members of the Baltic not only easy communication with their offices but with the specialist exchanges in other parts of the City which had taken the place of the Royal Exchange as the commercial resort of shipping men and brokers.

In April 1881 a body consisting largely of Baltic members, the Linseed Association, became incorporated as the Incorporated Oil

The Corn Exchange,
Mark Lane, completed
in 1828

London docks, 1831

Mr John Hubbard, afterwards Lord Aldington, an influential member of the Baltic, depicted by Spy in *Vanity Fair*, 1884

Opposite above: South Sea House in Threadneedle Street in the early nineteenth century

Opposite below: The Reading Room of the Baltic at South Sea House in 1900

The Floor of the old Baltic at South Sea House

The Baltic, Threadneedle St.

Benjamin Lancaster, second Secretary of the committee of the Baltic Coffee-House

Septimus J. Glover, Chairman of the Baltic committee 1892-4 and 1898–1901

June 1884

To The Committee of the "Baltic".

We beg to refer to the Resolution passed by a special Meeting of the Members of the "Baltic", held 20th July 1865, That the cooking should be limited to Steaks Chops & Potatoes; and Petition that said Rule be enforced in future, and that nothing hot except the above be supplied, the room being at times nearly unbearable.

[numerous signatures]

Petition to the Baltic committee, 1884

Seed Association. It held its first annual general meeting on June 20. Dr G. D. Longstaff was its first chairman, and he was succeeded in 1888 by Stephen Ralli. Henry Plummer was its first secretary.

Even more Baltic members belonged to the General Produce Brokers' Association of London which in February 1883 posted a petition to Parliament in the sale room of South Sea House and invited signatures. A letter from R. J. Hossack, the secretary, explained its purpose.

An effort is about to be made to relieve London Brokers from the Annual Tax, known as Brokers' Rent, imposed by the Corporation [of London], by submitting a short Act to the House of Commons at the ensuing Session: Mr Magniac MP, Chairman of the London Chamber of Commerce has consented to take charge of such a Bill, and other Members of Parliament will also take an interest in the question.

It is considered that this Tax should be abolished because: –

1. No equivalent is received in any shape or form.
2. It is simply a relic of barbarous times.
3. In no other city in the United Kingdom is any Tax levied upon Brokers, who all exercise their calling without it.
4. Merchants, dealers, agents (who receive commission) and all other traders are untaxed.
5. The Tax, as it is now levied, is most unequally collected; some pay it, some compromise by paying in part, and some evade it altogether. All Brokers certainly do not pay it.
6. No benefit accrues to the Broker by the payment.

Their campaign resulted in the withdrawal of the £5 annual 'rent' in 1886 – a restraint on trade castigated by *The Economist* as far back as 1847 when they accused the City Corporation of creating a privileged class.

Most of the executive committee of the London Corn Trade Association were members of the Baltic, and in May 1884, Edward Majolier, Samuel Keene, Francis Lenders and Seth Taylor were joined by W. Bridges Webb. In the same month Ernest Forwood became a member. In the six years following their formation the drawing up of uniform contract forms had been applied to most areas of the world, and in February 1884 the association's St Petersburg and Baltic wheat contracts for cargoes were issued. An Australian contract was in draft, and a sub-committee was working on Chilean and Californian contracts in co-operation with the Liverpool Corn Trade Association. But six members of the committee opposed and only four were in favour of the association taking action solely on contracts which they had made or approved.

At their annual general meeting in the Baltic sale room their chairman, Richard Reid, said he hoped the Merchant Shipping Bill before Parliament would result in a more just bill of lading than many of those then in force, and announced that they had sent a deputation to Joseph Chamberlain, President of the Board of Trade, to impress on him the correct definition of the word 'charterer'. (At a meeting chaired by John Glover, the Baltic also protested against Mr Chamberlain's bill, objecting to the clause which proposed a limitation of insurance on ships and their cargoes.)

In deciding to carry forward £1002, the whole balance for the year ending September 30, 1884, the directors of the Baltic Company agreed that the sum was somewhat larger than usual but 'looking on the possible effect of the general depression of trade, both in checking the usual accession of new members, and in interfering with the speedy re-letting at full rates', they considered it the prudent course to take. It was the culmination of many years of slack trade, and several firms had gone out of business. One who suffered was Baltic member William Wordsworth Lyndall who in January, 1882 wrote to the committee seeking re-admission.

He had been a member of the Baltic he said for twenty-four years, and his father was one of the founders of the Old Baltic. Owing to the continued yearly depression in shipping matters and owing to the large number of his best country correspondents at the outports coming up to London and establishing offices, his business had been seriously affected. His firm lost £3000 honourably paid in cash by them in consequence of a foreign correspondent failing to carry out his own engagements. They lost another £4000 which they had invested in the Confederate Cotton Loan at the request of one of their largest and most influential customers, who otherwise would have withdrawn their business.

My failure in November 1880 arose from the following circumstances. My correspondent as Broker at St Petersburg was Mr Charles Maynard who occasionally telegraphed me the quotations and orders he received from bona fide merchants at St Petersburg for their requirements of steamers. The mode was for him to cable the quotations for me to secure as Broker the offer of steamers and cable them to him to fix, and when chartered he cabled back the confirmation; a share of the chartering commission *alone* being our payment. I never offered any steamer to St Petersburg until I had first offered her to all our London merchants and they had refused to charter.

In 1879 I thus obtained charters for several steamers belonging to Mr Barwick of Sunderland by getting the offers through his agent, Mr Frederick Woods of London, and upon all these the freight was fully paid by the Russian merchants altho' when the steamers arrived at Cronstadt the freights were in almost all cases lower than the chartered rates, and Mr Barwick the owner thus received a considerable amount from the merchants by chartering his steamers beforehand.

All went well until he received a cable from Maynard in St Petersburg reading 'Near end of June loading placeable 2   East Coast 2/6 continent'. He took the blank between the '2' and 'East' to be a telegraphist's error for '3' (the original telegram as received is reproduced opposite), as the difference between the continent and London was invariably 3d. and not 6d. A tangled sequence of events followed which included Frederick Woods not allowing him time to telegraph to St Petersburg to confirm the wording, and the falling of freight rates, which resulted in Barwick claiming £400 from Lyndall which his solicitor told him he would be obliged to pay.

The previous bad state of business had compelled me to borrow from my friends to enable me to tide over what we all considered a bad year in the expectation of the next being better; but this last blow left me no resource and Mr Barwick pressed legal proceedings upon me and would not take into consideration the previous years' benefit he derived through my means, and I was thus compelled to fail by that which, I think Gentlemen, you will consider as a pure business accident.

His plea for re-admission to the Baltic deserved consideration from the successors of William Wilson and Thomas Tooke, who had formed the committee sixty-five years before in disapproval of the tallow gamblers. William Wordsworth Lyndall was no Richard Thornton.

THE GREAT NORTHERN TELEGRAPH COMPANY.

No. of Message

3894

MESSAGES for all Stations in

CHINA, JAPAN, RUSSIA, SWEDEN, NORWAY and DENMARK,

Accepted at the Company's LONDON STATION (ALWAYS OPEN), 7, Great Winchester Street Buildings, and at all Postal Telegraph Stations, marked: VIA **NORTHERN.**

| No. 279 4255 | Time received. 6·25 p. | Service Instructions. | Time Sent. a. p. | GREAT NORTHERN TELEGRAPH 28 MAY 80 LONDON. |
| Words. 13 | h. | | by | |

Given in at *Witersburg* on the 28 at 9 H. 5 M. A m. To

Maynard   Lyndall, London

Near end June loading placable a East Coast 2/6 Continent.

Arm Henrick's on West Coast

Maynard's telegram to Lyndall, 1880

In the above-named, as in all my transactions, I never speculated for gain. I simply acted as Agent and worked only for my share of the commission, and if there had been any money made upon the charter it would never have been for my account; my business has been simply that of a Broker in all my transactions.

The Baltic committee were more co-operative with the Shipowners' Society over the negligence clause in the Adelaide charterparty for grain cargoes, which they agreed should read:

The Act of God, Perils of the Sea, Fire, Barratry of the Master and Crew, Enemies, Pirates and Robbers, Arrests and Restraints of Princes Rulers and People, and other Accidents of Navigation excepted, Strandings and Collisions, and all Losses and Damages caused thereby are also excepted even when occasioned by negligence, default or error in judgement of the Pilot, Master Mariners or other servants of the shipowners.

But shipowners were not exempt from liability for damage to cargo occasioned by bad stowage, improper drainage or ventilation.

As merchants, brokers and shipowners had once been members of a number of coffee-houses, so in the 1880s their successors made up the circle who met and re-met, week in week out, in the voluntary exchanges and associations of specialists which had taken over from the Privy Council the role of regulating their respective trades – though, of course, in their own, not the public's, interest.

The Baltic was not such a body. William Adams had a very clear idea of what its function should be. In a letter deprecating the proposal to shut the Room on the Saturday after Good Friday, he pointed out that subscriptions were paid on the understanding that the member should have access on all days except on certain specified non-business days.

While not questioning the right of the Committee to close the room on further great public occasions, such discretion should, we submit, hardly be exercised whenever a few score of good natured people can be induced to sign a request for such closure in the supposed interest of those who wish to have an extra holiday. We say 'supposed', as it is ludicrous to imagine the closing of the room would influence any sensible man of business in giving or withholding a holiday. This must be regulated by the exigence of his business. The keeping the room open should if anything facilitate the holiday making as rendering the work easier for those who remain in towns. Those who ask for the closing of the room appear to forget that the Baltic is simply a convenience for, and not the cause of, business, and that the letters and telegrams of foreign or country correspondents will come forward and require attention as usual. It is not so with holidays arbitrarily arrived at by private fiat. The holiday becomes a fiction in the majority of cases; the inconvenience alone remains and is a serious evil which we protest against being called upon to submit to. [March, 1888]

When the Canterbury Chamber of Commerce in New Zealand wrote to ask for information about how the grain trade was run in Britain, the committee told Oxley to say they were unable to do so, 'their duties being confined to management only'. They referred the Chamber to the London Corn Trade Association, which in 1886 became incorporated. Baltic members John Ross, Edward Majolier, Samuel Keene, Seth Taylor, John Todd and R. J. Duck were the subscribers to the memorandum with its comprehensive articles of association which were to serve it for nearly ninety years.

When the LCTA became incorporated members of the grain trade in London formed a social club called 'the Cereals'. In September 1886 Albert Christie, the chairman, wrote to the Baltic committee asking if he could put up a notice board in the vestibule of South Sea House to save having to distribute notices. The club, he said, had been going for a year 'with the object of promoting good fellowship amongst the younger members of the grain trade and their friends'. The printed rule book said the object of the 'society' was 'the promotion of social intercourse amongst the members of the Grain and allied trades and their friends'. The subscription was five shillings a year. On January 1, 1886, there were fourteen members, but by June 30, when they issued a half yearly report, there were forty-four. In their first six months they ate five dinners and held a smoking concert which raised £20 for the Corn Exchange Benevolent Society.

The Baltic committee's seven-year lease of rooms at South Sea House from the Baltic Company again expired in 1888, and throughout the period leading up to the expiry date there were rumours that the strained relations between committee and company might end in a complete break. There was talk in the City that they might leave South Sea House and take a lease of the Wesleyan Centenary Hall in Bishopsgate Street, and Sir William McArthur, who was a trustee of this building, asked Stephen Ralli what truth there was in the rumours. He said he would speak to Oxley and on November 13, 1886, he wrote to confirm to the secretary of the Baltic committee – who passed the information to the secretary of the Baltic Company – precisely what had passed between him and McArthur so there should be no misunderstanding.

25 Finsbury Circus, London, EC
13 Nov 1886

Dear Mr Oxley,

> On the 11th Nov. I have written to my friend Sir Wm McArthur as follows:

> 'In consequence of the conversation which I had the pleasure of having with you, I have spoken to the Secretary of the Baltic. There is no intention on the part of either of the Committee to move from their present place.

I have to-day received his reply as follows:

> 'I thank you very much for your letter, and for the trouble you have taken. I now learn from your note that there is no intention on the part of either of the Committees of the Baltic to move from their present place. I had heard to the contrary, and it is satisfactory for me to know the real facts of the case, before taking any further steps in the matter about which I spoke to you.'

I remain, Dear Mr Oxley
yours faithfully,
S. A. Ralli

It is not clear what the *two* committees were – the committee and the board? – but Ralli was obviously concerned to scotch rumours that the Baltic were on such bad terms with their landlords that they seriously planned not to renew their lease and move elsewhere.

But it was the relations between members and committee, never very amicable at the best of times, rather than tension between committee and board, which now threatened to produce a rumpus of major proportions. Owing to the protracted illness of William Oxley, which necessitated his absence from the scene of action, his dual duties were carried on by another (often his son, Charles Oxley) who unfortunately failed to keep the correspondence of 1888 and wrote very limited minutes of committee meetings. Tracing the precise sequence of events at this critical time is therefore more difficult than usual.

On November 3, 1887, the committee discussed the expiration of the lease with the company and 'the Secretary was instructed to arrange for a renewal', which would have taken place in May, 1888.

In November the Baltic Company held its thirty-third annual general meeting. Insecurity of tenure was obviously worrying chairman Michel Rodocanachi, as can be seen from the note he scribbled (see illustration overleaf) on his copy of the accounts.

Suppose we get rooms upstairs say cost 500 or 1000 will the Com. become liable for a certain number of years at the present revenue – think of the Comp's position if we turn out our tenants or rather buy them out and the members for one reason or another should leave us and go elsewhere.

If they require us to make such a risky spec, they must give a guarantee for 7 years.

These are probably notes for his chairman's speech which the growing body of dissatisfied members would have heard him deliver in their capacity as shareholders of the Baltic Company. The committee were now lumbered with a lease of South Sea House for another seven years, but that would not prevent members from staying away from the building if its amenities were below their requirements. The disinclination of the committee to meet these could be the 'one reason or another' which led them not only to stay away but 'go elsewhere'. It was worth having a try; there was little to lose and much to gain, if the pressure they applied bore fruit. The group of members who saw the attraction of pressing for the improvements they sought with a threat of 'or else' included H. W. Barnett, F. B. Garrard and Seth Taylor.

They wrote a long letter to the Baltic committee, dated November 27, 1888, offering suggestions for 'terminating the existing state of tension between the Members of the Baltic and their Committee' and removing 'all hindrances to the Committee and the Members working harmoniously together for common aims – the welfare and comfort of the Room.' They should shelve the matter of which members should form the Baltic committee until October 1889 and concentrate on the requirements for enlarged and improved accommodation – the addition of the sale room, using the space now used for dining (which could go up or down stairs) and revising the arrangements with the Baltic Company. If none of these could be accomplished to members' satisfaction, steps should be taken to secure suitable accommodation elsewhere by a tempor-

The Baltic Company, Limited.

NOTICE IS HEREBY GIVEN, That the THIRTY-THIRD ORDINARY GENERAL MEETING of the Shareholders or Members of this Company will be held at the Offices of the Company, South Sea House, Threadneedle Street, in the City of London, on Thursday, the 8th November Instant, at ONE o'Clock precisely, to receive the Report of the Directors and the Accounts for the past year, to elect Three Directors in place of those who retire by rotation, and an Auditor, and to declare a dividend.

The Transfer Books will remain closed until Friday, the 9th day of November.

By order of the Board,

WILLIAM C. OXLEY,

Secretary.

THREADNEEDLE STREET,
1st November, 1888.

Notice of the Baltic Company's thirty-third ordinary general meeting, 1888

ary committee 'approved by the Room' and appointed by members for the specific purpose of conferring with the existing official committee on 'the best mode of giving effect to this Cause'. The writers also listed improved ventilation, improved shipping and general intelligence, and a revision of the rules as three further points for consideration.

The letter ended:

These matters all press for early action, and are less the demands of any section of Members than the natural requirements of a vigorous and (consequently) developing community. While its vitality continues, it is plain that similar requirements will assert themselves from time to time, and will require providing for if the prosperity which has attended the Room hitherto is to be maintained.

Charles Oxley, son of William Oxley, was instructed to reply to the 'Shadow Committee' on December 6 that as the members of the official committee, which included Stephen Ralli, John Glover and Edward Majolier, considered themselves caretakers only, waiting for their promised dissolution and the election of a new body in their place, they did not feel able to discuss the matters raised. They regretted the shadow committee had not seen fit to give the thirteen names of those they wished to see forming the new official committee.

F. B. Garrard, who was the leader of the pressure group, was not to be fobbed off with nonsense of this sort. In the summer of 1889 he conceived a complete plan which he submitted in writing to Peter Rodocanachi. This was to take a lease of the whole of the ground floor, basement and first floor (except for one suite) of South Sea House from the Baltic Company for seven, fourteen, twenty-one or twenty-eight years at a yearly rental of £6700; to pay £900 in rates and taxes; increase the cost of staff and information from £3000 to £4000 and spend £12000 on structural alterations. He proposed raising £30000 on 6 per cent debentures and depositing £18000 of this with the Baltic Company as a security for rent. The plan continued:

To meet the above outlay *and so have the Room the property of the Members* [this was the key to future harmony] it is suggested to make the following alterations in the entrance fees and subscriptions

1005 town members at £10 10/–	10 552
369 clerks at £6 6/–	2324
126 country £5 5/–	667
Entrance Fees	
Members £15 15/–	
Clerks £10 10/–	

Garrard's plan accounted for an income of £15683 and expenditure of £13400. The surplus would be used to pay off the debentures 'so that in the course of a few years there would be large surplus standing to the credit of the members'.

To carry out the above scheme it is necessary to ascertain the feeling of the Members: if those Gentlemen who are in favour of the proposed alterations would kindly sign this paper as consenting to take one debenture not exceeding £100 it would greatly assist in carrying them out. The alterations suggested: to clear the whole of the ground floor for the subscription room and to give improved information, shipping &c.; in the basement to make such alterations as the Committee may think necessary; on the first floor to make a large restaurant and reading room.

On July 15, 1889, Garrard's plan was considered by the Baltic committee who inevitably appointed a sub-committee to study it in detail, and also to make recommendations for new rules. Garrard was not a member of the committee but he was allowed to attend this meeting, as was George Edwards, the solicitor, who pointed out that the main alteration in the rules would be in raising the subscription to allow Garrard's plan to be put into operation. It would be desirable, Edwards told them in five pages of 'Observations', to have the alterations ready to submit to the general meeting. However,

the General Meeting does not appear to have the power to alter the rules, but it would be well to proceed as if it had, instead of at once providing to dissolve the Society and establishing a new one. If the Members acquiesce in the alterations and pay their new annual subscriptions upon the footing of them, I think the rules will be perfectly valid and binding.

This tortuous piece of legal word-bending was going to save the face of the men who had made all the rules so far without the aid of a solicitor. The recommendation was to alter the rule which said a general meeting could pass 'additional regulations' so that it read that *a rule* could be altered by a resolution passed in the ordinary way or by a two-thirds majority, 'or by altering the rule so as to make it clear that any alterations in the rules can be made provided they are confirmed by a General Meeting'. In other words, you cannot alter the rules, but shut your eyes and pretend you can; then pass a pretend rule to say you can alter the rules; then under this rule alter the rule so that you can alter the rules 'legitimately'; open your eyes and then proceed to do so 'legitimately'. Their distrust of the law and lawyers had led them on to thin ice.

The sub-committee presented its report on Garrard's plan on September 5.

After careful consideration of Mr Garrard's proposal and having in view the fact that the present Committee is much less than the usual number, and that important changes in the Rules are essential to enable the full committee which it is expected will be constituted at the next annual meeting to carry out either Mr Garrard's plan or modification of same or any other arrangement between the Baltic Co Limited and the Members of the room,

the sub-committee recommended that the solicitors be instructed to draw up a new code of rules for consideration of the whole committeee and that further consideration of Garrard's plan be deferred until the new full committee was constituted and the new rules were settled. Edwards asked if they wanted the present rules altered or a complete new set. The committee opted for the latter. He told them,

The postponement of the increase in subscription for one year is very desirable. As pointed out in my 'observations' page 1, the General Meeting has no power (by the present rules) to alter the rules, therefore the collection of subscriptions (on the present basis and on the present rates) will give time for considering the course to be adopted if the new Rules be opposed.

The situation was fluid, to say the least.

There was little time for so big a task but the new rules, as can be imagined, went through many drafts. If Edwards had had his way there would have been thirty-four of them. They transferred the committee into another kind of body altogether. Under his proposed rule 5 they were to be given the management and control of all matters relating to the subscription rooms and all the property and affairs of the Baltic; power to appoint and remove the bankers and secretary and to purchase or lease the Room or any other rooms; sell them, make repairs and alter them as they saw fit, provide furniture, borrow money. James Charles wrote on the draft 'Can hardly be adopted without far more mature consideration than can be given to them before the general meeting in October next. The new powers proposed to be now given to the Committee on these rules can be dealt with after proper deliberation by extraordinary general meeting.'

The new rule 7 enabled the committee to appoint trustees; rule 8 was going to raise the annual subscription to £10 10s. for members elected after October 1, 1889, and to £7 7s. if elected before that date.

Edwards proposed a new rule 34:

The Rules or any of them may from time to time be rescinded or altered and new rules may be made by a resolution passed at any General Meeting or at a ballot taking as aforesaid, provided that at least 40 members be present at the meeting, and that the resolution be passed by a majority consisting of at least two thirds of the number of votes given; and also that the resolution be confirmed by another General Meeting to be held within thirty days after the passing of the resolution.

William Oxley had died on April 4, 1889 after fifty years in the service of the Baltic and twenty-three of them as secretary of the committee or clerk of the Room (since 1866), and the Baltic committee had made a grant of £150 to his widow, and the Baltic Company (whose secretary he also was) allowed her a pension of £50 'terminable at discretion'. In his place the company had appointed 'a gentleman for many years a Member of the Room', Frederick Curtis, who on May 2, 1889, was also appointed secretary of the Baltic committee for six years at a salary of £200. Charles Oxley continued as a member of the secretariat at South Sea House and his salary was raised from £30 to £45 a year.

It was Frederick Curtis, therefore, who, two days before the committee meeting called to discuss the Garrard plan, received the large package sent round by Edwards containing proofs of the new rules signed by the chairman, the agenda for the meeting, and the proposed new form of application for membership which, said Edwards in his covering letter, 'will tend to confirm the new Rules and annul the old ones'. He added 'I think it desirable after the Rules have been adopted, to send a copy to each member with a notification that they have been substituted for the previous Rules, Regulations and Bye Laws by a resolution passed by the General meeting held &c (giving the day of the meeting at which they were adopted).' As a postscript he added 'I have sent the print for perusal by counsel after the various manipulations by the Committee and he has returned them with his opinion that they "may be passed and recommended for adoption".'

Fred Curtis's first printed Baltic committee report went as follows:

The great anxiety of the Members for additional accommodation which led to somewhat unsatisfactory results at the last annual general meeting placed your Committee in some embarrassment, as the Rules contained no provision for the calling of Special Meetings competent to deal with such difficulties. It will be in the recollection of the Members that after the election for the vacancies in the Committee failed, the remaining Members of the Committee intimated that it was their desire to resign, should the Room find it practicable to get a new Committee constituted. This, however, was found impracticable, and the remaining Members of the Committee received assurance that it would be convenient that they should carry on the business of the Room until this Meeting. They therefore decided to do so. They have had prepared, and now submit for your adoption, a new code of Rules, which amongst other things provides: –

1. For General Meetings being held when necessary and for enlarging the powers of such Meetings.

2. For granting to the Committee powers to make other arrangements than those now existing with the Baltic Company Limited, such as have lately been suggested, or any modification of the same, and for raising money on debentures, and increasing the Entrance Fees and Subscriptions if thought fit.

Your Committee has carefully enquired the opinion of the Members as to the additions to the Committee which would be likely to be most acceptable to the Room, and they would gladly have elected the gentlemen who have been nominated as interim Members of the Committee, subject to your ratification today, but they were advised that, as the vacancies had not occurred during the year, the Rules did not enable them to take that course. . . .

Your Committee have only to add, in concluding this report, that in all the communications they have had with the Baltic Company they have found, on the part of the Chairman and Directors the most anxious desire to meet the growing wants and convenience of the Baltic, and they have every ground for hoping that the enlarged Committee will find the same disposition.

The new rules were adopted – there were twenty-nine of them finally – and it seemed that at last the Baltic was steering into calmer waters. But then four leading members of the committee – Stephen Ralli, William Galloway, John Glover and Henry Yeames – who retired by rotation, withdrew their names for re-election, and in the next few days Curtis received letters of resignation from William Muller ('in view of . . . the want of support the Committee received at the hands of the general body of the Members'), Lord Revelstoke, Peter Rodocanachi and Baron J. Henry W. de Schroder, who also resigned his seat on the board of the company which was taken by Henry F. Tiarks.

The report of this meeting in the next annual report stated:

It was expected at the last General Meeting the position of the Committee would have strengthened, but owing to retirements and the resignations which immediately followed the proceedings at that Meeting, the reverse was the case. The result was a reduction of the number of the Committee from 13 to 7 [?] and under these circumstances your Committee decided to postpone all proceedings with regard to carrying out the suggested new arrangements with the Baltic Company, Limited, until the additional number of Members had been elected.

This could not take place until the twelve months had passed. They had become hamstrung by their own rules.

7. The Baltic Challenged

As success was threatening to stifle the Baltic and ineptitude paralyse its management, a rival contender for the subscriptions of the mercantile and shipping community of London, the Jerusalem, had been re-grouping. In December 1889 it began soliciting new custom.

H. McDowell, secretary and manager of the Jerusalem Limited issued a four-page leaflet headed

THE JERUSALEM
SUBSCRIPTION ROOM AND EXCHANGE
(established over 200 years)
Cowper's Court (32–33), Cornhill, London, E.C.

> The Company desire to call attention to the numerous advantages this old-established City Rendezvous offers to gentlemen interested in Exports and Imports, Freights, Shipping and Mercantile affairs generally.
>
> The old building has been replaced by the present handsome and convenient premises.
>
> 'Change' is held daily, attended by a large number of gentlemen interested in Shipping and Mercantile relations with the Colonies, the Cape and the East, for the purpose of arranging Freights, Charters and generally transacting business.

H

An engraving of the Jerusalem Subscription Room and Exchange

At the Jerusalem would be found the latest information about arrivals of vessels and mails from the West Coast of South America and North Pacific, notices of freight wanted, Government tenders, and lists of homeward-bound wool, wheat and nitrate ships; market fluctuations of the London Stock Exchange, continuation rates, bullion returns, rates discount; latest prices of metals, provincial mining market prices, European Bourse prices, shipment of specie, 'and important Political and General News, also received in the Room by wire and conveniently arranged for reference'. There was a telephone in the Room for the use of members. Every facility for correspondence was provided, including private drawers at a small rental.

The entrance fee was only £2 2s., and the annual subscription for a firm which admitted two members to the Room was £5 5s., with £1 1s. for each additional representative or clerk. For an individual the subscription was £4 4s.; country members living fifty miles outside London paid £2 2s., commanders and officers of ships £1 1s. 'Gentlemen resident in India, China, the Cape and

Australasian colonies in London for a period not exceeding Six Months' paid £1 1s. too.

The leaflet (see illustration overleaf) displayed a fine coat of arms on the front page with the motto *Auspicio Regis et Senatus Anglia*, and inside was an engraving of the building in Cowper's Court with gentlemen in tile hats clustered round the corner entrance which was surmounted by a large sculptured version of the same heraldic device. It showed a basement, a first floor with high windows presumably the main subscription room, two floors above, and at the top a row of narrow attic windows. Facing the building on the right was a tower coming forward into the street built over the porch.

The 'Jerusalem' had been registered on November 10, 1880 to carry into effect an agreement dated November 8, 1880 between George Forman, James Thomas Browne and James McDonnell, and to take a lease of, acquire and carry on the business of the 'Jerusalem' Coffee-House in Cowper's Court as a commercial resort, sale, exchange and news rooms. It had a capital of £50000. The coffee-house at the time of the agreement was occupied by Edward Norton Harper, and before him William Harper, heirs presumably of the partner of the Horatio Hardy who had run the Jerusalem in the eighteenth century. George Forman was the owner and was charging Harper £2000 rent.

The old coffee-house had been demolished in 1879 and the new building had been built by the 'Jerusalem' Ltd on the same site. Nine years later it was a modern 'rendezvous', custom-built for the purpose in the centre of the City, providing all the amenities of the Baltic but on a smaller scale and with no qualification for membership other than an ability to pay the entrance fee and subscription.

But it was to the old, over-crowded Baltic, and not the new Jerusalem, that the London Produce Clearing-House Ltd turned in the summer of 1889.

Gentlemen,

As this Company is about completing arrangements with the Corn Trade for dealings in wheat under its Rules, and as the Corn Trade desire that the business should be carried on at 'The Baltic' rather than at

THE JERUSALEM

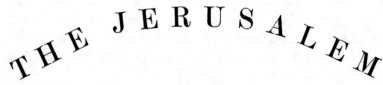

Correspondents at

Calcutta	Manila
Bombay	Cape Town
Madras	Algoa Bay
Colombo	Port Natal
Singapore	Mauritius
Hong Kong	St. Helena
Shanghai	

Correspondents at

Sydney	Auckland
Melbourne	Wellington
Adelaide	Lyttleton
Fremantle	Dunedin
Brisbane	Nelson
Rockhampton	Oamaru
Townsville	Timaru

SUBSCRIPTION ROOM AND EXCHANGE

(ESTABLISHED OVER 200 YEARS),

COWPER'S COURT (32-33). CORNHILL,

LONDON, E.C.

THE JERUSALEM LIMITED.
2,000 /12/89.

The front page of a leaflet issued by the Jerusalem in 1889

the Mincing Lane Sale Rooms, we beg to request your sanction that daily meetings for the purpose of fixing quotations may be held in your Sale Room when not otherwise occupied and in one of the alcoves of 'The Baltic' when the Sale Room is not available. Similar meetings, usually denominated 'Calls' are held on the floor of 'The Atlantic' at Liverpool for the purpose of fixing quotations for wheat and are not found inconvenient. We may explain that each 'Call' does not occupy more than about 10 to 15 minutes and simply consists of the process of naming each month and asking those present at what price they are prepared to sell or buy so that reliable quotations may be arrived at. There would be two calls daily, say at about 12 noon and 4 p.m. (Saturdays, noon only).

But the committee jibbed at having a twice daily influx of non-members in corridors and 'alcoves' already jammed tight with dissident subscription payers. They had to refuse. And besides if they admitted a crowd of strangers unfamiliar with the geography who, like Mr Lohden, insisted on entering the smallest rooms covered, their funds would soon be seriously depleted.

c/o H. L. ADAMSON & Cº.
STEAM SHIP BROKERS.

TELEGRAPHIC ADDRESS,
"SUPERNAL. LONDON."

10, Great Sᵗ Helens.

London, 3rd February 18 90.
E.C.

To the Secretary of the Baltic
E.C.

Dear Sir,

I beg to inform you that when entering the lavatory of the Baltic, owing to there being insufficient height in the doorway I struck my new silk hat against the top with the result that it was so badly damaged as to render it unfit to wear,. and shall be pleased if you will canvey this to the right source notifying that I shall claim the cost of a new hat. Hoping to hear from you be return.

Yours truly,

Fredᵏ Lohden

Mr W Burley With interviewed Mr Lohden.

Letter from Mr Lohden, a member of the Baltic, to the Secretary of the committee,
1890

In pencil at the foot of the letter a patient Fred Curtis wrote 'Mr W. Bridges Webb interviewed Mr Lohden'. It was good training for more arduous duties to come.

Time and fashion came to Fred Lohden's rescue. By 1893 the Baltic was already 'where *once* men wore clothes of sombre hue and the sleek top hat shone over every head'. Crowns were lower in 1893.

THE COSTUME OF THE BALTIC IN 1893 – A PROPHECY

> When a bold member first from Brighton's shores
> Came bounding to the Baltic in a hat
> Of snowy straw, all stood around and stared,
> Struck dumb, astonished at the wondrous sight;
> For never yet had such a thing been seen.

Heightening doorways was not a feature of any of the schemes submitted by Goymour Cuthbert, the Baltic Company's architect, between March and April, 1889, all of which were rejected for not going far enough. The new rule which had been passed raising the subscriptions and entrance fees to provide the money for the alterations was rescinded as there was no need for it. In any case, there was no lack of new candidates to keep the subscription income buoyant.

At the annual general meeting on October 17 it was announced that the total number of subscriptions received up to December 30, 1890, was 1534, an increase of twenty-eight over 1889. For thirty exasperated members this was much too many. They at once wrote a memorial to the committee drafted by their leader Marmaduke Lawther urging them to consider the necessity of restricting the number of members and call a special general meeting to pass resolutions that since membership was in excess of the accommodation preference for election should be given to filling vacancies created by death or retirement. Such a meeting was in fact held before the AGM but when Marmaduke Lawther put his resolution none of those who signed his petition were prepared to second him and he had to withdraw it. With that quickly disposed of, the gathering became the adjourned annual general meeting to elect a new committee. Further anti-climax. Chairman John Ross rose to announce that all the gentlemen who had offered themselves for election had withdrawn. Eleven new committee members however were elected on January 22, 1891, and they included Frederick Garrard and Septimus Glover who renewed their attempts to gain acceptance for the Garrard plan.

In June 1891 Curtis sent out a notice to all members calling them to a meeting to consider yet another and more thorough scheme by Goymour Cuthbert, and to approve the increase in subscription which would once again be necessary.

When Robert Bovey received the notice he wrote at once to say he was opposed to an increase in subscription in any form whatever. 'It appears to be evident that some increase in accommodation has become necessary and *entirely* through increased membership; the revenue therefore must have been considerably increased of late years without any additional accommodation being provided.' Miall Green and Francis Holland sent a joint letter of protest at the proposed increase in subscription 'which is already sufficiently high to admit of the proprietors according to the subscribers infinitely better accommodation'. 'The fees are already excessive' wrote an anonymous member in red ink across the notice which he posted back, 'and the accommodation is bad. The latter ought to be improved and the former reduced. If this is not done two members at least will withdraw altogether.' 'Enormous expense for little improvement' was another comment.

It was a warning of what was to come. The plans were turned down. The Baltic committee report for 1891 stated,

In consequence of the rejection of the scheme proposed at the Special Meeting of the Members held on 23rd June last, your Committee have opened negotiations with the Baltic Company Limited with a view to the Company's increasing the accommodation for Members upon another plan which your Committee are assured will be placed before them at an early date. In the meantime, in consideration of the crowded state of the Room, your Committee have thought it advisable to postpone the election of new Members for further consideration.

There were five vacancies to fill.

On September 2, 1891, John Ross received the following:

Dear Sir,

The object I had in view when I joined your Committee having so utterly failed, I beg you will kindly accept my resignation.

Yours faithfully,

F. B. Garrard.

The Garrard plan was dead.

But at the annual general meeting William Bridges Webb, of Dewar & Webb, became one of the four new members of the committee and three weeks later Seth Taylor, of Harris Bros & Co., was elected chairman of the committee, and Septimus Glover of Glover Brothers, deputy chairman, a team which gave the Baltic the sense of direction and firm stewardship which for so long it had lacked.

The new leaders of the committee recognized that the time for courtesies was over, that the Baltic Company directors must be treated as a completely separate body of businessmen with completely separate objectives – as indeed they were. Bridges Webb wanted to go one further and moved that the election of the candidates waiting to be admitted at that meeting be postponed (the first time in the history of the committee). In spite of oppositon from Mavrogordato and Glover, the resolution was carried eleven to two. At the December meeting they minuted that they strongly objected to a further payment to the company in respect of any increase of members over 1500, assuming a fixed rental.

Now that the gloves were off, news of the fresh confrontation with the company quickly circulated around the small circle of mercantile and shipping men in the City, and inevitably became the subject of comment in the shipping press. In its issue of November 13, *Fairplay*'s leader on the 1891 annual general meeting of the committee pointed out,

The rent paid is very high and there really seems to be no reason why, with such an income available to the Company, more suitable accommodation could not readily be obtained . . . It is no news that for a long time there has been considerable friction between the Committee and the Company, and the question is whether it may not be for the interest of the company to give the accommodation required, rather than drive the committee to go elsewhere.

But in that autumn of 1891 it looked rather as if the *members* might choose to go elsewhere. For that very next issue of *Fairplay* carried news of a development which threatened to beat the Baltic at its own game.

THE BALTIC,

VISITORS ADMISSION CARD.

30 Sept 1897

Admit Mr Sam Ellmann

Introduced by Alx Villar MEMBER.

Countersigned by L. Allston MEMBER OF COMMITTEE.

THIS CARD MUST BE GIVEN UP ON LEAVING. ADMISSION MAY BE RENEWED IN ACCORDANCE WITH RULES AT BACK.

RULE 21.—Members shall be permitted to introduce friends as visitors to the subscription room; visitors, if in business, must reside not less than 40 miles, if not in business, not less than 20 miles from London; their names and addresses shall be entered in the visitors' book with the signature of the Member who introduces them. No visitor shall be introduced more than six times in one year, and the aggregate of his visits shall not exceed one month, unless with the approval of three Members of the Committee; with this approval a visitor may continue as such for a further period of two months, upon payment of 40s. per month, and the Committee shall have power in special cases to grant an extension of time to a visitor, on terms to be agreed.

Baltic visitor's admission card, 1897

Steps are being taken to form a Shipping Exchange in London and already several influential firms in the City have given their names. The object is to secure ultimately some large place in a commanding position where merchants, shipowners and others may meet for an exchange of views or to transact business. The social element will not be neglected, for it is likely that a club will arise in connection with the new institution. In the meantime temporary accommodation is being looked for.

The extent to which it was a threat to the Baltic was underlined in the long announcement in the issue of November 27 which was so greatly at pains to show it was nothing of the sort.

THE idea of establishing a Shipping Exchange in London has been entertained for upwards of two years, but it is only during the past few weeks that the matter has taken practical form. The want of such a facility has been specially felt by the managers of the various steamship lines trading to New York, etc., now included in what is known as the 'New York Conference'. Until recently the rivalry existing between some of the Transatlantic lines has prevented the formation of a combination sufficiently strong to carry out the idea of establishing a Shipping Exchange, but the harmony now brought about by the 'conference' has removed this difficulty and at the same time revived the desire of the several managers for a common meeting-ground where they might transact business together, and where also they could see shippers. Liverpool merchants and shipowners have always had such facilities, and have found them of the greatest possible service. On the Continent shipowners and merchants, or their representatives, can always be found on the Bourse, and a great deal of time is thus saved all round. In London shipowners and merchants have generally to go from office to office to see one another, and the simultaneous 'cross calls' result in the loss of much valuable time. London is too large for one central general Exchange, and the different sections of trade have founded their own Exchanges at centres convenient to them; but the shipping interest, which is not the least important one in the metropolis, has hitherto been without a business institution of its own. The 'Baltic' is a grain and grain-chartering market, and by no means representative of the shipping trade generally; and even as the home of grain-chartering it has become too small to accommodate properly the shipbrokers, charterers, and others who flock to it.

It is thought possible by the promoters of the new Shipping Exchange that their institution may in time so develop as to afford suitable accommodation for those who now find the Threadneedle-street centre too limited – though there is no present idea of setting up in rivalry with the famous and extremely fortunate 'Baltic' Company. The objects which the committee of the new Shipping Exchange have before them are the providing of a more convenient meeting place for shipping business than now exists, and the establishment of improved facilities for discussing trade questions, at present handled in so perfunctory a manner by the leisurely merchants and faddists who constitute the Chamber of Commerce. Questions small and great, and some of considerable importance, arise from time to time between shipowners, dock Companies, shippers, and others; these, it is believed, could be discussed to the best advantage on the common ground which the proposed Exchange would afford. The social element will be studied by the formation of a club, to be called the Argonaut Club, in connection with the Exchange. The committee will, in the first instance, secure temporary premises, starting in a small way, but hoping to grow into a large undertaking. Judging from the promises of support received from a large number of firms interested in shipping, it is anticipated that the movement can be carried to a successful issue. Only persons engaged in shipping business will be allowed to join. The proposed subscription is two guineas per annum for principals, and the same for clerks; a certain number of original members will be admitted without entrance fee.

Mr W. Becket Hill of Wilson-Hill Line to America and Allan Line to Canada was given as chairman, and Mr T. L. Feild of Atlantic Transport Line as honorary treasurer of the Argonaut Club and Shipping Exchange, and Mr H. Neville Ward of Johnstone Line honorary secretary.

An inaugural dinner of the Argonaut Club and Shipping Exchange was held at the London Tavern in Fenchurch Street on December 4 and there was such a demand for the 150 tickets, at 7s. 6d. that they put the price up to a guinea. The diners passed a resolution that it was desirable in the shipping interests of the City of London that the club and exchange should forthwith be established.

Two weeks later an important notice was circulating in the City issued from 23/25 Billiter Street, dated December 15, 1891. It was headed

LONDON SHIPPING EXCHANGE

NOTICE IS HEREBY GIVEN that the Meeting of those
interested in the establishment of a
Central Shipping Exchange
for London
will be held at the 'Ship & Turtle' on Thursday next,
December 17th at 2.30 p.m.

On February 2, 1892, the London Shipping Exchange was registered with a capital of £10000 in 1000 £10 shares. The object of the company was to provide a suitable building for a shipping exchange in the City of London, to disseminate useful information connected with the shipping interest throughout all markets and generally to promote the shipping trade. Thirdly, it aimed to communicate with chambers of commerce and other mercantile and trade associations. Subscribers to the memorandum were W. Becket Hill, shipbroker, Alexander Howden, shipbroker, Thomas Feild, shipbroker, Richard Cattarns, gent, Edward Gellatly, shipbroker, Adam Kettelwell, shipbroker, G. R. Birt dock manager, Thomas Skinner, shipowner, E. H. Forwood, merchant, John Hield, shipowner, H. W. Ronaldson, shipbroker.

The first meeting of the directors of the London Shipping Exchange was held in the Ironmongers' Hall in Fenchurch Street at the beginning of February 1892. *Fairplay* reported,

The authorities of the Ironmongers' Company, being wishful to forward a movement that is thought likely to benefit the shipping and mercantile interests of London, are considering the advisability of placing their ground floor and court at the disposal of the Shipping Exchange for a year or so, as temporary premises. The action of the authorities of this excellent old Company will be much appreciated by shipowners and shippers in London as, coupled with certain changes which I have always regarded as indispensable, it will help greatly to give the new Exchange a business-like and satisfactory start.

Sir Donald Currie MP was now chairman, Alexander Howden and W. Becket Hill vice-chairmen.

The prospectus showed that the first 500 members were to be asked to pay an annual subscription of £3 3s. without entrance fee, the second 500 £5 5s. also without entrance fee, and after the first 1000 the entrance fee would be £5 5s. and the subscription £5 5s. A firm of more than two partners would pay £10 10s.; clerks would pay £3 3s. It was all very much cheaper than the Baltic.

All seemed set fair for the new project's happy début when out of the blue came a rival project – and it was not the Baltic.

Jerusalem Shipping Exchange

— AND —

Subscription Rooms.

APPLICATION FOR MEMBERSHIP.

E. G. KIMBER, Esq.,
    Secretary,
       The "Jerusalem," Limited,
          Billiter Buildings, London, E.C.

Sir,

      Being desirous of becoming............Member.........of your Exchange,...................subjoin address, and request you will be good enough to submit.................Name.........for Election.

        Yours faithfully,

....

Name in full..

Occupation ....

Address ....

....

Application form for membership of the Jerusalem Shipping Exchange

On February 26, 1892, the following announcement appeared in the *Shipping Gazette & Lloyd's List*.

Since the introduction to the public of the proposal to establish a Central Shipping Exchange for London which has led to the formation of a Joint Stock Company with a capital of £10000, the directors of the Jerusalem (Limited) have closely followed the course of events, and the chairman of that institution [James Browne] has attended and spoken at all the public meetings on the subject. At the outset the directors of the Jerusalem held out the hand of friendship to the promoters of the suggested Exchange, in the belief that a comprehensive scheme would at once be proceeded with on such a scale as would render unnecessary the existence of two concerns for similar purposes, and would have admitted of the interests of the proprietors and members of the Jerusalem being adequately considered and cared for. They were also under the impression that the project would have received the united support of the shipping trade, and was certain of such powerful financial assistance as would have rendered any opposition practically hopeless [including the Baltic]. Differences of opinion however have arisen in the ranks of those who were originally concerned in the movement, many of whom complain of the delay that has taken place and object on various grounds to certain features of the plans and methods contemplated; it being also felt by some that the overtures of the proprietors of the Jerusalem have not been met in the spirit in which they were made. The directors of the Jerusalem therefore came to the conclusion that they would be studying the interests of their proprietors and members, as well as the commercial interests concerned, if they moved in the matter themselves without further delay, and this conclusion has been acted upon. They felt that by adopting this course they would not in any way lay themselves open to the charge of unnecessarily adding to the number of institutions that already exist.

In the 'last few days' continued the piece, the directors of the Jerusalem Ltd had been negotiating for the purchase of Billiter Buildings at No 22 Billiter Street and they had now secured this property. They were furnishing the rooms, and they would open the building as a shipping exchange 'within the ensuing week'. The old Jerusalem Coffee-House in Cowper's Court would be closed. Although they had taken No 22 Billiter Street for a term of years, the directors considered it would only meet their requirements for a time, and they were already treating for a site in a central and most prominent position upon which buildings were proposed to be erected 'which will be an ornament to the City'.

In connection with this latter scheme, the directors, we understand, have already been assured of co-operation from a sufficient number of powerful interests to occupy the building from cellar to roof. We have been asked not to make public the details of this building project for the present, but it is declared that if the scheme be carried out as contemplated the directors will well deserve the gratitude of the commercial community of the City of London. We can only say, therefore, that the project as shadowed forth is of a very bold and comprehensive character, and the promoters are confident that it will receive such support as will ensure the sanction of the necessary authorities.

They proposed having the exchange managed by a committee representing the different interests to be provided for, 'their desire and intention being to leave as much as possible in the hands of the members themselves'.

This article was reprinted and circulated as a pamphlet by E. G. Kimber, the secretary of the Jerusalem Ltd, to solicit members.

At what point the promoters of the first shipping exchange scheme also acquired temporary premises in Billiter Street is not clear, but they had certainly done so by March 4. Not to be out-done F. Savage, who had been appointed secretary in place of the temporary Mr Pegg, also acquired (and probably wrote) an article in the *Shipping Gazette* which he too had reprinted and circulated (see illustration overleaf).

He obviously wrote it. He also mentioned that they intended to supply the latest shipping news and information on movements in the markets. A room committee, on which the subscribers were well represented, would arrange for 'high change'. 'As the subscribing members already number nearly 700, it is expected that there will be no lack of business to negotiate at these meetings, or of business to get through it promptly.'

Savage also sent out a circular bearing an impressive list of directors, bankers, solicitors and auditors and announcing the opening of the London Shipping Exchange in temporary premises at No 19 Billiter Street at 12 noon on March 16. He added that the directors were negotiating 'for some very convenient permanent premises in the immediate neighbourhood'. Naturally he felt obliged to add a second paragraph which sadly blunted the impact of the whole project: 'I am desired to inform you that this Company

LONDON SHIPPING EXCHANGE,
(LIMITED.)

From Shipping Gazette of March 4th.

This Company has now secured most eligible temporary premises at No. 19, Billiter Street. Mr. M'Nab, the owner of this handsome building, which was erected some 20 years ago for the then famous firm of Pinter, Perez & Co., has placed the first floor at the disposal of the directors of the London Shipping Exchange for temporary occupation until the ground floor becomes vacant, which will be on or before Michaelmas. This first floor, lately occupied by Messrs. Swire & Sons, is lofty and spacious, having an area of about 2,500 square feet, and is well lighted by a range of 10 windows. The energetic Secretary, Mr. Savage, is fast making it habitable. Of course, when the ground floor becomes vacant, a space of nearly twice the size will be secured, with three capital entrances direct into Billiter Street. It is intended to supply not merely the latest and most reliable shipping news, but also the promptest and most detailed information of the movements of all the markets in which besiness men are interested. A room committee, upon which the subscribers are well represented, will arrange hours for "high change," and, as the subscribing members already number nearly 700, it is expected that there will be no lack of business to negotiate at these meetings, or of business men to get through it promptly.

A circular from the London Shipping Exchange, reprinted from the Shipping Gazette, *1892*

is in no way connected with the Shipping Exchange, which it is reported is about to be opened at Billiter Buildings.'

It was an extraordinary, if not ludicrous, situation in which neither of the participants was prepared to give an inch. Only the press reporting from the sidelines could afford to acknowledge the absurdity of it all, though its serious implications demanded an attempt to analyse how it had ever been allowed to come about. 'Look-Out Man' in *Fairplay* on March 11 wrote:

So far as what might be called the rival Exchanges are concerned I do not think that those connected with the 'Jerusalem' come very well out of the matter. I have reason to believe that proposals were made by gentlemen connected with the 'Jerusalem' to the effect that if the London Shipping Exchange would appoint as secretary the present secretary of the 'Jerusalem', no opposition would be offered; but that the last-named institution would eventually come to be wound up.

He then added the information that the directors of the London Shipping Exchange did not think the Jerusalem secretary (Edmund Gibbs Kimber) suitable as he was very young and studying for the Bar which he would join when he qualified in two or three years' time. So they appointed Savage whom they knew could stay with them longer.

Just before the opening of the Exchange at 19 Billiter Street, those who projected one at No 22, the directors of the Jerusalem, held a luncheon party for their friends and discussed the coming fight. 'Look-Out Man' was in no two minds as to who would be the winner.

To those behind the scenes who really know what has taken place and understand the little wheels that move the larger wheels, the accounts of the position in the papers are amusing . . . An attempt to resuscitate the 'Jerusalem' is about as likely to succeed as an attempt to resuscitate the old Jamaica Coffee House. The concern has survived from ancient days, and it may be added that it has survived its utility.

Before the London Shipping Exchange opened at 19 Billiter Street on March 16, 1892, two leading members of the Baltic joined its board of directors, Theo Angier and Francis Lenders. Alexander Howden was in the chair for the opening and his speech was followed by orations from Becket Hill, Theo Angier, Richard

Cattarns and the American Thomas Feild, who, according to a press report, said that what the trade needed in London was what it had in every other great commercial centre, a genuine Shipping Exchange. 'There is no doubt whatever that the movement will succeed', commented *Fairplay*; 'anything that some shipowners regarded as objectionable in the early stages has been got rid of, and not a word of adverse criticism is to be heard.'

Though all this must have led to considerable merriment in the subscription room of South Sea House, those who gave the matter serious thought must have deplored the initiative being taken out of their hands, and wondered to what it might lead – not to a welcome depletion of their numbers, but wholesale secession to one or other of the rivals in Billiter Street? They would have noted the alleged by-passing of the Baltic as a possible general exchange on the grounds that it was predominantly the meeting place of the grain trade, and had become a centre for one part of the operation, tramp shipping, as the Jerusalem was of the liner trade. But they should have derived comfort from the knowledge that it was not the accommodation which had ever given the Baltic its popularity and prestige, but its seventy-year-old Code of Conduct and the international reputation attached to membership which no money or clever promotion could ever suddenly create out of nothing.

But while recognizing the value of these intangible assets and refusing to abandon them in the knowledge that it would take another seventy years to build them up again, members of the Baltic were equally adamant in their refusal to pay a higher annual subscription. What future members might be asked to pay, however, was another matter. On March 24 they agreed to take a new seven-year lease of South Sea House at a rental of £8000 from September 30, 1892, provided certain structural alterations were made. Subscriptions would be kept at their current level for all present members until they resigned, but new members elected after September 30, 1892, would have to pay ten guineas instead of seven, and an entrance fee of £21.

Meanwhile young Edmund Gibbs Kimber pushed on regardless of rivals and impudent press correspondents to promote the 'Jerusalem' Shipping Exchange and subscription rooms for all he was worth. On April 12 he sent out a chatty letter to members telling them of latest developments. His letterhead bore the crest of the Jerusalem Ltd below the legend 'Established 1625'. Arrangements for the reception of additional subscribers were complete, he said, and they were in a position to afford their members the benefits of the lofty and commodious rooms they had acquired, a handsome reading room with current daily newspapers and a hundred back files. Telephonic communication was available with Liverpool and all the principal northern towns by the National Telephone Company's system. The exchange room of large and symmetical proportions was supplied with a full and prompt service of shipping, cotton, woollen, Stock Exchange and general market reports, and over a hundred directories, a valuable collection of shipping records from 1760 and files of *The Times* from 1875. High change was held daily from 3 to 3.30 at which there was a large attendance of merchants, shipowners, brokers and agents. An engineering exchange would also be held on the premises. Subscriptions for London members were £4 4s. a year. The List of Merchants which Kimber attached to this letter included A. L. Elder & Co, Findlay Durham & Brodie, Antony Gibbs & Sons, Hudson's Bay Company, Ralli Brothers, and John Evan Tibbs, tallow merchant.

An Australian journalist visiting 22 Billiter Street in March 1892 (the building still stands, as does No 19*) described the scene.

From 5 minutes to 3 until the doors were closed at 5 minutes past 3, free arrivals took place, and as the clock struck the hum of business voices was at its full. The strict regulation of closing the door at 3.5 sharp works well, and should be continued in all its exactness as, although perhaps two or three late comers may grumble at first, it will work well in concentrating business ... There was no doubt at all about actual business being done, and we were particularly struck with one circumstance. There is one of those horrid instruments in the room called a 'tape' i.e. a Stock Exchange record of prices, a thing that is to the Stock Exchange gambler what an imaginary snake is to the hard drinker; well, the 'tape' was perfectly unheeded, one man walked up and looked at it in a careless sort of fashion and another surveyed it with his hands in his pockets, as if it was a curiosity. A good sign this struck us to be. Long may shippers attend to shipping business, and it is clear that the

---

*See illustration between pages 252 and 253

'Jerusalem' Shipping Exchange means business and is bound to be a great success. Our representative says he was much impressed by the fact that this Exchange seems already to have filled a want in the Billiter neighbourhood viz, a centre around which the shipping trade may revolve and the shipping trade has taken very kindly to the new centre.

But the Jerusalem Shipping Exchange only lasted the spring and summer of 1892. For most of that time the occupiers of No 19 and 22 Billiter Street were discussing ways and means of joining forces. The initiative finally came from No 19, with an offer from Ernest Forwood, chairman of the LSE committee, to purchase the Jerusalem outright. At first the directors of the Jerusalem asked for a totally unreasonable sum, but on September 27 they signed an agreement by which they sold the business and goodwill of their commercial resort, sale, exchange and news rooms for £1500, plus £250 for their records (still in the possession of the Baltic Exchange). The Jerusalem agreed to close their rooms at 22 Billiter Street and not to open others within five miles of the Royal Exchange, and to encourage their members to join the club next door. Jerusalem members were taken on by the London Shipping Exchange without re-election for the unexpired portion of their subscriptions.

The sensible move was widely welcomed, but the manner in which the Jerusalem so abruptly capitulated without telling its members caused considerable offence. The *Daily News* reported:

Members of the 'Jerusalem' yesterday found the doors of their building closed and were not a little put out by the absence of notice that they were to be transferred to the London Shipping Exchange. It is true that the latter is only next door, has good accommodation and demands a smaller subscription, nevertheless it was regarded as a sort of coup d'état; the object of the surprise being, no doubt, to prevent the formation of a new 'Jerusalem'.

'Old Jerusalemite' wrote to *Fairplay* to protest at an injustice to old members who had their cards printed and addressed with the well-known name. If only the joint establishment had been called the Jerusalem and London Shipping Exchange ill feeling would have been avoided. 'The name is second only to Lloyd's and known throughout the known globe as the oldest established Subscription Room in London.'

But, by whatever name, the new combined exchange was a success from the start. Overnight it had 1500 members. It had the whole of the ground floor and most of the first at Nos 19, 20 and 21 Billiter Street. The big exchange room at street level was 90 feet long and 25 feet wide. Upstairs were a luncheon room and reading room. It was all lit by incandescent electric light.

Edmund Kimber, director and secretary, was presumably called to the Bar, and Frank Savage resigned as secretary at 19 Billiter Street in July 1892. Ernest Forwood and his colleagues in charge of the new Jerusalem/LSE took a great deal of trouble to find a new secretary and manager, and after interviewing a large number of candidates picked James Arbuckle Findlay.

The crest of the London Shipping Exchange,
founded in 1893

On January 30, 1893, the London Shipping Exchange was formally opened by the Lord Mayor of London, appropriately enough a wharfinger, Mr Alderman Knill. The universally popular ship-owner Sir Donald Currie, the president of the Exchange, was in the chair, and his speech was followed by remarks from Becket Hill, 'father' of the Exchange, Thomas Feild, Alexander Howden, Henry Langridge and others. In proposing the health of the Lord Mayor, John Glover said no other trade beside shipping was so harassed by the perpetual legislation of faddists; no other would be able to survive the incubus of chief clerks, officialdom in general and faddists in particular. More than one of the speakers referred to the apathy of merchants towards the Exchange. *Fairplay*'s Look-

Out Man thought this would prove to be transient. 'These are not days of over abundant credit and London merchants take nothing for granted.' But such facilities, he wrote, led to business, and business bred business. The absence of facilities afforded elsewhere had long been a drawback to London. (Glasgow and Liverpool already had them, as had many cities abroad.) To get rid of this reproach had been the object of those who founded the London Shipping Exchange – 'a movement which certainly in recent years has had no parallel in this city'. The opening ceremony was destined to form an epoch in the commercial history of London.

Some of the correspondents were not clear whether it was intended as a club or a business centre. 'Whether the exchange will be entitled to control wages and to keep competition within bounds is not very clear at present. The idea only originated last year, so that not much time has been allowed to elapse between its conception and its embodiment.'

It was a field day for versifiers. 'Bernardino' in *Fairplay* had a page-length piece on these lines:

> There was champagne and a sandwich for the company at large
> And a pillar to lean up against provided free of charge.
> I apologise for bringing in an ancient joke, but still
> I can't refrain from saying that the business done was K(nil)l.
>
> We are going to start a smoking room and billiard saloons,
> And we give a little 'kettledrum' on Wednesday afternoons,
> Tableaux vivants and theatricals, and dances too, as well
> As our merrysmoking concerts at the Cannon Street Hotel.

When the Exchange proposed closing the doors at Afternoon Change to ensure punctuality, many objected. If a shipbroker had a charter-party to negotiate subject to telegraphic reply by 3.45, he visited one merchant after another, finally concluded the charter, sent off his telegram and went back to Billiter Street to find the doors closed. 'By the way' commented Look-Out Man, 'if brokers should find themselves frequently shut out of the London Shipping Exchange they might transfer their patronage to the Baltic; how would this suit the Exchange?'

But it was no joke. It seemed as if the Baltic had been eclipsed.

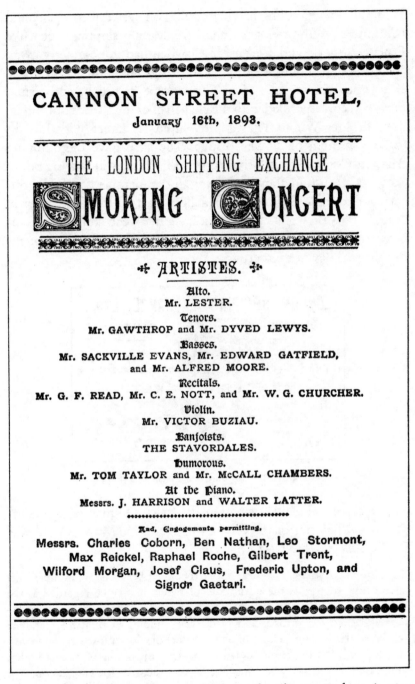

CANNON STREET HOTEL,

January 16th, 1893.

THE LONDON SHIPPING EXCHANGE
SMOKING CONCERT

⚜ ARTISTES. ⚜

Alto.
Mr. LESTER.

Tenors.
Mr. GAWTHROP and Mr. DYVED LEWYS.

Basses.
Mr. SACKVILLE EVANS, Mr. EDWARD GATFIELD,
and Mr. ALFRED MOORE.

Recitals.
Mr. G. F. READ, Mr. C. E. NOTT, and Mr. W. G. CHURCHER.

Violin.
Mr. VICTOR BUZIAU.

Banjoists.
THE STAVORDALES.

Humorous.
Mr. TOM TAYLOR and Mr. McCALL CHAMBERS.

At the Piano.
Messrs. J. HARRISON and WALTER LATTER.

And, Engagements permitting,

Messrs. Charles Coborn, Ben Nathan, Leo Stormont,
Max Reickel, Raphael Roche, Gilbert Trent,
Wilford Morgan, Josef Claus, Frederic Upton, and
Signor Gaetari.

Programme for a smoking concert given by the London Shipping Exchange in 1893

While all the wrangling had been going on between company and committee, committee and members, leading shipping men like Ernest Forwood and Alexander Howden had gone quietly away and created the London Shipping Exchange under their very noses. But James Findlay and Fred Curtis kept in touch, and Ernest Forwood corresponded with the chairman of the Baltic committee, now Bridges Webb. They jointly hired a steamer with Lloyd's for the opening of Tower Bridge. The LSE gave the Shipping Auction Company exclusive right to hold sales in the big room downstairs; in June they took over all the members of the Engineering Exchange Ltd, which had been part of the Jerusalem; in August 1894 they gave James Findlay a five-year contract of employment at £450 a year for two years and £500 for the remaining three. They were there to stay.

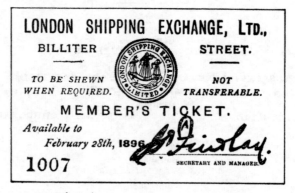

London Shipping Exchange member's ticket

Three years after its formation Frederick Dolman gave a comprehensive description of 'Where Merchants Do Most Congregate' in *The Ludgate Illustrated Magazine*.

The Shipping Exchange has now about 1600 members, a larger number than at any time supported the institution, of which it may be regarded as the business successor [the Jerusalem]. The Exchange proper is a large and well-lighted hall on the ground floor of the fine building in Billiter Street. The official who is seated in a kind of sentry box at the door turns a vigilant eye – which even 1600 different faces hardly baffles – upon you on passing in, lest you should be neither a member nor have a member for companion. It is comparatively early – not quite eleven o'clock – but there is already a goodly gathering; many members are interested in the latest shipping news – posted around the room – some are ascertaining the latest speakings or reports of vessels they are the agents for, whilst others are anxious to discover, if possible, the fate of a vessel which has had to face a recent gale. A member who makes a business of salvage is, perhaps, coming to terms respecting a recent wreck, or a tug-owner may be fortunate enough to obtain orders to tow a vessel up to the docks.

At about half-past eleven – when Chartering Change is held, and at a quarter to four in the afternoon – which is the hour fixed for High Change – the floor is crowded with Members. 'Chartering Change' almost explains itself – it is the time when ship owners, freight agents and others meet to 'fix ships' and arrange rates for the conveyance of cargo. 'High Change' is a more miscellaneous gathering, which transacts all kinds of business more or less connected with ships and shipping. At a quarter to four the doors are closed, and no one is allowed to enter till High Change is over at four o'clock. A score or more of members are sometimes in this way left lamenting outside. The object of the manoeuvre which inflicts this hardship upon them is to facilitate the business of the members generally. With the doors closed, those who wish to meet and do business with each other are, it is thought, likely to do so much more easily and speedily than if members are constantly coming in. The closing of the doors at High Change is, I believe, the con- tinued observance of one of the old customs of 'The Jerusalem'.

At High Change the shipowner can meet his broker, or the merchant can arrange terms for the conveyance of his dried fruits or baled goods by the various liners. It should be said that the ship-brokers who frequent the Exchange are of various kinds. There is the 'loading broker', a man who gathers together, so to speak, the cargo of ships which are prepared to take miscellaneous goods, whose sailings he announces in good time on the Exchange. The chartering brokers, on the other hand, occupy themselves with the search for cargoes of one particular kind, such as cotton, grain, coals, iron rails, etc. They are mostly employed by the owners of what are called 'tramp ships' – vessels, that is, which have no regular trade, but are willing to go almost anywhere if a profit is to be made on the run – and often if it is not. Lastly, there are buying and selling brokers – men who know everything about every ship in the market; what she cost, who built her, owns her and so forth, and are well-informed about the most likely purchasers.

Not all the members of the Shipping Exchange, however, have joined it for the purpose of doing business there. Some make it a place of call merely for the purpose of obtaining information on matters affecting their business interests. In the Exchange Room there is a duplicate service of Lloyd's intelligence, and a record of 'Sailings' and 'Arrivals'. There are files of a number of newspapers, including the leading Colonial papers and directories, and reference books relating to the commerce of all parts of the world. With this regard for the business interest of the members of the Exchange is combined ample provision for their social comfort. On the first-floor is a large luncheon-room, and on the second, smoking and reading-rooms. The whole building is electrically-lighted and, taking all things into consideration, it must be admitted that the members of the Shipping Exchange, who pay an annual subscription of four guineas, if residing in London, and of only half that sum, if residing in the country, get very good value for their money.

The exchange is the property of a limited liability company, whose shareholders form a distinct body from its members. But the object of the Company is the welfare of the shipping trades, rather than the making of dividends, and this much might be inferred from the strong list of the Directors, who number twenty-three out of about 150 shareholders. Sir Donald Currie is Chairman of the Board, and Messrs Alexander Howden, and E. H. Forwood, Vice-Chairmen. Sir Frank Evans, M.P. (Union Steamship Company), Mr C. H. Wilson, M.P. (Thomas Wilson, Sons and Company, Limited), Col. G. R. Birt (Millwall Dock Company), and other men of leading in the shipping world are also on the directorate. Mr Alexander Howden, the senior vice-chairman of the Directors, has taken an exceptionally keen interest in the success of the Exchange. He is often spoken of as 'the Father of the ship-brokers', having been in business as a ship-broker for upwards of fifty years. The arrangements of 'the Room', are under the control of a Committee annually elected by the whole body of members and known as the Room Committee. It numbers twelve, and Mr Henry Langridge is Chairman.

Although the Shipping Exchange is only three years old its members are already beginning to display the *esprit de corps* which comes of association together for a common purpose. A fund has been started for the temporary relief of such members as may be in need through various causes, and in its administration secrecy is held to be of the first importance. The name of any member who may apply for assistance is known to only two members of the small committee which administers the fund and they are under an honourable obligation to keep the name religiously to themselves. This secret service fund, if one may apply the phrase to a work of such unqualified excellence, has so far prospered greatly.

On one occasion in the year this incipient feeling of good-fellowship between the members of the Exchange is greatly stimulated and evoked. This is the rowing match to which 'The Baltic' – the old and well-known centre of commerce in Threadneedle Street – is challenged by eight of the most skilful oarsmen to be found among the members of the Exchange. The race takes place at Putney, and last year was witnessed by members of the two institutions numerous enough to fill two of the large Thames steamers. Mr W. D. Barclay was the first to propose this aquatic contest, saying 'we have to make our living out of craft below bridge, why not get our recreation out of craft above bridge'.

Occasional 'house dinners' at the Exchange have further promoted this *entente cordiale* between the members of the Exchange. The toasts at these dinners have enabled prominent members to discuss various public questions as they affect the interests of the shipping community. On a recent occasion of this kind, for instance, a claim was put forward for a Ministry of Shipping, and it was urged that they should secure the return of a member of Parliament 'who would block all measures calculated to injure shipping and act in the interest of shipping generally'. The members of the Exchange may not live to see the realisation of both these objects, but as an organised and united body their influence will certainly have to be taken into account when legislation affecting their business concerns is brought forward. It was mainly owing to the large meeting recently held in the Exchange, and arranged by the Directors, that a deputation of shipowners, &c, was received by Mr Bryce, the President of the Board of Trade, to hear their views on the new regulations relating to the Rule of the Road at sea.

At South Sea House it was a question of reducing expenditure to a minimum – illumination of the building for the wedding of the Duke of York and Princess May, the future King George V and Queen Mary, on June 23, 1893, at a cost of £340 was declined and the committee left it to members 'to arrange for a few flags' which they bought from Piggott Brothers for £8 11s. At their annual meeting in October the company announced the completion of all the alterations which 'seem in every way to give satisfaction not only to the Committee but to all the Members of the Baltic'. The cost had been £8020. Investments valued at £4700 had been realized for £5256 and went in part payment. The company's income was £12075 and their expenditure £5139, including £1459 interest on preference stock, which gave them a credit balance of £7836. Shareholders were still being paid 17½ per cent.

On the back of the chairman's copy of the accounts Michel Rodocanachi scribbled (as notes for his speech?)

except Restaurant the alterations do not increase value, if we should have to let to others – on the contrary.
Lift – increases cost of working, but is an improvement. we still have an empty room to let first floor. Rent of 8000 furnished & all tax paid – with loss of 1038 average from sale room, is not much, but has given satisfaction receipts from sale room hirings were only £376.

£556 windfall on sale of securities, when so many have depreciated, is a proof of our wise discretion in investing our surplus cash.

Then, in 1894, came the first decrease in the number of members in the history of the committee – 1395 as against 1448, a drop of fifty-three. 'The falling off in the number of Members was to be expected in view of the increased subscriptions and the severe commercial depression which has characterised the year.' Committee income only exceeded expenditure by £174.

Early in 1895 came the inevitable comparison of services between the Baltic and the London Shipping Exchange. A hundred and eleven members signed a petition to the Baltic committee drawing their attention to the fact that although a large proportion of members were engaged in the shipping trade and that a majority of members were interested in the movements of shipping, the information to be obtained in the Room was of the meagre and unsatisfactory description and fell far short of that obtainable at any other leading exchange.

At the 'Shipping Exchange', where the subscription is comparatively nominal, copies of all Lloyd's telegrams are regularly posted, and we shall be glad if you can see your way to make arrangements with Lloyds to have similar information supplied to the 'Baltic' without delay. We would further point out that Members of the 'Baltic' interested in the Grain Trade are most fully supplied with telegraphic information relating to their trade; and it seems to us, therefore, only reasonable that the Shipping Trade should be supplied with all possible information relating to their trade.

Among the signatories were J. Henry Schroder, Ralli Brothers, C. H. Rugg, and Theo Angier. It was not exactly a new request. Bridges Webb, the chairman of the committee, who was a grain man himself, would have seen the typed letter going the rounds for signature, and a week before it was presented had a word with Colonel Henry Hozier, the secretary of Lloyd's, who wrote to him to say he had given the matter thought. 'I do not think you would want anything like the same amount of service as the Shipping Exchange.' He suggested important casualties, arrivals of grain ships at Queenstown and Falmouth, arrivals of grain steamers and sailing ships at Odessa and Black Sea ports, of sailing vessels at

Californian ports and steamers and sailing vessels at Australian ports.

'The above applies only to grain vessels. There may be a difficulty in determining which are grain vessels and which are not, but I have no doubt this would adjust itself as time went on.' He proposed the service should start on March 25, and the petition was dated March 28.

The Baltic's shipping connection was reinforced when at the end of 1895 Nelson Cameron, a director of C. W. Kellock & Co. of Water Street, Liverpool, who was a member of the Baltic (they later moved to London and are still operating today) wrote to Curtis:

We think that your Sale Room would probably suit us to hold our shipping auction sales, and we shall be glad if you will inform us terms and on which floor the room is situated. We presume it must be on the first floor. Please also say whether it is fitted for auctions, with rostrum etc.

On hearing the terms were £2 a time he wrote back to say this was higher than they were accustomed to pay to Lloyd's for the use of their Captains' Room. Nonetheless they booked the room and it was the beginning of a long series of ship sales conducted by Kellock's at the Baltic.

But whether they were shipping or grain orientated the current generation of members were not as sensitive as hitherto to the delicate unformulated relationships on which the whole reputation and tradition of the Baltic depended. 'Several complaints have been made to the Committee during the last two years', reported the committee in 1894, 'of the introduction of Visitors who would certainly not be admitted as Members. The Committee feels that it is desirable their power should be increased to enable them to deal with such cases.'

As Septimus Glover had not been able to attend the committee meeting at which this had been discussed he wrote to Curtis to give his views on the incident which had caused the complaint – the introduction of someone called Reischer – and the steps they should take to prevent a recurrence.

Reischer was introduced on the 1st Feb by Mr F. Smith, clerk in the employment of Messrs Smales, Eeles & Co. My judgement is that the Committee ought to express very strongly to these gentlemen their sense of the impropriety on introducing a gentleman into the Room upon whom a Writ is served shortly after, and I think the question ought to be put to Mr Eeles whether he did not know at the time of introducing Reischer that there were serious claims made against him for breaches or alleged breaches of contract by Members of the Room. No doubt the Committee will admonish all parties that it must not happen again . . .

He proposed posting a notice in the Room as follows:

The Committee feel very strongly that in some recent instances the privilege of introducing Visitors to the Room has been grossly abused, and desire to direct the attention of Members to Rule 14 and to point out that the introduction of persons of doubtful character into the Room may in the judgement of the Committee render the Member so introducing liable to be dealt with under the Rule.

He wanted the rule altered so that members should be made responsible for the visitors they introduced and if a visitor was known by a member to have been charged with conduct derogatory to his character as a businessman, the member would himself become liable to suspension or expulsion.

In April the following year, Bridges Webb wanted members of the committee to be elected by ballot, and three members agreed with him and three disagreed. Septimus Glover cast his chairman's casting vote against Webb, who brought it up again at the meeting in May when it was passed unanimously.

Bridges Webb then made 'formal and serious complaint', to use the words of the minutes, 'that the proceedings of the Committee which met on April 4 were not only reported in The Room but that the names and action taken by individual members of the Committee were reported to Berlin.' He read a letter showing that 'in consequence of such action a refusal to deal with the firms of certain members had taken place'.

'The Chairman spoke very strongly as to the impropriety of this and hoped that all proceedings of that room would be considered privileged, and as a point of honour members would regard them as sacred.'

The Baltic Company, Limited.

DIRECTORS.

MICHEL E. RODOCANACHI, Esq., *Chairman.*

RICHARD BRANDT, Esq.

SIR HENRY EDWARDS.

EDWARD MAJOLIER, Esq.

HENRY F. TIARKS, Esq.

THOMAS USBORNE, Esq.

EDWARD WILSON, Esq.

FORTIETH MEETING OF THE SHAREHOLDERS.

REPORT OF THE DIRECTORS.

Your Directors annex their usual Annual Statement of Accounts made up to 30th September last.

It will be observed that the Balance of Revenue falls rather short of last year.

Under these circumstances your Directors recommend, instead of the usual 17½ per cent., the payment of a dividend of 17 per cent., free of Income Tax, on the Ordinary Stock of the Company (7½ per cent. having been paid in May last), leaving a balance of £79 2s. 9d. to be carried forward.

The Directors who retire by rotation are Sir Henry Edwards, Richard Brandt, Esq., and Edward Wilson, Esq., and, being eligible, offer themselves for re-election.

The Auditor, Mr. H. Bishop, of the firm of Messrs. Turquand, Youngs & Co., also offers himself for re-election.

THREADNEEDLE STREET,

24th October, 1895.

The Baltic Company's annual report of the directors, 1895

London 5 Nov '95

To the Chairman & Committee
of the Baltic

Dear Sir

As a member of the Baltic I advise you
to think twice before electing Mr. Epaminondas
Vardopulo, as a member of the Baltic –
I am informed that he is a bad lot
your truly,

X Y Z

An anonymous letter to the Chairman of the Baltic committee, 1895

Perhaps the attitude of members at this time of great prosperity had become too cynical and frivolous for points of honour and sacred trusts, though the danger of misinterpreting the informality was a real one, as 'Baltico' was quick to point out in *Life on 'the Baltic'*, and *Shipping Idylls for Shipping Idlers*, a series of sketches first published in *Fairplay* in 1895–6 and reprinted as a book by Ward Lock in 1903.

The wily Greek and the almost wilier Hebrew, the cute Yank and the German with spectacles on both outer and inner eyes, are to be found there, together with some of the shrewdest Britons, metropolitan and provincial, who ever wore out shoe leather. Of course these worthies do not look as preternaturally sharp as they really are – that wouldn't suit their book. A stranger would reckon them up as an easy-going lot, a shade stupid perhaps, rather than otherwise; but let that stranger get into business relations with a few of them and then deliver his verdict. If he is a truthful man he will confess, possibly in language interlarded with wicked cuss words, that he has been as clay in the hands of the potter. When it is remembered that every hour of the business day the Balticers are competing keenly for what is going and sharpening their wits upon one another, it is not to be wondered at that most of them should have become double-distilled business diplomatists, and that some exceptional ones should have developed powers placing them on a par with the miracle-working deities of ancient Greece.

Much of what he wrote was caricature, and, in spite of a sustained heartiness of style typical of the period, 'Baltico' evokes a lively picture of the misleadingly dilettante atmosphere of the Old Baltic with its young bloods like Beautiful Bountie Bertie, the leader of the *jeunesse dorée* of the Room, resplendent in frock coat with well-squared shoulders 'and a vast display of "garden truck" in the button-hole' who, adjusting his topper, casually remarks to Tom Forsit, ' "Got anythin' spiffin' for my bally boat?" '

He described how Micklepipe with the impressive manner did his best to get 14s. for an Azoff boat from Bruggles who was sticking at 13s. 6d.

'Split the difference' splutters the agent 'and we'll call it a fix.' 'I have no authority under 14s. and you must take it or leave it. I don't want to go to Dryasdust, but of course if I must I must, and I don't think he'll haggle over threepence.' The wily Micklepipe knows his man; a little more persuasion and the fateful stamp is affixed. 'A solid threepence above the market'

I

murmurs the cute old hand as he saunters off to his office to wire acceptance –
while a little later in the day Bruggles learns, much to his disgust, that
Dryasdust had already been approached and declined the boat at anything
over 13s. 6d.

There was nothing in the code of conduct against tricking a
customer like this; it was clever and expected. If the tack had
taken him off his guard, so much the worse for him. He would
never complain of the other's 'sharp practice', only admire him for
being so 'cute'. At the eighth anniversary Baltic dinner at the
Trocadero John Wrenn said 'neighbourly feeling, fair dealing and
straight speaking have come to stay and increase and multiply
among us' and meant it. 'With us', he continued, 'dwells a decorum
of demeanour which I think is above the average of most commercial concourses. Other and perhaps neighbouring institutions
may have their bear fights and their bull fights, their cockpits and
their corners, but the delicate dignity of the Baltic revolts at even
the innocent innovation of a guileless grain ring.'

There was little delicate dignity, however, behind the scenes, out
of view and hearing of members – in the booth where Henry
Goodfellow, the telephone attendant, worked.

The National Telephone Company wrote to Curtis,

I must really ask you to instruct your telephone attendant to endeavour to
work more amicably with our exchange operators. I am having continual
complaints of the difficulty there is in working with him, & it is now complained that he uses very objectionable language to them, going so far as to
threaten one that he would 'screw her neck'.

But instantaneous communication which needed neither attention nor attendant was not far away. For in that year of 1895,
when Micklepipe sauntered off to his office to wire acceptance, a
young English telegraphist, called G. F. Creed, was inventing the
Morse keyboard tape perforator to actuate a typewriter mechan-
ism; this was to lead to the machine which revolutionized communications at the Baltic and similar institutions even more than
the telephone – the teleprinter.

But for many years yet life on the Baltic was to be as 'Baltico'
so amusingly described it in his opening piece:

It is only reasonable that the pictures we propose to take of men and things connected with Britain's national industry should deal more particularly with the Baltic, the central institution of the world's greatest port, though for how much longer London will retain this honourable position remains to be seen. What with 'Made in Germany' scares, and grasping and short-sighted Dock Boards, the time may not be far distant when a few coasting steamers and begrimed colliers will constitute the entire trade of the port. A view of the future shipless Thames is not, however, included in our gallery, and for the sake of those budding brokers whose subscriptions have so recently been paid, let us hope that 'a few more years shall roll' before the last stamp has to be licked, and the last charter signed within the sacred precincts of the Room.

Dealing for a moment with the building itself, sandwiched at the north-east end of Threadneedle Street between the once infamous South Sea House and what was until lately the new Oriental Bank, one feels that in size and accommodation we are put to shame by such noble structures as the Liverpool and Glasgow Exchanges. True, within the last few years some improvements have been wrung out of the impoverished shareholders who have to put up with a petty forty or fifty per cent annually on their capital, but considering the magnitude of the trade carried on within its dingy walls by its 1400 members, one cannot help feeling that a more commodious, comfortable, and imposing structure would be in better keeping with the proprieties and the times. But in such matters poor old London advances slowly. Doubtless to the *habitués* of the old Baltic Coffee House a couple of centuries ago the present arrangements would appear palatial. A vision of electric lights and whirring air distributors would be apt to distract the attention of the old-time merchants, while the click of the tape and the irritable 'Are you there' of the telephone would certainly have hastened their departure to the creepy stillness of St Botolph or Crutched Friars. The most fearsome innovation would have been the Brobdingnagian speaking-trumpet of sixteen-inch calibre and 200 i.h.p. through which the gentleman with the gold braid and buttons announces that James John Jenkins or Theophilus Maurogadotarus is wanted.

Any misguided visitor who chances to get within close range (gold braid is an adept at drawing ahead on an innocent) and encounters the full blast of some fifteen syllable Greek name, is never quite sure whether he has been caught in a tornado or whether this is the 'sudden fall in the market' he hears so much about in the country. At any rate, he is never quite the same man again, in spite of a prompt request at the spiritual end of the Room for something that will keep the sound out – and soothe the startled nervous system.

A nice, quiet, comfortable time they must have had of it in those bygone days, when they met over their posset of sack or glass of Canary, inter-mingled with a whiff of their churchwardens. No telegrams arriving to upset their equanimity by announcing that Simon and Sludge were buying wheat freely, and wouldn't they follow their lead as the market was stiffening? No imperative instructions to charter a 15000 qrs. boat and sell the cargo at a given price, all within a couple of hours. Then, as now, the grain trade figured largely at this resort, and there is no reason to doubt that, in a quiet and health-giving way, the forbears of our wily Levantines were very much in evidence in their endeavours to sweat an extra ha'penny a quarter out of the British buyer. It was never theirs to know the cold chill which runs down the back of the spec charterer, when he hears by wire of the unexpected (no pun intended) arrival at Constantinople of the s.s. *Pusher*, with her orders due in twelve hours, and not a pound of cargo arranged for. Nor did the arrival of a Greek brig, or a Turkish palacca, at a Danubian port necessitate the departure up country of the charterer 'to look for his cargo'. They had time then to do things decently, and in order, and if there were any pigeons to be plucked the operation was performed leisurely, but thoroughly, with a total avoidance of the unbecoming haste which so frequently characterizes the operation nowadays. Not but that the thoroughness remains.

Apart from the active (sharp is so ambiguous) and up-to-date descendants of the early Greeks, so prominent to-day in the Room, we jostle against numbers of an essentially modern and daily increasing class, the combination managing shipowner and broker. Some very fine and jolly fellows among them, too, and later on we hope to come to closer quarters with lots of them. It is hardly their fault that they are placed in the somewhat paradoxical position of, as owners, declining with scorn business which the next minute they, as honest brokers, do their level best to induce their brother owners in the country to accept. There are, of course, among them the very wide-awake gentlemen who, with the command of boats, take up a contract, and if freights drop below the figure they have guaranteed, do not hesitate to go into the market and charter cheaper tonnage, the profit going to themselves as *brokers*, and when freights rise upon them, then the poor shareholders have to stand the onus of their manager's little job.

Rubbing shoulders with them are fewer in number, owners pure and simple, who confine their entire attention to looking after the interests of their fellow shareholders. Their own stake is usually greater than that of any of their colleagues, and unlike the modern [1895] manager with his £100 stake and an unlimited capacity for brokerages and pickings, their business is to make as much profit as possible for all concerned. The old-fashioned owner who used to put his entire capital in a ship is now, alas! seldom to be met with. The single ship-companies have pushed him into the background. If lucky, he may have retired on the profits of half a century ago, or as the result of continuing the struggle too long, be chopping firewood in the local Union.

Following close upon the heels of the shipowner proper are scores of nimble brokers. No need for them to waste time on the manager-broker genius. They know that what crumbs are going in that direction are promptly assimilated by the joint affair; but there is still business to be done with the other kind of owner, and many are the mysterious and confidential whisperings between the two as they lounge against a central pillar, or gaze into each other's optics across one of the narrow tables which adorn the room.

Then we have the merchants or charterers, the men who deal in full cargoes of produce, and who fix with the cheapest man. These gentlemen can sign a charter right off, and with perhaps a million or so behind their signature one can imagine that said signature is eagerly sought after on a document. Not always do these lords of commerce mingle with the common herd, but their trusted representative may generally be found the centre of a respectful group of owners and brokers.

Occupying a little lower grade in the scale, though not in their own estimation, come the chartering agents, the men who act for charterers 'on the other side', which may mean any port from Antwerp to Adelaide or Havre to Hong Kong. Their motto is 'By cable authority' and with half a dozen of the tribe working on one and the same order the competition for a boat makes things 'hum' occasionally. Perhaps the most exhilarating display of this kind of business is to be found in the Danube and Black Sea market, where the agents have not only to compete with one another, but with many resident principals.

Then, not necessarily conspicuous by a general air of shabbiness, we here and there encounter the men who run to 'seed', dealers in all kinds of the Eastern article, not forgetting cotton-seed from Alexandria. Various studies in oils may be observed dotted round the room, while tallow makes shiny the pillars and corners of seats. Timber has its votaries, and even vendors of black diamonds forsake their own special domain in Billingsgate to capture a few bunker orders. The Stock Exchange sends emissaries to keep an eye on foreign markets and to provide against a too sudden attack on the bulls and bears of Capel Court.

As a result of a ballot in 1897 the Baltic was closed every afternoon at 4.30 instead of 5. It was the wish of the majority but at least one member objected to the way the daily closing was carried out.

If it is the general sense of the members that official change shall be over at a certain hour well & good, & it should then be left to each individual to leave the building as may suit himself, the attendants should not drive them out like police or Park keepers clearing the Park. Further I protest against the attendants proceeding almost to personal violence to prevent a member entering after the bell has gone. At Lloyd's they manage matters in a very different manner but members are not excluded from the room.

More unflattering comparisons.

A contemporary description of South Sea House in 1896 in *Chambers's Journal* (July 11) called it a large, dingy, red-brick building with 'The Baltic' in bold relief above the granite doorway. A visitor

finds himself in a spacious room, with a low roof supported by Corinthian pillars. Pillars indeed are everywhere, the whole appearance of the building, both externally and internally, being suggestive of a patchwork arrangement which, he learns, is the result of certain structural alterations effected within recent years, with the object of increasing the space available for members. The wall on his left contains a succession of handsome mirrors, also a large clock and a wind-dial, which, he afterwards discovers, are specially useful as well as evidently ornamental. Ranged along this wall is a leather-covered Sybaritic settee, whose continuity is broken only by the large fireplace in the centre, also suggestive of comfort. He is told that when business is slack, members loll and take their ease on this seat, chatting – not always 'shop' – or reading the daily papers and periodicals, a liberal supply of which is provided. He finds at the western end of the room an alcove, with a table in the centre, upon which are the principal illustrated papers and several foreign journals – French, German, Greek, and Italian; the corresponding portion of the opposite side forming the Secretary's office. At the eastern end, just outside the private entrance to the building, he sees on the left a luncheon room and refreshment bar, where the members fortify the inner man against the wear and tear of their afternoon 'contracts', or search for 'contracts'.

After passing at the right hand corner, a pulpit-like structure, in which yet another leather-lunged official shouts out the names of members who are wanted by fellow-members, he discovers a telegraph office, outside of which is a succession of pigeon-holes containing inland and foreign telegram forms. Lower down, he finds a very complete telephonic system, embracing nine felt-walled cells, which effectually deaden all sound to and from the speaker, after he has been 'switched on' by the attendant in the telephone-box. Pursing his explorations, he comes across a variety of foreign telegrams from the leading grain centres of the world, and these give him the first clue to the nature of the business transacted within the building. His attention is next attracted by one of the Exchange Company's tape machines, where he may see an anxious speculator eagerly noting the fluctuations of the stock markets in which he is interested. Close by is a door leading down a flight of steps to the underground apartments, which consist of a lavatory, well looked after by attendants, and an inner room where newspaper files are carefully preserved. He learns that there are also other subterranean rooms, in one of which the Committee of Management meet for their deliberations. A casual glance during his peregrinations up-stairs has revealed to him the fact that the comfort of members in the matter of writing-tables, books of reference, and so forth, is attended to in a way which leaves little to be desired.

Assuming that the room is well filled, which it invariably is at noon and between four and five in the afternoon, the hum of voices which arises from the silk-hatted, keen-faced throng is suggestive of a huge beehive. Between four and five, the sound increases in volume, until just before five, when the doors of the building are closed for the day, it reaches its maximum, and so does the volume of smoke for cigars and cigarettes are permitted after 4.30 P.M. Daring spirits have introduced, in summer, straw-hats into that conservative institution, but no one has yet had the temerity to light up a 'briar-root'. An unwritten law tabooing pipes is in existence, and the stony glare of the staid old members, to be followed, possibly, by a report to a shocked Committee, would probably meet the daring innovator, and annihilate the innovation. Ere our supposed visitor has found himself once more outside the building, a wiser, and possibly not a sadder man, he will have learned that the 'Baltic' is the great emporium in London for foreign grain, with ramifications, however, which embrace other trades of smaller dimensions.

South Sea House is the property of 'The Baltic' Company, Limited, who receive a rental of £8000 a year from 'The Baltic' Committee, a body of leading men elected annually by the members of the room to manage their affairs for them. The Company is in a very flourishing condition, its £100 shares being worth about £700.

Wheat, of course, is the chief market of all, and its power is such that it often exerts an indirect influence over articles which have to all appearance only the remotest connection with it. Often the price of wheat affects, not only that of maize and of barley, &c, but also to a more or less appreciable extent that of linseed and cottonseed, owing to the cake products of these articles being used for [animal] feeding purposes. And the freight markets are directly influenced by the state of the grain markets; when the latter are brisk, chartering proceeds with a swing; and conversely, when grain [trade] is stagnant, there is little demand for tonnage, and rates of freight generally fall. The various branches of business on 'The Baltic' are therefore interlaced in a remarkable manner, notwithstanding their apparent diversity.

Occasionally speculation is rife in a particular article; but during recent years the speculative spirit has been largely dormant. Prices have ruled so low that 'bear' sellers have fought shy of going 'short' to any considerable extent, whilst there has been an absence of the 'bull' element, in view of the downward trend of prices generally. A good many years ago, tallow was an article which formed the subject of extensive gambling, but it now occupies a comparatively subordinate position in the affairs of the Exchange. Auction sales of this article take place every Friday in a small room in South Sea House, and members are duly apprised of them by an official ringing a bell at noon, followed by the announcement in stentorian tones: 'Tallow sales are about to commence, gentlemen.'

Huge operations having as their object the 'rigging of the market' are unknown on 'The Baltic'. 'Wheat corners' and 'maize rings', names of dire portent on the other side of the Atlantic, are never attempted here; in view, indeed, of the increase in the number of exporting countries, and in the quantities of their exports, operations of this description would be altogether too Herculean a task to undertake, unless under circumstances which are unlikely to arise. But Brother Jonathan nevertheless too often rules the English grain markets with a rod of iron. For wheat and maize markets on this side follow America very closely; and any large rise or fall in New York or Chicago is at once reflected in prices here. Needless to say, the fluctuations in America are due very frequently to the most unscrupulous tactics on the part of 'shorts' and 'longs', who manipulate the markets, and send prices up or down according to the strength of the opposing cliques. The English consumer thus has sometimes to pay for the so-called cuteness of Yankee operators. When the grain markets are brisk on 'The Baltic', the arrival of the American cablegram giving the opening prices of wheat and maize in New York and Chicago is awaited with, occasionally, feverish anxiety, and prices close better or worse according to the news from 'the other side'. The great influence thus exerted by New York and Chicago is of course primarily due to the dependence of this country on America for wheat and maize, a condition of affairs which will probably undergo a gradual change as other grain-exporting countries, more particularly perhaps the Argentine Republic, develop their rapidly expanding resources and export trade. At present South Russia ranks next to America in importance as a grain-exporting centre; Australian wheat is now a factor to be reckoned with; and India is always ready to export wheat when prices encourage shipments. Calcutta and Bombay still rule the linseed market, although their supremacy is being yearly more and more disputed by La Plata, whose exports generally, owing to a fertile soil, cheap labour, and a paper currency, have increased enormously in recent years. Cottonseed is entirely in the hands of Egypt, and she shares – but it is the lion's share – the bean trade with Morocco and Smyrna.

By a tacit understanding, for the sake of convenience, each trade has its own particular corner of the room, where those members who are engaged in it meet and transact business. Near the entrance to the room is the freight market, where current rates from Odessa, from the Danube, from Alexandria, from the River Plate, are discussed, and where expressions such as 'laydays', 'cancelling dates', 'deadweight capacity' are heard all around. In the centre of the room, linseed is the prevailing topic, and one can learn the price of 'spot Calcutta' or 'May–June Plate'. The same brokers will tell one the current value of 'November–January cottonseed', or of 'July–August brown Cawnpore rapeseed'. At the farther end of the room, wheat and feeding stuffs reign supreme. The prices of 'No. 1 Californian' wheat on passage; June–July 'Plate' maize; May–June 'Azof' barley; and March–April 'Libau' oats become familiar to the ear. One learns that the months refer to the periods during which the produce must be shipped; that the mysterious expression which sounds like 'siff' means c.i.f. – say cost, insurance, and freight; that 'rye terms' are more favourable to a buyer than '*tale quale*'; that produce is often sold before it is shipped, and sometimes before it is grown; that f.a.q. means 'fair average quality', being a guarantee which obviates the necessity of showing samples, the display of which in the room is indeed forbidden.

Produce valued at many thousands of pounds daily changes ownership, without the production of a single document binding the bargain, until the contract notes are drawn out and signed. Confidence in mutual integrity after the conclusion of a bargain forms the basis of this apparently loose system, and any one abusing this confidence, say by repudiating a bargain, would be reported to the Committee, and upon conviction would be instantly relieved of his membership. Any disputes arising out of contracts are settled by arbitration, each side appointing an arbitrator; should the arbitrators fail to agree, an umpire is called in, whose decision is final. In this way disputes are settled quickly, inexpensively, and satisfactorily by practical men, a method infinitely preferable to setting in motion the cumbrous and expensive machinery of the law-courts.

'The Baltic' affords the opportunities so important to a commercial man, of transacting a maximum of business with a minimum of time and trouble. A merchant can sell a cargo of produce for shipment at some future period, and can then proceed to another part of the room and charter a steamer against the sale. Assuming that he has secured a profit on the transaction – a contingency which frequently the future course of markets can alone determine – he can afterwards, without leaving the room, seek out a stockbroker, and through him either invest his profit in 'gilt-edged securities', or speculate with it in the Kaffir Circus or in Westralians. Some years ago, when trade was in a more flourishing condition than at present, members of the Stock Exchange were largely in evidence on the floor of 'The Baltic', but their visits have of late been less frequent. In a sense, they may be termed the 'barometers of The Baltic', for by their presence or absence may be gauged pretty accurately the volume of business which is being transacted, and the profits which are being made, within the walls of the building. A certain pregnant saying might here suggest itself to the irreverent mind, but one refrains from associating the stockbrokers who frequent 'The Baltic' with the gathering together of birds of prey, 'eagles' or otherwise, or their clients with the 'carcase' which provides a sumptuous feast.

And if the vocations of the members vary, how much more their nationalities. A more cosmopolitan assemblage of business men it would be difficult to imagine. Even 'English as she is spoke' by Englishmen on 'The Baltic' varies materially in accent and purity. The Irish brogue may occasionally be heard mingling with a *soupçon* of the Scottish Doric; Jew and Gentile, Frenchman and German, Greek and Russian, Belgian and Italian; all creeds and no creeds, and nearly all European nations, are represented. The Germans and the Greeks form a considerable proportion of the foreign element, both in numbers and influence; some of the Greek merchants, particularly, are among the wealthiest members of the Exchange.

On Mondays, Wednesdays, and Fridays, members may be seen in large numbers at the Corn Exchange in Mark Lane, where the brokers meet their country clients, and exhibit samples of grain which they have for sale. And every afternoon there is an exodus of those members engaged in the oilseed and cognate trades to the Royal Exchange, where sellers and buyers come into free contact with one another. 'Going on 'change' is a daily duty which is rigorously observed, whether or not it is likely to be productive of business.

8. Absorption by City of London Exchange Syndicate

Members of the Baltic would soon have stopped going on 'change if it had not been productive of the kind of business they knew would only come their way on the floor of 'the great emporium in London for foreign grain' and the corners of it which every day became freight, linseed, feeding stuffs and wheat markets.

It was a monopoly which Ernest Forwood told his shareholders he hoped the London Shipping Exchange would one day emulate. 'I have full confidence' he told the fourth annual general meeting at Billiter Street in 1896, 'that when it [the London Shipping Exchange] has acquired the position of other similar monopolies such as the Baltic, it will be a most remunerative investment for those shareholders who have the patience to wait.' At their next annual general meeting he told them their premises would shortly be inadequate, and that should suitable premises worthy of the shipping interests of London be offered at a reasonable rent they would consider them.

Theo Angier was one of the many members of the Baltic who also belonged to, and was a shareholder of, the London Shipping Exchange, and in 1921 (when he was the second oldest member of the Baltic at seventy-eight) he wrote a letter from Menton where he was in retirement reminiscing about this period at Billiter Street.

When the exchange was first formed, he recollected, only a minority of its directors wanted a big company with a capital of

half a million pounds or so which would enable it to buy land
and erect a building on it worthy of the great national industry of
Shipping. This was at a time when the Jeffreys Square site would
have been obtainable. In his view, the majority of the London
Shipping Exchange promoters lacked the necessary courage, and
so opted to lease premises in Billiter Street and raise only sufficient
capital for this smaller project. 'This served its purpose for a few
years but the small progressive minority of the directors, Mr
Forwood, Langridge and myself (reinforced by Mr Findlay's un-
varied tho' tactful and modest support) never let go the conviction
that the position warranted, demanded and would guarantee
success for the bolder and large enterprise.'

By 'the position' Theo Angier presumably meant the increasing
number of applicants for membership of the London Shipping
Exchange. Only timidity seemed to hamper the progress of that
exchange, but any next move by the Baltic committee had to wait
for the expiration of the lease of South Sea House which was not
going to be until September 29, 1899. When three directors of the
Baltic Company, Sir Henry Edwards, Edward Majolier and
Richard Brandt, died in 1897, and Thomas Usborne the following
year, there seemed to be a changing of the old guard. But there
could be no short cuts.

The company's income in 1898 was £11998, about the same as
the year before. Expenditure was only £4916. The value of South
Sea House was still put as £70000. Chairman Rodocanachi's notes
for his speech at the AGM were, as usual, revealing:

Whenever altered
valuation of 70000
if we wish to pay cost
valuation will be nearer
280000 – Revenue 7000
would equal 3,66 !

We are reasonable in only asking them
not to be troublesome in asking little
things to be done from time to time

lease of 6 mths notice is no security & no one
wd let to them on such terms. We could get as
good a rent from others & we cannot alter the
terms proposed
Lease expires 29 Sept 1899; 6 mths notice they can
give it up. Comp. pays all the rates & taxes; furnished.

including basement the area is 10390 ft
where can they find that & at what price

the position of the comp. is satisfactory and
with the prices now paid in the city for
freeholds and the increase of rents I will tell
you that we have a safe and good property

There had been an interesting change of mind from 1893 when Rodocanachi's notes showed he did not consider alterations would increase the value of the building. Now in 1897 he estimated that with alterations the book value of £70000 would become £280000. But the Baltic Committee were not to be deterred from exploring the possibility of a break with the old rooms and making a fresh start elsewhere. In November 1898 they engaged a separate solicitor, J. A. Tilleard, and estate agents S. Quinton & Son to advise them regarding a 'proposed new building'.

The sub-committee handling the matter met Goymour Cuthbert, the architect, on Monday December 6 to discuss the plans, and over the weekend the news leaked. On Thursday Curtis received a letter from Findlay proposing a merger (illustrated overleaf).

Curtis was told to write back to Findlay asking him if he would be good enough to call upon the chairman of the committee, Septimus Glover, at 88 Bishopsgate either the next day, Friday, or on Monday. Whether the chairman met James Findlay and or Ernest Forwood at his office is not known, but on the Monday (December 12), probably following a meeting, Ernest Forwood wrote to Septimus Glover at Bishopsgate Street as follows:

TELEGRAPHIC ADDRESS,
"TRIREME, LONDON."
TELEPHONE Nº
11370 & 11371.

BILLITER STREET,

LONDON. E.C. 8ᵗʰ Dec 1898

Dear Sir,

My Directors have noticed in the Press that your Committee have under consideration the question of removing to other premises & I have been requested to ascertain if they will receive a deputation from them to consider the expediency of bringing both bodies of Members under one roof.

I shall be glad to have your reply as soon as possible

Thanking you in anticipation.

Yours faithfully,

The Secretary,
The "Baltic" Committee

J... ....
Secretary.

---

*Letter from James Findlay, Secretary of the London Shipping Exchange to the
Secretary of the Baltic committee proposing a merger, 1898*

Forwood Bros & Co
3 Crosby Square, London, EC.
12th December 1898

Septimus Glover Esq.,
88, Bishopsgate Street, EC.

Dear Mr Glover,

As promised you to-day I now write you with reference to the proposed idea of seeing whether some arrangement could not be arrived at that will enable the members of the Baltic Exchange and the members of the Shipping Exchange joining together and building an Exchange worthy of the City of London. Ever since I have been in London – some twenty eight years or more – I have found it irksome to have to attend so many Exchanges in order to be able to carry on my business; I also have found it very costly in as much as I have to subscribe for my clerks being members both of the Shipping Exchange and the Baltic. Now, if anything could be done to concentrate the trade of the City under one roof it would prove a great boon to the City commercial world, especially seeing now that everybody has to get through more work in a day than was the case in the past. I have for two years studied all the different sites in the City and the only site which would give the area necessary for such a General Shipping Exchange I find to be in Jeffrey's Square. This site was found not to be out of the way and by arrangement passages through certain buildings could be made which would make it half way between Mincing Lane and the Baltic and would come within a few yards of Billiter Street. I would point out to you that owing to traffic etc. the Mansion House is virtually out of the City Community, and between that and the Baltic is mainly taken up by the financial world, and therefore the bulk of your members are located more in the direction of Jeffreys Sq. than the Baltic. I have analysed your members and I find that 662 are located nearer to Jeffreys Sq. than the Baltic, and 807 of our members are similarly located.

I need not now go into details with reference to the cost of the site, building etc. but you may take it from me that for a rental of £5000 a year very fine premises could be obtained, both for Exchange and Club purposes. The ground area would be about 12000 feet with good light at three sides, and in basement dining rooms etc. for the use of members could be provided. I calculate that within 12 months of signing the contract everything would be ready.

I would suggest that your Committee should look well into the matter as I feel sure the more the matter is studied the more feasible it will become.

Yours faithfully,
E. H. Forwood

Jeffery's Square, Jeffrey's Square or Jeffrey Square was at least 250 years old. It was shown in John Rocque's map of 1746 as Jeffery's Square lying between St Mary Axe and 'Berry Street' to the north of Leadenhall Street on land reputed to have belonged to monks in Bury in Suffolk. It was a small cul-de-sac hidden from St Mary Axe and approached from it by a narrow alley flanked by No 26 and No 28, much as Sun Court with the Baltic Coffee-House in it was approached from Threadneedle Street by the narrow Hercules Passage. Beneath the square ran a broad stream on its way from Highgate to the Thames. At the end was a single mansion of two storeys with a bowed front and twelve large windows of equal size surmounted by a balustrade. A wide pavement enclosed a cobbled courtyard at the end of which, in front of the mansion, stood a solitary lamp-post. It was a fashionable place of residence in the reign of Queen Anne (who died in 1714). Thomas Coutts, who was born in 1735, was for some time a partner with his brother Patrick in a house there. There was once a coat of arms in the square and as far as it could be deciphered its motto read '*Je Ferai . . .*' No such motto or armorial bearings were registered at the College of Arms and it was assumed that Jeffery Square was a corruption of the French motto '*Je Ferai*'. It was further presumed that a French nobleman once had a residence there. In the church of St Andrew Undershaft, at the corner of St Mary Axe and Leadenhall Street, are monuments to a family called Jeffreys but no connection is known between them and the square so named.

It was in Jeffrey's Square that Dickens located the firm of Cheeryble Brothers; here Tim Linkwater resided, and here came Nicholas Nickleby to make the beginning of his prosperity.

In the street called St Mary Axe – the 'Simmery Axe' of John Wellington Wells, the Sorcerer of Gilbert's operetta – once stood the church of St Mary the Virgin, St Ursula and the Eleven Thousand Virgins which housed as a holy relic an axe used in the legendary massacre of St Ursula and her virgins at Cologne in the fifth century. This church became a warehouse in the sixteenth century. The church of St Andrew Undershaft, which still stands today, is famous for its tomb of John Stow, the London historian, whose

The façade of the City of London Tavern which became the Wesleyan Centenary Hall (on the site of the Bank of India demolished in 1976) in Bishopsgate, facing South Sea House, which members were asked to vote on as a possible location for 'The Baltic'

Jeffrey's Square, demolished in 1900 to make way for the new Baltic Exchange

Sketches from the *Shipping World* of April 29, 1903, made during the opening ceremony at the new Exchange. *Note:* the Chairman of the Baltic at the time (depicted right) was W. Bridges Webb

Opposite above: An architect's model of the Baltic Exchange in St Mary Axe, as it was built

Opposite below: The Lord Mayor of London lays the foundation stone of the new Exchange at St Mary Axe on June 25, 1901

The end of the room

The Lord Mayor declaring the new exchange open.

What might have been. A
proposed, and later rejected,
design for the new Exchange

Opposite below: The
Floor of the Baltic
Exchange, *circa* 1916

SKETCHES AT "THE BALTIC."—I.

James Arbuckle Findlay,
Secretary of the Baltic
1899–1932

Opposite above: A rival of
the Baltic, Moxhay's Hall
of Commerce in
Threadneedle Street, seen
here as Parr's Bank shortly
before its demolition. A
drawing in *The Sphere*, 1921

Opposite below: The
building which housed the
London Shipping Exchange
at 19–21 Billiter Street, as
it is today

Gilbert Findlay, Secretary
of the Baltic, 1932–54

Above: Jack Walker, Secretary of the Baltic, 1954–68

Left: Derek Walker, the present Secretary of the Baltic

father was a tallow chandler. It was at the corner where this church stands that Samuel Pepys described how on January 24, 1644,

at noon going to the 'Change and seeing people flock in the City, I enquired and found that [James] Turner [a solicitor who had robbed a merchant called Fryon] was not yet hanged. And so I went among them on Leadenhall Street at the end of Lyme Street near where the robbery was done; and to St Mary Axe where he lived. And there I got for a shilling to stand upon the wheel of a cart, in great pain, above an houre before the execution was done; he delaying the time by long discourses and prayers one after another, in hopes of a reprieve; but none came, and at last was flung off the ladder in his cloake. It was believed there were at least 12 to 14000 people in the street.

Less infamous people than the thieving lawyer had lived in St Mary Axe, which was once a Harley Street with the houses of leading physicians and surgeons – Sir Astley Cooper, the surgeon, lived at No 12. J. L. Toole, the actor, was born at No 50.

A special meeting of the Baltic committee was summoned for Wednesday, December 14 to consider Forwood's letter. Septimus Glover was in the chair, and the others were Bridges Webb, Seth Taylor, Ashton, Henderson, Mendl and Seymour. The minute read:

A Letter was read from Mr E. H. Forwood inviting the Baltic Committee to join the Shipping Exchange to purchase a site and build a large Exchange in Jeffries Square so as to unite the two institutions. After due consideration the chairman was requested to reply and state that this Committee was not at present free to consider the proposal, being somewhat committed in another negotiation.

Septimus Glover confirmed the decision to Ernest Forwood in a letter from his office the day after the meeting. (see illustration overleaf).
And that, for the time being, was that.

The negotiations which made the Baltic committee unable to entertain the idea of fusion with the London Shipping Exchange in December 1898 were for the building about which Stephen Ralli had written to Sir William McArthur in 1886, the Wesleyan Centenary Hall at 17 Bishopsgate.

This was a less forbidding and more suitable building than its name implied. For in fact it was something that has already featured

88, Bishopsgate Street

15/12/98

Dear Sir,

I read your letter re the suggested
fusion of the Baltic & Shipping Exchange and
the building which might be erected in
Jeffries Square, to the Committee of the Baltic
today.

I am instructed to express to you
their thanks for the suggestion and their
regret that at present they are not able to
entertain the matter as they are already in
negotiation for other premises.

Allow me to add my personal thanks, especially
for your courtesy in shewing me the Site&c.

Yours faithfully,

(sd) S.J.Gl over.

E.H.Forwood Esq.

Letter from Septimus Glover to Ernest Forwood rejecting the proposed merger, 1898

in this story under another guise – the City of London Tavern (not to be confused with the London Tavern, also in Bishopsgate Street). The heart of the building was a mansion built for Sir Roger Hudson, a wealthy merchant, to a design of Christopher Wren to replace the building destroyed in the Fire of London. For a period in the mid-eighteenth century it stood empty and was acquired by Messrs Terry, Peacock and Terry who added to it and converted it into the City of London Tavern. A writer of 1809 described its assembly room as 'the most spacious apartment of this nature in this or perhaps in any other city'. It could seat 400 to dinner. Many state banquets were held there. On the first floor were a grand saloon and drawing rooms 20 feet high. Below the street were cellars and vaults 'not unaptly compared with the Catacombs' and a well for holding 400 loads of ice. In 1838 the proprietors put the tavern up for sale including its chandeliers, plate, and 2000 bottles of port, sherry and madeira. A representative of the Wesleyan Methodist Connexion attended the auction and bought building and contents for £15000. They had just received a grant of £30000 with which to celebrate the centenary of Methodism, and with the other £15000 they made substantial alterations, particularly to the front. For the next sixty years they used it as their headquarters and Mission Hall. But by the 1880s they had outgrown it and were planning to go elsewhere. But there were not many who were ready to buy it; considerable rebuilding would be needed.

Septimus' Glover's letter to Ernest Forwood of December 15 was far from bluff; on the 19th Curtis gave notice of a special general meeting of members to be held on January 3 'for the purpose of considering and if so resolved, of approving, the provisional arrangements made by the Committee for acquiring new premises in the Wesleyan Centenary Hall'.

But before they considered this members were invited by Septimus Glover who was in the chair to give their views on the offer of the Baltic Company to renew the lease of their rooms at South Sea House for another seven years on the understanding that members paid for alterations and repairs. He told them that the company had said they were in the course of other negotiations to let or sell the building, so their offer was only open till the 31st. They had ascertained that the property was worth more than was being asked for, but in deference to the number of years the members had occupied the Room they had decided not to increase the rent.

Both Edouard Majolier, son of Edward Majolier and a director of the company, and Michel Rodocanachi, chairman of the company, as well as Ernest Forwood of the London Shipping Exchange were present as members of the Room. The proceedings began with Majolier being invited to put the views of the company. He dismissed as unfounded the assertion that the company wanted £2000 a year more in rent.

I believe now that if the committee were to appoint as a sub-committee a certain number of reasonable gentlemen (loud laughter) – well, a certain number of gentlemen (laughter) – to meet the company, matters could be arranged satisfactorily. As to the idea that the company could allow you to remain another year while the new room is being built [at the Wesleyan Hall] I am sorry to say that I do not think that can be done. We are already far advanced in certain negotiations and until this – what shall I call it? – agitation (laughter) we really had not the slightest idea as to the value of our property (loud laughter and cries of 'Oh!'). At the same time I am sure the Baltic Company has no desire whatever to dislocate this important part of the commerce of the City of London and would make very considerable sacrifices – though possibly it might be against the interests of their own pockets to make any arrangements as I believe they could very possibly do better if the Baltic left them – in order to avoid breaking off the friendly relations that have hitherto existed between the committee and themselves.

Septimus Glover then turned to the second offer which was for a seven-, fourteen- or twenty-one-year lease of the ground floor and basement of the Wesleyan Centenary Hall at a rental of £6500 a year for the first period, £7000 for the second and £7500 for the third (South Sea House was costing them £8000 a year).

The two propositions were debated at length, and finally a resolution was put to the meeting: 'That having heard the statement of the Chairman on behalf of the Committee, this meeting of Members of The Baltic, having entire confidence in the Committee, gives them full authority to do what they think best in the circumstances in the interest of the Members of the Room.'

It was a great climax to the hard work of the committee and a personal triumph for Septimus Glover.

Before he received this comforting confirmation of his victory Glover wrote to Curtis as secretary of the company on January 7, clutching at the olive branch of conciliation so patently held out by Edouard Majolier in his strange speech:

> The Committee of the Baltic will be glad if two Members of the Baltic Coy would meet Mr Power [Vice-chairman] & myself to talk over present difficulties and see if it is possible to bridge them over before the Committee take any further action. Please communicate this to the coy.

But those who were dissatisfied with a turn of events which took further initiative out of their hands and gave it to the committee made a final attempt to influence their fellow-members by issuing a circular, the contents of which have not survived but presumably was putting the case for Jeffrey's Square. Frederick Curtis, the servant of the committee, allowed himself to be persuaded to countenance their design by authorizing the posting of it inside the Baltic and helping to draft it. The minute of a special meeting of the committee called to consider the matter read:

> The Chairman having reported the issue of the Circular signed by Mr Forwood and others as having been prepared and posted by Mr Curtis and other employes of the Room, the Committee passed the following Resolution moved by Mr Seymour and seconded by Mr Osborne: –
>
> > That the Committee having considered the Chairman's statement and heard Mr Curtis's explanation hereby censures him for his conduct which was most disloyal to the Committee.

A month later Curtis felt his position no longer to be tenable and he offered his resignation. At the moment of parting Septimus Glover could not bring himself to address his lieutenant by any more friendly title than

Dear Sir,
    I am sorry to hear you are so unwell and trust that a few days rest will put you right again.
    I am glad you have tendered your resignation as the painfully strained relations between the company and the committee would have

involved this change before long. I will read your resignation to the Committee on Thursday.

The newspapers, of course, knew that the Baltic's lease of South Sea House ran out in September and there was the usual speculation about possible next moves. One of those who read this was R. L. Franks, clerk of Christ's Hospital, EC.

14th January 1899

Dear Sir,

      I notice in the Money Article of 'The Times' 12th January that the Committee of the Baltic have lately been trying to obtain a suitable site for the erection of new and larger quarters, and the suggestion that an opportunity now occurs for centralising the ship-owning, shipping and allied businesses.

      The site of this Hospital will shortly be vacated, and as there is a station of the new Electric Railway adjoining, it may not be too far off to suit the requirement of your Committee. It is large enough to accommodate the Baltic, the Shipping Exchange, Lloyds and the other interests connected with the Shipping Trade, and most of the existing buildings, which are in a substantial condition, could be utilised.

      Perhaps you would kindly let me know if this property is likely to be of use for the purpose indicated.

Septimus Glover pencilled on the letter to thank but say 'too far east (say West)'.

The committee under Glover's chairmanship now met weekly. On January 17 the Baltic Company's written confirmation of their terms for a renewal of the lease of South Sea House was formally considered and a resolution passed: 'That the offer of the Baltic Company Limited be declined.' While the secretary was told to turn down Christ's Hospital, the first mention was made of a fourth possible site – in Fenchurch Street.

This offer came through a distinguished member of the Baltic and leading shipbroker, James Dixon of the old-established firm of Harris & Dixon of 81 Gracechurch Street. It referred to a block of land at the corner of Fenchurch Street and Lloyds Avenue and Northumberland Alley, facing Fenchurch Street Station. Members were invited to take part in a postal ballot indicating for or against the committee negotiating for this site.

Just before they received the ballot sheet they were sent a leaflet from the Stay At South Sea House Lobby headed by Stephen Ralli and Frederick Garrard, which concluded:

Is it not more than likely that our successors would cease to bless us if we relinquish our present magnificent position, and transplant them to an out-of-the-way locality at the further end of Fenchurch Street, and nearer to Whitechapel than to Lombard Street? We venture, therefore, earnestly to beg of you not to sacrifice our present splendid position for one so vastly inferior as that suggested and to vote for our present site.

A memorial from ninety-two members, excluding one who signed twice, respectfully desired that before any decision was taken about Fenchurch Street a letter be sent out with reference to the Jeffreys Square site, and that full particulars and plans of both be posted up in the room. But the Fenchurch Street ballot went ahead as arranged and on January 21 371 declared in favour and 403 against.

The Jeffreys Square lobby probably turned the balance. On February 2 Ernest Forwood wrote to Septimus Glover to say that as rumours had reached him that the reason the committee had not taken the Jeffreys Square site into consideration was that they were under the impression that it was not in the market, he would inform him that he held the firm offer of the site in writing for fourteen days.

Should your Committee write me that the site is one they would recommend to the members of the Baltic, I should be prepared during the 14 days to give you a firm offer to rent the proposed exchange to be built or should your Committee wish to do the same themselves I will be happy to transfer the offer to them.

This letter was considered by the committee the same day and the chairman was told to write to Forwood that they did not see their way to taking any steps in the matter.

Forwood was not to be put off. In spite of the Baltic not being prepared to back his judgement he was so confident in the rightness of the site that he was ready to risk acquiring it himself; and before the option ran out on February 16, with the aid of a group of friends, he did so.

Obviously Septimus Glover was more attracted by the Fenchurch Street idea than any of the other schemes. On February 1 he had written to Dixon: 'The plans are highly approved and from your letter it does not look as tho' we should have any difficulty in agreeing the terms of the lease.' But he had his reservations. If Dixon wanted members of the Baltic as tenants he should withdraw the hypothetical proposal that in the event of Lloyd's coming to Lloyds Avenue the price would be higher, and that ultimately the rent would be raised to £8000. James Dixon's reaction was immediate. He offered to build a building designed specifically to accommodate the Baltic. The rent would be £7000 inclusive of rates and taxes. He would give the lessees an option to buy the freehold of the site for £100000 and the entire building to be erected on it for another £80000. But the option would have to be taken up before August 6. The building would have 8447 square feet on the ground floor and 6628 square feet in the basement. When Glover raised further objections, Dixon said he would accept £6000 a year for the first seven years, £6500 for the next seven years, and £7000 for the last seven years.

Glover was satisfied with this, and got the committee to agree to put Dixon's offer to a general meeting of members together with a definite proposal for the Wesleyan Centenary Hall, which although shelved was still a possibility. A letter went out on February 13 calling a meeting for the 28th.

Septimus Glover opened the proceedings by apologizing for troubling members again after they had given the committee full powers to take what decisions they deemed fit at the meeting of January 3, but the reason for doing so would become plain. He quoted parts of Majolier's speech at that meeting in which, on behalf of the company, he had offered to make considerable sacrifices to make any arrangements to prevent the dislocation of the important part of the commerce of London which was the Baltic.

I ask you particularly to note the expression 'would make very considerable sacrifices'. Now this, gentlemen, is the first reason I have to give you why we did not act under the absolute discretion you gave to us. The committee considered this speech, and I think rightly, as a direct overture from the Company. It was so accepted by the committee, who at their first meeting after that speech was made, passed a resolution unanimously that before proceeding further in any other direction a response to this overture should be made, and I was instructed to invite the company to depute two of their directors to confer with your vice-chairman and myself 'to talk over our present difficulties and see if it is possible to bridge them over.' The answer we got to that modest request was most discouraging; it made no reference to the invitation to confer, but simply restated the terms we had already declined, namely, a seven years' lease without the option of the six months' notice and the tenants to do the repairs; that is, the committee must accept the Company's terms or no discussion. I am quite sure that Mr Majolier is incapable of stating what is contrary to fact; and, I think every man who knows Mr Majolier will agree with me that Mr Majolier is incapable of stating what is contrary to fact or of attempting in any way to do anything to mislead a meeting (hear hear) of influential gentlemen engaged in commerce in the City of London (hear hear), but I confess my utter inability to reconcile his statement that 'the Company was prepared to make very considerable sacrifices rather than dislocate this important part of the commerce of the City' with the answer we got to the invitation to confer.

He went on to refer to the committee's serious disappointment. For they had not been without hopes that if they had conferred with the company, they might have persuaded them to rebuild South Sea House and to retain the Baltic as tenants. He had had proposals put before him which indicate this could be done at a comparatively small cost; and that by improving and increasing the office accommodation an increased rent could be obtained which would amply cover the interest on the outlay. If that had been entertained he was assured there were many members of the Room who would have liberally contributed to the cost. The Baltic Company had thought it expedient to issue a copy of correspondence which members might find useful for reference. In the main it was accurate, and the committee were quite content to be judged by it. The company and the press had blamed the committee for delaying negotiations for the renewal of the lease. He merely wished to put the record straight.

He then gave figures of the comparative spaces of the rooms (see illustration page 264): 5195 square feet at South Sea House, 6120 square feet at the Centenary Hall and 7827 square feet at Fenchurch Street. The rent of South Sea House was £8000; that of the Centenary Hall would be £7000, of Fenchurch Street £6000 –

both for the first seven years. Only in the case of Fenchurch Street
had they the option to purchase the freehold. The great advantage
of South Sea House was that they remained undisturbed; the disadvantage of the Centenary Hall was that the existing building
would have to be demolished and it would be eighteen months to
two years before the new building was ready. The new building
on the Fenchurch Street site would give 50 per cent more space
than South Sea House and building could start at once, but its
great disadvantage was its position. Having outlined the pros and
cons fairly and without bias he invited members to speak for not
longer than five minutes at a time.

Many took to their feet but few minded the time limit. A Mr
Berlandina favoured Fenchurch Street but felt the building would
not meet the requirements of merchants, shipowners, shipbrokers,
produce-brokers and the grain trade. They should look to the
future. They wanted committee rooms, arbitration rooms, telephone and telegraph rooms. He would like to see not only the
present 1500 members of the Baltic, but another 1500 (cries of
'No'). Repeated cries of 'Time' forced him to his seat.

Sigismund Mendl MP agreed, that after Majolier's speech on
January 3 the general opinion was that a *modus vivendi* might be
found. He believed the members of the shipping trade were the
main supporters of the Fenchurch Street site. 'But it should be
borne in mind that the Baltic was not started in the interests of the
shipping trade (hear hear); it was started to provide facilities for the
grain trade, the seed trade and the tallow trade.' Their friends of
the shipping trade had come to them since for their own convenience, though they were very glad to see them. He would vote to
stay at South Sea House because he believed a move to Fenchurch
Street would be disastrous to those commercial interests for which
the Baltic was primarily intended. Harry Webb agreed with him;
if the pilgrimage was made to Fenchurch Street it would be made
without the seed and oil trades.

John Wrenn, from whom everybody expected a display of his
customary wit, began by referring to the foetid fog facetiously entitled the atmosphere of the Baltic (laughter). But besides its inconvenient and insanitary condition the Baltic building was an

altogether unworthy setting for the great business conducted within its walls and was the mirthful scorn of their foreign visitors. He was surprised that any serious suggestion had been made still to subsist in its squalid surroundings. He would vote for Fenchurch Street and a fresh deal.

Stephen Ralli rounded off the discussion by suggesting that member firms of the Baltic should between them raise £5000 with which to make the necessary repairs at South Sea House, and his own firm would take the lead with a gift of £500. If they voted for Fenchurch Street many of them would doubtless do so to have revenge on the Baltic Company. He urged them to vote for remaining where they were.

What is the Baltic? The Baltic is, I think, to you by far the most important and most useful commercial club in the City of London. (hear hear) We are all very proud of the Baltic and I, as one of its oldest members, am more proud of it than any of you. What then is the Baltic composed of? The grain trade is a very large trade, but it is not as large as the other trades combining to make the Baltic. The seed trade is a very large one, so is the oil trade, the seed-oil trade, the trade in petroleum and in tallow, besides which we have a pretty large business in Stock Exchange securities. I am informed that we have 26 members of the Stock Exchange who are members also of the Baltic and that these gentlemen attract a good deal of business to the Baltic. Are you going to run the risk of dislocating this Baltic and making it not what it is now but a mere annex of the corn market?

Every member was given a printed sheet with three boxes marked South Sea House, Centenary Hall, Fenchurch Street, and the recipient was asked to put a cross in the box of the proposal he preferred and return the voting paper signed with his name to the secretary not later than 2 p.m. on March 3.

The committee met on March 6 to hear the result. Only 28 voted to take over the Centenary Hall; 388 voted to remain at South Sea House and 439 to move to Fenchurch Street. They ordered the figures to be posted in the Room and turned to routine business.

After losing to the Centenary Hall by 32 votes on January 21, Fenchurch Street's victory over it by 368 votes was heartening news to James Dixon after all the work he had put into the presentation of his case. Having received the will of the majority clearly

THE BALTIC.

24th February, 1899.

Sir,

I am desired by the Committee to forward you a statement showing in detail the several proposals for The Baltic.

Yours faithfully,

S. J. GLOVER, *Chairman.*

COMPARISON OF PROPOSALS FOR THE BALTIC.

Comparative areas. In each case the Outer and Inner Lobby, the Secretary's Desk and Caller's Desk, Waiting Room or Annex to Lobby and Stairs to and from Basement are excluded.

SOUTH SEA HOUSE.	Superficial Area.
Main Hall, Annexes, Old Porch, Reading Room, Telephone Boxes. Telegraph Desks and Landing ...	5,195
Dining Room and Gallery ...	1,421
Total ...	6,616
	Cubic feet.
Business portion ...	97,000
Dining Room ...	21,000
Total ...	118,000

Lease—7, 14 or 21 years*

Rent—£8,000, less £100

The Tenant to do internal repairs and decorations

CENTENARY HALL.	Superficial Area.
Front portion ...	2,750
Back portion ...	2,770
Reading Room ...	600
	6,120
Dining Room ...	1,450
Total ...	7,570
Air Space.	Cubic feet.
Business portion ...	127,000
Dining Room ...	23,000
Total ...	150,000

Lease—7, 14 or 21 years*

Rent—£7,000, £7,500, £8,000

The Tenant to provide the furniture, and do internal repairs and decorations

FENCHURCH STREET.	Superficial Area.
Exchange Room ...	7,317
Telegraph Office ...	405
Telephone Boxes...	105
	7,827
Dining and Coffee Rooms ...	2,496
Total ...	10,323
	Cubic feet.
Business portion ...	164,500
Dining and Coffee Room ...	31,200
Total ...	195,700

21 years certain

£6,000   £6,500   £7,000
1st 7 years   2nd 7 years   3rd 7 years

With option, until 6 months' after occupation, to purchase the freehold and rooms and offices therein at £180,000

The Tenant to provide the furniture, and do internal repairs and decorations

* At option of the Tenant.   *Kindly bring this with you to the Meeting on 28th inst.*

and distinctly, the committee's next step was obviously to give expression to it. But regrettably, though realistically, the committee saw it was not a matter of dismissing South Sea House as easily as that. With so large a section of the membership still anxious to remain where they were, who knows if they were forced to move they might resign – and join the London Shipping Exchange? In readiness for even further weary confrontations with the board of the Baltic Company they appointed Charles Oxley as their secretary in place of the discredited Fred Curtis 'on the understanding that he was the servant of the Committee only'.

As soon as the result of the voting was known, both sides at once made representations, to the committee direct and via the company, to add to the message of the poll, in helping them to make up their minds. For with the powers given them on January 3 the committee were still the sole arbiters, and since objections had been made to the deviation from the usual method of balloting by making members sign, in an effort to be ultra-judicial they decided to hold a final poll between a rebuilt South Sea House and a new building in Fenchurch Street.

The committee's decision had been made at their meeting of March 9 when they had carried a motion by Seymour and Eumorfopolous that 'a second vote be taken between the Baltic and Fenchurch Street site, without signatures, and that a different coloured paper be sent to clerks'. Sigismund Mendl wrote to say he would resign from the committee if the decision went in favour of Fenchurch Street.

The result, declared on March 16, realized the worst fears of the Fenchurch Street lobby and so far from giving the committee the overwhelming majority for one or other of the projects which they sought, the margin of 51 was reduced to 26 – but for the other side. Members voted 478 to go to Fenchurch and 504 to stay at South Sea House. Some 982 members voted this time – 127 more than on March 3.

James Dixon was nonplussed. He thanked Septimus Glover for sending him the result of the new poll. 'The figures 26 against as

FACING PAGE *'Comparison of proposals for the Baltic'*, issued to members in 1899

compared with 51 majority for on the last occasion are curious.'
He could not claim personally to have sacrificed either much time
or money over the negotiation, but had rather played the part of
a very patient and interested looker-on. He presumed he would
receive a definite official refusal of his offer, but

> somehow or other I have an impression that the building and Exchange in
> Fenchurch Street will be built. The Baltic Company appear not yet to have
> said their last word. When it is spoken perhaps Fenchurch Street may be
> given an opportunity of saying theirs, if the property is not disposed of
> meantime.

The following day (March 17) he wrote again from his home
in Sevenoaks.

> On reconsideration I think I prefer to withdraw my proposal to the Baltic
> rather than it should receive the cold shoulder on Monday. I trust your
> colleagues and yourself will not think me acting in the least discourteously
> to them. Such is far from my intention, but my disgust of the tactics adopted
> by some of the South Sea House party with whom I thought I was fighting
> a fair fight for what we respectively considered for the interests of the Baltic
> members, has overborne all other considerations with me.
>   I sincerely hope that in a new South Sea House if it can be rebuilt so as to
> be in a commercial sense advantageous to landlord and present tenants, your
> mutual relations may be more genial and harmonious than hitherto.

At the meeting of February 28 members had been given the
impression that rebuilding of South Sea House was a possibility,
if not a certainty, and this would have been a main reason for their
voting for 'the present Baltic' site at the second vote on March 14.
Specific reference was made to it by the ninety-five firms who
favoured remaining at Threadneedle Street in their memorial to
the directors of March 9. The directors of the company allowed
them to believe this to be the case until *after* the vote had taken
place. Only in their reply of March 18 did they casually mention
(in the second paragraph) 'in regard to the proposal to rebuild we
are advised that at present the Company has not the necessary
powers for that purpose, and it would be impossible therefore for
us at present at all events to negotiate on that basis'.
  Rodocanachi added that for some time they had been engaged
in making changes with a view to the reconstruction of the com-

pany and obtaining the necessary powers to deal with the property, and as soon as that had been effected they would be prepared to give proper consideration to any proposals which might be put before them.

Michel Rodocanachi enclosed a copy of this reply when he wrote to Glover, on hearing the result of the poll, to remind him that the board's offer was still open – the same rent of £8000; seven, fourteen or twenty-one years; the company to allow the committee £100 a year for repairs; the committee to undertake any other improvements at their own expense and subject to approval of the company's architect; the company to give the committee the entire basement without charging extra rent.

Septimus Glover and his committee met to consider this latest letter on March 20. They decided to decline the offer, but declared themselves willing to take the Room for one more year on the terms of the present lease, that was to September 30, 1900. If the company agreed to do this, the committee would be pleased to confer with two of their directors to try and agree terms for rebuilding South Sea House.

Septimus Glover wrote to the company asking for a reply by March 27. He received it – in the affirmative. The committee now had eighteen months' breathing space.

With the Centenary Hall, Fenchurch Street and Christ's Hospital to one side and temporary possession of South Sea House assured, what had become of the Jeffrey's Square project?

Its supporters, of whom Ernest Forwood was the protagonist, had never lost faith in what they considered its overriding attractions. For them it was the best solution of them all. In the months which followed the collapse of all plans to move the Baltic from South Sea House to any of the sites that had up to then been put to members, the Jeffrey's Square lobby went into action in earnest. No record of this preparatory work has survived, apart from the invoice of Notley, the solicitor, covering the period March 1899 to January 1900. The Bousfield Trustees were persuaded to sell No 26 St Mary Axe for £33 000; No 24 Bury Street was bought for £11 000 'after prolonged negotiations with the owner on account of his reluctance to sell', and No 22 from a Mrs Northcote for £8400. Sums ranging from £1500 to Messrs Grantoff for 3 Jeffrey's Square to £30 were given to tenants as compensation. Edwards & Co, who still had eighteen years of their lease of a warehouse at 23 Bury Street, were paid £4000 and Robert Whyte & Co, who had twelve years to run at No 22, were given £5000.

Ernest Forwood explained the motive behind this activity to shareholders of the London Shipping Exchange at their annual general meeting. He referred to the unsuccessful efforts of the Shipping Exchange to obtain other premises and to the equally unsuccessful efforts of the Baltic committee to secure a suitable new site for their exchange. The directors of the London Shipping Exchange, he said, had feared that if the Baltic committee should eventually pick the Jeffrey's Square site, the Baltic's sole possession would materially injure the Shipping Exchange as it would enable the Baltic to offer such facilities and club comforts as would be bound to attract many of the Shipping Exchange members. 'A committee was thereupon formed to purchase the Jeffrey Square site and buildings and to create a new Exchange Company.'

It called itself the City of London Exchange Syndicate.

Five members of the Baltic committee met on June 6, 1899, with Septimus Glover in the chair, to consider a letter addressed to their chairman from 88 Bishopsgate Street, Within, dated June 5, as follows:

Dear Sir,

CITY OF LONDON EXCHANGE SYNDICATE

I am instructed by my Directors to inform you that they are in a position to offer you as a freehold site for the New Exchange Building the whole of Jeffrey Square including the houses in front in St Mary Axe, containing an area of about 25 000 square feet for a sum not exceeding £175 000 which includes all expenses. Possession within a reasonable time.

Inasmuch as the offer must be formally dealt with by the 20th inst., the Syndicate hope that you will be able to submit the proposed site to the Members of the Baltic for approval before that date.

As regards the building of the Exchange, the Syndicate are, as I have mentioned, prepared to transfer the property to the Baltic Committee leaving them to make the necessary arrangements for the building of the Exchange and the formation of the Company to acquire it. If, however,

it be preferred, my Syndicate are prepared, in conjunction with the Baltic
Committee, of course, to undertake all these arrangements.

Should you wish them to do so, Messrs E. H. Forwood and
Hy. Wm. Barnett will attend the Committee Meeting tomorrow if you
kindly let them know at what hour it may be held.

Yours faithfully,
A. Thorp
Secretary

Henry Barnett and Ernest Forwood did attend the meeting
which was adjourned to the 9th when a larger attendance could be
rallied.

The City of London Exchange Syndicate Ltd was in fact registered on that June 6. Its Memorandum of Association stated that
its object was 'to acquire land in Jeffery's Square [the spelling
varied from document to document] and to turn the same to
account as may seem expedient and in particular by . . . construct-
ing . . . exchanges for mercantile or other purposes.' The thirty-
seven subscribers to the memorandum were all members of the
Baltic and included E. H. Forwood, merchant, Edward Gellatly,
shipowner, A. S. Kettelwell, shipowner, Theo Angier, shipowner,
Robert Pim, corn broker, Stephen Ralli, merchant, Henry Langridge, shipowner, H. W. Ronaldson, shipowner, L. F. Ozanne and
Richard Peirano, grain merchants, E. M. Rodocanachi, banker,
H. W. Barnett and Howard Houlder, shipbrokers, H. Bevan,
director of the Produce Brokers Co. Ltd. They included fifteen
shipowners, six shipbrokers and three merchants. The capital was
£30000 in sixty shares of £500 each.

On June 9 Thorp sent Glover another letter.

Dear Sir,

Referring to the interview of Messrs E. H. Forwood and H. W.
Barnett with you and your colleagues on Tuesday, at a meeting of my
Board held yesterday I was instructed to place before you the following
for the consideration of your Committee: –

That we shall form a Company with a total Capital of £275000
divided as follows:

£150000 3½% Debenture Mortgage Bonds
£125000 in 12500 Ordinary Shares of £10 each
Of these Ordinary shares 9000 shall be offered to your

K

Committee for subscription by the members of your Exchange, the balance of 3500 shares being held in reserve.

It is understood that no member shall be entitled to hold at any time more than 200 Ordinary shares; further nobody but a member of the Exchange shall hold these shares and therefore if from any cause whatever a holder ceases to be a member, the shares held by him are to be offered by public auction in the room within six months of his death or retirement, provided always that such arrangement shall not nullify a holder's right to transfer his shares if he desires to do so, to other members of the room, such members being eligible to hold them.

The debentures, he went on to say, would be offered in the first instance to members of the Exchange and, should they not be taken up by them, to the public. A joint committee composed of members of his committee and the Baltic committee should be formed, they suggested, to meet and settle the prospectus which would have to be issued to raise the capital. 'My Board regrets it cannot see its way to offer your Committee the new premises it is proposed to build on the Jeffrey Square site on the basis of a rent.'

At their meeting on June 9 the Baltic committee agreed to treat with the Exchange Syndicate on the basis of this letter, but they must first see the articles of association. The syndicate acted very swiftly. Ten days later they had issued their prospectus and were allotting their £500 shares. On June 30 Paines, who had been appointed the Exchange Syndicate's solicitors, wrote to Charles Oxley, now secretary of the committee, sending him draft memorandum and articles of association. The constitution of the new company, they said, was based on the assumption that practically the whole of the money required for acquiring the property and building the Exchange would be obtained by means of debentures and preference shares, and that the ordinary shares, which had alone had voting rights until the preference dividend was twelve months in arrear, could only be held by members of the Exchange. The business of the company would be conducted by a board of directors and by an Exchange committee which alone would have the management of the room and control over members. The board would have powers of forfeiture and re-issue of shares. The rules of the Exchange would dictate the minimum number of shares each member could hold.

City of London Exchange Syndicate £500 Share certificate, 1899

In July a five-page private and confidential document was issued containing the 'Suggestions of the Sub-Committee of The Baltic Association [*sic*] on the proposals for the removal of the "Baltic" to an exchange to be erected on the site in Jeffreys Square belonging to the City of London Exchange Syndicate Limited'.

In these the proposed company was to have a capital of £175 000 divided into 10 000 £10 preference shares and 7500 £10 ordinary shares. They suggested that there should be no limit to the number of shares each member could hold so long as he had at least one. To prevent the management falling into the hands of a few members holding a large number of shares they recommended that the voting power should be limited to one vote for each of the first five shares, plus one vote for each extra ten shares. The directors should be able to sell to any member shares which following death or retirement had not yet been transferred to another member. There should be between twelve and eighteen directors each holding at least twenty-five ordinary shares. A separate committee of management was not necessary; this function should be carried out by a sub-committee chosen from the directors – 'this will have the advantage of removing causes of friction which might arise between the directors and a committee'. If they were dissatisfied with the management they had the remedy of exercising their votes as shareholders at a general meeting. Membership should be limited to 2000. The objects of the company as defined in the memorandum should not be so wide that the company was enabled to embark on any trade which might be carried on by members using the Exchange.

The sub-Committee is of the opinion that, as the members of the Baltic are asked to transfer their membership to the new Exchange, it would not be unreasonable to suggest that the Company should allot to each existing member without payment the one share which it is necessary he should hold as a member of the new Exchange.

The Baltic would be making over to the new concern valuable goodwill with subscriptions amounting to about £12000 a year, and if this suggestion was agreed to, the assets of the Baltic could be made over to the company.

Having got as far as this in so short a time, the Baltic committee took a long, deep look at what it was they were being asked to do. Before committing members they considered the proposal from every angle. Determined not to jump out of the Rodocanachi frying pan into the Forwood fire, they entered on a long period of negotiation. It was obvious they were going to need more time than the eighteen months which had seemed ample in March, and in August the committee instructed their secretary to write to the secretary of the company (both of whom, contrary to the committee's wishes, were Charles Oxley) asking for an extension of their lease of South Sea House beyond September 30, 1900. On August 11 Oxley wrote to Oxley, as his father had so often done before, to say the directors were not in a position to give the undertaking required.

On August 10 the Baltic Company had sold South Sea House to the British Linen Company for £350800.

But, said Oxley, secretary of the company, his directors would be happy to communicate the committee's letter to the buyers of

THE BALTIC,

March 10*th*, 1899.

The Committee regret exceedingly that it is necessary to ask you to vote again, as the matter is reduced to a question between THE BALTIC in its present condition and the Fenchurch Street site. The Centenary Hall scheme is eliminated by the last vote.

As the question is of the utmost importance the Committee earnestly request every Member of the Room to record his vote, as this will be the final ballot.

The comparative areas of the two sites are republished for your guidance and enclosed.

The Voting on the last occasion was as under :—

Fenchurch Street	...	...	...	438
South Sea House	...	...	...	387
Centenary Hall...	...	...	...,	28
Illegible	...	...	...	,..	2
Spoilt ...	...	...	...	...·	28
				883

SOUTH SEA HOUSE.	FENCHURCH STREET.

Please record your vote in one of the above columns with a **X** Do not sign your name.

Any Mark other than the Cross will render the vote null and void

To be returned by noon of Thursday, 16th March.

Results of the voting on the three sites proposed for the Baltic, 1899

the property, recommending their request to their most favourable consideration. In the meantime Oxley, as secretary of the committee, was told to write to likely estate agents for temporary accommodation to tide them over.

To effect their contract with the British Linen Company, the Baltic Company Ltd had to be wound up voluntarily, and this took place on September 14, 1899.

At the beginning of September the solicitors of the Baltic committee and of the Exchange Syndicate were still bargaining and all other options were still open. Indeed, with the situation seemingly fluid once again, James Dixon re-entered the lists on October 10 by renewing his offer of Fenchurch Street which he had himself withdrawn rather than have it officially rejected. His terms were the same – and the Baltic was to have the opportunity of purchasing the freehold of the land and the building for £180000. But Fenchurch Street was not an official runner at the annual general meeting on October 19 when members listened patiently to the latest proposal which Septimus Glover had to lay before them.

When the scheme for providing a Baltic at Jeffrey's Square was first mooted, my committee did not feel justified in adopting it, seeing that a heavy responsibility would have been incurred in signing contracts for the purchase of land and for the erection of a very large building. That responsibility has however been undertaken by gentlemen, chiefly members of The Baltic, who have formed a syndicate to purchase the property.

They could not force the condition of membership to be the holding of at least one £5 share, so a qualifying share would be given free to each of the 1250 town members. Thus Baltic members would command 1000 to 1500 votes if anything were threatened contrary to their interests. These arrangements would prevent a state of things arising similar to that from which they were escaping. The management of the Room would pass out of the hands of the present committee to the directors of the new company.

Henry Barnett gave details on behalf of the Exchange Syndicate. There would be a nominal capital of £400000; £200000 in 3½ per cent mortgage debenture bonds, £100000 in 5 per cent preference cumulative shares, and £100000 ordinary shares. They would only issue £50000 of the latter at first. The capital on which they would have to pay interest was £350000. Subscriptions at £7 7s. a head and entrance fees were expected to bring £16000 a year, office rents £15000, with sundry receipts £1000. With a total income of £32000, their working expenses would be £6500, and rates and taxes £5500, which would leave a balance of £20000 with which to pay interests on shares. The purchase of the site had already cost £170000 and the erection of the building and its equipment was expected to cost another £134000. The syndicate's profit would 'as agreed' be £15000.

The meeting ended with Stephen Ralli moving

That this meeting of the Members of 'The Baltic' hereby signifies its approval of the proposed removal of 'The Baltic' to the new Exchange to be built in Jeffrey's Square, and gives full authority to the Committee to conclude and agree terms with the City of London Exchange Syndicate Limited, and with the proposed new Company, upon the basis explained by the Chairman at this Meeting, with or without such modifications as the Committee may deem desirable.

Only three voted against. The 'overwhelming' majority at last.

There was a last-ditch stand for Fenchurch Street when A. C. Adam moved an amendment that before approving the Jeffrey's Square site a vote should be taken on Fenchurch Street, but it was lost. The ball was back in the committee's court, and at a special meeting on December 21 they authorized a sub-committee to approve a draft agreement with the syndicate for the full committee's eventual signature.

Septimus Glover was unable to attend the meeting and he wrote to Oxley to say he regretted this, as the business included the appointment of chairman. He hoped the committee would make arrangements to relieve him of the chair which he had occupied for some years and had entailed a good deal of labour and thought. 'With so many good men to choose from there ought not to be any difficulty.' But there was, and he was re-elected.

A month after the AGM of the Baltic committee Ernest Forwood was telling the story of the new Exchange to the shareholders of the London Shipping Exchange called to an extraordinary general meeting on November 30. At the beginning of the month the Exchange Syndicate had approached the Shipping Exchange with a view to purchase and amalgamation, and a committee of Shipping Exchange directors, composed of Becket Hill, Tom Ellis, Edward Gellatly and John Johnston, none of whom had any interests in the new project, had been formed to consider the question. They recommended to reject the syndicate's offer, but the meeting had been called to ascertain the feelings of members at large before accepting their report. The offer was £10 in cash or shares in the new company for every share held in the London Shipping Exchange on which only £9 had been paid. The estimated gross profits of the new concern were £32000 and net profits £20000. 'The new exchange will influence many of our members to leave us and join it. This would be a serious matter for your company which had in any case only been able to pay one dividend – 2½ per cent last year.'

Becket Hill said one of the reasons for their rejecting the offer was the members of the Baltic were to be given a free share, but subscribers to the Shipping Exchange would have to pay £5 a share and a large subscription. (Septimus Glover had told *his* shareholders that the syndicate proposed trying to secure the Shipping Exchange as temporary accommodation, and that ultimately it was hoped that many members of Billiter Street would join the Baltic and without entrance fee.)

Becket Hill said his committee had offered to accept £13000 for the assets and goodwill of the Shipping Exchange, but the syndicate were only prepared to give £10000.

Tom Ellis said if they refused to close, even though they lost 300 members to Jeffrey's Square, the Shipping Exchange could manage to get along in spite of the pains and penalties foreshadowed. Henry Langridge thought the assets of the Shipping Exchange worth no more than £5000. It was incorrect to say that Baltic members would get their £5 shares 'free'. They would be paid for out of the surplus funds of the Baltic.

Finally a resolution was put that the offer of the Exchange Syndicate to purchase the undertaking and assets of the London Shipping Exchange Ltd as a going concern from February 28,

1900, for £10000 in cash be approved. A show of hands gave twenty-seven for and eleven against. A poll was demanded resulting in 619 shares for, 99 against – representing 188 members out of a total of 760.

A letter was read from Sir Donald Currie to say he had no connection with the Exchange Syndicate, and the following week he resigned his chairmanship of the Shipping Exchange.

Fairplay's comment on the whole affair was:

Considerable dissatisfaction exists among a large body of the shareholders of the London Shipping Exchange with the proceedings of some of their directors in respect of their action in connection with the Jeffrey's Square business. I believe the matter will not be allowed to rest where it is. The feeling appears to be that the shareholders should have been consulted before steps were taken calculated in their opinion to prejudice their interests.

The Jeffrey's Square building was not going to be ready for some time and the immediate problem of the Baltic committee was still to find somewhere to go when their lease of South Sea House ran out in less than twelve months' time. They renewed contacts with estate agents. A possible was the Bishopsgate Institute. The Royal Exchange itself might have made a temporary home but it was not adaptable. Then, on December 22, Septimus Glover received a letter from the manager of the hotel and refreshment department of the Great Eastern Railway from his office in the Great Eastern Hotel, Liverpool Street, asking for an appointment for his chairman Lord Claud John Hamilton.

The Boer War had broken out and morale on the home front was being maintained by jingoism and the easily parodied verses of Rudyard Kipling. 'Baltico' contributed his ration with 'The Absent-Minded Broker'.

> When you've finished your subscription for the widdys and the kids,
>   (Which the fathers are a-fighting at the front)
> You may cast your thoughts a moment on the man who's asking bids,
>   And who's got to stay at home and bear the brunt.
> He's an absent-minded broker, and his needs are very great
>   In the matter of commission on a charter;
> See him bustling in the Baltic, and endeavouring to state
>   To an owner just precisely what he's arter.

Woolpack, Turtle, Palmerston, Hill's or Ring's,
   Spending his ha'pence and taking his kicks,
Chasing the owners, and saying things
   When they won't respond to his Fix! Fix! Fix!

When he leaves the dear old Baltic and adjourns to Jeffrey Square,
   Where he'll find a purer atmosphere for thought,
We may take it he'll continue to be very much all there
   When a charter or commission's to be sought.

The year 1899 – a turning point in the history of the Baltic –
ended with the annual Baltic dinner at the Trocadero, 'the most
effective *mis-en-scène* for the display of the camaraderie and mutual
goodwill which is so characteristic of the Baltic community'.
William Weeks, the evening's chairman, proposed the toast of
The Shipping Interests. 'A year ago', he said, 'the Jeffrey Square
site was in the clouds, but the Baltic will be safely anchored in
St Mary Axe by September 1901.' It was a statement, wrote
Fairplay's Look-Out Man, received with cheers of hope mildly
tempered by scepticism, while a shudder passed over the audience
on the reminder that the present Baltic would close its doors to
members in September next.

The body which was to own and administer the Jeffrey's Square
project was neither the Baltic committee, the Baltic Company,
the London Shipping Exchange nor the City of London Exchange
Syndicate. All were agreed it was to be a completely new and
separate body, and the immediate problem was what to call it.
Though separate, it was to be a reincarnation, if not a continuation, of the Baltic and it was therefore the Baltic committee who
were principally concerned with determining its form – and its
name.

New Year 1900 found Septimus Glover confined to his home
with his leg on a chair – an inflamed varicose vein rendered him
helpless, 'as I cannot put my foot to the ground'. It was an un-
fortunate time to be laid up and he wrote to Oxley on January 2
to be sure to remind Edward Power, his vice-chairman, that he
favoured admitting members of the Shipping Exchange without
entrance fee and for the seven-guinea subscription. They had gone

a long way to meet the difficulties which existed between the syndicate and the Shipping Exchange and he hoped there would be cause for no further delay.

I think the name of the company should be The Baltic Exchange Coy Ltd and I would not consent to The Baltic & Shipping Exchange Ltd unless it was shown that the refusal would prevent the floating of the company that is to be.

Henry Dillon, who also could not be present, wrote to Glover advocating the very name he disliked. 'I am strongly of the opinion that it would be advisable to call it The Baltic & Shipping Exchange – this seems to be the general wish of our community and as I understand we have about 50% of the members attention should be paid to their wishes.'

The Baltic committee met on January 4 to discuss the name of the new company, and Theodore Bassett proposed and Seth Taylor seconded that 'to meet the requirements of the Syndicate this Committee agrees that the name of the new company should be styled The Baltic Mercantile & Shipping Exchange Limited'.

The Baltic committee next settled the more complicated matter of their relations with the Exchange Syndicate.

On January 16 this fifteen-man committee of an unincorporated association of 1250 subscribers made a covenant with the Exchange Syndicate who agreed to form the Baltic Mercantile & Shipping Exchange Ltd with a Memorandum and Articles of Association approved both by Septimus Glover and his committee and by Jacques Mendl, chairman of the Exchange Syndicate, and within two years to erect a building in Jeffrey's Square on plans also approved both by the Baltic committee and Jacques Mendl. They mutually agreed that no ordinary shares would be issued to anyone who was not a member of the Baltic either before or after the completion of the building. The syndicate agreed to open the ground floor of the new building within two years as a subscription room and to establish a new Exchange 'having the same objects as and governed by rules and bye-laws similar to those of the Baltic subject to any modifications as the Baltic Committee may approve'.

The Baltic committee undertook to sell to the syndicate 'the undertaking and business of the Baltic and the goodwill thereof together with the exclusive right . . . to use the names of the Baltic and Baltic Subscription Rooms . . . as part of the New Company' and all the Baltic's assets, credits and effects, its investments and liabilities; and the syndicate to purchase them for the purpose of reselling to the New Company. The consideration for this sale was to be the allotment to each town member of the Baltic who wished to become a member of the new exchange of one fully paid ordinary £5 share which would entitle him to become a member of the new subscription room, subject to the payment of his annual subscription of £7 7s. The committee agreed not to make any alterations in the rules or subscriptions without the consent of the syndicate but before the completion of the building the syndicate had no right 'to interfere in any way with the conduct of the affairs of the Baltic' or with any way in which they applied their funds. Before the business was conveyed to the syndicate the committee agreed to pay their debts. Each member of the committee would use his best endeavours to support the new Exchange, and agreed not to form any other of a similar nature connected with grain or produce or shipping anywhere in the City of London. The committee agreed, if necessary, to procure trustees to accept a lease of the Billiter Street premises of the London Shipping Exchange from October 1, 1900, for three years (as temporary offices?). At the first annual general meeting of the new company its directors would retire and the ordinary shareholders would elect the board of directors of their choice.

Two days after the signing of this indenture, the syndicate borrowed £50000 from the National Bank (which they repaid on March 25).

The Baltic Mercantile and Shipping Exchange Ltd was incorporated on January 17, 1900. In its Memorandum its objects were stated to be to acquire any land etc., but in particular Jeffrey's Square, and to turn it to account for the purpose of the business of the Baltic subscription rooms for many years carried on at South Sea House, and of the business of the London Shipping Exchange; and to enter into an agreement with the City of London Exchange

Syndicate for the purpose of acquiring Jeffrey's Square, and the goodwill of the Baltic and the London Shipping Exchange. The capital of the company was to be £200000 divided into 10000 £10 preference shares and 20000 £5 ordinary shares. The seven subscribers to the memorandum were Jacques Mendl, merchant, Thomas Ronaldson, shipowner, Henry Barnett, shipbroker, Frederick Garrard, managing director, Robert Pim, grain broker, Hanry Langridge, shipbroker, Ernest Forwood, merchant.

The articles of association stated that the number of directors should be not less than twelve or more than nineteen; the first directors were to be the seven subscribers to the Memorandum. All of them were members of the Baltic but none of them of the Baltic committee. They were required to hold at least £250 worth of ordinary shares, and they would share an annual sum of £1500 as their remuneration.

Four directors would retire each year and be eligible for re-election. The original members of the new Exchange would be the members of the Baltic who were principals and held at least one ordinary share in the new company, and had paid the annual subscription of £7 7s. 'Until the Exchange is established by the opening of the part of the Company's buildings appropriated for the same, no other persons shall be elected to be Members of the Exchange.' Only when the Exchange was opened would new members be elected, and companies could then nominate representative principals as members who were their directors, managers or secretaries. The total number of members would not exceed 2000. Members of the Shipping Exchange would be admitted members of the new Exchange without entrance fee for a period of three months after the closing of Billiter Street.

All powers for election, admission, suspension and expulsion of members would be exercised by the directors or a committee appointed by them and the directors were charged with the responsibility of drawing up rules for the Exchange before January 31, 1902. Until that had been done the rules of 'the Baltic Subscription Rooms' would apply.

The directors of the Baltic Mercantile and Shipping Exchange Ltd met for the first time on January 17, 1900, at 88 Bishopsgate

Street, the offices of Forwood Bros and of the Exchange Syndicate, together with J. E. Huxtable, the solicitor, James Findlay, secretary of the London Shipping Exchange and Alfred Thorp, secretary of the Exchange Syndicate. Jacques Mendl, who was chairman of the syndicate, was asked to preside, and Huxtable told them that the company had been registered that day, and the directors formally appointed. James Findlay was appointed company secretary, a post he coupled with secretary at Billiter Street.

William Bridges Webb was elected chairman of the board. He had entered the grain trade as a young man of twenty-one in 1870 and later entered into partnership with James Dewar to form Dewar & Webb, corn merchants. He became a member of the Baltic in 1872 and of its committee twenty years later. He lived in style off Portman Square and was president of the London Corn Trade Association from 1896 to 1899. He had a commission in the Honourable Artillery Company and liked to be known as Major Bridges Webb. 'As smart a business man as one can find in this great city of business men' was how *The Miller* described him. 'His courteous manner and open hearted demeanour are quite refreshing.'

Henry Barnett was elected vice-chairman. Seth Taylor declined the offer to sit on the board, but agreed to become a trustee for the debenture stock. The full board met for the first time on February 2. Having settled its obligations to the Baltic committee, the Exchange Syndicate next turned to the London Shipping Exchange. By an indenture of February 13 the syndicate agreed to buy the goodwill and assets of the Shipping Exchange by February 28, 1900, together with the right to use the name the London Shipping Exchange or any part of it as part of the name of the new company, and the right to represent that they were carrying on their under-taking 'in continuation of the London Shipping Exchange Limited and in succession thereto'. The Shipping Exchange's lease of 19, 20 and 21 Billiter Street at £850 a year (reduced from £1900 in 1893) expired in 1913, and they would endeavour to secure an assignment of the lease. When the purchase was completed the Shipping Exchange undertook to go into voluntary liquidation within a month. In consideration of all this the Exchange Syndicate agreed to pay the Shipping Exchange £10000 on signing the indenture and another £9000 on completion of the purchase, and payment of the proceeds of the sale of Billiter Street.

With the assets and goodwill of both the Baltic and the London Shipping Exchange safely in their hands, the Exchange Syndicate then handed them over to the Baltic Mercantile and Shipping Exchange by an agreement signed on March 2. The new company was then free to issue its prospectus on March 5 for £250000 3¾ per cent irredeemable first mortgage debenture stock and £100000 4½ per cent 'B' mortgage debenture stock. The subscription list closed on March 14. Of the seventeen directors given on the prospectus five were shown as being members of the Baltic committee: William Bridges Webb, Edmund Carver, Charles Howard, Edward Power and Arthur Serena; and eleven as shareholders in the Exchange Syndicate: Henry Barnett, Thomas Feild, Ernest Forwood, Frederick Garrard, Arthur Kettelwell, Henry Langridge, Francis Lenders, Edouard Majolier, Jacques Mendl, Robert Pim and Thomas Ronaldson. The seventeenth was T. L. Devitt of Devitt & Moore.

The object of the company was to acquire from the Exchange Syndicate the whole of Jeffrey's Square, 26 and 28 St Mary Axe, 22, 23 and 24 Bury Street and to build on the site an exchange 'which will replace the present Baltic in Threadneedle Street and the London Shipping Exchange in Billiter Street'. Plans for this building had been prepared by W. Wimble, FRIBA, and T. H. Smith to cover an area of 18515 square feet. When complete the property would be worth £440000 and the offices would yield a gross income of £18900. There were 1350 present members of the Baltic and 1410 of the London Shipping Exchange, and the directors were justified in assuming that within a few weeks of opening the new Exchange would have the maximum membership of 2000. Gross revenue of £35000 was envisaged; £15000 from subscriptions and entrance fees, £19000 from office rents and £1000 from refreshment rooms etc. Working expenses would be £13000. Payment on the debentures would amount to £13875 leaving £8125 for the ordinary shareholders. The new company would repay all the money spent by the Exchange Syndicate plus a sum of £15000 as the agreed profit in cash. Such obligations

77 Gresham House EC
February 12th, 1901.

To
The Secretary of the Baltic Mercantile and
Shipping Exchange.

Sir,

    We estimate the cost of work to be done in completing the Superstructure of The Baltic Mercantile and Shipping Exchange, St Mary Axe and Bury Street, E.C., in accordance with the Drawings, Specification and Bills of Quantities all the work to be done to the satisfaction of the Architects at the sum of One Hundred Sixty-three Thousand Nine hundred Eighty £ s d

	£	s	d
	163980	0	0

    If the finishings of Offices, &c. are executed in mahogany in lieu of deal the extra cost will be Seven Thousand one hundred fifty Pounds

	£	s	d
	7150	0	0
Total £	171130	0	0

    We will undertake to complete the whole of the works within 22 Calendar months from the date of taking possession of the Site.

We are, Sir,
Yours obediently,

Geo. Trollope & Sons

G. W. Trollope & Son's estimate for building the superstructure of the new Baltic Exchange at St Mary Axe, 1901

would absorb £220000 and another £6000 would cover the single ordinary shares being given to each town member of the Baltic as qualification of membership of the new Exchange. The balance would go towards meeting the cost of erecting and equipping the new building which the architects considered should not exceed £175000. The company undertook to complete the new building by January 15, 1902, and have the Room ready for that date. The London Shipping Exchange belonged to the company from March 1, and it would be run by it at Billiter Street until the new Exchange was ready.

Unlike the floating of the Baltic Company, there was considerable over-subscription and an allotment committee was appointed. All applications for forty shares or less were granted in full. There were 136 applications amounting to £412500 for the £250000 3¾ per cent debentures and 170 amounting to £211760 for the £100000 worth of 4½ per cent stock. The purchase of Jeffrey's Square was completed on April 4 and Bridges Webb handed over the cheque for £87693 to Ernest Forwood and congratulated him and the syndicate on the successful outcome of efforts begun more than twelve months before. At the same meeting a cheque was signed to settle with the London Shipping Exchange, and a committee of the new company was appointed to manage it, consisting of the chairman and vice-chairman with Forwood, Langridge, Kettelwell and Feild. It had its first meeting on April 10 and all those directors of the company who did not already belong were made honorary members of the Shipping Exchange.

The Jerusalem Ltd was wound up voluntarily on April 24 and the City of London Exchange Syndicate paid their sixty shareholders £250 a share on May 17 and went into liquidation shortly afterwards. On July 18 they made a final distribution of another £250 a share, less income tax of a shilling in the pound.

The Baltic Mercantile and Shipping Exchange altered its articles of association for the first of many times on June 5 and held its first statutory general meeting on June 12 when it received tenders for building the foundations of the new Exchange and accepted Trollope & Dove's at £34918.

III

THE BALTIC EXCHANGE

The City is a mysterious place to most people. We don't really go out and try and tell people about the City and the finer sides of the City as being one of the few places in the world where a man's word is his bond. If I told you that I would buy something at a price, then I would do it the next day and you wouldn't have anything more to worry about. It doesn't happen in every city in the world.

SIR KENNETH KEITH, 1970

9. St Mary Axe

For Septimus Glover and the Baltic committee the last days at South Sea House were dominated by the need to find temporary accommodation from October 1 to the postulated January 15, 1902, when they would be able to occupy the new Room at St Mary Axe. Lord John Claud Hamilton of the Great Eastern Railway duly kept his appointment to see the Baltic early in the new year. The railway company, he revealed, was building an extension to its Great Eastern Hotel at Liverpool Street Station to form a big banqueting hall, bars, restaurants and masonic temples, and before the annexe was equipped for the purpose it was designed to serve, he thought it might make a very suitable temporary home for the Baltic. Hence his lordship's visit. Septimus Glover accompanied him to the corner of Liverpool Street and Bishopsgate Street and saw the building going up. It seemed the answer, and the committee set in motion the formalities for obtaining a short lease and adapting the rooms to their purpose. By the end of January a document was in draft, and on June 18, 1900, the committee signed an agreement with the Great Eastern Railway Company to have the rooms ready by October 1, and for the Baltic to have exclusive use of them every business day from 9.30 to 6 for an annual rent of £3000 for two years. The railway's catering department would run the restaurant in the basement and 'The Baltic Menu', showing prices, was annexed to the agreement – grilled sole and boiled salmon at 1s. 6d., saddle of mutton 1s. 2d., roast beef 1s., asparagus 8d., pudding du jour 4d.

There was a lot to be done – fitting the rooms up with the telegraph office, the tape machines and telephones, dealing with the staff at Threadneedle Street, arranging the fittings and furniture, the speaking tubes and counters at the Great Eastern, trying to find a purchaser for bound copies of *The Times* for the previous forty-three years – since the Baltic moved to South Sea House in 1857. Hampstead Public Library were showing an interest.

For the members of the Baltic the last days at South Sea House meant business as usual in the Room which contemporary photographs show to have been a cross between the big conservatory at Kew Gardens and the concourse of a main line railway station. It had a long rectangular pitched roof of glass, supported by tall, slim iron pillars surrounded on the bare herring-bone wooden floor by circular leather seats, or chest-high reading stands. On either side of the wall of mirrors facing the entrance were long leather benches, divided by a monumental marble fireplace. Arches separated the main section of the Room under the glass ceiling from the foreign telegrams corner on one side and the reading room, with its writing table and chairs, on another. Ornamental iron light pendants hung from the roof, and glass shaded brackets protruded from the walls. How much the interior changed during those forty-three years it is difficult to say, but the photographs of 1900 compared with early prints show an additional storey had been added to the building, and the pavement overlapping the basement.

The stark interior came to life at noon and half past four. When a hot sun shone through the clear glass on to a crowded floor, the atmosphere must have been stifling and little affected by the turning of the ugly electric fan slung from the ceiling. The air would have had as little circulation as the members who clung to their traditional groups: the shipowners, chartering agents and brokers near the main entrance discussing coal freights and grain freights or the sale of a steamer; the dealers and brokers buying and selling cargoes and parcels of grain on passage, or for future shipment, by the 'quarter', which Liverpool, with its more civilized 'cental' or 100 lb weight system, considered an anachronism.

In 1897 an option or futures market in grain had been established on the lines of that at Liverpool, a counterpart on a small scale to the wheat pits of Chicago and New York.

In the past when a farmer wanted money in advance, the bank would only lend him money if a 'sale' had been made on growing corn. In this way raising money on the security of an offer for corn to be delivered some time in the future was the origin of what became a feature of trading on all the grain-growing countries of the world. In many places it constituted purely a means of financial speculation and gambling by those who had no interest or intention of every taking delivery of the actual grain. But its apologists claimed that it tended to stabilize prices.

Operations at South Sea House in 1897 were confined to American wheat and maize which were bought and sold in loads of 1000 quarters, and the gain or loss on each transaction was determined immediately. More often than not no delivery of actual produce took place; it was simply a matter of settling the differences. There were two daily 'calls' besides numerous less formal occasions for deals. The contracts were registered daily by the London Produce Clearing House which received from seller and buyer alike a deposit of £50 a load and guaranteed the differences would be met.

Elsewhere on the Floor there was dealing in linseed from India, the River Plata and Russia, and cotton-seed from Egypt, both of which were caked for cattle and sheep food and used for oil making. Weekly sales were still held in tallow from Australia and South America.

But it was soon September, and the Baltic's forty-three years at South Sea House were coming to an end. At the beginning of the month there was doubt about the Great Eastern rooms being ready in time, and an attempt was made to extend the stay at Threadneedle Street a little. The manager of the British Linen Company's bank at 41 Lombard Street wrote to Septimus Glover on September 8 to say he was instructed by his head office that everything was arranged to begin the work of demolition whenever they got possession so they must decline his offer (of taking a further lease). And demolition it was – the building which stands on the site of 37 Threadneedle Street today was built in 1901 and no part of it belongs to the South Sea House which became known as 'The Baltic', let alone the headquarters of the South Sea Company.

As Charles Malcolm wrote in his *History of the British Linen Bank* (1950),

In 1899 Andrew Kingsmill reported that the historic South Sea House in Threadneedle Street would soon be vacated by the Baltic Company which had been there since 1855 [*sic*]. As the site was most desirable Kingsmill was instructed to complete the purchase. South Sea House was not adapted for the needs of a bank and John Macvicar Anderson, a former president of the RIBA, was commissioned to attend to the rebuilding which he completed in a most satisfactory manner.

The stone carving over the entrance on the north side with figures symbolic of the South Sea Company's activities is the piece of sculpture, rejected by the owners of the original building, which was found in the sculptor's studio in 1900 and used in the new building of that date. In 1972 the British Linen Bank changed its name to the Bank of Scotland, who vacated it in 1976.

Edouard Majolier, who was acting as a liquidator for the Baltic Company, knew only too well that members would be using the Room up to the last minute of the very last day, and wrote to Septimus Glover on September 20 confirming that they had arranged to hold an auction of the furniture and fittings on the Monday, October 1.

I would therefore feel greatly obliged if the Gentlemen of the Committee would allow the inspection of furniture etc by intending purchasers to take place after closing time on Thursday, Friday and Saturday the 27th, 28th and 29th inst . . . This can cause no possible inconvenience either to the Members of the Committee . . . Regarding your offer for the furniture that you require for the new Room, I would gladly have considered it, had it been in my power to do so, but I am advised by my lawyers that I am unable to dispose of the property of other people, viz. the shareholders of the Baltic Company, except by valuation (which I have already offered you and I understand you decline) or by auction, and if I may be required to express an opinion I think you will find the latter the more preferable course.

The 'Valuable Furniture' of 'this Historic Exchange [see sale poster illustrated opposite], formerly known as "South Sea House"' included the mirrors on the wall in their Spanish mahogany frames, the ornamental steel stove, marble drinking fountain with plated dish designed as a shell, the settees in their maroon leather, the

By order of the Liquidators.

"THE BALTIC,"
THREADNEEDLE STREET, CITY.

CATALOGUE
OF

THE VALUABLE FURNITURE
Fixtures and Fittings,

Of this Historic, Exchange, formerly known as "South Sea House,"

INCLUDING

The Contents of the large Subscription Room, Committee Room, Refreshment and Luncheon Departments, Offices, Waiting Rooms, and Apartments connected therewith; comprising a large quantity of solid

OLD SPANISH MAHOGANY,

Board Room, Writing and other Tables, Desks, Chairs, Fauteuils, Settees, Circular Lounges, Whatnots, &c., Plate Glass Wall Mirrors, valuable Clocks, Wind Dial, Marble and Silver Plated Fountain,

SOLID MAHOGANY SLOPING DESKS AND SEATS

ALSO

THE MODERN PASSENGER LIFT, by Waygood & Co.,

SPANISH MAHOGANY & PLATE-GLASS PARTITIONING, WALL FITTINGS

TELEPHONE CLOSETS.

The Marble & Glazed Fittings of Lavatories, Urinals & w.c.'s, by Finch & Co.

POLISHED STEEL AND MARBLE FIREPLACES AND STOVES.

FITTINGS FOR ELECTRIC LIGHT AND GAS, MOTOR GENERATOR, ELECTRIC VENTILATING FAN, and other Effects,

Which will be Sold by Auction by Messrs.

HOBSON, RICHARDS AND CO.

Upon the Premises, "THE BALTIC,"

On MONDAY, the 1st of OCTOBER, 1900
At ONE o'clock precisely.

May be Viewed as follows: on Thursday, September 27th, and Friday, September 28th, after 5 o'clock; on Saturday, September 29th, after 2 p.m.; and on Morning of Sale. Catalogues may be obtained of F. W. PIXLEY, Esq., (of the Firm of Messrs. Jackson, Pixley, Browning, Husey & Co.), of 58, Coleman Street, E.C. (one of the Liquidators); of Messrs. PAINES, BLYTH & HUXTABLE, Solicitors, 14, St. Helen's Place, E.C.; at the "Baltic"; or of the Auctioneers, Messrs. HOBSON, RICHARDS & CO.,

79, Coleman Street, Bank.

The front page of the catalogue for the sale held at South Sea House, 1900

board-room table, the ventilating fans, the eighteen-day dial clock by Thwaites & Reed, and the wind dial to match supported by figures of mermaids, the 'Ancient Chair for the Use of the House Porter' with high hood, stuffed and covered in maroon leather on mahogany plinth (where is this now?), the eleven wash basins in the basement, the five-pull beer engine by Heath of Goswell Road from the restaurant, and *The Times* bound in quarterly volumes from 1850 to June 1900, with Palmer's index from 1874 – Hampstead Library had turned it down. And last the lift by Waygood & Co with car, fitted mirror and all connections.

On the day of the auction members were carrying on Saturday's left-off business in the Great Hall of the Great Eastern Hotel extension which over the week-end became 'The Baltic'. The Room in which they conducted their business at that first 'Change on Monday October 1, 1900, while the contents of their former occupation were being sold off, can still be seen today. It has a high ceiling elaborately decorated with plaster casts of mythical and floral groups, and tall light windows. It is 96 feet long and 40 feet broad and very spacious. The new annexe was known as the Abercorn Rooms; 'the Room' was what is now the Hamilton Room. In the basement was the restaurant, the Cambridge Room. There was a private telegraph office and telephone booths; members had their own entrance at the corner of Bishopsgate Street. James Findlay however operated from 19, 20 and 21 Billiter Street, the registered office of the Baltic Mercantile and Shipping Exchange.

They had not been in occupation very long before James Findlay received a letter from 'Broughton Black, B.A., Vocalist, Actor, Manager, Author' of Dulwich. He was the manager, he said, of the Great Eastern Railway Co.'s pavilion at Lowestoft and had organized the opening smoking concert in the new Hall of the Great Eastern Hotel for railway company staff (after the Baltic had closed for business) on October 2. He wrote to propose 'That the Baltic who occupy the above magnificent room in the day time should form a Musical Society from its own members, like the Stock Exchange, including if possible a Male Voice Choir.' He would be prepared to take over the entire musical direction and conductorship of the society and choir. It was an idea which was to lie fallow for seven years.

The completion of the sale of South Sea House to the British Linen Company on September 30 was the last function of the liquidators of the Baltic Company. As liquidators were not competent to pay dividends, in November 1899 they had made a payment of £10 per £100 of stock to the holders of the £40000 ordinary stock.

As it is expected that the liquidators will ultimately return to each shareholder a sum largely in excess of the nominal amount of his stock, the object of the present distribution, which is made exclusively out of current rents, is to continue, pending completion of the sale, the half-yearly payments which the shareholders have hitherto received as dividend.

They made a further distribution of 10 per cent on March 31, 1900. On October 3 Michel Rodocanachi wrote in the Baltic Company's annual report book:

Baltic

3 October 1900

deeds delivered
amount paid
the keys delivered by me in the presence
of Mr Crumple Blyth & the two Bank officials

But it was not quite the end. Eighteen shareholders met on October 22 to close the liquidation, and forty-eight proxies were received. The minute of this meeting read as follows:

Mr M. E. Rodocanachi said: –

Gentlemen,

We were appointed liquidators in August last year.
We had some troublesome and delicate negotiations that gave us some anxiety, but I am pleased to say that we have overcome all difficulties in due time.

We have delivered the deeds – we had to borrow some money to carry the business. Mr Pixley will present his statement up to date with accounts and the items and the following resolutions which require your confirmation to proceed with the liquidation that lasted 15 months to date.

RESOLUTIONS: –

(1) the sanctioning or confirming of certain compromises with persons having claims against the company; and

(2) the settlement of the remuneration of the liquidators and the consideration and adoption of their accounts up to the present time.

> On the 3rd October I delivered the keys to the Manager of the British Linen Bank and in the presence of the Solicitors of both banks received the value of the property – paid it into the London Joint Stock Bank. We are now prepared to distribute a very handsome sum to each of you.
>
> Cheques of £730 per £100 stock will be sent to you as soon as possible.

Why and when they had to borrow money 'to carry the business' when they were paying themselves 730 per cent is not clear; nor what was meant by the 'certain compromises' unless it was the income tax commissioner. Uncertainty seems to have arisen over whether the £300000 profit made from the sale of South Sea House might not be liable to tax, and counsel's opinion was sought. Mr A. V. Dicey, of Brick Court, assured them, however, that the price of land sold by its owner, even if it was higher than the price for which years ago he bought the land, did not constitute annual profits or gains from any profession, trade or employment within the income tax laws of 1853. He was, therefore, very distinctly of the opinion that no portion of the purchase price obtained from the company's property was chargeable with income tax for which the liquidators were liable to account to the Inland Revenue. But it was a nasty moment.

The final account of the liquidators showed the disposal of a sum of £366217, of which £350800 was for the sale of South Sea House. It showed a bonus of £2887 paid to the directors and the secretary; £1806 liquidators' remuneration and bonus to Mr Oxley; and £327391 paid to stockholders since liquidation – 10 per cent on October 24, 1899, 10 per cent on March 31, 1900, 730 per cent on October 26 and 43 per cent on November 21.

The person who most benefited from this was Michel Rodocanachi who, as the largest shareholder with 1400 shares, between liquidation and November 21 collected £11102 apart from his share of the £2887 directors' bonus and £1806 liquidators' remuneration, on all of which he only paid a shilling in the pound income tax. He had been on the board which founded the Baltic Company in 1857 and was thus a director for the whole of the company's forty-three years of existence. Stephen Ralli was the next largest shareholder with 1200 and his final collection was £9515; he also held 650 preference shares. Edouard Majolier's 920 ordinary shares brought him £6975 in this final pay-out. After thirty years as Baltic housekeeper Mrs Brown was given a pension of 10s. a week.

A conspicuous absentee from the share register of the Baltic Company was the chairman of the Baltic committee who the week the 730 per cent dividend was paid out was enjoying a 'much needed rest and holiday' at the Queen's Hotel, Eastbourne, and wrote to the committee to say he would not, therefore, be at the next meeting.

My object in writing is that I wish first of all to express my thanks to the committee for their great confidence in me and for the loyal support they have always given me and for their repeated kindness in electing me over and over again as Chairman of the Baltic, an honour which I have very highly appreciated.

As I must necessarily leave the committee next year, I think it is most desirable that another Gentleman should be elected as Chairman. Of course I know nothing of the intention of the Committee, but if there should be any proposal to re-elect me, I write to say that I cannot accept same and I shall be much obliged by your making this clear to the committee.

Yours faithfully,
S. J. Glover

The close ties which the Baltic also had with the United States at this time were shown by the fact that the New York Produce Exchange closed on the day of Queen Victoria's funeral (February 2, 1901) 'as a mark of respect for her character and of their sympathy with Britain in the loss it has sustained'. The Chicago Board of Trade and the Philadelphia Commercial Exchange did likewise. The Baltic, at the Great Eastern Hotel, naturally suspended business that day but there was too little support for the subscription list for the Queen Victoria Memorial Fund, so the amount was sent to the treasurer as 'from certain members' and not from the institution as such.

Throughout the short period between the evacuation of South Sea House and the occupation of St Mary Axe, three bodies operated independently which were later to merge into one: 'the Baltic' at the Great Eastern Hotel, supervised by the Baltic committee; the London Shipping Exchange at 19, 20 and 21 Billiter Street, supervised by a management committee of the Baltic; and the Baltic Mercantile and Shipping Exchange Ltd, being run by James Findlay and his staff at Billiter Street, whose main function was to supervise the building of the new Exchange in St Mary Axe and prepare for the new 'Baltic' which was to operate there. The Baltic Company Ltd, the City of London Exchange Syndicate Ltd and the London Shipping Exchange Ltd were no more. The overheads were very much less at the Great Eastern, so the committee commendably decided to reduce the subscriptions for town members from £10 10s. to £6 6s., and for country members from £4 4s. to £2 10s. On leaving Threadneedle Street 143 members resigned, but 114 joined. At September 30, 1901, membership stood at 1357.

Seth Taylor took over as chairman of the Baltic committee from Septimus Glover, and at the end of 1901 both he and Bridges Webb, of the new company, formed committees to consider the rules for the new Baltic. Two members of each of these committees formed a joint steering committee to hammer out the draft.

The first printed proof had forty-six rules. No one was to be eligible for election other than a British subject until he or his firm had been domiciled in the UK for twelve months. The board of directors would elect members by ballot but could not propose or second candidates. One blackball in four would exclude; a second ballot could be called for an excluded candidate and if not admitted again he would be excluded for twelve months 'after which period his candidature may be allowed or not at the Directors' discretion.' The board could censure, suspend or expel a member 'who, in their opinion, has been guilty of improper conduct or who shall make use of the Exchange for purposes other than the proper purposes thereof or who shall have violated any of the rules or regulations or who shall have failed to comply with any of their decisions.' As with 'conduct derogatory to his character as a man of business', so 'improper conduct' and the 'proper purposes' of the Exchange were left undefined.

The directors saw that they had the power to notify other members or the public that they had expelled or suspended a member. And they stated that no action in respect of such notification was maintainable by the person referred to against the board. All complaints against a member should be made in writing to the chairman of the board who had to post a copy of the complaint to the person concerned before he was summoned to appear before him and his colleagues. No more 'being called in' without knowing what for. If a non-member made a complaint against a member, the directors would first of all consider whether it was one fit for their adjudication, and if they did, before hearing the case, the complainant had to sign a written consent binding himself to carry out their award as if he were a member of the Baltic. He promised not to prosecute or take part in any civil or criminal proceedings in respect of the case. He agreed that his letter was a submission to arbitration within the meaning of the Arbitration Act 1889.

By the time they had hammered out the framework of a constitution, a ceremonial gavel had laid the foundation stone of the building in which it would come to life – on June 25.

The Lord Mayor, Sir Frank Green, drove in state from the Mansion House down a St Mary Axe decorated with flags of all nationalities. The civic party was met by Bridges Webb who showed them over the excavations and foundations of the building. They returned to the crimson carpeted dais on which stood the stone in which had been placed coins of the realm and copies of that day's national newspapers. Inviting the Lord Mayor to perform the ceremony Bridges Webb said the building would accommodate 3000 members. When completed it would be a great acquisition to the City of London. With the trowel handed to him by T. H. Smith, the architect, the Lord Mayor declared the stone to be well and truly laid, 'and may the structure to be raised upon it be creditable alike to the architects and the builders, and may it fulfil also the purpose which you all deeply desire it to fill.'

In thanking the Lord Mayor, Henry Barnett said the pioneers of the scheme were first told that the Corporation of London would never consent to Jeffrey's Square being blotted out but in the event they had received nothing but encouragement. Ernest Forwood seconded his vote of thanks.

A luncheon for eighty-one followed at the Merchant Taylors Hall in nearby Threadneedle Street (arranged by Ring and Brymer at 21s. a head, including Moet et Chandon 1892) and the thirty-two visitors included the members of the Baltic committee, the late directors of the London Shipping Exchange, the leading lights of Lloyd's, Lloyd's Register and the Stock Exchange (see illustration between pages 252 and 253). Shareholders had been invited to the ceremony but not their ladies as that would have meant asking the Lady Mayoress and upsetting the luncheon arrangements. Seth Taylor was there not only as chairman of the Baltic committee but as Master of the Merchant Taylors' Company. In his speech Bridges Webb said he hoped the opening of the building would be honoured by royalty. It was a sensitive subject. The opening date of January 15, 1902, given in the company prospectus was only seven months away.

There were mitigating circumstances for their inability to open on the promised day, however, as Bridges Webb told shareholders at the second annual general meeting on May 14, 1902. The new building had not progressed as rapidly as they had hoped, he said but so that it could be oblong (had it suddenly changed shape?) further property had had to be acquired in Bury Street. Not only its shape but its size seems to have altered. It was now to be much larger than originally contemplated, he told them – an area of at least 16000 square feet instead of 10000, and the height had been increased 12 feet. As a result, fifty neighbours had put in claims for Ancient Lights, and all of them had had to be compensated which had taken time. It had also been decided to give the building its own electric light plant and its own artesian well. It was all going to cost rather more money and the meeting was asked to extend the borrowing powers to £500000. Not unnaturally, the chairman was unable to commit himself on the opening date.

L

The directors' report and accounts showed that £272000 had been paid to the London Shipping Exchange for its assets and property. Findlay wrote to their members to find out which were going to join the new Baltic and reminding them that if they were not elected within three months of the opening 'which was expected to be at the end of 1902', they would become liable to the twenty guinea entrance fee. In fact, however, the building was not to be ready till the spring of 1903.

This put considerable strain on the relations between the Baltic committee and the Great Eastern Railway Company who commendably rose to the occasion, however, and gave them an extension of the Abercorn Rooms to March 31, 1903. At the approach of the end of their financial year in September, 1902, Oxley was instructed to collect only half a year's subscription, as the next full subscription would be to the new Baltic and start from April 1, 1903. Seth Taylor presided over the last annual general meeting of members of the old Baltic at Winchester House on October 16, 1902. He found time, among more pressing business, to congratulate Fred Lohden on the formation of the Baltic Rifle Club, prompted by the military training everywhere in evidence for the South African War.

Before the year was out James Findlay was laying plans for the opening of the new Exchange on Tuesday, April 21, 1903, and for the first day of business on the following Monday. In the first three months of the year he was tying up final details – deciding to use the Post Office telephone system only – to the disgust of the National Telephone Company – applying for a liquor licence and borrowing another £25000. On April 1 the first batch of London Shipping Exchange members, numbers 1 to 686, were elected to the Baltic and it was found that number 1, Mr Stevenson, had recently died. At the final meeting of the board before the opening they refused to meet a deputation from the National Telephone Company. The Baltic committee made arrangements to evacuate the Abercorn Rooms; H. E. Moss and others held their last ship sales at the London Shipping Exchange at Billiter Street.

Only the ground floor was ready when 3000 members and friends saw Bridges Webb, Ernest Forwood, Henry Barnett and other directors escort Sir Marcus Samuel, Lord Mayor of London, to the dais inside the new marble Room on April 21 to declare the new Baltic open. Introducing the Lord Mayor the chairman recalled the Baltic's early history. 'The Baltic Coffee-House from which this institution bears its name,' he said, 'was soon found by those merchants to be inadequate to their requirements.'

'The chairman was not jesting', ran one newspaper report, 'but this remark provided a storm of laughter and the audience laughed and jeered as only a City audience can.' Describing the new facilities, Webb said 1500 telephone calls were made by members every day and they had adopted the Post Office system. The Postmaster General was opening a post office in the building.

The Baltic Mercantile & Shipping Exchange

Admit ....

on the occasion of the
opening of the Exchange,
by The Rt. Hon. Sir Marcus Samuel, Kt
Lord Mayor of the City of London,
on Tuesday, April 21st 1903, at 3 o'clock p.m.

The Entrance in St Mary Axe   *J. A. Findlay,*
will be closed at 5 mins. to 3 p.m.   *Secretary.*

Invitation to the opening of the new Exchange on April 21st, 1903

He concluded,

I hope that a great and noble career of usefulness is open for this exchange today, dedicated to the advancement of commercial and friendly relations with our world-wide connection, and the consequent development and consolidations of international concord. Commerce and mutual interest have done, and are doing, more to draw nations together than all the artifices of diplomacy, and these peaceful achievements of the merchant will out-rival even honourable success in war, while they cannot but lessen the possibilities of international misunderstanding, and will draw closer the bonds of mutual respect and of our common brotherhood.

Sir Marcus Samuel said that he was a member of the Baltic. Only the broad-minded views of the City Corporation had enabled the Exchange to be built at all. When the Court of Aldermen deputed his friend, Alderman Pound, and himself to show cause why it should be allowed to be built and Jeffrey's Square demolished 'we took the line that businessmen should always take action, and disregarding all ideas of red tape, seeing that it would injure no one but might benefit a great many, we reported to our colleagues that there was no objection to the scheme'.

Thanking the Lord Mayor, 'the chief magistrate of the first city in the world', Ernest Forwood said in opening the building he had impressed on it the character and position it would hold in the long future as the great centre of the shipping and commercial life of London. 'I predict that all businesses and trades will meet here, not only to do business but also to exchange views on current questions of the day, and to become knit together in friendly intercourse.'

It was back in Lombard Street before the Royal Exchange.

I believe this exchange will serve to strengthen the hands of our commercial men in meeting the severe foreign competition to which we are exposed today, and which I fear will be more acutely felt in the future. It will give us combination, and we in this country do not I think fully realise the power that combination has. I do not mean combining wealthy companies to squeeze out small firms or traders, but a combination to keep our commercial competitors from markets rightfully our own – markets which have been gained and retained by our forefathers and ourselves by much sacrifice of Britain's sons and Britons' money – as I am sure that every man in this room believes this exchange will strengthen our hands to uphold our commercial supremacy.

It was the greatest and most complete exchange in the country if not the whole world. He asked everyone there to conduct their new City home on broad-minded principles, always bearing in mind that it was for rich and poor alike, and that men should not be excluded by heavy entrance fees and old-fashioned rules.

It was no empty cliché for Ernest Forwood to say that it was a proud and happy moment. For few can faith and dogged persistence have been crowned with such complete success. The Jeffrey's Square project was entirely his brain-child. No one would have envied him more than James Dixon.

The building, which cost half a million pounds in 1903, still stands, with few modifications, for all to see today, though because of the narrowness of St Mary Axe, even more pronounced then than now, it is difficult to view the front in its proper perspective. The style chosen by architects Smith and Wimble – the latter died before opening day – was monumental. It is what at the time was considered 'palatial', an adjective much used in contemporary accounts. The design of the front is mock Renaissance in polished Norwegian, some said Swedish, granite. From the first floor rise six monolithic Corinthian columns, also of polished granite, with carved capitals surmounted by a pediment bearing a sculptured group representing Britannia, Neptune and Ceres to symbolize the Exchange's chief interests of shipping and grain. 'Severe grandeur' was the verdict of most of the reporters.

The Room, of 20000 square feet, is a marble hall in every respect except for the oak parquet floor and the glass domes and windows. The *Magazine of Commerce* described it as 'a veritable fairy palace'. Around the visitor were gathered the choicest marbles of Europe. 'Every column, every inch of wall space is of marble, carefully chosen to fulfil its purpose in a chromatic scheme. The result is a rare effect of architectural polychromy, rich and magnificent beyond anything else that London can show.'

The choice of marble was given to Messrs Fenning & Co. who searched Europe for material which, besides giving the required tone, could be obtained in columns of sufficient length. In St Peter's, Rome, they saw the kind of marble they would have liked, but the quarry from which it had been obtained four centuries before had long been closed. But Fenning had it re-opened, and from it extracted a number of seventeen-foot monoliths and had them shipped to England in specially constructed cases. Each weighed three tons and cost about £100. Owing to their brittleness they were worked entirely by hand. On arrival at St Mary Axe they were lifted into position by an ingenious device for distributing the strain longitudinally instead of transversely. The columns were cased with monolithic slabs of Skyros marble from a quarry in Thessaly in Greece. The broad arches of the bays were of yellow marble from Brescia in Italy. The 13-foot monoliths in the main vestibule were from Piastraccia. Here the windows carried the stained-glass arms of the principal London livery companies and the grain ports of Britain. In the high-ceilinged room on the left of the main entrance from St Mary Axe James Findlay ran the Exchange as secretary and manager. The exit to Bury Street was under a marble balcony; a marble staircase led down to the sale, arbitration and sample rooms, lavatories, dining and luncheon rooms and bars in the basement on the north side. There was a large 'Merchants Hall' for auctions, meetings and banquets below street level on the south side. In a lower basement were the boilers and the ventilation system which the directors, mindful of the fog of South Sea House, insisted should purify as well as heat the air. The artesian well, sunk to a depth of 480 feet, made the Exchange independent of the public water supply. The upper floors, which were not opened till later, were for letting as offices to tenants. Several members asked to be allowed to show the new building to their wives and mothers and sisters, and Findlay gave permission to bring ladies to the Exchange between 4.30 and 5.30.

Flushed with the success of the opening, the board of the Baltic Mercantile and Shipping Exchange met the next day and raised the membership limit from 2000 to 2500 (but in the event the peak of 2419 members reached in 1904 declined until, in 1910, it was 2270).

The Baltic committee met two days after the opening and re-solved that 'in order to ensure the thorough success of the New Exchange, this committee is of the opinion that a committee should be elected by the Members of the Room whose duties should be confined to the election of new members'. The question of wind-

ing up the accounts of the committee and transferring the investments to the new company was deferred – presumably to give
them some bargaining ammunition. But unless they were careful
they would have a 'committee and board' situation of the kind
which had run into trouble before and which the new constitution
was designed to avoid.

They asked the company to find employment for Mrs Reader
and Miss Charteris who had been for many years in the Baltic
dining room, which they agreed to; and donated gratuities
amounting to £100 to a number of people, including £10 to
Henry Goodfellow, the telephone attendant, who was later
pensioned off at £1 a week, and £20 to Charles Oxley who was
going to transfer to St Mary Axe as assistant secretary of the
new company under James Findlay.

There was a presentation to Mr Groves, chief 'caller' at South
Sea House for very many years. Handing him a silver tobacco box
John Wrenn said the old Baltic had gone and unfortunately many
old members with it.

A new building and, to a great extent, a new generation stand in their stead.
But the tones of your sonorous voice which so frequently summoned us to
meet the good luck or the bad luck which was handed in to us at the door,
will long linger in the recollections of the old members and arouse echoes
of old friendly feelings in which you bear your full share.

The committee did not meet again until June 16 when their
agreement with the Baltic Mercantile and Shipping Exchange Ltd
was submitted, and 'it was agreed that the books of the Baltic
Committee be closed and the accounts audited and the balance
sheet approved by Mr Taylor; also that the investments be sold
and the cash placed in deposit.'

The last meeting of the Baltic committee, with Seth Taylor in
the chair, took place on July 9, 1903. The others who attended
were Henry Seymour, John Wrenn, Sigismund Mendl, Edward
the last resolution:
Power, Edmund Carver and Septimus Glover. The latter moved

That a draft memorandum of agreement said to be agreed between the
solicitors of the New Company and the Baltic Committee, resolved That
the same be referred to the Chairman and Mr Glover to confer with Mr

Tilleard with instructions to sign if, consulting with Mr Tilleard, they are satisfied and that the Committee is fully protected against any liability which may attach to the Committee under previously signed agreement or otherwise.

A guarded conclusion to fifty years of positive achievement with which Thomas Tooke, William Wilson and the other cautious founders of the committee of 1823 would have approved thoroughly.

Five days later (on July 14) the final contract between committee and Exchange Company was signed and sealed, but, according to the board minute,

the Baltic Committee before handing over the assets to which this company is entitled under the contract, asked that they might be indemnified against any further claims, and after consideration it was decided to give the indemnity. As the assets of the Baltic Committee have not been handed over to this company, the secretary was instructed to defer for the present sending out the circular to the members as to the shares they are entitled to under the contract between Company and Committee.

The committee's experience with Michel Rodocanachi and his board was not swiftly forgotten. But the circular went out two days later. The Baltic committee's assets – £10587 in cash at the Bank of England – finally became the property of the Baltic Mercantile and Shipping Exchange Ltd on July 16. The Baltic committee was no more.

The Baltic was dead, long live the Baltic! A new reign began under a dictator who gave it prestige and vitality as never before. It was said that James Arbuckle Findlay took the decisions at St Mary Axe, and the board was nothing but a rubber stamp which confirmed them. However true that may have been, Findlay's unpopularity with the rank and file seems undeniable. It is the fate of all disciplinarians. Having come from the Shipping Exchange, he naturally had a bias towards shipping matters, but he was always open to any suggestion for the expansion of the body of which he now found himself the supreme head, and ready to consider any means of widening its reputation.

He agreed to allow members of the Timber Trades Federation to join the Exchange on equal terms with original Baltic members

Balance standing to the credit of the account of

The Baltic Committee

on the evening of the 15th July 1903.

£10,587 . 15/-

Ten Thousand five hundred & eighty seven pounds fifteen shillings ————

BANK OF ENGLAND,

16th July 1903

Asst **Chief Cashier.**

(546) 10/00

Examined,

Bank of England receipt for £10 587, 1903

Average Market Letter.

THE "BALTIC," LONDON.

WEDNESDAY, DECEMBER 9th, 1908.

			s.	d.	
Town Tallow	....	℔ cwt.	30	6	**PARTICULARS OF TALLOW**
					Returned Dec. 1st, 1908
Fat by ditto	....	℔ 8 lb		9	
Australian Mutton do.	℔ cwt.		32	3	Stock Packages 12,329
Ditto Beef ditto.	....	,,	30	–	Tons Gross 4,833
Melted Stuff	....	,,	20	–	
Rough ditto	....	,,	8	3	Delivered .... 5,250 *(Last Month)*
Tallow Greaves	....	,,	13	–	Landed .... 7,588 *(Last Month)*

COMPARATIVE PRICES OF TALLOW, &c. FOR FIVE YEARS.
WEDNESDAY, DECEMBER 2nd, 1908.

Corresponding Week.	1904		1905		1906		1907		1908	
	s.	d.	s.	d.	s.	d.	s.	d.	s.	d.
Price of Town Tallow	27	6	28	3	34	3	33	0	30	6
Ditto, Australian Mutton, ditto	28	6	31	0	35	6	34	0	32	3
Ditto, Beef, ditto	26	0	27	6	33	0	32	3	30	0
Ditto Melted Stuff	17	0	17	6	23	6	23	0	20	0
Ditto Rough ditto	8	0	7	9	10	9	9	9	8	3
Stock	6.069		5.676		6.555		11.388		12.329	

JAMES GAZE, Clerk,
297, Liverpool Road, Islington, N.

London Average Market Letter Committee report for 1908

in 1903. Some eighty took advantage of his offer, but the idea of a timber exchange within the Baltic never materialized. When members of the petroleum trade asked for similar privileges, Findlay turned them down. In 1905 he appointed 'honorary' agents of the Exchange in ports on various trade routes throughout the world and invited them to submit monthly reports on trade and conditions in their docks. He supported the formation of the Baltic and White Sea Conference in 1905, designed to regulate freights and reconcile the opposing interests of merchants and shipowners on such matters as the strike and ice clauses in charter-parties. He encouraged the formation of the London Cattle Food Trade Association in August 1906 to establish uniform contracts and arbitration systems for the cake and meal trade. Frederick N. Garrard and Herbert Grimsdale were the first president and vice-president.

The amalgamation of the London Shipping Exchange with the Baltic gave a new fillip to the formation of groups with common cultural and sporting interests, and in 1907 a member, called Leopold Marx, and others formed the Baltic Amateur Dramatic and Orchestral Society which Broughton Black of Dulwich had suggested in 1900. Marx persuaded C. W. Gordon to be the society's president and among the vice-presidents was ex-Baltic member, Beerbohm Tree. Their first production was a play called *The Second in Command*. In August 1907 the group changed its name to the Baltic Amateur Dramatic and Operatic Society with John Harrison as honorary secretary. A series of straight and musical plays were mounted every year, mainly at the Scala Theatre in Charlotte Street, and the performances were great social occasions – everyone turned out in evening dress. A member of the cast of *The Rose of Persia* in 1910 was a clerk in the accounts department of shipbrokers Watts, Watts & Co. called Ronald Colman, who became the well-known Hollywood star of silent films and early talkies. With interruptions only from the two world wars the society flourished* under producers like Cecil Howard,

*Its activities were only brought to an end when the Scala Theatre was demolished in 1967 and there had already been a falling off of attendances. In its hey-day it was one of the half-dozen leading amateur dramatic societies of London and set a very high standard of singing, acting and production.

Sydney Ewart and Dudley Moore, and under the musical direction from 1928 of Norman Bidgood. It was responsible for many 'amateur premières'. It was good public relations for the Baltic, and James Findlay could not but approve. So was the annual dinner at the Savoy Hotel at which in 1906, for instance, A. J. Balfour was guest of honour (see poster illustrated opposite).

It gave Findlay greater satisfaction, however, when leading shipbrokers came to see him in 1911 to suggest the time had come for *them* to form an organization to safeguard their interests and improve their status. They included Charles Gee, J. F. Fawcett, Howard Glover (son of Sir John Glover, knighted in 1900, whom he had succeeded as senior partner of Glover Brothers), H. G. Kellock, the ship auctioneer, Sir Thomas Devitt, Howard Houlder and Marmaduke Lawther. After a meeting at the Baltic to explain the aims of forming such a group, the Institute of Shipbrokers was born. Its objects were to provide for the better definition and protection of the profession of shipbrokers by a system of examination, to report on subjects of interest to shipbrokers and communicate them to chambers of commerce and other public bodies, and to protect and promote the interests of everyone concerned in shipbroking. James Findlay acted as honorary secretary of what at first was a committee and was not formally associated until 1913. It obtained a royal charter in 1920 as the Institute of Chartered Shipbrokers.

For reasons which cannot have been wholly unconnected with the talks he had on these matters, in April 1911 Findlay issued a warning about 'the serious losses which have been incurred by shipowners through agents acting for irresponsible principals and who have failed to carry out their contracts'. In the event of chartering agents acting for principals abroad who to their knowledge had failed to carry out contracts, they would be deemed guilty of improper conduct and dealt with under the rules of the Exchange.

Before the days of the Welfare State, the Baltic, like similar institutions, had a role of providing social insurance, and in November

FACING PAGE *Poster announcing the annual dinner of the Baltic Exchange, 1906*

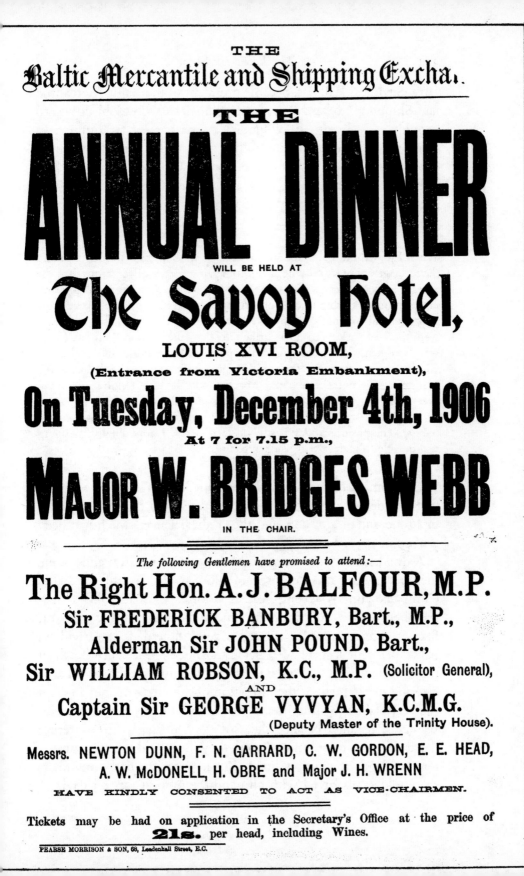

1912 Sir Lucas Ralli Bt, became president of the Baltic Mercantile and Shipping Exchange Benevolent Society whose object was to provide assistance to its voluntary subscribers of two guineas a year, whose circumstances, as the rules had it, 'rendered them deserving of help'. It was complementary to the older 'Cereals'.

Bridges Webb died in 1913 at the age of sixty-four and was succeeded as chairman by Henry Barnett who told a newspaper reporter,

When I joined the Baltic the steam tonnage was far less than today. In fact the tonnage has practically doubled, for against vessels of 3000 tons then the average is 6000 tons now. For some years there was a time of great depression in the tramp steamship trade, but fortunately the year 1912 saw a very great improvement in English shipping. Many causes led to this, but the chief were the coal strike, the dock strike and the Turkish war. This last factor was of immense benefit to English shipping, for the majority of Greek boats which are the great competitors in the tramp business, were bottled up in the Mediterranean ports and could not get out. English freights went up, everybody was busy and in consequence companies were able to pay from 15 per cent to 25 per cent dividends and put considerable sums away as reserve. The position today is still satisfactory and I hope English shipping will be able to maintain its place in future.

The number of members of the Baltic, which had dipped in the first decade of the new century, rallied to 2377 in 1913, bringing in an income of £20428, and the credit balance, which had been £9389 in 1910, rose to £14224 in 1913.

A dividend of 7 per cent had been declared in 1913, and to one member at least this savoured of the bad old days of the Baltic Company and its wrong-headed priority of shareholders first, members second. At the annual general meeting on May 26, 1914, Stamati Eumorfopoulos moved a resolution that 'the dividend be $5\frac{1}{2}$ per cent instead of 7 per cent and the difference between these amounts be devoted to improvements in the room and catering department at the discretion of the directors, but to meet the complaints so often heard from users of the room'. He also wanted a detailed balance sheet of the working of the catering department to be submitted to shareholders, and a more competent manager to be appointed. But a majority of the member-shareholders disagreed with him and the motion was rejected.

When the world went to war in August 1914, it was not un-expected that an institution like the Baltic, which was the world in microcosm, should find itself divided into the warring camps of the belligerents in the field. To the directors of 1914 their responsi-bility to members was crystal clear. It had been the prime aim of the founders of the Baltic committee, which was intensified by those who had succeeded them, to enable members never to have any doubt in their minds about whom they were dealing with when they met another member, or his clerk or his guest, in the Room at 58 Threadneedle Street, South Sea House or St Mary Axe. To be a member of the Baltic was synonymous with financial stability and business probity. When Britain declared war against Germany and her allies, which included Bulgaria, Austria and Turkey, the directors considered it their duty to distinguish not only the commercial sheep from the commercial goats, but the King's friends from the King's enemies. There seemed no middle course, and they shirked none of the expected 'unpleasantness' which would inevitably arise from publicly denying old and commercially trusted merchants and shipowners access to the Room of which they had been members for so long, on account of their German birth. In behaving as they did, members of the Baltic were only reflecting the general mood of the country, intensified perhaps by the sense of *esprit de corps* which any closely knit group always engenders.

In any event there was not much time for clear thinking. Three days after war broke out on August 4, James Findlay received a telephone call from Scotland Yard asking for a list of foreign members of the Exchange, indicating whether or not they were naturalized, and a list of foreigners employed by members and their home addresses. At their meeting of August 12 the directors considered the position of German and Austro-Hungarian mem-bers of the Exchange and their clerks, and resolved 'until further notice no German shall be allowed to enter the exchange' but that this would not apply to naturalized British subjects. In September the directors decided to exclude any clerk whose principal had been excluded, whether he was German or not. Principals who were excluded were refused the right to appoint a substitute for the duration.

Six member firms were suspended in September 'in which the major portion of the capital belongs to aliens of German or Austrian nationality', most prominent of which, ironically, was British Petroleum Company. This was the marketing organization established in Britain in November 1906 by the Europäische Petroleum Union which had been promoted by the Deutsche Bank and other European oil interests in June of that year. At the outbreak of World War I in 1914 German interests held 50·5 per cent of EPU's issued capital, and Russian, French and Belgian interests the remaining 49·5 per cent.

The list of suspended firms was given to the Admiralty. All of them protested; all were told there was 'nothing to add'. The chairman of British Petroleum however was granted an interview, but Findlay was instructed to confirm the previous formula – 'nothing to add'. The board refused to reconsider their case even when British Petroleum had another try, enclosing a pamphlet and a press report of a statement in the House of Commons. In August 1916 the Board of Trade issued an order declaring that British Petroleum Company Ltd and Petroleum Steamship Company Ltd, also formed by EPU, were to be classed as enemy concerns and their shares vested in the Public Trustee and the nominees. In this way the one per cent German control was eliminated, and in 1917 the Anglo-Persian Oil Company which had been formed in 1909 purchased the outstanding shares. The latter changed its name to Anglo-Iranian Oil Company in 1935 and to *The* British Petroleum Company Ltd in 1954.

Though Belgian-born refugees were admitted to the Exchange without subscription, no substitutes or visitors of German or Austrian birth were admitted for the duration, notwithstanding naturalization. Aliens introduced as visitors had to bring and show their passports – to show they were not Germans or Austrians or Turks.

The Baltic acted swiftly, but not swift enough for some. The anonymous head of a leading firm of shipbrokers told a *Daily Mail* reporter in October 1914,

Only now after the war has been in progress two months, has its [the Baltic's] committee awakened to the fact that the foreign members have been privileged to gain day after day from the notice boards and otherwise, information most valuable to the enemy. At last the doors of the Baltic have been closed against them, but they would still be open now if some of the older members had their way.

There was general satisfaction however when W. W. Kellock, of C. W. Kellock's, auctioned the first German steamer to be condemned by the Prize Court, the *Marie Glaeser*, at the Baltic on October 21 – no such sales had been held since the Crimean War. It was the first of many. When Ernest Hartley, of Lachlan & Co., brokers to the Admiralty Marshal, auctioned four German schooners in December 1914, he used the hammer last wielded by John Lachlan for the same purpose in 1855. At the end of the sale he presented the hammer to H. W. Lovell, the Admiralty Marshal.

Inevitably there were accusations of shipowners making large profits from high freights, and inevitably there was a member of the Baltic to rebut them. 'H.P.R.' wrote from the Baltic to the *Morning Post* in January 1915 pointing out that 12s. 6d. freight obtainable from South America before the war left no profit in view of the delays from scarcity of labour, congestion and lack of lighterage. A 5000 tonner took a fortnight to discharge its cargo of grain in London. Costs were very much higher – war risk premiums, provisions, coals had doubled – wages had risen 20 per cent. No wonder freights had quadrupled.

When a prominent shipbroker declared shipowners were making profits of 200 and 300 per cent, the *Daily Mail* sent a reporter for a statement from Henry Barnett, the Baltic's chairman.

Freights which as recently as early December were offered at 25s. and 26s. a ton are now offered at 57s. a ton, and a merchant does not hesitate to pay that figure because he knows that if he does not the shipowner will be offered that or a higher price elsewhere, and he will be unable to move his goods. The reasons for the shortage of ships are many. All the German ships have ceased to carry goods. There are many British ships laid up and unable to get out of the Baltic and Black Sea ports. The British Government has commandeered a tremendous number of ships. The Allied Governments have done the same. Russia chartered a large number of British ships. Other factors are the extra length of voyages owing to the necessity of travelling by longer and safer routes, and the congestion at all ports and docks. The delays mean that voyages on the average are 25 per cent longer than before the war. Shipowners have had many lean times when they could make no profits, and are entitled to recoup themselves now that ships are in demand. If the Government fixes maximum charges for freights, as is suggested, the first problem that will arise is, who shall hire the boat? There will be six merchants wanting it, and only one can have it. Many boats will be diverted to foreign trade, where huge freights can be earned, and there will be a still greater scarcity of boats to carry cargoes to Great Britain. My opinion is that freight charges have nearly reached their maximum, and that as soon as the Argentine wheat crop and the American maize crop are moved there will be a tendency in the direction of lower rates.

The shipping of Russian grain, except for a trickle through Archangel, had stopped entirely but Indian wheat began coming in April 1915.

The *Daily Express* pursued the same line. How far was the ship-owner to blame, they asked 'a leading member' of the Baltic, for the enormous freight rates which helped to raise the price of wheat and meat? He expostulated,

It is not fair, it is most unjust. The shipowner is absolutely helpless in the matter. All he can do is to accept the price which the world offers him. He would be unjust to his shareholders if he did otherwise; and in these days shipowners are not individuals, they are directors of companies with share-holders. It is their duty to make the best dividends that they can for their shareholders. If they neglected to do so they would be betraying their trust.

The word 'blockade' began going the rounds for the first time since Napoleon's Berlin Decrees. This time it was by submarine. But, as a writer commented in the *Morning Post* in February 1915,

for all the effect upon the markets most likely to be affected one would have thought yesterday that no such thing as a blockade of these islands existed. The matter was never referred to without a jest upon the Baltic Exchange which, after all, is the centre of the world's shipping. In fact it must be a severe blow to the pride of the Germans to learn of the levity with which their threats are being treated by a body of the hardest-headed community in the world. If anything can cause a shipowner to treat a subject seriously, it is the danger of losing his ship.

The *Morning Post*'s correspondent took a serious view, too, of the Government's interfering with normal trading by bulk pur-chase of wheat, whether for reserves or otherwise, and made strong representations to the Board of Agriculture and Fisheries along with members of the London Corn Trade Association. As a result of these the Board sent a letter to the LCTA, which was published on the Baltic, to say they would make no further purchases of wheat. Uncertainty had been created by recent selling in London and Liverpool of wheat bought on Government account which had certainly brought the prices down, but, complained a *Times* leader, the trade had been kept ignorant of the Government's intentions.

Shipowners took an angry view, too, of the Germans' sinking of the *Lusitania* and Findlay's slow reaction to it. The *Daily Telegraph* of May 11, 1915, reported,

When the notice was posted at The Baltic there was a perfect howl of indignation at the timidity displayed by the committee. A meeting was immediately called, which was attended by about a thousand members, and it was resolved to petition the committee to expel all members of enemy origin.

The latter, knowing they would receive no sympathy from their own committee, presented a memorial to the Lord Mayor of London:

We, the undersigned naturalised British members of the Baltic Exchange desire to put on record our horror and detestation of the abominable methods and actions of barbarism foreign to all civilised usage adopted by our enemies in carrying on the war. We take this opportunity of reaffirming our devoted loyalty to our King and country, as undertaken by our oath of allegiance in becoming citizens of this great Empire with which we have identified ourselves for so many years.

The directors decided 'that all members and clerks of German, Austrian and Turkish birth, although they may be naturalized British subjects, be suspended'. This was not to apply to any member or clerk over sixty years of age or to any member or clerk with a son serving in the forces. No member could employ a clerk who was a German, Austrian or Turkish subject.

At the close of High Change on the day this decision was announced (May 11), a member climbed into the rostrum and protested that the directors had not gone far enough. He carried those on the floor with him in resolving to urge the directors to *expel* all Germans, Austrians and Turks, not merely suspend them; that members over sixty should not be exempt; and that British clerks of expelled firms should be refused admittance. A strong opinion was expressed, however, that the ruling should not apply to members born in enemy countries whose sons were serving in the British forces. A committee to make representations to the board was formed on the spot.

A prominent shipowner told a *Journal of Commerce* reporter,

I have been a member of the Baltic Exchange for 36 years, but I have never seen anything like the demonstration this morning. Members were exasperated almost to the extent of losing their heads. And a lot has to happen before a British business man feels as bad as that! The time was over for polite requests and half measures. All Germans had to be kicked out . . . This *Lusitania* business had put the lid on it, and the innocent must suffer with the guilty. We must pull out the roots of this cancer.

A deputation from the Baltic, Lloyd's, the Corn Exchange and the Stock Exchange visited the House of Commons to seek the internment of all 'alien enemies' in London. They walked in procession from the Royal Exchange but were stopped at Somerset House. However at the House of Commons the Attorney General promised to lay their views before the Cabinet. The anger was intensified by stories of ill-treatment of prisoners of war, the use of poison gas, the air raids and 'atrocities'.

A notice posted in the Exchange warned shipowners:

The directors have received information that several firms of alien nationality, domiciled in the USA, are assisting the enemy and have agents on this Exchange quoting their business. Notice is hereby given that the directors will seriously consider the conduct of any member of the Exchange who may deal directly or indirectly with such alien enemy firms or any firms employed by them on their behalf to negotiate their business.

Findlay compiled a blacklist of firms and people with whom members were not allowed to trade. It was open for any member to see but no copies or extracts could be made. Findlay put up a notice saying the directors would suspend or expel any member who might trade or deal with any firm on the list. A public list was posted of twenty-five names of those who had ceased to be members 'owing to the state of hostilities existing between this country and the German, Austro-Hungarian and Ottoman Empires'.

The headline of the news story in the *Financial News* of August 28, 1915, ran,

SUSPENSIONS ON BALTIC CREATE GREAT SENSATION

Considerable excitement exists in commercial circles in the City in connection with the reported suspensions on the Baltic. The drastic action of the directors involved, it is said, seven or eight members, some of them the representatives of steamship companies trading with Holland, and wealthy firms who have been admitted to the Baltic for very many years. The charge, so far as we can gather from rumours, is that of trading with the enemy. One report even goes so far as to say that one of the suspended members was the founder and controller of the Dutch Overseas Trust through which business this country and Holland is now conducted.

They appealed to the directors to make a disclosure so as to end rumours, but no announcement was ever made from St Mary Axe.

In spite, or perhaps because, of a proliferation of instructions, many members were far from clear just where they stood. Their confusion was expressed by Ernest Glover, son of Septimus, now himself a director, who wrote to Frederick Garrard, chairman, on August 27, 1915:

Our notice re W.H.M. and the other one about Yankees still continue to agitate the room generally. A very pertinent request is, I think, one asking for a statement of the directors' desires as to what they will consider members may or may not do. One comment is that some member might find himself suspended without reason being given for some action that he had no idea would meet with our disapproval. Of course we are reasonable people but still the cry is not an unreasonable one – viz: Tell us what you want us to do & we will abide by it. I have been thinking a good deal about it and have sketched a notice which I think might be stuck up in the room – or something to this effect.

But members were required to show not only their lack of disloyalty but their loyal willingness to play their part in defeating the enemy in the field. On December 14, 1915, it was decided 'that no person shall be admitted as a member, clerk to a member or a substitute who is of eligible age for military service who has not offered himself to the authorities'. At the same meeting the board put their words into action by handing a white feather to Mr C whose election was 'not entertained, he not having offered himself for military service'. Two months after war was declared Marmaduke Lawther had received permission to use the Exchange for three evenings a week for drilling members eligible to enlist, and by January 1915 an official 'Baltic Drill Corps' had been formed. The enlistment of large numbers of young men who earned their livelihood with members' firms created an acute staffing problem and clerks were at a premium. All kinds of under-hand methods were used to lure an over-age or physically unfit executive from one firm to another, and when the practice grew to regrettable proportions, Findlay put a notice up saying no member was allowed to engage any clerk of another member firm until permission was given. Any member who contravened this ruling would be suspended. This was regarded as *ultra vires* and produced a petition in protest. Findlay replied with another notice sympathizing with the view expressed by the petitioners but re-stating that 'owing to the war the necessity has arisen of protecting members whose staffs have been denuded by responding to the Country's Call'.

In 1917 James Findlay's staff of four girls was augmented by one office boy of the name of Jack Walker, whose duties included helping Charles Oxley, younger than Findlay, who, as we have seen, had stayed on as assistant secretary. A Saturday morning duty for the young Walker was to buy from Leadenhall Street Post Office the postal orders which the Exchange were sending as allowances to the wives of staff in the forces. On such a morning in August, as he turned the corner by St Andrew Undershaft on his return from this errand, he heard someone shout, 'You'd better take cover!' and saw a man coming down the street with a placard bearing the words 'TAKE COVER'. He looked up and saw twenty-eight German Gothas in V formation coming over Houndsditch and heard the gun on the Tower of London open up at them. He ran back to the Baltic and into the Bury Street entrance to find Findlay running down into the basement. 'Come down here!'

shouted Findlay, but remembering that the basement also sheltered the gas meter Jack Walker preferred to stay where he was and, crouching in the passage, he heard the explosion as a bomb hit the staircase and blew open the doors and windows. Arrangements were afterwards made for the Exchange to be closed within ten minutes of an air raid warning. Should the building be hit Findlay was authorized to close all the doors of the building at once.

After Paine's, the solicitors, had told Findlay that the articles of association had become so altered 'as to become difficult of interpretation', in May 1917 new articles were drafted and presented to a general meeting, but the resolution approving them was withdrawn, and a counter-proposal by yet another ginger group of members urging a major constitutional change was discussed in its stead.

This was probably aimed at relaxing the iron discipline of James Findlay, for it recommended the appointment of a floor committee to give members a bigger say in the management of the Room. It was to be composed of four directors and four non-directors. It was the idea which had been submitted and rejected some years back. It had the same reception in 1917. The directors agreed with the ends but not the means, which they saw as restoring the dual control which had led to the unhappy antagonisms at South Sea House. They made a counter-proposition. They proposed augmenting the board by three directors balloted for by members on the principle of one member one vote, and having a floor committee composed of three 'shareholder' directors and three 'ballot' directors'. Henry Colebrook and his ginger group were prepared to accept this, but insisted that the ballot directors should be balloted for by everyone with entrée to the floor, including clerks of seven years' standing as well as pre-1892 clerks who had the status of full members. Moreover they wanted clerks to be able to own shares. Findlay would not agree to this, but was persuaded to refer the matter to the whole membership.

In his letter to members Findlay pointed out that there were then 1400 members (including twenty-three clerks elected before 1892 who ranked as members) and 702 clerks elected after 1892 who were not 'members'. Of that 702 it was estimated that 387 would become eligible under the conditions of the new scheme. The chairman of the board would preside over meetings of the floor committee and would have a second or casting vote. 'By authority of the Board, this Committee shall act as an Advisory Committee to the Board on all matters relating to the management of the Floor and the convenience of Members.'

The controversial sixth clause in the new proposal which led to the referendum was as follows:

Every Clerk who has been on the Room for a continuous period of at least seven years shall be entitled to obtain and own one share in the Baltic Company and upon so doing shall become a Clerk entitled to vote in the election of Directors, but shall not be eligible for election to the Board of Directors.

Members were asked to answer Yes or No to three questions. Less than half bothered to return their papers – 521 out of the 1440 sent out – and the majority (366) voted for the scheme as proposed; twenty-three voted for the scheme but without representation of clerks; 122 preferred to have no alteration in the management of the Exchange. Findlay and the board bowed to the wishes of the Room and the scheme was confirmed at the general meeting of February 5, 1918, and incorporated in new articles. The first three ballot directors were nominated from among the members in April – each nomination being signed by at least twenty members. The first three to be elected as directors by ballot were D. Hick, F. V. Japp and H. L. Routh. They became members of a general purposes committee.

The Baltic was still predominantly a grain exchange and throughout World War I the Government allowed members to trade individually. There was food rationing after a time, but there was no complete control of supplies. There was also a pooling system of ships but not through the Ministry. But there were necessarily certain restrictions which affected the corn trade more than any other.

The state of the trade had been bad for some years before 1914. Price cutting was rife and many traders had found it hard to make a decent living. The acceleration given by the war to the development of the petrol engine and the motor industry led to the quick disappearance of horses from most of the farms and their replacement by motor trucks. Agricultural merchants had to adapt to the changing conditions brought about by large-scale mechanization.

Soon after the outbreak of war merchants in Lincolnshire, Birmingham, Cornwall and other provincial centres set up local associations to exchange views and act for their mutual benefit. Some of these felt it was something which should be done nationally, and on January 19, 1917, an informal meeting of corn merchants was held in the board room of the Corn Exchange Tavern in Mark Lane under the chairmanship of A. L. Sadd of Norwich to discuss the formation of an association of buyers and sellers of home-grown grain, and the National British and Irish Corn Trade Association came into being. A. E. K. Wherry, of Bourne, Lincolnshire, was appointed honorary secretary and the first meeting of its council took place at the Great Eastern Hotel in London on May 8, 1917, with L. Hampson, of King's Lynn, as president. The name was later changed to the National Association of Corn and Agricultural Merchants (NACAM).

When on April 17, 1917, Lord Davenport, the Food Controller, published orders fixing maximum prices of wheat, oats and barley, the association received telegrams from all over the country urging them to press the Government to withdraw them – 88s. to 90s. for 504 lbs of wheat – as many merchants had stocks on hand which had cost much more. The next morning the council of the association went to the Ministry of Food which had taken over the Duke of Westminster's home, Grosvenor House in Park Lane, and demanded to see Lord Davenport. When they were told the minister could not see them for at least a fortnight, they threatened to occupy Grosvenor House unless they were allowed to see him that afternoon. They were told Sir Henry Rew, the Permanent Under-Secretary, would grant them an audience of ten minutes. At the end of a two-hour session a new order for prices was drafted; it was approved by six that evening. It was a good start to its avowed objective to protect the interests of its members, a large number of whom belonged to the Baltic.

In 1919 a National Federation of Corn Trade Associations was established to act as the liaison between the Government and the Corn Trade Association at the seven grain importing centres of London, Bristol, Liverpool, Glasgow, Leith, Hull and Belfast to organize the release of stocks, and this was kept alive as the link between the trade and the Government of the day. At the back of everyone's minds was the possible outbreak of another conflict when Government control would again be needed. For the same reason certain quarters pressed for the nationalization of Britain's mercantile marine. In 1916 the Trades Union Council sent a deputation to Mr Asquith, the Prime Minister, to demand state ownership and control of all merchant shipping, but in spite of the Parliamentary Secretary to the Shipping Controller advocating outright nationalization, the Government rejected the proposal. But by November 1918 a large state merchant fleet had come into being including prize ships and vessels bought and registered in the name of the Controller of Shipping. The action of the TUC in 1916 haunted shipping interests in Britain for many years to come.

Looking back on the war period in 1921, Sir Theo Angier wrote:

All through the long years of bitter struggle, the Baltic gave freely of its men in every branch, fighters and workers at home, and money. From its members the Government found its Controller and best organisers of the great mercantile marine, the right hand of the Navy and feeder of the nations. The merchants and brokers provided the leaders and staff of the corn and seed import control. Wherever experts in commerce and other branches were needed they were to be found among the Baltic members and freely they offered their services, in most cases without remuneration. No institution set a more noble and patriotic example, one to be remembered and writ large in the nation's record and Roll of Honour.

One of the most remarkable and praiseworthy activities of the Baltic during the 'Great War' was the raising of money for war charities. Between August 1914 and September 1918 members of the Baltic gave £155722 to causes including Romanian Relief (£1855), the Baltic 'Our Day' Fund (£13495), the Baltic YMCA Christmas Gift Fund (£10559), the Baltic Belgian Relief Fund (£1255), the Baltic French Red Cross Collection (£1810), the

Serbian Red Cross Fund (£1199), the Baltic and Corn Exchange List for King George's Fund For Sailors, the Lady Markham Lamp and George Robey's Appeal. The largest sum was raised for the Baltic and Corn Exchange Base Hospital at Calais – £98 000. The Baltic also bought a hostel in Cairo for the YMCA.

James Findlay allowed collectors for funds with which the Baltic was not specifically connected to make their headquarters at St Mary Axe so long as they did nothing to detract from its position as a solely male preserve. He gave Dame Clara Butt permission to sell emblems for Joan of Arc Day *outside* the Exchange; but turned down the application of the Croix de Rouge for their 'lady friends' to go on the Floor for a flag day. He refused to allow a member to make a speech from the rostrum at lunch time about Russian prisoners.

Sir Edward Hain was the instigator of a scheme to raise a £50 000 Guarantee Fund to provide pensions for the widows of Baltic members who should lose their lives. Most impressive of all, a sum of £483 871 was 'lent' to the Government by members of the Baltic free of interest 'to be used in case of need, as payment of death duties and/or taxation . . . for the duration of the war and three months thereafter, or at the lender's option to be repayable on demand'.

But the Baltic's greatest contribution to the war was the lives of its sixty-two members, fortunately a very small proportion of those who went to serve. Memorial services at St Andrew Undershaft for those who fell were held at regular intervals throughout the four war years. The last, for fourteen members including Krikor G. Gulbenkian, and two staff, was held on September 17, 1918. The names of all of them were inscribed on marble panels unveiled in the Room in July 1920, to which five stained-glass windows were added as a war memorial in 1922.

If any had thought that with Armistice Day on November 11, 1918, and the end of the fighting on the fields of France, would come an end to the old animosities on the floor of the Baltic, they were soon disillusioned. The following week the board met to consider the admission of naturalized Germans or those of enemy origin, and whether they should continue to insist on visitors showing their passports. After a long discussion it was decided to allow matters to remain as they were until the terms of the peace had been signed. They were told that some members thought the Baltic as such should express a corporate view on the form the terms of peace should take and the payment of an indemnity by the enemy. But when a group of members asked Findlay permission to post a letter in the Room urging the extradition of the ex-Kaiser and the ex-Crown Prince he refused it. Following a petition the directors received in December on the admission of enemy born and neutral subjects, they agreed to see a deputation. They decided to adopt a new set of rules on the subject by which no application for membership would be entertained from anyone of present enemy birth until further notice; anyone having a partner of enemy origin would be expelled. Applications for membership by foreigners other than of enemy origin would only be entertained provided the applicant had been engaged in business in Britain for seven years.

But Findlay found the new rules far from straightforward to apply. What should he do with the company which had a director of enemy origin and another a naturalized German, but two-thirds of whose shares were in British hands? Or the firm with a naturalized German as chairman whose son had been at the front for the last four years? It was difficult. But he had no difficulty in declining to contribute to the British Empire Union fund for publishing a booklet giving a list of Germans who had adopted English names.

When the Treaty of Versailles was finally signed, at their annual general meeting in June 1919 members altered the rules to extend membership only to those who had been born in the British Empire or were children of British subjects resident in any foreign country, or were British subjects by naturalization before December 31, 1915.

The Great War was over.

10. The Twenties and Thirties

Returning to normal involved more positive action than settling old scores with the defeated enemy. It was for the Baltic, as the clearing house for the cereal produce of the world, to overhaul the mechanics of the exercise and in doing so eliminate the evils which had developed during the conflict. Members realized the importance of putting their own house in order, and regulating their operations to their own satisfaction, before another Labour Government of the kind which had been in power for a few months in 1924 did it for them.

A problem which particularly affected the Baltic as an exchange was the role of the broker. Was a broker really necessary? To find an answer to this question – or to confirm that it was only rhetorical – the directors called a series of conferences in 1927 with grain merchants, millers and seed crushers, and grain and oilseed brokers. Apart from giving their views on brokers, many inevitably expressed opinions on the Baltic's own role as the self-appointed regulator of the natural course of trade. Many criticized the Baltic's assumed right to impose unified procedures. How far could, or should, rules 'interfere' with free methods of buying and selling? How far was it desirable for the Baltic to become a Brokers' Protection Society?

Sir Ernest Glover, chairman, opened the conference with the thirteen grain merchants by telling them it was felt by many that there was a tendency for the broker to be eliminated in transactions between merchants and buyers. F. Gamburg said it was no advantage for the merchant to sell direct as he had to give his $\frac{1}{2}$ per cent commission either to the buyer or broker. Before the war there were some forty buyers, but in 1927 there were only four or five representing immense interests. In the seed trade there were practically no brokers any more.

The only way for the trade to continue to exist, in the opinion of Sir Arthur Holmes, was for the Baltic and other exchanges to use their plenary powers to prevent the gigantic combinations from freezing out those who had made the trade. The Baltic should withhold rights of membership from those millers who did not buy through the usual channels, a merchant or broker. Sir Herbert Robson thought the trouble was direct buying by the large combines; 60 per cent of North American wheat was bought direct by combines in the US or Canada without the intervention of a broker. F. Kahl blamed the committee of the old Baltic. They had allowed a miller, Seth Taylor, to become a member and direct buying could be traced from that period. The Government had aggravated the position during the war by placing the broker on the dole. The trade had suffered too much from control; any interference would be detrimental to the interests of the broker. He doubted if any compulsory scheme, however desirable, would prove feasible since firms which figured as merchants could immediately become brokers. A. Hurst pointed out that in New York and Chicago, where the exchanges were not as powerful as the Baltic, it was clearly laid down that all transactions must pass through a broker. G. Eumorfopolous felt that to fetter trade in any way would drive it away from the Baltic, and if any attempt was made to lay down conditions as to buying and selling big firms would buy from the continent instead of on the Baltic. R. H. Hein agreed with him; it was extremely dangerous to lay down any hard and fast rules as to how business should be done. The broker's position could only be improved by goodwill.

Joseph Rank Ltd, Hovis Ltd, British Oil & Cake Mills Ltd, Associated London Flour Millers Ltd were among the seven millers and seed crushers who discussed the broker's position. J. W. Pearson of BOCM said the elimination of the broker was due to natural world development of commerce and he now dealt direct where he formerly dealt through an intermediary. In the past a broker had often provided credit and so was a necessity. That was no longer so. During the last twenty years there had been a marked change in commerce owing to combinations of buyers and sellers; trade was getting into fewer hands. Unless the broker was a necessity it would be a mistake to take artificial means to keep him alive. No Baltic regulations could prevent a buyer from sitting in his office and buying direct from the seller in his office. Should the Baltic decide that every contract between seller and buyer must pass through a broker it would probably result in a company like his withdrawing its representatives from the Exchange, and sending them to see sellers in their offices instead of on the Baltic.

S. B. Askew of Rank thought the broker served a useful purpose before the war when there was speculation on the continent, but now the majority of wheat sold was for direct consumption. The Russians sold direct to the big houses. Any steps to make the services of a broker compulsory would be to try to put the clock back. O. E. Robinson, of OLFM, agreed that the lack of work for the broker was the absence of speculation. The violent fluctuations in prices of wheat in 1925 had checked speculation. If the London option market could be re-established more business would come to the broker as he was essential for this type of trading. A. H. Hobley of the Co-operative Wholesale Society was convinced that the trade must be left free and unfettered. The policy of the pools was to get the grower to reach the consumer direct.

When finally thirty-three grain and oilseed brokers were consulted, H. A. Francis said the grain brokers themselves were largely to blame for the situation in which they found themselves. They had failed to co-operate. A lead should be given by the Federation of Corn Trade Associations. The directors of the Baltic could not force the trade to conduct its business in any particular way. The London Corn Trade Association contract was paramount throughout Europe and was a powerful weapon for forcing everyone to dovetail in with methods considered best for everyone. H. L. Routh disagreed; the LCTA contract was no longer paramount. Drastic action by the board of the Baltic would do more harm than good. F. E. Fehr thought it necessary to stop big combines forming their own brokerage business. In Horace Reynolds' opinion brokers got what they asked for; it was a case of survival of the fittest. G. N. Chapman advocated a change in the Baltic's rules requiring importers' and merchants' undertaking to do their business through a broker. B. Woodward said the Labour Government when in power brought forward a rather comprehensive scheme for working the grain and flour trades, and it would probably be put in the forefront again should they return to power. There should be a triple combination of millers, merchants and brokers to combat any Government interference. The London people should seriously consider evolving a new speculative contract. No trade could exist without a certain amount of reasonable speculation. A. Antunovitch said the use of the Baltic should be denied those firms which refused to deal through a broker.

The chairman invited the brokers to submit a concrete scheme for the re-instatement of brokerage business for consideration by the directors. On May 17 the Oil and Oilseeds Brokers' Association circularized their members seeking support for a scheme to categorize their membership into shippers, consumers, merchants and brokers, so there was no overlapping of activities.

No members of the first three categories would be permitted to trade except through the intermediary of a firm classed in the fourth category. Members declaring themselves brokers would have to be content to do strictly brokerage business only. They would not be allowed to operate in any way without a principal.

The grain brokers, said Hugh Trenchard, secretary, appeared to be entirely unorganized, but they were forming a committee with which the Oilseed Association would collaborate. 'Unless something is done promptly it is feared that direct dealing will eliminate the Broker.'

The Baltic directors took a year to digest all this and in July 1928 they decided 'in view of the deplorable condition of the grain and seed trades that a referendum be taken of members whether it is desirable for the rules to be amended that all transactions be effected through the medium of merchants and brokers'. On August 15 they sent out a circular to all members.

Urgent representations have been made to the directors by members of the Exchange engaged in the Grain, Seed, Oil and Produce trades that it would be an advantage if the rules of the Exchange were altered so as to make the employment of an intermediary obligatory in those trades, such rules to be drafted on similar lines to those which are in force on the Stock Exchange, Cotton Exchange, Rubber Exchange etc.

They were asked to say Yes or No to a question asking if they were in favour of this being done. Of the 1444 letters sent out, only 753 were returned. Of these 529 answered Yes; 210 No. Some fourteen were incomplete. Most of those who answered in favour were shipping members (267); 137 were in the grain trade, 101 in oilseeds, 24 were 'miscellaneous'. Having got this very definite expression of opinion – surprising in the light of the views put at the conferences against Baltic interference – the directors (perhaps for this reason) decided to take no further steps in the matter other than informing the LCTA and other interested bodies of the result.

The scale on which the buying and selling of grain took place on the floor at St Mary Axe in the 1920s was very considerable – around 250000 tons, worth £2½ million, a day. And, in spite of the attempts of the big combines on the continent and elsewhere to avoid the expense of a middleman, it was increasing. S. K. Thorpe, who supplied James Findlay with some notes on the subject for his book which was published in 1927, considered anyone who was so venturesome as to operate on c.i.f. terms in grain other than through the medium of a Baltic broker would soon find that he was frequently landed with a cargo at so much above the market value that it would pay him to avoid conducting the operation direct. There were many instances, he said, where the buying and selling department of the same house had dealt with each other through a broker without knowing that they were trading with themselves. Each department needed a broker to know that they were paying and receiving the market value.

The brokers of 1925 ascertained as early as possible what shippers were offering – the kinds of grain and the periods of shipment. In doing so they picked up a great deal of valuable information to help them judge probable market fluctuations during the day with which to advise prospective buyers and sellers. A broker was able to get buyers and sellers to concede on price and terms which neither could manage if they met face to face. Most hedging transactions

M

for merchants were done on the Baltic; they were better than buying or selling on the speculative option markets of the US, Canada or South America. The merchant or his agent on the Baltic each morning had offers of grain on c.i.f. terms at a price depending on what he could obtain for the cargo and what he could charter a vessel for. In the course of a series of brief conversations on the floor of the Baltic he obtained a firm offer of a vessel and a firm bid for the cargo by her, arranging all the details very much more easily and swiftly than by telephone and telegram or letter.

The work of a chartering clerk of the 1920s needed intelligence and energy. He had to be twenty-one before being admitted to the Baltic, but he would have started as an office boy at fourteen at ten shillings a week. His first duties would have been to run errands, take telegrams, copy letters in a press or duplicator. Hours were nine to six on weekdays and nine till one on Saturday morning. But once eligible for the Baltic he would earn about £150 a year, and would spend much of his time calling on outward charterers to ascertain their business – they disliked quoting their wants on the telephone – and there was considerable walking from Lloyds Avenue to Finsbury Circus. Tramp shipping depended on the outward coal trade from Newcastle, Hull and Glasgow, but principally from South Wales, to Italy, Spain, North Africa and Egypt as well as the various coaling stations at Gibraltar and the Atlantic Islands. The most important market was outward with coal to, and homeward with grain from, South America. The homeward grain business was in the hands of about six merchants, and a self-respecting chartering clerk, would have visited all of them, or found their representatives on the Baltic, by 10.45. He would then report to his seniors in the coffee room between 11 and noon, and telegrams and cables would be drafted to owners in the provinces and abroad. In the 1920s most principals still sported top hats; and many of them kept them on as they ate, as their coffee-house predecessors had done. Clerks wore bowlers or occasionally a boater. Most had lost their beards but large moustaches prevailed. There was no bar until 1930; what is now the main bar was the clerks' luncheon room. There was no snack bar;

the main luncheon room, with its paintings of Catherine the Great and other Russian tsars on loan from the Russia Company was patronized only by principals. In any event clerks could rarely afford to lunch at the Baltic in the 1920s; they preferred a good two-course meal for a shilling at Wilkinson's round the corner.

But a chartering clerk had the satisfaction of knowing that he was working on the ship chartering centre of the world. London was not only the shipping, but also the financial and insurance centre of all international trade. For this reason shipbrokers on the Baltic represented not only shipowners based in Britain but all overseas owners who had tramp tonnage to manage. The London market was so important that no foreign shipowner could afford to ignore it or be without regular information about its activities. Every ocean-going steamer had some representative on the Baltic who could advise its owner on what freights were available. Every merchant in every part of the world was similarly represented. It was the 'floor situation' of the Royal Exchange all over again, with daily intercourse between those with empty holds and those with cargoes to fill them, and the quick exchange of information and contracts on a basis of mutual trust and respect. Brokers were no longer merely fixing cargoes for the spaces of British shipowners; they were marrying up foreign merchants with foreign shipowners, neither of whom would have easily been introduced but for the common ground, the crowded Floor, at St Mary Axe. The tightness of this community, and the familiarity of its members the one with the other, had the effect of stabilizing rates and ensured that no shipowner needed to take any lower rate than his neighbour, and, however far he was from London or from the ship he was going to charter, no shipper of goods had need to fear he would have to pay anything more than the market rate of freight for his shipment.

The personal responsibilities of shipbrokers were considerable. By the nature of their work they constantly found themselves in a vulnerable position and never more so than when effecting fixtures under pressure of time, or caring for unfamiliar vessels in their port. To insure them against any professional negligence in the course of their duties, the Chartered Shipbrokers' Protection and Indemnity Association was formed in December 1925, under the chairmanship of Joseph F. Fawcett. This was the creation of a solicitor called Eric J. Edward who was the association's first secretary, a post he retained for thirty-five years until his death in 1960. The body became incorporated in 1937 as the Chartered Shipbrokers' Protection Association Ltd.

The Baltic's complicated rules defining the rights and responsibilities of clerks in their relation to principals, particularly during the war, had led to anomalies. Foreign principals could be admitted so long as they had been domiciled in Britain for seven years, for two of which they had to have been in business on their own account, but all clerks had to be born in the British Empire or of British parents. A man whose parents had been naturalized since his birth was not eligible as a clerk even though he had served in the army throughout the war. A foreign clerk of even twenty years' standing if promoted to principal had to go off the Room for two years. A naturalized clerk ineligible for election as such could leave his firm, set up as principal and at once become eligible. When the directors received a petition on the subject they thought the time had come to put it right. The one thing they had to guard against, the chairman told a meeting of members called to discuss the matter, was the possibility of laying the Baltic open to being flooded by foreign clerks who wished merely to learn the language and business methods and accept low pay or none at all in order to get the experience, thus excluding clerks of British nationality. The reasonable thing was that clerks and principals should be put on the same footing.

It was an attitude more in line with the increasingly democratic climate of a decade which in 1926 saw a general strike whose effects caused sixty-five members to demand a meeting to urge the Government to reconsider the Trade Disputes Act and to deal with the question of the so-called 'peaceful picketing'. James Findlay urged Sir Ernest Glover, Bt, to rule that the moment was not opportune. Fraternity for clerks and principals, but not *too much* equality. Findlay refused to use the company's funds to insure the building against riots and civil commotion at 1s. per cent. He had the doors of the Exchange closed at 3.30, however, and handed on

LONDON RIFLE BRIGADE
BALTIC EXCHANGE UNIT.

It is proposed to form a Baltic Exchange Unit in the London Rifle Brigade.

The Directors of the Baltic wish to bring this to the attention of the young men on the Exchange in the anticipation that the required numbers will be forthcoming.

It is hoped that Members will encourage and assist in every possible way any members of their staff who wish to join.

Leaflets giving full details are available at the St. Mary Axe end of the Exchange.

Chairman of the Directors.

Vice-Chairman of the Directors.

Representative of the Baltic Exchange on the City of London Territorial Force Association.

Officer Commanding London Rifle Brigade.

BALTIC,
16th December, 1925.

London Rifle Brigade poster for the Baltic Exchange unit, 1925

a resolution from members pledging support of the Government in those times of grave emergency to the proper quarter. So right and responsible an action, however, did not prevent 'the disorderly scene' which took place in the Exchange on Friday, December 23. The notice in the Room stated,

The 'Ragging' was apparently organised by a small number of members to the great annoyance and inconvenience of the large majority of members desirous of using the exchange. The directors are determined that such disorder must be stopped and desire it to be known that they regard the introduction, or letting off, of fireworks, playing football or other similar behaviour as misconduct under Rule 37 and they will in future deal drastically with any members guilty of such misconduct.

For one who spent much of his time pulling members up for leaning against the pillars and reprimanding members in coloured shirts for wearing 'pyjamas' as if they were naughty schoolboys, such a display of high spirits will have seemed beyond the tolerance allowed even at Christmas time. Obviously to Findlay their behaviour was yet another symptom of the general lack of discipline which had manifested itself in the recent outbreak of dissatisfaction with board awards. 'If a member lodges a complaint with a request that directors should investigate same' insisted Findlay in a notice he posted for all to see, 'a condition precedent to such investigation must be an undertaking from the complainer to refrain from discussing the matter sub judice, and accept decisions of the Board unreservedly.' (July 26, 1927.)

Only eighteen months before it had been brought to the notice of the directors that some members who were partners in firms, or directors of companies, dealt privately on their own account with members of the Exchange as well as on account of their firms and companies. 'The directors desire to make it known to members', announced Findlay, 'that in such cases any concealment of private dealings from their partners or directors would in their opinion be detrimental to the interests of the Exchange and render them to be liable to be dealt with under Rule 37.'

In May 1927 James Findlay's privately printed 'Short History' of the Baltic Exchange (1744–1927) was published at 21s. a copy. 'Mr Findlay has spent many years in completing this work', stated the leaflet soliciting buyers. Sir Ernest Glover in his foreword wrote:

As we study the record of the Baltic we cannot but be impressed by the fact that at every point the withdrawal of restriction has at once resulted in healthier trading development, and we realise that it is only when Government interference is removed that the delicate plant of international commerce can flourish as it should. In fact, it is not too much to say that under the trammels of officialdom the position which London holds to-day in the markets of the world, and for which it stands indebted to the individual energy and initiative of the mercantile community in establishing facilities for banking, insurance, shipping and buying and selling, could never have been won.

A development which came too late for James Findlay's book was pioneered by S. Instone & Co. Ltd who, on February 15, 1929, issued Britain's first air charter-party. This was between themselves as ship, insurance and aircraft brokers acting as agents for the charterers, and Imperial Airways for a flight from Croydon to Berlin. It was merely an adaptation of a shipping charter-party. They charged 10 per cent brokerage. The time for loading was one day with demurrage of £35 a night. Discharge was on day of arrival, and the time for unloading was to start on receipt of notice by telephone, telegram or in writing. Freight was payable on signing of a consignment note and to be non-returnable in the event of the plane being lost. There was a strike clause, and in all matters arising under the contract the owners were entitled to privileges in the Carriage of Goods by Sea Act 1924.

S. Instone & Co. were a coal exporting and ship-owning firm which became the first trading concern in the world to employ aeroplanes in its ordinary business. For some time after the Armistice in 1918 there was a delay of a week to ten days in the post to the continent. The non-arrival of bills of lading sent by post to ports in northern France was holding up the discharge of the ships which Instone's had on time charter and was costing them large sums in demurrage. So they bought a plane and obtained Government permission to fly their bills of lading to the ports so their ships could clear at once. They saved themselves thousands of pounds.

Encouraged by this, in 1919 they started the Instone Air Line, at first to carry documents such as bills of lading, then passengers and goods (Charlie Chaplin was a passenger in 1920) and finally airmail. Instone, Handley-Page and Daimler Hire were the three pioneers. But owing to competition from heavily subsidized French air companies, Instone's discontinued the service to the continent in 1921, and in 1924 they were absorbed by Imperial Airways. They continued, however, as brokers. (Instone Air Transport was sold to a French consortium in 1958, and in 1967 was a member of Matthews Wrightson Group.)

In 1929 the formation of the Millers Mutual resulted in a considerable reduction in the brokerage business done by members of the Baltic. By buying up and, in many cases, closing down small mills, the large combines concentrated their buying of grain and dealt with merchants direct. To help bring back brokerage business to the Baltic, in March 1929 the London Corn Trade Association established a 'futures market' at the Exchange in Canadian wheat on c.i.f. terms. It was conducted on similar lines to the futures markets in American wheat and maize opened at South Sea House in 1897. For the purpose, the London Corn Trade Association created the London Grain Futures Association as part of its organization, but with rules and regulations of its own. A ring and price marking board were set up on the Floor in the north east corner. All members of this new association had to be members both of the LCTA and the Baltic. There were five trading positions – September, November, January, March and May. The contract unit was 1000 quarters of 480 lb each. To be tenderable, a parcel of wheat shipped from a Canadian port on the east coast had to have a bill of lading dated within the contract month. If it was shipped from a west coast port, the date when the vessel passed Colon was substituted for the date of the bill of lading. The basis was No 3 Manitoba wheat, with other grades at differentials.

There were two trading sessions from 11.30 to 1, and in the afternoon from 2.45 to 4.15, Monday to Friday, with a morning session on Saturday. Each session was opened and closed by the striking of a gong by an official appointed by the LCTA, who was also responsible for marking on the board the prices of the trades done. All contracts had to be registered in the LCTA clearing house by 11 o'clock the following morning accompanied by an 'original margin' of £50. Further margins were called by the clearing house on all contracts which showed losses against the daily 'call prices' which were fixed at 12.30 p.m. and moved up or down by five shillings a quarter.

The main function of the market was to provide a medium for 'hedging' transactions in physical Canadian wheat, but it also attracted some speculation in the value of Canadian wheat for future shipment. According to A. A. Hooker who published his first book, *The International Grain Trade* in 1936, a certain amount of speculation is welcome in a futures market, because it gives it breadth and because successful professional speculation renders an economic service by correct forecasting. Pure gamblers help to broaden the market, but as a fraternity the odds are against them.

The Manitoba Wheat Futures Market was a slow starter, but it attracted a large business in 1931 when sterling suffered its first devaluation.

Options or futures markets were not entirely in tune with the spirit of 1823, and of course there was no reference to them in the rules and regulations of the institution which had once turned its face on the tallow speculators and stock gamblers. But their successors, who had already opened the door in 1897, had no qualms, and were only concerned that broker members of the Baltic who wanted to join the London Grain Futures Association should sign the Exchange's so-called 'Broker's Letter' and agree to certain other conditions before trading in the futures market as a principal. The Baltic 'Broker's Letter' had been introduced in 1910 or earlier. It stated simply,

With reference to my election as a Member of the Exchange, I beg to state that I am carrying on business as a broker or *agent only*. I understand that I have to give the name of my principals in any contracts to the buyer or seller, if called upon so to do, and further I undertake that I will not at any time deal directly or indirectly on my own account.

That was for a produce broker. There were variations for a company and for a shipbroker, but they all made the same basic declaration. In 1929 142 brokers had signed the letter; by 1931 the number had risen to 192, of whom 138 were shipbrokers, 39 grain brokers and 15 oil brokers.

Findlay realized they might wish to operate in other futures markets, and stipulated that a broker member could act as a principal in any such market provided that, when transacting business with a member of the Baltic Exchange, he disclosed to him the name of his principal and declared him to be a member of the Baltic, the LCTA, London Corn Exchange or other relevant trade association. If the broker's principal was not a member of any of them he had to make a deposit of £50 a load, if the commodity was grain, or 10 per cent of its value if something else. Findlay asked broker members to let him know whether they were ready to accept these conditions. If they were not they had to adhere to the terms of the Broker's Letter and confine their activities in options to the London Grain Futures Association.

The establishment of a futures market on the Floor of the Baltic Exchange was a step in the right direction, but the plight of brokers worsened, along with every other kind of employment, with the arrival of the world economic crisis of 1930. It was an unhappy moment, therefore, for Findlay to try and re-adjust the rules of the Exchange which under the stresses of wartime had legislated so harshly against the employment of foreign clerks.

On November 29, 1930, members received a printed letter from John Parry, their chairman, as follows:

As it is now 12 years since the cessation of hostilities it is suggested that the war-time policy of restricting membership to British subjects is no longer necessary and is prejudicial to the interests of the Members inasmuch as it limits the scope and volume of business that can be transacted on the Exchange, and it is further suggested that a naturalised British subject who is liable to our taxation and military service, should be eligible for election under the Rules. It will be remembered that five years' continuous residence in this country is necessary before naturalisation is granted.

The business of the Exchange being international in character, the Directors are unanimously of the opinion that membership should now, as in past times of peace, be open to the nationals of all countries, provided they are of the standard required of Members, pass the ballot box, and conform to the Rules.

He enclosed a notice of an extraordinary general meeting planned for December 12 to obtain members' approval for a change in the rules to make five years' residence the qualification for a foreign candidate to be elected a principal member instead of seven (rule 6), and for clerks to be admitted who were British subjects by birth *or naturalization,* or foreign subjects who had been resident five years (rule 15). As rule 15 stood clerks had to be born in the British Empire or be children of British subjects resident in any foreign country.

It was a reasonable, laudable and overdue proposal, but Findlay had reckoned without the sensitivity of the Baltic Sub-Branch of the British Legion who staged a mass meeting in the Merchants Hall below St Mary Axe to declare that the proposed alterations were detrimental to the interests of ex-servicemen. 'The admission of foreign clerks can bring no commercial advantage to the Exchange but only lessen the openings for British employees.'

'The Storm On The Baltic' was the headline to the City Man's Diary feature in the London *Evening Standard* (see illustration overleaf).

The *Evening Standard* was only echoing points made by an unnamed member of the Exchange to the *Daily Telegraph* on December 3:

We object most strongly to the proposals and to the way they are being brought forward. A year ago a proposal to admit foreigners was put before the members as a body and thrown out. This time it is to come before the shareholders only, and voting instead of being by the head, will be proportionate to the shares held.

The proposal amounts to nothing less than selling the birthright of the younger generation – the clerks who are budding principals and senior members of the room. Many of our clerks, as it is, are looking for work, and an influx of foreigners would make things much worse; and it is just these men whose hands are tied, since they are not shareholders.

Foreign merchants who have been accustomed to transacting business through British brokers in London will undoubtedly set up their own offices, with their own nationals as employees. If the measure is carried there is nothing to prevent the Soviet Government from being represented on the Baltic Exchange.

I have no doubt, personally, that the measure is inspired by a desire to admit two or three specific foreigners on whom our present rule presses

The Storm on the Baltic.

Question of Employment of Foreign Clerks—Liners and the Grain Trade—The U.S. Motor Industry.

FEW questions of policy on the Baltic Exchange have ever aroused the same intensity of feeling and widespread interest as the present dispute concerning the amendment of the rules in such a way as to prevent the employment of foreign clerks and agents on the exchange.

* * * *

Apparently the members are wholeheartedly opposed to the amendment while the directors are in favour of it. The fact that only a small proportion of the total share capital of the Baltic is held amongst the general body of its members explains why the board if it wishes can take a course so opposed to the will of the majority. And it is this fact almost as much as the question of the clerks and agents which has so aroused the members.

Pre-war Conditions.

PREVIOUS to the war a vast number of the foreign, and in a number of cases British, firms employed foreign clerks and agents on the exchange. Many of these being chiefly concerned with learning the business and language, and were willing to work for little or no salary. Some, I am told, even paid a premium for the privilege of working in certain firms.

* * * *

Now it is feared if this rule debarring them is rescinded, especially at the present time a great number of British clerks will be forced out of their jobs.

* * * *

The general feeling of resentment has not been alleviated in any way by the fact that several foreign firms are known to have been buying up shares for a considerable time, thus giving them a preponderating influence on the board.

* * * *

In view of the strenuous canvassing now going on by partisans of both members and directors it will be decidedly interesting, I think, to see what happens at the special meeting called by the directors for next Friday.

'The Storm on the Baltic,' a press cutting from the Evening Standard, 1930

rather heavily. But we felt that no individual hardship can justify so radical a change of principle.

The directors met on December 9 to consider this unexpected opposition and also the warning of their solicitor and counsel that if they tried to rescind the resolution excluding foreign clerks, which had been passed in December 1918, they might find themselves involved in a lawsuit. The only thing to do was to postpone the meeting, and on December 10 Findlay sent members a letter informing them that the meeting would be adjourned to December 16 'to meet the convenience of members. . . . The Directors further propose to suggest at the adjourned meeting the elimination from the Resolution regarding Rule 15 of the following words: "or foreign subjects having been continuously resident in this country for a period of five years preceding their nomination".' They were climbing down. Two days later they received another letter to say the adjourned meeting arranged for December 16 had been abandoned.

The directors considered the foreign clerks situation over Christmas and on January 15, 1931, John Parry sent out yet another letter.

Referring to the circular letter which I sent you on the 13th ultimo, in deference to representative opinion on the Exchange that in these times of bad trade the proposal to make foreign clerks eligible was inopportune, the Directors as you are aware decided not to proceed with that suggestion.

With this exception therefore it is proposed to abolish the other war-time restrictions on membership of the Exchange previously mentioned, and to make naturalised British subjects eligible as clerks. The directors consider that if such are accepted as British citizens with all the rights and responsibilities attaching thereto, they should be eligible for admission to the Exchange as clerks, subject of course to the ballot box.

As regards foreign principals, instead of the twelve months' residence qualification required before the war, it is proposed that five years' continuous residence immediately prior to the application for membership shall be necessary.

He called a meeting for January 27.

He took the chair, flanked by Sir F. Vernon Thomson, Sir Arthur W. Holmes, Sir Herbert Robson and eight other directors. When the alteration of both rules was put, a motion was carried from the floor to put each separately. Substituting five years for seven in rule 6 was carried with a show of hands. Before putting the alteration to rule 15 about foreign clerks, the chairman assured Marmaduke Lawther that the board had closely considered all applications from British naturalized subjects to see that they were not taking advantage of the naturalization laws merely in order to gain admission to the Baltic. The resolution to alter rule 15 was then lost on a show of hands. The board demanded a poll, but Howard Houlder suggested that instead the resolution should be re-submitted so that he could propose an amendment, which was that clerks seeking admission should be naturalized British subjects *of not less than two years' standing*. This was carried.

Encouraged by the success of this organized opposition, members then proceeded to deal with the matter which had caused them to act as they did, and which had been referred to by City Man in the *Evening Standard*: voting rights.

In the typed notes for his introductory remarks at the meeting of January 27, John Parry's first point was 'The proposed alterations are only put forward, after careful consideration, in the interests of the Exchange and the Shareholders.' But he crossed out 'and the Shareholders'. It was wise. But his first thoughts were correct. The state of affairs which the constitution (the Articles of Association) of the Baltic Mercantile and Shipping Exchange of 1903 had sought to prevent – the separation of members and shareholders, of managed and management – had overtaken them. The decision-making had come into the hands not of the members, all of whom had to be shareholders and numerically were the majority, but of those who had put the most money into the company, who were a minority. Once again the question arose, what was the object of the exercise? To provide a commercial resort for businessmen or to make profits for shareholders?

James Findlay who had not served the Baltic during the Septimus Glover/Michel Rodocanachi contest at South Sea House was unlikely to ask himself such questions, let alone know the answers. Cecil Brightman asked them, however, and was in no doubt about the answers. He served notice on the company of his intention to propose a resolution at the annual general meeting on May 28, 1931, that article 81 was inequitable in so far as it provided that the number of votes to which each individual shareholder was entitled at a poll for the alterations of the rules was dependent on the number of shares he held, and that the directors should call a meeting to alter the article to read, 'On a show of hands every member entitled to vote under the provisions hereof shall have one vote only.' He won his point with an overwhelming majority on a show of hands, and the directors had to call a meeting to consider it on July 14. With the notice calling the meeting, Sir

Vernon Thomson, now chairman, set out the board's reasons for opposing Brightman's scheme. He reminded shareholders that under the articles each shareholder had one vote for the first share and an additional vote for every ten additional shares. The number of votes each shareholder had was commensurate with his pecuniary stake in the company, the usual practice of joint stock companies.

The position has been carefully considered by your Board, and twelve of the fourteen Directors are strongly opposed to the alterations as not being in the best interests of the Exchange. In their opinion it would involve a fundamental and drastic change in the constitution of the Company by introducing the principle of 'one shareholder one vote' and would virtually hand over the control of the Company and the Exchange to a section of the shareholders, numerically large but whose holding in the capital of the Company is small, whilst the remainder of the shareholders, though fewer in number, hold in the aggregate nearly all the capital of the Company. . . .

To-day there are about 1250 shareholders of whom 913 have only one vote each, so that if the alteration were effected these 913 shareholders, though actually owning in the aggregate only £24 425 capital, or even only 650 of them, could control matters affecting the interests of £260 400 capital and £321 728 Debenture Stock, i.e. over £580 000 in all.

The Board are always willing to consider any suggestions made for the improvement of the Exchange or furthering its interests, but in the opinion of the large majority of the Board the proposed resolution is unnecessary and contrary to the true interests of the Company and the Exchange, which are supplemental to each other and mutually dependent.

Cecil Brightman and his fourteen supporters countered with a broadside dated June 26 pointing out that the proposed alteration was confined to the rules of the Exchange, and that votes for resolutions about subscriptions and entrance fees would continue to be on the existing basis. Thus shareholders' rights would be conserved where financial considerations applied. He pointed out, in black print, 'that the share register contains approximately 1230 members. According to the shareholdings, the Board, together with only 35 of the largest shareholders, hold a majority of the company's shares, with the preponderating voting power at a poll attached thereto'. It was the large shareholders whom they asked to realize that the suggested alteration was likely to result in more harmonious working of the Exchange, and in its general improvement, with consequent improvement in the security of investment in the company. The resolution would stimulate the interest of members who used the Exchange from day to day in its proper conduct.

A show of hands at the AGM gave Brightman his special meeting, but when the stockholders turned up in force to defend their threatened rights their share power defeated him and the *status quo* was calmly confirmed. Cecil Brightman was unabashed. In the face of his failure, he felt the board would not react favourably to a revival of the floor committee idea. He suggested that the three ballot directors, the chairman and the vice-chairman should meet once a month to consider suggestions from members and clerks for the improvement of the Exchange. 'The idea commended itself to the Board', wrote Findlay in the minutes. They agreed to do as Brightman proposed.

For James Findlay it was only partial surrender of the part of his power which he considered secondary to his prime function as company secretary of the joint stock company dedicated to earning for the shareholders the highest dividends. If this was the yardstick of Findlay's success he had done well. The last pre-war dividend (in 1913) was 7 per cent and throughout the war 5 per cent was paid. The credit balance of £14 224 in 1913 had become £9619 in 1918. But by 1920 the company was paying 7½ per cent and the balance was £23 500. Total income was £70 827 compared with £60 264 in 1914. The cost of rates and taxes and insurance almost doubled after the war: £12 470 in 1920 compared with £7698 in 1914. Subscriptions, which had been raised in 1917 from fifteen to twenty guineas, brought in £28 104 in 1920 and rents another £27 356.

In 1922, the peak year for subscriptions (2771), they had a balance of £29 732 and paid 10 per cent; but when by 1929 the number of subscribers (2368) had fallen to below the 1913 figure (2377), they were able to pay 12½ per cent and had a balance of £39 098. The £5 share was worth £8. It was Findlay's finest hour. The income from office rents seemed so lucrative that in 1920 he thought of adding another floor to Exchange Buildings. But the London County Council restricted the heights of buildings to 80 feet and the extension would have brought the Baltic to 83. This meant a special application and the architect thought it unlikely it would be granted, so the idea was dropped.

Membership figures had been less buoyant. The 2377 members of 1913 shrank to 1908 in 1919, but by 1920 the figure was up to 2510, reaching a peak, as shown, of 2771 in 1922. But from that year it fell away – to 2735 in 1923, 2591 in 1925, 2486 in 1927, down to the 2368 of 1929. The world slump took even greater toll. Fewer and fewer members could afford the subscription. In the year ending March 31, 1931, 296 members resigned. But membership only fell to 2228, as 168 new members were elected. The following year another 199 resigned with only 119 to take their place, so membership fell again – to 2106.

'The figures for 1931', the chairman told shareholders, 'were the lowest we have had for the past ten years, and I am sorry to say that this year's total is lower still.' Total income for 1931/32 was £85 260, however. The book value of the property stood at £57 5203. They again paid 12½ per cent dividend out of a profit of £31 559. However badly members' businesses were suffering – a Baltic Employment Bureau was set up with A. R. Brabazon Jones as hon. secretary in 1931 – the shareholders were not weathering the crisis at all badly.

But it was by no means over. 'Though I have seen bad times and even very hopeless looking times', wrote 'Shipowner With 50 Years in Tramp Shipping' to *Fairplay* in January 1932, 'I have never seen anything to compare with the year that is now closing. 1930 was bad, but 1931 has been worse and at the time that I write I should hope the very worst depth of all has been reached.'

It had not. According to the Tramp Shipping Administrative Committee's 6th Report, 1930 to 1935 was the worst period 'ever experienced by British shipping'. Exports fell from £729 million in 1929 to £389 million in 1932. Between 1931 and 1933 three to three and a half million gross tons of British shipping was laid up. Real improvement did not come till 1936 but not enough to arrest the decline of the British merchant navy compared with other nations. In 1914 48 per cent of the world's merchant tonnage was British; in 1937 only 32·5 per cent. Though the British tanker fleet tonnage increased between the wars – it was 2·7 million in 1938 – dry cargo tonnage declined.

James Arbuckle Findlay retired in the spring of 1932, and at his last meeting as secretary on March 22, after thirty-three years' tenure, he was formally thanked by Sir Vernon Thomson, the chairman, for 'his many and signal services to the company, having seen the present Baltic built and having always been a devoted servant of its interests'. Their business relations, he said, had always been of the pleasantest. They assured him of their best wishes in his retirement. Later members had an opportunity of saying farewell at a meeting in the Room at which the chairman described him as 'the architect of our great institute'. The institute, he said, might be likened to a cathedral. It would constantly increase in importance and usefulness to chartered shipbrokers, as well as to shipowners and merchants, for its conception had that three-fold object. Mr Findlay prepared the plans, they were the builders. In presenting the secretary with his portrait by Maurice Codner, Sir Vernon chose his words carefully. Mr Findlay's retirement, he said, recalled the lines: 'How Sultan after Sultan with his pomp, abode his hour or two and went his way'. He then unveiled the portrait which James Findlay presented to the Exchange as a gift. Sir Vernon thanked him for the gracious words in which he had made the gift and stated that it would be accorded an honoured place in the rooms of the Exchange as a reminder of his services to them and their successors. It now hangs in the house of his son Gilbert Findlay who became assistant secretary of the Baltic in June 1929 at the age of forty-six and succeeded his father as secretary on April 1, 1932.

With the world depression deepening membership of the Baltic declined even further. There were only 2016 who subscribed in 1932/33. The following year it sank to 1929.

It was a moment to insure against whatever even greater blows lay ahead, and on June 2, 1932, the Baltic Exchange Clerks Pension Fund was constituted by Trust Deed with Richard Hopwood as secretary. 'The urgent need for organised provision for the future is rapidly becoming more apparent', stated the explanatory pamphlet. Centralized facilities were now available for the super-annuation of those employed in the various trades represented on the Exchange. Through the Fund pensions on retirement could be secured at reasonable cost by the joint annual contribution of the employer and employee. It was managed by a committee of eight – four representing employers and four the clerks. The investments were held in the names of four trustees, and apart from agreeing to nominate future trustees when vacancies occurred, the directors of the Baltic had nothing to do with the fund.

When the world's economists met in London in June 1933 to try to sort the crisis out, the Baltic Exchange invited 280 of them to lunch at St Mary Axe. Guests of honour were R. B. Bennett, Prime Minister of Canada, and J. H. Thomas, the Dominions Secretary. Sir Theodore Angier, now ninety-one, was among the guests.

Sir Herbert Robson, the chairman, told these delegates to the World Monetary and Economic Conference,

We who labour daily in this exchange live by international trade. Our business is connected with ships and the merchandise which moves in ships. The enormous decline in international trade has hit us harder than any section of the commercial community. It is we who have felt the full blast of the economic storm. The decline in the volume of trade has caused vast numbers of our ships to be laid aside.

The free trade which the members of the Baltic Coffee-House had celebrated with such ardour ninety years before with the repeal of the Corn Laws had vanished.

Sir Herbert continued,

Our ships are largely idle because so many nations have seemed determined to limit international trade by enormous tariffs, and even by prohibition of imports except under a quota of negligible proportions. Our merchants are hampered at every turn because from hour to hour no man knows the value of the exchanges. Your business as delegates is to seek means of restoring international trade. If you fail there is a dark future before us all, not only on this exchange and in this country, but throughout every civilized country.

How could the purchasing power of the world be restored? asked R. B. Bennett. A rise in the price of commodities must be brought about all along the line, if the world was to get back to normal trading. Confidence could spring from great commercial organizations like the Baltic. Jimmy Thomas pointed out that the world's trade was a third of what it was in 1929 and if every non-British merchant ship were wiped out Britain's merchant fleet could do the whole of it. The real and permanent solution was the removal of those trade barriers and the re-establishment of confidence.

For those who had had no occasion to witness the Baltic acting as a single body expressing a corporate view, the attendance of the representatives of sixty-six trading nations at this great luncheon at St Mary Axe demonstrated not only the premier national role of the Exchange, but the world's recognition of its right, born of the unbroken experience of over a century, to dispense advice and prescribe remedies for the recovery of the international operation of which it was the centre.

Though the Great Depression had sprung from the wild speculation which caused the bottom to fall out of the market in the United States in 1929 and led to world trade slumping to half its volume in the next three years, the idle state of British merchant shipping was due to earlier and less dramatic events. Even before the Great War the United States had demonstrated her enormous economic strength; and her neutrality until 1917 enabled her to win markets in Canada and Latin America while Britain's energies were engaged in the fighting. At the same time Japan took advantage of Britain's diversion to military matters to encroach on her markets in the Far East. When the war ended, the harsh economic terms of the Treaty of Versailles made Germany no longer a customer but a determined commercial competitor. The re-drawing of the map of Europe into nation states led to the building of tariff barriers to keep them in being. Britain's coal industry was faced with strong rivalry from Germany and Poland; her cotton industry from Japan and India; her iron and steel industry from the United States. By the end of the war America and Japan had taken away a large part of Britain's carrying trade. Not all would have agreed with Sir Ernest Glover that in such circumstances the delicate plant of international commerce could only flourish when

Government 'interference' was removed. The mood of the times in the City of London was against what it stigmatized as 'interference', but hindsight might lead one to the view that some degree of enlightened state direction of economic policy, backed by a national effort of the kind only stimulated by war, might have brought recovery more quickly than allowing economic *laissez-faire* to linger till the nation was hit by the crisis of 1929 and unemployment rose to three million. 'In practice', as E. E. Reynolds wrote in 1966, 'the difficulties were too great to be overcome by the familiar mixture of nervous caution at the top and self-interest below.' Protection came, belatedly, in 1931. The principle of imperial preference, rejected at the beginning of the century, was accepted only in 1932 in circumstances less favourable to its success. The British merchant navy received no protection in the form of loans or subsidies before the mid-1930s and then it was too late and too small – the British Shipping (Assistance) Act of 1935 introduced as a result of pressure from British shipowners.

Such assistance was not, of course, 'interference'. The Baltic directors noted in their 1935 report,

International trade is at a low ebb and in consequence the volume of business conducted on the Exchange remains smaller than was the case in years gone by. The directors note with pleasure that H.M. Government has decided that the time has come when the Tramp Shipping Industry must be assisted and an Act of Parliament was passed on 25th February last whereby the sum of £2 million is allocated for the purpose of subsidising tramp shipping. Agreements have been adopted by the shipping industry on minimum rates of freight on grain from Australia, Canada and the Argentine Republic. It is therefore to be hoped that the Shipping Trade has now passed the worst phase of depression.

The subsidy would be available so long as the average level of rates did not rise above 92 per cent of the 1926 level and on the understanding that the industry would introduce rationalization. The Tramp Shipping Administrative Committee was formed under the aegis of the British Chamber of Shipping and the minimum rate scheme was initiated, at first only with British vessels. When freights failed to improve, other owners supported the scheme.

The River Plate market exercised most control over world rates.

The initial minimum rate here was fixed at 13s. 9d. a ton from up-river ports in Argentina to selected ports in Britain, but there was no guarantee that an owner would find a charterer willing to pay the minimum. At times there were more than fifty vessels lying idle in the River Plate. Several owners tried to find some way of fixing at less than the minimum rate so that their vessels could get away. This was done by paying charterers a 'back-hander' of two or three shillings a ton by cutting a size or giving cheap options, which was called 'ratting'. By fixing their tonnage on time charter it was possible to charter a 9200-ton vessel at nine knots on 22 tons of coal at 2s. 4½d. for a 'Plate Round'.

This caused a considerable amount of ill feeling on the Baltic and a number of owners who had mysteriously fixed their waiting vessels out of rotation were called before the directors and asked how they managed to do it. The scheme was enlarged to cover other areas such as Western Australia to Britain. The break-even rate for the round coal trip from Wales to Buenos Aires and back was 35s. for British vessels. Bunker coal was 20s. a ton in Wales and the running cost of a British vessel £40 a day. With a freight index of 100 for 1929, the index for 1920 was 76·84, 75·43 in 1932, 72·90 in 1933, 76·28 in 1935. The volume of world trade had shrunk in 1934 to less than it was in 1913, and in 1934 there was 49 per cent more tonnage available than in 1913.

The London Corn Trade Association established a La Plata Maize Futures Market on the Baltic in August 1933, and received permission to erect a ring and prices recording board alongside the Wheat Futures Market, with the same kind of control and conditions of trading. Trading was confined to members of the London Grain Futures Association. There were talks once again about starting a timber exchange earlier in the year but nothing came of them. But in July 1935 clerk members formed a London Grain Trade Clerks Association for male clerks of over twenty-one, which in November of that year resolved

that in view of the importance, from the point of view of employment, of maintaining the maximum number of intermediary firms and also of avoiding any action which would appear contrary to the efforts now being made by the Trade Reconstruction Committee . . . it was not in their interests that shippers, brokers or merchants should be subsidiaries of the milling industry.

In spite of attempts of this jobs-for-the-boys nature to keep employment high, the number of people and firms still in business and able to afford the manifest advantages of belonging to the Baltic dwindled in 1935 to the lowest figure ever – 1893. But the gross revenue was £78 193 and they could still pay a dividend of 12½ per cent and continue to make the Lord Mayor of London a annual luncheon guest. Indeed, as the chairman pointed out to shareholders at the AGM, the financial position of the company was very sound. To make his point he looked back to the first year of the company and the pessimistic prognostications made by the *Pall Mall Gazette* of July 21, 1903.

When, in March, 1900, the Baltic Mercantile and Shipping Exchange (Limited) prospectus was submitted to the public it was severely handled in our columns. The capital was £200 000. Two classes of Debentures were also created – £250 000 First Debentures, bearing 3¾% interest, and £125 000 'B' Debentures bearing 4½% interest. This seemed an enormous burden of debt for an association like the Baltic to assume, and moreover there was good reason to believe that the value of the properties acquired afforded but a poor margin of security for all this capital. The original estimate (in 1899) for the St Mary Axe site was £324 000, but by the time the prospectus was issued this had grown to £400 000, and we hazarded the opinion that it would be at least £50 000, more. We have now the balance sheet before us made up to March 31st last, and there we find that the total expenditure to date amounts to about £516 000. The whole of the Debenture Stock has been issued and £75 000, in Ordinary Shares, in addition to which a loan of £58 000, has been obtained from the Company's Bankers and £8660, is due to creditors. Possession of the ground floor has been obtained, but the rest of the building is still incomplete, and it would be interesting to learn how much more will have to be expended on it. The cash balance is only £398, and no statement is made as to the fees and subscriptions received, but it seems to us highly probable that the Company will have to be reconstructed before long if it is to be placed on a sound footing.

In 1935 the chairman said,

Let us look at the present position. On the repayment of this 'C' Debenture Stock, the Company will have repaid over £220 000, since its inception, namely: – £25 000 Mortgage to the Metropolitan Life Assurance Co., in

1914, £125000 'B' Debentures in 1921 and the £80000 'C' Debentures in October 1935. I can, therefore, say without fear of contradiction that the Company is in a very sound financial state. But today it is not possible to buy the *Pall Mall Gazette*.

A country which believed it could help relieve the slump but was not being allowed to do so as fully as it would have liked was the Baltic's traditional trading partner, Russia, in its new guise as the Union of Soviet Socialist Republics. Throughout the crisis considerable British tonnage had been brought into the Soviet export trade, but the Russians complained that owners of British tankers could work only at a rate of 1s. or 2s. above the market rate. In the winter some British owners refused to send their vessels into ice-bound ports or the Black Sea, although vessels of other nationalities willingly agreed to be fixed for these ports. Moreover the London market could not supply sufficient tonnage of the size and draft suitable for certain shallow French and Scandinavian ports to which Soviet exports were delivered. For the same reasons British shipowners could not accept Soviet export cargoes of grain and timber intended for certain British and Irish ports.

A shipping company in London which in 1932 thought it could iron out many of these difficulties if it became a member of the Baltic Exchange was the Arcos Steamship Company Ltd, which in 1928 had changed its name to the Anglo-Soviet Shipping Company Ltd. The chairman of the Baltic, Sir Vernon Thomson, talked it over with the Board of Trade who in their turn saw the directors of Anglo-Soviet Shipping. Discussion continued for another two years by which time a Trade Agreement had been signed with Russia. In March 1934 Sir Vernon was telling the Board of Trade:

No one, neither the Prime Minister nor the Chairman of 'the Baltic' can guarantee that a particular candidate will be admitted to membership. Each case is considered by the Directors on its merits and a ballot box is then circulated round the table of 12 or 14 directors. One black ball cast in four disqualifies and the candidate cannot again apply until after 12 months.

The applicant must comply with the conditions of membership and his reputation and standing be suitable. In the case of foreign or foreign controlled firms applying for membership, the Directors have to be satisfied that there are assets in Britain to meet possible claims etc., and would have regard to whether or not the candidate was likely to bring business to the Baltic Exchange.

For some time past in this country, as you know, Russia has not been very popular and they have taken away from London business hitherto done in London. Of course the Directors of 'the Baltic' know this and they (who are elected by the members) have the sole decision.

The Russians should seek to make their business attractive here by offering clean (instead of objectionable) terms of charter etc. This seems to me only common sense and as I have told Mr Leonidoff [chairman of the Anglo-Soviet Shipping Company] frequently, will enable them to get their tonnage at the lowest current market rates,

If the Russians undertook to bring back to London (i.e. to 'the Baltic' as the Chartering Centre) the trade formerly done here, I would favour their admission. Without such a guarantee I do not think they would be elected at present, notwithstanding the Trade Agreement.

There is also an awkward point due to the Soviet trade system of Government monopoly. If a duly made arbitration award is given against a member or someone represented on 'the Baltic', and that one does not honour it, the Directors would probably suspend the member concerned, or if it was a foreign client of the member, would not allow any member of the Exchange thereafter to represent him on 'the Baltic'. During my term of office I recollect a charterer in Japan being brought up to the mark in this way. If then by any chance the Anglo-Soviet Shipping Co. Ltd. (which is really the Soviet technically complying with our Companies' Acts requirements) were to decline liability for such an award or for a verdict of the Court, and were in consequence suspended, international political questions might arise.

At their meeting of March 13, 1934 the directors decided that it was not desirable in the interests of the Exchange to elect as members representatives of monopolistic or Government organizations, 'especially in view of the precedent created in February 1929 in the case of David Smith of the Canadian Co-operative Wheat Producers Ltd, whose membership was not allowed'. Under this policy decision, they minuted they were not prepared to admit the Anglo-Soviet Shipping Company.

11. The Ghost Exchange

When Walter Runciman, as President of the Board of Trade, had to make a speech in the House of Commons in 1935 on the debate on the Great Pepper Scandal when the market was cornered by a single supplier, Sir Herbert Robson gave him some notes for the references he wished to make to the Exchange as an example of the right way of doing things:

As Chairman of the Baltic I have no hesitation in stating that any attempt to corner or manipulate any of the commodities which are dealt with on the Exchange would be considered as conduct detrimental to the interests of the Exchange, and a member so acting would be suspended or expelled according to the degree of his delinquencies. If at the time of election a member is unable to show that he is worth at least £5000, he signs a letter undertaking only to act as a broker. There is no record of any attempt to corner any of the commodities dealt with on the Baltic Exchange which, I beg to remind you, is the most important Exchange in the world for transactions in cargoes and parcels of wheat, maize and other grain, as well as oilseeds and similar products.

The man who had been so largely responsible for making that claim a reality, James Findlay, died in 1935 – the architect, as Sir Vernon Thomson had said at his retirement three years earlier, of the modern Baltic Exchange.

In his actual speech on March 7, Walter Runciman said that by experience the Baltic had learned that for wheat and other grain a settling should take place once every 24 hours at 11 o'clock every morning.

It is a matter of very great concern to the Baltic that that system should be maintained. Had there been anything like this in pepper I doubt very much if we should have heard anything of the recent operations. What is done in the Baltic and the Liverpool cotton exchange is done informally in one or two important commodities in the City of London now.

But the days of the Baltic as a commodity market were numbered. In 1928 shareholders were reminded that the two retiring directors represented grain and shipping sections of the Exchange, and that it was considered desirable that the interests of both should continue to be adequately represented on the board. A similar reminder went out in 1936 – the vacancies which occurred were in the ratio of two grain; one oil and oilseed; one shipping. But by the end of the decade with the revival of shipping and the concentration of business into big combines like ICI and Unilever, and with the development of telecommunications and the increasing size of tankers, the Baltic was changing from a commodity market into a freight market.

'The signs are to-day', said the confident directors' report of 1938, 'that a point has now been reached when improved conditions in trade can be expected to develop gradually, provided no international complications arise.' But the signs included the rising cost of maintaining an office in the City – bigger rates, taxes and insurance, higher wages for clerks and executives (young Leslie Phillips received 10s. a week when he started work as a boy of fourteen in 1919), higher postal and telephone charges – and the consequent easing out of the one-man and two-man partnerships which had constituted so large a part of the Baltic membership up to the mid-1930s. The partnership was no longer the economic way of running a business. As millers amalgamated and the shipping companies grew into larger units, though the number of people on the Floor each day remained roughly the same, any hundred of them, instead of representing fifty firms, by 1938 covered some five or six companies each with twenty or thirty representatives.

Between the wars membership of the Baltic was divided into 50 per cent shipping and the other half grain (37 per cent) and oil seed (13 per cent). But in 1938 a fourth division emerged – air freight.

The first steps were taken by Captain Alfred Instone of S. Instone & Co., the company which, as already shown, pioneered the carrying of air cargo in 1919. In April 1938 he sounded out a number of airline operators on the idea of setting up an air freight section at the Baltic. One of these was Imperial Airways, and their Dennis Handover was not at all sure it would work. 'Our freight rates', he told Instone, 'are not a matter about which there can be any bargaining, but are more analogous to those fixed by rail and road concerns and do not vary according to the amount of cargo to be uplifted as compared to the tonnage offering.' But he was keen to make it work if it could, and suggested a meeting of both of them with Gilbert Findlay at St Mary Axe.

The talks were encouraging and that summer Gilbert Findlay issued the following notice:

Many consignments of goods are being carried daily by aeroplane. The number of companies engaged in aerial transport is increasing and with the impending acquisition of an Air Port by the City of London, it has been suggested that consideration should be given to the possibility of increasing the air transport business transacted by members of the Exchange and centralising the point at which such business can be transacted.

There are a number of firms on the Exchange who are interested in the booking of freight by air, and as long ago as February 1928 an aircraft charter-party was executed by a member firm of the Exchange, an aeroplane being chartered for a complete cargo out and home. The aircraft companies operating in London at present are not numerous, and in most cases they have their own agents, but it would be to the advantage and benefit of all concerned if those interested in the various branches of the Aircraft Industry could have a central point where they could transact their business, and it would seem that no better centre could be suggested than the Baltic Exchange.

It is proposed to hold a meeting in the Merchants Hall at an early date, presided over by the chairman, to consider what steps should be taken to establish an aircraft section of the Exchange membership – all firms on the Exchange interested in this question are heartily invited to attend, and at the same time non-members interested in the industry will also be welcomed. It must not be taken for granted as a result of the meeting and publicity given that the present moment is the right one for founding an aircraft section on the Exchange, but with the growth of the industry, that day cannot be far distant and, therefore, it would be advisable to explore the situation without delay.

There was a large attendance at the meeting, which took place on June 10, 1938. It was chaired by Frank Fehr, chairman of the Baltic, who said that the idea of bringing in air interests had emanated from Gilbert Findlay. When Britain's armament requirements had been met, ran his notes for his speech, builders would undoubtedly devote attention to new kinds of aircraft capable of carrying big loads over long distances. Germany expected to run a daily air service to New York in three years' time. If the Baltic became the point where all business connected with air transport could be centralized, it would make for fair rates of freight, prevent unfair competition, provide a meeting place for builders and buyers and means of ascertaining freight requirements.

Alfred Instone said shipping and air transport had much in common. His own firm did both. The shipbroker was not far away from the flying shipbroker. Just as they had the tramp ship, so in the near future they would have the tramp aeroplane. There was not the same competition in rates as in the shipping industry, but this would come. He moved a resolution 'That in the opinion of this meeting of members of the Exchange and others interested in air transport, the time has arrived when membership of the Exchange should be open to those engaged in air transport and the aircraft industry, and ask the directors to accept such nominations for membership.' It was carried unanimously.

He wrote to Gilbert Findlay after the meeting to say he had spoken to the representatives of air companies who had been very impressed with the possibilities opened up at the meeting. 'I think you can be very satisfied that the movement has started well and having opened the door, it is for them to come in in due course.'

Alfred Instone hoped the time for forming the air freight section was opportune, but of course it was not. Circumstances were more favourable to the formation of the 159th City of London Anti-Aircraft Battery, Royal Artillery (TA) Baltic Section under Captain Cecil Pike. Lufthansa was not preparing to fly to New York, but the Luftwaffe, building on their experience in the Spanish Civil War, were training to strafe Warsaw and Prague. After only twenty years, German aggression had once again come to command all attention. The Baltic air market was stillborn, and the short lives of the Manitoba Wheat and La Plata Maize Futures Markets, and linseed oil futures trading were brought summarily to a halt.

When another war breaks out the only precedent is the last one. To what extent would precedent influence the Government in determining the amount of control, if any, they planned to exercise over the various activities which took place on the Floor of the Baltic? It was the question which every member asked himself that week-end of September 3/4, 1939, when all the hopes of revival from the slump of 1929 which had looked so promising were sadly forgotten. If things were not going to be better, how far were 'they' going to allow them at least to be the same?

In their report dated May 2, 1939, the directors of the Baltic pointed out that the political disturbances during the past year had affected industry in all its branches and had tended to render trade in many cases difficult and unprofitable. 'It can only be hoped that many of the obstacles to the free flow of commerce will be removed and that the strenuous endeavours of all concerned will succeed in restoring commercial relations throughout the world to a more normal and sounder economic basis.'

The grain section had few qualms. The trade had maintained contact with the Government throughout the inter-war period through the National Federation of Corn Trade Associations which, as we have noted, was established in 1919 for this purpose, and had never been disbanded. Planning for food control in the event of another war had been begun by the Food (Defence Plans) Department of the Board of Trade in 1936. J. V. Rank, eldest son of Joseph Rank, played a leading role in the delicate operation of buying for the Government under conditions of private trade a security reserve of wheat, and when war broke out he was appointed chairman of the Imported Cereals Committee of the Cereals Control Board of the Ministry of Food which took over from the Board of Trade. In 1940 the Board became the Ministry's Imported Cereals Division, subject only to the broad direction of the Food Policy Committee of the War Cabinet. It put into operation well-formulated food defence plans for a smooth transition into control *through the trade*. From J. V. Rank's house at Godstone, which he put at the disposal of the Ministry, was organized the buying of foreign grain through shippers and its distribution through merchants with the aid of brokers. The expertise of the trade was harnessed through the Port Area Grain Committees and the National Federation of Corn Trade Associations, of which Sir Leslie Phillips was president for a large part of the war.

The Baltic played no part in this operation, but it was Baltic members who made it work by being allowed to continue to practise their trade in the various port organizations and on the staffs of the Government bodies concerned. The supply side of the Ministry consisted of commodity divisions which also drew for staff on private trade and in some cases had been Government-sponsored trade organizations. With fatstock and cereals, the Ministry of Food became the major or sole importer and purchaser of home produce.

For the oil and oilseed section of the Baltic, however, matters were not so straightforward. The Food (Defence Plans) Department under Mr (later Sir) Henry French had appointed the key personnel in the oils and fats section well before the outbreak of war – Mr (later Sir) Herbert Davis became director of oils and fat and Jasper Knight director of imported oilseeds. Both came from the Unilever stable (as did most of their assistants) and between them became responsible for all purchases and allocations of oils, fats and oilseeds from September 1939. As in the grain trade, the Department had made substantial strategic purchases of whale oil during 1938 and spring 1939. Herbert Davis had also initiated discussions with the National Association of Oil and Oilseed Brokers regarding pooling and redistribution of commission on a 'past performance' basis. These discussions went on for many months after the outbreak of war and each member firm's quota finally proved to be barely sufficient to support life, but the scheme did enable many of the smaller firms to survive the war, even though some of the weaker brethren succumbed or were swallowed up soon after it ended.

Initially it seems the Government had no clear plans for priorities of animal feeding stuffs as against food for human consumption. In the absence of his minister, Sir Reginald Dorman-Smith, Sir Donald Fergusson, Permanent Secretary of the Ministry of Agriculture and Fisheries, wrote to Sir Horace Wilson, economic adviser to the Prime Minister, Mr Neville Chamberlain, on February 16, 1940, about a memorandum which was to come before the War Cabinet the following week. The Ministry of Agriculture, he said, had no direct relations with the Ministry of Shipping. The Ministry of Food was responsible for importing feeding stuffs and the Ministry of Supply for importing fertilizers. This constituted 'a flaw or gap in present arrangements which may lead ... to grave difficulties for us and a very embarrassing position for the Government as a whole'. The Ministry of Food's allocation (19·8 million tons) covered foodstuffs like wheat, sugar and meat, and animal feeding stuffs like oilseeds, oilcake and cereals. The Ministry of Food had to give priority quite rightly to essential foods like wheat, sugar etc., and animal feeding stuffs took second place in allocation of tonnage.

'What ought to happen in the event of a shipping squeeze in my view is that there ought to be someone to decide whether oil seeds and oil cake . . . should not be given priority to certain of the materials included in the 23·9m tons of shipping allocated to the Ministry of Supply.' At present it seemed the Ministry of Shipping would virtually decide 'and they certainly cannot be regarded as competent to do so'. At a Ministry of Food meeting on Tuesday he heard the supply position of oilseeds and oilcake had 'quite suddenly deteriorated'.

'This came as a great shock because hitherto we had been led to believe that whatever might be the position about cereals, the position as regards oil cake would be satisfactory.'

Dairy cows had to have a 'production ration' in winter as well as hay and roots if they were to produce normal quantities of milk, and cake was a main constituent. There would be a serious drop in milk production if cake supply diminished. This would not only affect the financial position of farmers but raise a political storm from the consumers. (Prime Minister's Office Papers, PREMIER 1/429, 1940 Trade.)

By 1942, however, a 'buying agreement' was reached with the United States under which Britain became the exclusive purchaser for the allies of animal feeding stuffs from Commonwealth countries, French Africa and the Belgian Congo.

Once they had settled among themselves which of the ministries was to have the final say, the Government left the implementation of their policy to the trade through the machinery they had set up. For members of the shipping section of the Baltic, too, there was doubt not only about which of the various ministries would initially give direction to the Government policy, but also about what precisely that policy was. By the 1930s, as we have seen, brokers at the Baltic, the international chartering centre, no longer depended solely on the British merchant navy as such; their business was concerned with 'fixing' cargoes for the ships of all nationalities and from ports in one part of the world to another without ever touching the British Isles. The whole of the world's shipping was their business. But from September 3, 1939, the world overnight became divided into three: Britain and her allies, the enemy, and the neutrals. The size and carrying power of the British mercantile marine, and in particular the tramp shipping part of it, immediately re-assumed special significance. It was a pale shadow of its former self.

Tramp owners throughout the 1930s had laboured under considerable difficulty owing to the fall in British coal exports and to the protection given by foreign governments to foreign ship-owners by subsidizing their own merchant fleets. 'In varying degrees' as C. B. A. Behrens wrote in *Merchant Shipping and the Demands of War* (HMSO 1955), 'the foreign seafaring nations of the world were reverting to the practices which had prevailed at the time of the Navigation Acts'. At the end of the 1930s the dry cargo tonnage that a British Government could bring under its control if it wished was 18 per cent less than in 1914, in spite of the population having increased and the consumption of imported commodities per head being very much larger.

The British merchant navy was still by far the largest in the world, but in 1939 44 per cent by weight of the commodities imported into the UK came in foreign ships. How far the allied and

N

neutral shipowning countries of Europe would help Britain out
was unknown at the beginning of the war. The United States was
neutral, but nothing could be expected from her in the light of the
Neutrality Acts. There was no parallel for shipping in any body
resembling the Food Defence Plans Department which was preparing for a war situation from 1936 onwards. 'The likely nature
of the shipping situation' wrote Behrens, meaning the relationship
between the demand for ships and the effective available supply,
'fundamental though it would be to the whole war effort, was not
considered by the Committee of Imperial Defence until the time
of Munich (1938).' Up to then the greatest danger to Britain's sea-
borne supplies was thought to be an attack on ports and not ships
at sea. A review of resources in 1938 by the Mercantile Marine
Department of the Board of Trade, with whom responsibility for
merchant shipping had been vested, showed British tonnage
would be able to import about 48 million tons of dry cargo in the
first twelve months of a war, and the needs were calculated to be
47 million.

The position seemed secure, therefore, for this estimate of 48
million tons related only to British ships and it had been assumed
that no neutral shipping would be available. 'It is however in-
conceivable', stated the Department in explaining its estimate, 'that
we should not in fact have substantial help from neutral shipping.'

According to Behrens, 'the department assumed that it would be
possible to charter even more neutral shipping than in peace because it argued that once the British blockade cut off the sea-borne
trade of the Axis [Germany, Italy, Japan] the neutral owners would
be forced into British service for lack of other markets.'

Ironically enough, while these secret plans were being laid for
an eventuality which everyone hoped would never occur, others
were being made to enable the British merchant navy to take the
fullest advantage of the improved conditions in the expectation of
a very much more stable situation for many years to come. In 1939
the Liverpool Steamship Owners' Association was engaged at the
initiative of the Government in the formulation of proposals for
temporary state assistance to British shipping, designed to enable
it to maintain its strength and position pending the full restoration

of international trade. Plans for the renewal of the tramp subsidy were embodied in a parliamentary bill which at the outbreak of war was on its way to the statute book. The war caused the bill to be abandoned.

In November 1938 the Liverpool Steamship Owners' Association had submitted a memorandum to Sir W. Norman Raeburn, of the Mercantile Marine Department of the Board of Trade, querying the right of the naval authorities to control the movements of British shipping in peacetime. In their opinion there was no justification for the claim. It would be strange, they said, if the Emergency Powers Act of 1920 was intended to cover the emergency of war, or threatened war, when Britain had just finished a war which was supposed to have ended war. They were told that the authority was not an emergency Act but the Royal Prerogative.

Their concern was about the payment of compensation and automatic indemnity to shipowners by Government as the result of damage and loss following carrying out Government orders. The file in the Public Record Office from which this correspondence is taken (M.5937/1939, Shipping Defence Advisory Committee, T.02828) shows that the Board of Trade was on very shaky ground, and clung to an opinion of the Treasury Solicitor which pinned everything to the prerogative right of the Crown. It also shows that plans 'for the regulation of merchant shipping' were in the forefront of their minds at least as early as the Munich crisis of 1938, though their disbelief that there would be an immediate need to put them into action was equally evident.

The appraisal of the situation in the event of war by the Mercantile Marine Department was accepted by the Committee of Imperial Defence and was not questioned until the Department's memorandum was re-examined just after the outbreak of war by a group of economists under Lord Stamp, appointed in the summer of 1939 to survey economic and financial plans for war. They immediately exposed absurdities of the estimate, not only for the country's needs but for its importing capacity.

In many respects the shipping plans of the Second World War began where the experience of the First World War had stopped. Notably plans were made to set up a Ministry of Shipping should it be required, and schemes for

N*

insuring ships and cargoes against war risks went into operation. Only one of the immediate consequences of war was not foreseen – shortage of ships ... Because it had assumed that shipping would be plentiful it had concluded that ships need not be requisitioned except to meet the needs of the fighting services. (Behrens.)

To their relief, therefore, the shipping section of the Baltic heard that the Government's policy was to be a licensing system, the main effect of which was to control freight rates, and the Government was going to run the country's merchant shipping through the trade as it was doing with food. There was not to be what most feared, a Ministry of Shipping.

The directors of the Baltic Exchange met on September 12, 1939, nine days after war was declared, at which the chairman, Frank Alexander, who took over from Frank Fehr in May, explained to his fellow directors that now war had been declared arrangements had been made to form committees to organize the chartering of vessels on behalf of the Government for the Food Defence Plans Department of the Board of Trade. He said he had written to the Board of Trade asking for a portion of the commission usually payable to the charterer to be allocated for the purpose of forming a pool from which those chartering brokers whose ordinary business had disappeared owing to the war, might receive an income bearing a relation to their peacetime income.

They met again on September 21 to approve the names of those selected to serve on the chartering committees, of which there was to be one for each market. But within six weeks the licensing system was showing itself wholly unsuitable to meet the situation. A Ministry of Shipping was set up on October 13 with Sir John Gilmour as minister. As Behrens, with the aid of hindsight, explains:

For just as the prevailing unwillingness to contemplate the possibility of total war, with its restrictions on individual liberty, had made it seem unnecessary, and therefore unwise, to requisition, so another dominant belief of the nineteen-thirties – that there must be equality of sacrifice and that no one should be allowed to benefit from a national emergency – had led to the determination to control freights. But the two assumptions led to contradictory results, for the control of freights removed one of the principal incentives that might otherwise have operated (although it could not have operated to a sufficient extent) to get the tramp ships into the dangerous but necessary trades, notably the Narvik ore and the Atlantic grain trades, where they were particularly needed because the foreign ships which engaged in them in peace were only available in greatly diminished numbers.

In general, in fact, in the conditions in which it was required to operate, the licensing system increasingly exhibited every conceivable defect, although the enormous administrative problems involved in requisitioning the whole dry-cargo fleet, as well as the objections, which still remained, to applying compulsion, made it impossible completely to abandon it for some time. Though it prevented any ship-owner from making profits on the scale that had sometimes been possible during the 1914–18 war, it ensured equality of sacrifice (or reward) between one ship-owner and another far less than requisition would have done, for it proved impossible to fix freight-rates in an equitable way; it placed on the ship-owners, and particularly on the tramp-owners, a burden of moral responsibility larger than they should have been required to shoulder, forcing individual firms to decide whether, or how far, the national interest required them to sacrifice their ships in trades for which they had not been designed, or to expose their crews' lives in dangerous voyages, when there were plenty of safe and attractive alternatives; so far from the ship-owners being able, by virtue of their experience, to exercise a useful discretion about the routes on which they sailed, the cargoes they carried and, in general, about the way they managed their ships, the bulk of the cargoes were increasingly purchased by the Government and the ship-owners, for this and other reasons, increasingly found their freedom of action limited by conditions over which they had no control – by the need, for example, to sail in convoy under Admiralty orders; by the impossibility of knowing, when sudden shortages of urgently needed commodities were daily occurrences, whether or not they would be allowed licences for the voyages they had planned; by constantly finding their plans upset at the last moment.

From the start enough tonnage could not be found for the unattractive trades except by requisitioning ships to meet the needs which the negative control exercised by the licensing system was incapable of meeting. The ships were, however, requisitioned when it was necessary. It seems unlikely, considering the other impediments at this time to harmonious marriages between ships and cargoes, that these hand-to-mouth methods, which prevailed until January 1940, when it was decided to requisition all deep-sea dry-cargo ships, significantly diminished either the total volume of British imports or even the importation of essential commodities. On the other hand they added to the difficulties, which admittedly continued long after the licensing system had been abandoned, of making reliable estimates about how much of this, that or the other commodity would come in during any given month or quarter.

The purchasing departments, in consequence, who saw their monthly quotas fluctuating in an exasperating and unpredictable way, naturally tended to suppose that all the Ministry of Shipping's predictions were wrong, and to the Ministry's admonitions that what was required was that they should set their house in order they could always find a *tu quoque* reply.

In fact, however, though in shipping as in other matters there was scope for better management than could immediately be supplied, it was the shipping authorities and not those who abused them who turned out right. The Ministry of Shipping's long-term estimates were almost exactly fulfilled; its warnings were justified by events; amidst all the false optimism it showed, in most respects, a remarkable prescience.

A main trouble came from the determination of acceptable controlled freight rates. In November 1939 the shipowners put to the Government what they considered these should be and on November 10 'E.T.' (E. Twentyman?*) wrote a memo to Sir Richard Hopkins in the Prime Minister's Office headed 'Shipping'.

The Shipping community have already been told that the schedule [revised schedule of freight rates] is under review and that any increase that may be decided upon will apply as from 1st November. Nor am I convinced that it is better policy to increase controlled freight rates now in the manner proposed than to requisition, and I confess that I do not understand Sir Vernon Thomson's position in this matter. He said yesterday that we were only a very little way off requisitioning. If this is the case, will not the revised schedule of controlled rates now proposed be likely to prejudice the issue as to the rates at which ships are to be requisitioned? In the event of requisition the rate can be fixed if necessary by independent arbitration under the Compensation (Defence) Act. In the atmosphere of uncertainty and doubt in which this whole matter is shrouded, I should be inclined to defer decisions at any rate for a short period rather than be rushed into a position the consequence of which may be serious. In any event I should feel much happier if we had a considered report from the Ministry of Shipping on the whole issue of requisitioning.

(Prime Minister's Office Papers, PREMIER 1/429, 1940 Trade)

Sir John Gilmour, Minister of Shipping, had discussed the new rates with Sir Kingsley Wood, Chancellor of the Exchequer, on November 9; they were to be roughly double the pre-war rate. A minute on the report of this meeting read, 'Such an increase is obviously startling'. Treasury examination of the proposal could

*He became Second Secretary, Ministry of Food, in 1941.

not be taken in time for the next day's meeting as figures promised by the Ministry of Shipping were not forthcoming. 'I am all against hasty decision here', minuted 'H. J. W.' (Sir Horace Wilson).

At their December meeting the directors of the Baltic had to revise the names recommended to serve on the chartering committees. Many had had to resign as it was not possible for them to give the time. Four days later they met again to confirm instructions that it was not the intention that members of a committee should take advantage of their prior knowledge of the market requirements for the benefit of their own business. This arose out of a letter received from Messrs V. in which they stated that they had failed to secure Danubian chartering committee business owing to clients of theirs being advised of this business by Mr A., a member of the Danubian chartering committee, before they had time to do it themselves. Mr A. explained that the firm in question was an old client of theirs and the business had been put through his company only because they were old clients and after Messrs V. had already been in touch. Frank Alexander reported that a certain amount of progress had been made with the Treasury over the amount of commission to be paid to the chartering pool on all Ministry of Food charters.

But it was wasted effort. The decision to abandon the licensing system and introduce direct requisition of ships was made on January 4, 1940. It put the Baltic out of court for the rest of the war.

Official war historian Behrens refers to the decision as being mainly dictated by the wheat shortage.

After a few weeks of war the country began to run short of wheat. Imports in September and October were only about half consumption; until the harvest began to come in there were, it was shown, stocks (over and above the distributional minimum) sufficient only for three weeks. As ill-luck would have it the harvest was unusually late. In the beginning of November it was reported to the War Cabinet that 'we have reached a condition of dangerous scarcity'. By the middle of the month there were mills that could not be kept fully employed for lack of grain.

The answer to this problem as long as it was considered in isolation was relatively simple, for wheat was a commodity of such vital importance that it seemed that the licensing system, which made it impossible to get enough ships into the North Atlantic grain trade in the autumn storms, could not be allowed to obstruct the importation of the necessary amount. The ships were requisitioned and the wheat transported to this country.

Frank Alexander called a meeting of all members of the Baltic five days after the announcement had been made to explain to them how requisitioning would affect each section of members. He told shipping members that he proposed writing to Sir Vernon Thomson pointing out that the Baltic as an institution was a vital pillar of the economic system and that the professions of broker and chartering agent should be preserved as far as possible during the time of war so that at the end of hostilities they might be in a position to resume their normal trading. Everyone agreed to this. No intercession with the Government was needed so far as oil and oilseed members were concerned, and an agreement had been made with the Government over payment though there were still details to confirm.

Fairplay commented on January 11:

In the event of the requisitioning of British tonnage lock, stock and barrel becoming the order of the day then the very lifeblood of British tramp owners as represented by the freight market must in consequence stagnate to no inconsiderable degree. In certain quarters the view is emphatically held that it is the intention of the bureaucratic element of the Ministry of Shipping to force the issue . . . Many errors of judgement or lack of judgement have been so apparent in the welter of requisition that has already occurred that it must be obvious that the counsel of practical shipping experts giving their services to the Ministry cannot possibly have been taken or, if so, ignored in view of the lack of elementary knowledge displayed in various tonnage dispositions whereby owners themselves have been completely nonplussed at such extraordinary and wasteful decisions . . . Requisition in itself apart from wresting the control from the hands of those so eminently fitted for the purpose will not add a single ton of carrying capacity to the British mercantile marine.

It was the policy of the Government that British shipowners should not be allowed to amass large profits out of the emergency of the state; but it was not possible, said *Fairplay*, to contemplate with any degree of equanimity the wiping out of so essential a service to the nation, much in the manner of a Gentleman with a Duster.

Sir John Gilmour defended his policy in an interview with the *Observer* published on February 1.

It is a common delusion that any ship we requisition is taken from the experienced hands of the owners and delivered to the mercies of a body of civil servants. This is not so. We do not in fact even hand the ships over to the shipowners or the ministry. We take the ship over as a running concern. The owners remain – continuing to operate it as though upon their own business. The ministry will instruct them from time to time as required to carry certain cargoes and to follow certain routes, and in these matters we have the advantage of expert shipowners to advise us. Chartering is on a time basis.

In a speech made the following month Sir John said he was one of those who thought any government must have their minds not only on winning the war and the use of shipping under war conditions, but also on the future and status of the mercantile marine.

After the TUC's effort to have the merchant navy nationalized in 1916, there was an inevitable fear that something similar might be in the mind of the Government for the end of the current war. Sir John Gilmour scotched these rumours by having his private secretary write to *Fairplay* to say that he had no desire to see the merchant marine nationalized at the end of the war.

At their meeting on February 6, 1940, three of the directors of the Baltic suggested that the chairman should announce from the rostrum what steps were being taken to safeguard the interests of shipbrokers and chartering agents on the Exchange. Negotiations between the Government and the grain trade were still not complete, the board were told, and though they had not been entirely satisfactory the intervention of Baltic directors was not required. Neither had the amount of money to be paid by the Government to members in the oil and oilseed section been settled; negotiations were still in train on how it was to be apportioned. A committee was formed to deal with claims under the chartering pool scheme and another to deal with sale and purchase in connection with Government business. An irate Frank Alexander wrote a letter to *The Times* which they printed on February 28.

The Government had told shipping, he wrote, that it would be policy to let them run their business on usual lines and not policy to requisition vessels wholesale. Thus there was strict control over freight rates by the Mercantile Marine Department of the Board of Trade and all ocean-going vessels could only go on a voyage under a licence. This control was accepted by shipowners who thought it would be exercised reasonably and by consultation between shipowners and brokers. In collaboration with the Ministry of Food, the Baltic established a number of chartering committees composed of various members qualified to operate in various markets of the world who gave services without payment and a commission payable to a fund administered by the Baltic. At the outbreak of war control of ships' movements was exercised by the Royal Navy and naturally there were delays due to devious routes, waiting for convoys etc. This worked well, so when the Government announced requisitioning of *all* vessels, the shipping industry was alarmed. 'The experience of other countries which have embarked on national control has shown the risk of loss to the public exchequer caused when private enterprise cannot reap any direct and personal advantage from extra zeal and work.'

Shipowners were not satisfied, he wrote, that requisitioning would produce economy of time, money or efficiency. It would for certain voyages. But if the ordinary type of cargo vessel was requisitioned it displaced the ordinary machinery of trade, threw brokers and agents out of work and made for an increased staff at the Ministry of Shipping. Agents and brokers were an integral part of the industry. If business was taken from them they were left without means of livelihood; they would disperse staffs and disappear. This would mean 'that this country will be in no position to recapture in happier times the important trade which up to now has been done in London, frequently between foreign countries, and our position as chief centre of the shipping business of the world will be lost'.

Sir Samuel Hoare, Lord Privy Seal, would not have read this letter when he prepared his report to the War Cabinet of February 23 headed 'The extent to which Shipping considerations call for a review of our import programme' (War Cabinet Memoranda WP(40)21–WP(40)70; Vol. V, p. 231).

This reviewed the situation in depth. One section (para II) attempted to make an estimate of the goods it would be possible to import into the UK in the first year of the war.

It might at first sight be thought that with a mercantile marine of over 21 million gross tons we should have no difficulty in war in importing to this country all the goods which we require even when account is taken of the large share (40 per cent) of our peacetime imports which in peacetime arrive in ships under foreign flags.

But more than half on the British Register, he pointed out, was not available for bringing in imports: $1\frac{1}{2}$ gross tons were river boats, dredgers, trawlers and similar craft; 3·3 million were tankers. The fighting services took up 2·2 million tons of merchant shipping. Thus only 9·8 million gross tons were available, not 21, to import dry goods into the UK. Of this 350000 tons were allocated to France, so the final figure was 9·467 which amounted to a deadweight capacity of 13·19 million tons. The cargo carrying capacity of this was 10·65 million tons. (In 1939, said Behrens, the tonnage registered in the UK over which the Government had control was $1\frac{1}{2}$ million gross tons less than in 1914.)

'Even when account is taken of our present increased ship-building programme our shipping difficulties, like our exchange difficulties, will be greater in the second year of the war than in the first and will continue to increase for so long as the war continues.' Once military operations had begun – it was the 'Phoney War' period – the essential requirements of the fighting services would be greater. 'Transition of the war from its present phase of relative inactivity to one of active military operations will bring other, and new, serious shipping difficulties.'

Arrangements had been made for the time-chartering of 235000 gross tons of neutral vessels of which 138000 gross tons had already been delivered – 397000 tons deadweight capable of importing 1·25 million tons of goods a year. 'There is reason to hope that during the last six months (March to August 1940) of the first year of the war, it will be possible considerably to increase the amount of neutral tonnage now under time charter.' In the first five months of the war (to January 1940) imports to Britain in foreign vessels (both those under time-charter and those trading independently) amounted to four million tons. 'The Ministry of Shipping hope that it may be possible in the first year of the war to secure a larger quantity of imports in vessels now under foreign flags.'

'We are faced with the problem', was the final daunting conclusion of the Lord Privy Seal's report, 'of having set ourselves to import 47 million tons of goods in the first year of war; shipping British and foreign is enough for only 41.7–44.7 million tons.'

As if mindful of Frank Alexander's carping, and as if to dissuade the War Cabinet from accepting the professional but comparatively hit-and-miss efforts of brokers on the floor of the Baltic, he was emphatic in his closing paragraphs that 'any attempt to deal with this problem in a piecemeal fashion would not only be foredoomed to failure but would also aggravate the difficulties in which we find ourselves'.

Members of the Baltic assembled at St Mary Axe on March 4 to pass a resolution protesting at the displacement by the Ministry of Shipping of the chartering committees and the establishment of the Ministry's City Central Chartering Office which they considered detrimental to the national interest. They placed on record the intense disappointment felt at the failure of the Ministry to remedy the serious hardship and loss of livelihood imposed upon shipbrokers and chartering agents by control and chartering of tonnage.

Frank Alexander presided at this gathering, and emphasized that it was a resolution of the meeting not of the board. He said he had only had notice of the disbanding of the chartering committees the previous week and only then had learnt of the proposal to set up a special department of the Ministry under Philip Runciman to deal with neutral tonnage. He told his receptive audience,

Whatever the government decides members of the Baltic will retain their freedom to endorse or oppose and criticize, because they are putting the national interest in the foreground, and their own interests and personal considerations second. But we will not do anything small, paltry or in the nature of pinpricking. If we have to oppose we will fight clean and will not lower the Baltic standards or cease to be actuated by the highest possible motives and the utmost integrity.

Frank Alexander told directors he had agreed with Sir Cyril Hurcomb, Director General of the Ministry of Shipping, on a commission of one per cent on all charter-parties effected by the Ministry's City Chartering Office to form a pool for agents affected by requisitioning. When his colleagues on the board rejected this as totally inadequate, Alexander wrote to the Prime Minister Neville Chamberlain (on March 20). At the April board meeting he told them about the reply. Mr Chamberlain had stated that he understood that the Baltic Exchange had been in touch with the Ministry of Shipping who had stated their readiness to consider any specific proposal that the Exchange might wish to be made, but the Ministry could not accept any arrangement on the basis of employing intermediaries between themselves and other Government departments, or between themselves and the shipowners. The Prime Minister referred him to the explanation of why the policy of general requisition was necessary which had been made in the minister's House of Commons statement on March 18 in which Sir John Gilmour said the scheme had followed closely that adopted in the 1914–18 war, introduced, only after two and a half years of war, in 1917. The Ministry must be the people to marry the ship to the cargo, said the minister, and in these circumstances there was no opening for the broker.

Alexander also talked to Sir Cyril Hurcomb about the rejected one per cent commission. Philip Runciman was present at the interview. He told the director general of the Ministry of Shipping how the points at issue could be overcome. Sir Cyril said the longer the delay the more difficult would it become to make the offer of one per cent retrospective to March 4. If a settlement was reached, it must be final, he said. He complained of the treatment the City Chartering Office were receiving on the Baltic, though Philip Runciman denied he had been the subject of unpleasant treatment in the Room. Sir Cyril insisted that it was up to Baltic directors to make the next move.

Agreement was reached with the Ministry of Shipping in May. A commission was to be paid into a pool of one per cent on freight earned on neutral vessels chartered by the Ministry's City Chartering Office. Provided one per cent was sufficient for it to be done, and without any guarantee, a maximum sum of £60 000 would be paid for the twelve months. Of this £30 000 would be payable after six months from March 4. The fund would be administered by the Baltic board for the benefit of chartering agents and ship-brokers whose business had been hit by Government policy. In consideration of this contribution to the pool, the City Chartering Office were given the facilities of the Exchange and the assistance of its consultative committees. Philip Runciman said Sir Vernon Thomson hoped Sir Julian Foley would be elected to represent the Ministry of Shipping on the Baltic. All clerks engaged in the Ministry's City Chartering Office were still members of the Baltic as representing their original firms, however, and the board agreed that in view of this Sir Vernon's proposal was neither practical nor necessary.

When shareholders met on May 23, 1940, for their annual general meeting Neville Chamberlain had been replaced by Winston Churchill as Prime Minister at the head of a coalition Government, a post he was to retain until May 23, 1945. For Frank Alexander it was another opportunity to dilate on the Government's treatment of the institution whose interests he held so dear.

You will I am sure agree [he told the shareholders] that the outstanding position of London and this country in the whole of the commercial world is very largely if not mainly due to the activities and enterprise shown by brokers and middlemen combined with the high standard of moral integrity which stands out pre-eminently, and it has always been the aim of the Board to watch jealously to ensure that this high standard is maintained unimpaired, and this is shown by the fact that throughout the world membership of the Baltic Exchange is looked upon as a hallmark of integrity.

The merchant princes and shipping magnates may with a great deal of truth be said to have built up their businesses on the activities of the middle-men and brokers, who in their incessant search to make commissions for themselves investigate and recommend fresh avenues of enterprise and commerce to their principals, and in all our negotiations with the Government we have stressed the importance and value of keeping the middlemen and brokers commercially as well as financially alive even in time of war when perhaps their usefulness is not so obvious, so that they may be able to resume their normal functions in happier days.

The directors were glad to report last week that they had come to an agreement with the Ministry of Shipping under which the personnel of their City Chartering Office would be granted the facilities of the Floor and the co-operation of our members in return for the payment of a commission into a pool which is to be administered by the Baltic.

It is satisfactory to know that to some extent the government departments who control our business life in war time are gradually recognizing this important fact, and have discovered that the brokers and the maintenance of a market are essential to institutions such as Lloyds' and the Stock Exchange, and there is hope that the Baltic is gradually achieving similar recognition.

I am happy to learn that the Ministry of Food, under the guidance of the Trade, are making use of some of our members in the world markets, thus proving that the activity of the broker and middleman, which as regards futures is sometimes considered by the uninitiated as merely an opportunity for gambling, in reality when properly used is just the reverse and would enable even a big operator like the Government to carry on enormous business transactions without suffering from the violent swings of the pendulum which inevitably occur when the middleman is eliminated.

In conclusion I would say that the future of the Exchange lies largely in your hands, and it behoves everyone of us to refuse to be depressed by controls or restrictions of business activity, but to employ his knowledge and experience to seek out fresh channels of service by which the business of the country may be increased, resting assured that the middleman and the broker will never be eliminated provided they render useful service, in which case they become the creators of business and not in any sense parasites on it.

The reality of the situation was more succinctly summed up in two sentences in the directors' report dated May 7, 1940.

The outbreak of war last September and the action of the Government in immediately taking over control of all imports into this country, together with control of shipping, has completely altered the business hitherto conducted in the Exchange. Many members have been faced with almost complete loss of their business and income.

Whether the war could have been won with the country's shipping handled by brokers on the Floor of the Baltic Exchange is anyone's guess. How far the demands of *total* war, in which men's lives were being thrown into the balance to tip the scales in favour of military victory, should be weighed against the livelihood of brokers and such, and the maintenance of their professional expertise for the benefit of post-war Britain, was one of those matters of policy which human politicians were called upon to formulate as best they could, and having made up their minds pursue it with all the courage of a conviction. The degree of involvement required in the military effort of 1939-45 had greatly changed since the business-as-usual and profit-making-more-than-usual days of World War I, let alone the happy-go-lucky atmosphere of the family cruise to Balaclava Bay in 1854.

There was no magic formula about requisitioning. It seemed to reduce the risks of things going wrong. As the editor of the *Guide to Documents* of World War II in the Public Record Office noted,

Requisitioning could not of itself produce more tonnage, and early 1940 saw the first of many attempts . . . to match the import demands as put by the responsible departments with the tonnage assessed as available by the Ministry of Shipping. Among the limitations of tonnage was the unwilling-ness of neutral owners to charter their vessels and this led in the summer to the institution of the ship warrant scheme by which world-wide facilities under British control were denied to vessels not engaged on approved voyages.

For better or worse the Baltic Exchange suspended its operations 'for the duration'. At Frank Alexander's instigation the City of London Air Training Corps was formed to prepare youngsters for entry in to the Royal Air Force, and they drilled on the Floor of the Baltic every day from 4 to 6. Everyone took their turn at fire watching, and a direct hit on No 14 St Mary Axe next door in April 1941 damaged the Exchange to some extent, and incendiary bombs fell on the fourth floor in December. A perspicacious member of the Baltic bought the No 14 bombed site from the Duchy of Lancaster as a possible post-war extension of the Exchange. Facilities were offered to the London Corn Exchange and the London Commercial Sale Rooms, both of which were very severely damaged by high explosive in 1941. Water from the well at St Mary Axe was 'lent' to the London Fire Brigade to help them fight the fires lit by Marshal Goering's merciless but un-successful *Blitzkrieg*. A sum of £8500 was raised to present three 'Spitfire' fighter planes to the RAF called 'Baltic Exchange 1, 2

The façade of the Baltic Exchange in St Mary Axe, opened in 1903

The rostrum, from which the 'waiters', as the attendants are still called, can summon members whenever thay are needed

The memorial window, installed in commemoration of those members and staff of the Baltic Exchange who lost their lives in the First and Second World Wars

The London grain futures market. The 'ring', where trading in futures in EEC wheat and barley is carried out

and 3'. By November 1941 £447870 had been given as a free-of-interest loan to the Government. The Baltic declined an invitation to join the Federation of Produce and Commodity Associations when it was formed in 1942 on the grounds that it was a meeting place not a trade, but the directors told L. W. Wilson, who was promoting it, that they would keep in touch.

Frank Alexander was knighted in the 1942 New Year Honours and became Lord Mayor of London in 1944. Though two members of the Baltic, Sir Charles Batho (1927) and Sir Charles Trinder (1968) were Lord Mayor before and after this, Sir Frank Alexander was the first *chairman* of the Baltic to hold that distinguished office. Later Leslie Phillips, who had been involved in the Food Defence Plans since 1936, became responsible at the Ministry of Food for the food shipping programme and the food warehousing programme. He was also knighted for his services

Fred Leathers, a director of William Cory, coal importers, and a leading member of the Baltic, was an old friend of Winston Churchill in whose constituency he lived, and had put him on a number of his boards while he was in the political wilderness between the wars. When Churchill became Prime Minister in May, 1940, he invited Fred Leathers to put his very considerable experience of shipping at the disposal of the Government. He made him a member of the House of Lords and put him at the head of the new Ministry of War Transport, a merger of the ministries of Shipping and Transport. The Ship Management Division of the new Ministry dealt directly, and through owners, with the employment of deep-sea tramps, chartered and seized foreign vessels, and purchased newly-built vessels. It also controlled the City Central Chartering Office. Its Shipping (Operations) Control was under the chairmanship of Sir Vernon Thomson of Union Castle, a past chairman of the Baltic, who undertook close supervision of shipping under Viscount Leathers. Sir Gibson Graham, another leading Baltic figure (who became chairman in 1953), was deputy director of Commercial Services at the Ministry of War Transport and represented the Ministry in the Mediterranean.

But the Baltic, as the London *Evening Standard* described it, became the City's 'Ghost Exchange':

once the hub of the world of commerce which is now almost deserted. . . .
The days when it was a hive of activity and echoed to the bids of merchants
and brokers are gone. Now it echoes only to the ghostlike footfalls of the
few members who use 'the floor' of the Exchange chiefly out of personal
habits. Pre-war footfalls would not have been heard above the buzz of
business. Now scarcely any business is transacted.

A few firms tried to nurse their reputations during the suspension
of normal activities. Sir Philip Haldin told Lamport & Holt shareholders in 1940 that they were trying to maintain their ninety-five-
year-old service from the United States to Brazil with neutral
tonnage chartered at very high rates, which ran them into a loss,
in order to protect their century-old goodwill and prevent it being
filched from them by foreigners. He complained that the rates
being paid for his ships by the British Government were small
compared with those paid to neutrals.

By the time the European war ended in May, 1945, membership
of the Baltic had fallen to 1287. Subscription and entrance fee income amounted to only £21 642, but rents brought in £44 082.
But after seven years (1939 to 1945 inclusive) the Exchange was
solvent, and, with a seven-year income of £480 299 and expenditure of £478 409, managed to end the war with a balance – £1890.
The company also had £16 000 in reserve, and a sum of £8000
for building contingencies. It had paid out £57 125 over the period
to shareholders as dividends.

V E-Day brought no immediate revival to the Baltic Exchange,
no overnight de-requisitioning of shipping. But it was not for the
lack of trying. Members had been prepared for control to be
maintained after the end of hostilities by the White Paper published in August 1944 which set out the plans of the United
Maritime Authority to continue co-ordinated control of all the
merchant shipping resources of the victorious allies now grouped
politically as the United Nations. One of its two secretariats was
set up in London by the Ministry of War Transport. Its planning
committee established procedures for programming and allocating
dry cargo and tanker tonnage, and the settling of freight rates.

In April 1945 representatives of thirty-eight firms, headed by
Norman Spratt, met at the Baltic and formed a pool for French

chartering business, encouraged by the Ministry's agreement to recognize the use of chartering agents; and Furness Withy urged the formation of a Russian chartering pool.

The Institute of Chartered Shipbrokers had pressed *their* post-war policy on Lord Leathers before the end of May 1945, encouraged by the minister's assurance that he fully appreciated the functions performed by brokers and the contribution they made to the national economy, and that he looked forward to the re-establishment of the UK chartering markets as an important factor in the revival of British overseas trade. When they presented their document to him, the minister stated that he had given consideration to the possibility of extending the range of business available to brokers without waiting for a return to peace conditions, and that he would be prepared from an early date for brokers to participate in fixtures for ministry-controlled deep-sea tramp vessels in certain additional export and cross trades, with a maximum commission of £75. This would treble their number of fixtures. The institute was opposed to the imposition of a maximum brokerage, but owing to the limited services brokers would be able to give, this was inevitable. But it was an emergency measure only for this period of transition from war to peace.

Sir Frank Alexander arranged for freight requirements of the Ministry of Food to be undertaken by chartering agents who were members of the Baltic Exchange. He told the Ministry that the system of having a large number of specialized freight committees of the kind created in the early days of the war was no longer practicable. Instead he proposed a small main committee of five members of the Baltic experienced in chartering grain, sugar, rice, oil and oilseeds etc. to meet under the chairmanship of Henry Brewer, the vice-chairman of the Baltic, with G. Neville as secretary, and to organize all the Ministry of Food's freight. Commissions would be collected from the Ministry of War Transport and paid to the credit of the Baltic Exchange Chartering Committee.

Oil and oilseed members of the Baltic, through whom animal feeding stuffs were being bought by the Ministry of Food, were upset in July when France and Belgium decided to buy without the co-operation of the British Ministry and sent buying missions to Argentina and Brazil cutting out the London merchants and brokers. Baltic members met at the Exchange to register their protest that prices would soar, but there was little else they could do. Their fellow members in the grain section were in a worse plight. For them wartime controls were to continue for another eight years.

On the shipping front, persistent lobbying of the Ministry of War Transport by the General Council of British Shipping began to bear fruit. Following prolonged talks with shipowners and Ministry officials, the council put out an announcement in September 1945 with the heartening title 'Restoration of Chartering Machinery'. It mainly concerned deep-sea tramp shipping. The Ministry proposed introducing a modified system of procedure for the allocation of vessels 'designed as a preliminary stage in the restoration of the ordinary commercial machinery for the chartering of tonnage'. By this the Ministry retained full control of the *direction* of voyages, but shipowners and their brokers could arrange chartering and conclude fixtures without altering their responsibilities or the Ministry's. Brokerages were allowed when tramp ships were employed and voyage charters were signed for the carriage of imports to Britain; but there would be a limitation of £100. 'The Ministry of War Transport are taking steps to bring these proposals to the attention of the Baltic Exchange and to consult them as necessary with a view to facilitating the smooth working of the scheme.'

The Baltic was back in business.

Chairmen of the Baltic had been holding office for two years, but Sir Frank Alexander, Bt, who received the then traditional baronetcy after his term as Lord Mayor of London, was chairman for the six years of the war without a break. When he retired from the board in May 1946, one of the three members nominated to take his place was Ernest Simpson, of Simpson, Spence and Young, chartered shipbrokers, whose ex-wife, Wallis, was now the Duchess of Windsor. He was not elected. Sir Frank's place as chairman was taken by Sir Norman Vernon, Bt.

Sir Frank's parting shot at his last annual general meeting as chairman was true to form. It could not be too strongly stressed, he told shareholders, that

this international business is largely dependent on the maintenance of free markets, and free markets whether in commodities or in freights cannot exist if the governments in consumer or producer countries decide to continue bulk buying or selling; and although it is recognized that the control of foodstuffs and many essential commodities may continue for some time during the present period of shortage and readjustment, yet it is hoped that at the earliest possible moment they will be relaxed so that free markets can again operate, not only to the benefit of our members but to the great benefit of the whole nation . . .

I hope it will be admitted [he concluded] that the prestige of the Baltic stands higher today than ever before, and that we have established a reputation for service to our country and to international trade based on the highest standard of upright dealing without undue regard to our own personal advantage.

Because of the character of the men who steered the Baltic Exchange through 123 years of social, political and scientific change, there was no question of the reputation which they had given it being in any way diminished by the six-year interruption of total war. The business activities of the majority of members had shifted from Grain to Shipping, but were still guided by the code of behaviour established by the Baltic Committee of 1823.

And in the 30 years since 1946 person-to-person contact which had begun in Lombard Street and was continuing on the Floor at St Mary Axe had yet to lose its value, in spite of the ease and speed of modern telecommunication. Attempts have been made in other cities to duplicate the service provided by The Baltic Exchange of London, but in 1976 the institution founded by the regulars of Monger's coffee-house in Threadneedle Street remains unchallenged as the ship-chartering centre of the world.

Postscript 1946–1976

For the Baltic, as for everyone else, there was no question of returning to the world of Before the War. But the project to form an air freight section was revived; the Airbrokers Association came into being in 1949. The Baltic became the world's first air freight exchange, but was never to regain its importance as a grain exchange. For the thirteen years in which the Ministry of Food was Britain's only purchaser the grain section was dormant. The first stage in de-control did not come until 1952. Sir Leslie Phillips and other members of the Baltic helped the Federation of Corn Trade Associations with the smooth release of the Ministry's stocks. But there were few successors for the large number of commodity brokers who had daily filled the Bury Street half of the Floor before the war; amalgamations and improved communications had reduced the need for the many commodity brokers who were trading in 1939. They were replaced by a few men trading on behalf of the large companies who nevertheless in due course handled larger quantities of grain and other commodities than the many had handled pre-war. Futures trading was resumed in 1954 in imported coarse grains, changing in 1964 to home-grown barley and extending to home-grown wheat in 1965. So the vast majority of new members were shipping men and by 1949 shipping interests were four times as numerous as those of all other trades represented.

In March 1955 Sir Winston Churchill laid the foundation stone of an annexe at 14–20 St Mary Axe which HM Queen Elizabeth II opened the following year, naming the big banquet hall in the basement the Queen's Room. HRH the Duke of Edinburgh had become an honorary member in 1953. Gilbert Findlay completed his twenty-two years as Secretary in 1954 and was succeeded by Jack Walker who on his retirement in 1968 was followed in office by his son Derek Walker.

The Rules of the Exchange were re-drafted in 1968, and again in 1971. Women were admitted to membership in 1974 and in 1976 a major revision of the Rules took place when the minimum age of admission was reduced to nineteen by the introduction of probationers. At the same time to the dismay of some of the older members clerks were renamed representatives. Additionally, foreigners with a residential qualification of three years in the United Kingdom were allowed entry to the Exchange as representatives. In 1971 a re-grouping of trade associations connected with the Exchange led to the formation of the Federation of Oils, Seeds and Fats Association (FOSFA) and of the Grain and Feed Trade Association (GAFTA). Both these had their offices in the Baltic Exchange building, as did the Institute of Chartered Shipbrokers, the professional body incorporated in 1920. Many of the members of the Baltic were now chartered shipbrokers.

Matching ships of any flag in any part of the world with cargoes waiting to be picked up in any other part of the world was their business. It was a highly skilled, complicated operation. They attended the morning and afternoon session at the Baltic to hand out to all who needed them duplicated sheets giving a list of the ships for which their clients were seeking cargoes that day. The information was given in a language meaningless except to the initiated:

1–2 TARRAGONA–MALAGA RANGE/ALEXANDRIV
Bagged Wheat Flour (stow abt 54/55′)
Any size 6000/10000 (try larger but max arrival draft 29′)
15/30 May, $4.90 1/1 FIOS, 200 HD max 800/200 HD max
1000, Synacomex C/P., $6\frac{1}{4}\%$.

TIMECHARTER
Require Vessel: About 500/600000 bale
Good gear inc H/L 25T or more

Able 7500 tons on 24 ft
Trip delivery Norrkoping 16/23 August.
Redelivery Tema-Douala Range
Duration about 55 days.
Adapted Produce 2.5% total.*

The reputation of the Baltic for impartiality had long meant that its members who were arbitrators dealt with many disputes over contracts and charter-parties and sponsored the formation of the London Maritime Arbitrators Association. Charter-parties usually specified London as the place of arbitration though often neither of the signatories was British.

The existence at the Baltic of a deep-rooted and strictly enforced tradition of commercial probity and financial reliability without parallel in any other city in the world was a major contribution to the continuing strength of the London freight market. Efforts have been made to establish similar centres but without success. The Baltic remains unique and has earned its position by its unbroken tradition of service and efficiency. Its position on the Greenwich Meridian, the dividing line between east and west, has also brought it considerable advantage. The rapid expansion of international telecommunications has not diminished the importance of the Baltic as a centre for the collection, collation and dissemination of shipping intelligence. But however efficient communications may be the Baltic's greatest asset will remain the open floor on which information can be passed from person to person and on which negotiations can be conducted face to face.

*For interpretation see Appendix D.

Bibliography

CHAPTER I. (1404–1744)

Addison, Joseph. *The Spectator*. (London, 1711)

APPERSON, G. L. *Byegone London Life*.

ASTROM, SVEN-ERIK. *From Cloth to Iron: the Anglo-Baltic Trade in the late 17th Century*. Part 1. (Helsingfors, 1963)

BESANT, WALTER. *London in the Times of the Tudors*.

BRYANT, SIR ARTHUR. *Liquid History*. (London: Port of London Authority, 1960)

Calendar of Treasury Books and Papers; Treasury Board Papers CCCXII, No 24, 1743; Book 46, pp 42–5.

CHILD, SIR JOSIAH. *A New Discourse of Trade*. (London, 1670/80)

COWIE, L. W. 'Paul's Walk', *History Today*, Vol. XXIV, No 1. (London: Financial Times, January 1974)

CRAIG, R. S. 'The Business Historian and the Shipping Industry: A Review and Prospect', *Business Archives*. (London: Business Archives Council, December 1970)

CURTLER, W. H. R. *A Short History of English Architecture*. (Oxford: University Press, 1909)

DAVIS, RALPH. *The Rise of the English Shipping Industry in the 17th and 18th Centuries*. (London: Macmillan, 1962)

DAWSON, WARREN. *The London Coffee Houses*. (London: Lloyd's)

DEFOE, DANIEL. *A Tour Through the Whole Island of Great Britain*, 1724. (London: Penguin, 1971)

DOWLING, S. W. *Exchanges of London*. (London: Butterworth, 1929)

ELLIS, AYTOUN. *The Penny Universities; a History of the Coffee Houses*. (London: Secker & Warburg, 1956)

FINDLAY, J. A. *A Short History of the Baltic Exchange*. (London: The Baltic Exchange, 1927)

Gentleman's Magazine, Vol. XIV, April 1744.

Grose's Antiquities. (London 1798)

HINTON, R. W. K. *The Eastland Trade and the Common Weal in the 17th Century*. (Cambridge: University Press, 1959)

HUME, DAVID. *The History of England to 1688*. (London, 1848)

JARVIS, RUPERT. 'Ship Registry to 1707', *Maritime History*, Vol. 1, No. 1. (Newton Abbot: David & Charles, 1971)

JOYCE, HERBERT. *History of the Post Office*. (London: Richard Bentley, 1893)

KING, CHARLES. *The British Merchant*. (London, 1721)

LILLYWHITE, BRYANT. *London Coffee Houses*. A reference book of coffee houses of the 17th, 18th and 19th centuries. (London: Allen & Unwin, 1963)

LINDSAY, W. S. *History of Merchant Shipping*. (London: Sampson Low, 1874)

MACAULAY, THOMAS BABINGTON. *The History of England from the Accession of James II*, Vol. 1. (London, 1848)

MACKY, JOHN. *Journey Through England*. (London, 1724)

MALCOLM, JAMES PELLER. *Anecdotes of the Manners & Customs of London during the 18th Century*, Vol. 1. (London: Longmans, 1810)

MASON, A. E. W. *The Royal Exchange*. (London: Royal Insurance, 1920)

MINCHINTON, W. E. (ed.). *The Growth of English Overseas Trade in the Seventeenth and Eighteenth Centuries*. (London: Methuen, 1969)

MORGAN, E. VICTOR, and THOMAS, W. A. *The Stock Exchange*. (London: Elek, 1962)

ODDY, J. J. *European Commerce*. (London, 1805)

PAGE, W. S. *The Russia Company*.

Pepys, Samuel. *The Diaries*.

PLUMB, J. H. 'The Mercantile Interest: the Rise of the British Merchant after 1689', *History Today*, Vol. 5. (London: Financial Times, 1955)

POOL, BERNARD. *Navy Board Contracts 1660–1832*. (London: Longmans, 1966)

PULLING, ALEXANDER. *A Practical Treatise on the Laws, Customs and Regulations of the City of London*. (London: 1842)

REES, GRAHAM L. *Britain's Commodity Markets*. (London: Elek, 1972)

ROBINSON, EDWARD FORBES. *The Early History of Coffee Houses in London*. (London: Kegan Paul, 1893)

ROBINSON, HOWARD. *The British Post Office*.

ROGERS, JAMES E. THOROLD. *The Industrial and Commercial History of England*. (London: T. Fisher Unwin, 1894)

RUDOLPH, ROBERT. *Chartered Companies.* (London: Bell, 1969)

SMITH, JOHN THOMAS. *An Antiquarian Ramble in the Streets of London,* Vol. 2. (London, 1846)

SMOLLETT, T. *The History of England to the Death of George II.* (London, 1848)

THORNBURY, GEORGE WALTER, and WATFORD, ERNEST. *Old and New London.* (London: Cassell, 1883)

WRIGHT, CHARLES and FAYLE, C. ERNEST. *History of Lloyd's.* (London: Macmillan, 1927)

ZINS, H. *England and the Baltic in the Reign of Elizabeth.*

CHAPTER 2. (1744–1823)

ANON [D. Morier Evans?]. *The City, or the Physiology of London Business with Sketches on 'Change and at the Coffee Houses,* in the series 'City Men and City Manners' published by Baily Brothers, 1845; a revised edition with a fresh chapter 'showing the commencement and decline of the railway era' was published by Groombridge & Sons, Paternoster Row, in 1852. D. Morier Evans was the author of a number of other books including *Facts, Failures and Frauds: Revelations Financial, Mercantile, Criminal,* 1859, reprinted by David & Charles in 1970.

ASTELL, CARLETON W. 'The Tallow Trade', *The Baltic Magazine.* (London: The Baltic Exchange, Winter, 1961)

BROODBANK, SIR JOSEPH G. *History of the Port of London,* Vol. 2. (London, 1921)

BRYANT, SIR ARTHUR. *The Age of Elegance, 1812–1822.* (London: Collins, 1950)

CHECKLAND, S. G. *The Rise of Industrial Society in England, 1815–1885.* (London: Longmans, 1964)

EDMONDS, CHARLES H. 'It Is This Day Mutually Agreed', *The Baltic Magazine.* (London: The Baltic Exchange, Summer 1960)

GAYER, A. D., ROSTOW, W. W. and SCHWARTZ, A. J. *The Growth and Fluctuations of the British Economy, 1790–1850.* (Oxford: University Press, 1953)

HAWKER, ROBERT. *The Royal Exchange.* (Plymouth, 1808)

KNIGHT, A. CHARLES. *The Tallow Chandlers Company.* (London: Tallow Chandlers Hall, 1918)

LEWIS, ROY and MAUDE, ANGUS. *The English Middle Classes.* (London: Phoenix House, 1949)

LOFTS. R. B. *A Short History of the London Average Market Letter Committee.* (London: Tallow Chandlers Hall, 1950)

MORTIMER, THOMAS. *Mystery and Iniquity of Stock Jobbing.* (London)

MUSSON, A. E. *Enterprise in Soap and Chemicals: Joseph Crosfield & Sons Ltd, 1815–1965.* (Manchester: University Press, 1965)

THACKERAY, WILLIAM. *Vanity Fair.* (London, 1848; Penguin English Library, 1971)

WATERS, CHARLOTTE M. *An Economic History of England, 1066–1874.* (Oxford: University Press, 1925)

WILSON, CHARLES. *The History of Unilever,* Vol. 1. (London: Cassell)

'The Light of Luxury and Necessity' by a member of the Advertising Staff of *The Times,* January 10, 1905.

CHAPTER 3. (1823–1837)

CLARK, RAYMOND. 'The Oil Man Who Never Was', *The Shell Magazine.* (January, 1959)

COBBETT, WILLIAM. *Rural Rides.* January 3, 1822, and July 28, 1825. (London: Dents Everyman Library, No 638)

MACLEOD, H. *The Theory and Practice of Banking,* Vol. II. (London, 1856)

MATHIAS, PETER. *The First Industrial Nation.* An Economic History of Britain 1700–1914. (London: Methuen, 1969)

OWENS, JOHN. *Plain Papers relating to the Excise Branch of the Inland Revenue Department from 1621 to 1878,* or *A History of the Excise.* (Linlithgow, 1879)

SHEPPARD, FRANCIS. *The History of London: London 1808–1870, The Internal Wen.* (London: Secker & Warburg, 1972)

SMITH, JOHN THOMAS. *An Antiquarian Ramble in the Streets of London,* Vol. 2. (London, 1846)

TOOKE, THOMAS, and NEWMARCH, W. *A History of Prices.* (London, 1838–57)

TOOKE, THOMAS, and NEWMARCH, W. *High and Low Prices.* (London, 1823)

Annual Biography, 1824.

Annual Register, 1823.

Corporation of London, Committee for Improving the Navigation of the River Thames and for Preventing Encroachments Thereon. Index to Minutes 1770–1857. Meeting of April 23, 1796, Book 8, page 1 *re* drift timber at Nine Elms; Book 30 for 1823. (Port of London Authority Library)

Correspondence of John Hubbard & Sons, Russia Merchants. MS/10364/1&2; MS 14280; MS 11463A. (Guildhall MS Library, London)

History of Price's of Bromborough 1854–1954. (Unilever Library)

John Knight Ltd Centenary Booklet 1817–1917.

Livery Court Book of the Worshipful Company of Tallow Chandlers. (Tallow Chandlers Hall)

Lloyd's List, March, April, July, August, September 1823. (Lloyd's Library)

Manuscript log of the brig *Benjamin* (John Lidgett, master), 1830–32 Cronstadt, Petersburg, London, LOG/M29 MS 806. (Manuscript Library, National Maritime Museum, Greenwich)

Pigot's Directory, 1823/4.

Post Master General's Minutes, Vol. 31 from January 2, 1821, to June 28, 1824, No 849 N. Post Office Records, St Martins-le-Grand. (*re* Ship Letter Bags and the Ship Letter Office)

Robson's London Directory, 1838.

Sharp Correspondence, 1830. (Baltic Exchange Archives)

Tables of the Revenue, Population, Commerce &C of the United Kingdom, Part III from 1820 to 1833; and Part IV 1834. (HMSO, 1835)

The Public Ledger ('Open to all, influenced by none'), May 1 and 4, 1823.

The Times, May 2, 1823.

CHAPTER 4. (1838–1858)

CLAPHAM, SIR JOHN. *Economic History of Britain: Britain and the Nations 1848–53.* (Cambridge: University Press)

FAIRLIE, SUSAN. 'Shipping in the Anglo-Russian Grain Trade, to 1870: Part One', *Maritime History,* Vol. 1, No 2. (Newton Abbot: David & Charles, September 1971)

GOSS, C. W. F. 'The Parish and Church of St Martin Outwich', *London and Middlesex Archaeological Society Transactions,* New Series 6. (London, 1927–31)

HARBEN, HENRY A. *A Dictionary of London.* (London: H. Jenkins, 1916)

LAMB, CHARLES. *Essays of Elia.* (*London Magazine,* 1820)

LATHAM, BRYAN. *Timber: a historical survey.* (London: Harrap, 1957)

NOORTHOUCK, JOHN. *History of London.* (1773)

SEALER, J. R. *History of Literary Associations of the South Sea House.* (1925)

STOREY, G. *Reuter's Century.*

WATSON, JAMES. *The Historic Interest of the Neighbourhood of the Corn Exchange and the Baltic.*

WELCH, C. *London at the beginning of the 20th Century.* (London)

WELCH, C. *The Royal Exchange.* (London, 1913)

Baltic Company File, BT 31/259 856. (Public Record Office)

Committee of the Baltic Minute Book 1857–72. (Baltic Exchange Archives)

Incoming Correspondence, internal memoranda etc, of the Baltic Committee at South Sea House, 1857–1901. (Baltic Exchange Archives)

Lane Hankey Papers. W. Stuart Lane's Notebook, 1856. MS 11462, MS 11463 1–8. (Guildhall MS Library, London)

Miscellaneous Papers 1823–57; including documents belonging to the Jerusalem Coffee-House. (Baltic Exchange Archives)

The Baltic Coffee-House 1837–57, Book of Candidates. (Baltic Exchange Archives)

The Baltic Coffee-House 1857–63, Book of Candidates (containing by-laws). (Baltic Exchange Archives)

w. w. 'London Gossip', *John O'London's Weekly.* (London; November 27, 1920)

CHAPTER 5.   (1858–1873)

ANGIER, SIR THEO. Manuscript notes for J. A. Findlay. (Baltic Exchange Archives)

DOWLER, JOHN F. *100 Not Out; 1820–1920.* Centennial History of C. W. Kellock & Co Ltd. (London: C. W. Kellock, 1920)

HOOPER, W. A. C. *A Brief Record of the founding and progress of the Incorporated Oil Seed Association.* Issued to mark the completion of 100 years' service of the oilseed trade. (London: IOSA, 1963)

HURD, ARCHIBALD. *The Triumph of the Tramp Ship.* (London)

MEYER, HUGO RICHARD. *The British State Telegraphs.* (London: Macmillan, 1907)

History of Glover Brothers 1853–1953. (London: Glover Brothers, 1953)

CHAPTER 6. (1873–1889)

BALDWIN, F. G. C. *The History of the Telephone in the UK.* (London: Chapman & Hall, 1938)
Committee of the Baltic Minute Books 1873–1901. (Baltic Exchange Archives)
London Corn Trade Association Executive Committee Minutes from 1885. (Grain and Feed Trade Association Archives)
'The Baltic and the London Corn Trade Association', *The Miller*, December 21, 1836.

CHAPTER 7. (1889–1896)

'BALTICO'. *Life On 'The Baltic' and Shipping Idylls for Shipping Idlers.* (London: Ward Lock, 1903)
DOLMAN, FREDERICK. 'Where Merchants Do Most Congregate', *The Ludgate Illustrated Magazine*, 1895.
'The Baltic', *Chambers Journal*, July 11, 1896.

CHAPTER 8. (1896–1902)

MALCOLM, CHARLES. *The History of the British Linen Bank.* (London: Constable, 1950)

CHAPTER 9. (1902–1918)

MYHRE, J. F. *About Chartering and Shipbroking Business.* (Maritime Technical Association, Copenhagen, 1917)
Baltic Mercantile and Shipping Exchange Ltd Board Minutes, Vols 1–8. (September 1943)
London Cattle Food Trade Association Minute Book August 28, 1906, to October 11, 1912. (Grain and Feed Trade Association Archives)
The History of NACAM. (London: The British Association of Grain, Seed, Feed and Agricultural Merchants Ltd, 1967)

CHAPTER 10. (1918–1934)

DODD, TOM. *The Chartering Clerk Between The Wars.* Typescript Notes. (Baltic Exchange Archives)
HOOKER, A. A. *The International Grain Trade.* (London: Pitman, 1936)

HOOKER, A. A. *The London 'Home Grown' Grain Futures Markets.* (London: A. A. Hooker, 1968)

INSTONE, ALFRED. *Early Birds: Air Transport Memories 1919–1924.* (Plymouth: Western Mail & Echo, 1938)

REYNOLDS, E. E., and BRASHER, N. H. *Britain in the Twentieth Century, 1900–1964.* (Cambridge: University Press, 1966)

'The Grain Market of the World; the Baltic Exchange'. (London: The Brewery Record, 1922)

'The World's Chartering Center'. (The Nautical Gazette, May 28, 1921)

CHAPTER 11. (1934–1946)

BEHRENS, C. B. A. *History of the Second World War: Merchant Shipping and the Demands of War.* (London: HMSO, 1955)

HOOKER, A. A. *The International Grain Trade.* (London: Pitman, 1939)

HOOKER, A. A. 'London Grain Futures Markets', Parts 1 and 2, *The Baltic Magazine.* (London: The Baltic Exchange, 1961)

JANES, HURFORD. *The Master Millers, The Story of the House of Rank 1875–1955.* (London: Harley Publishing Company, 1955)

TRINDER, SIR CHARLES. *The Baltic Exchange.* Typescript of address. (Corporation of London Records)

Co-ordinating Committee, Food Defence Plans September 21, 1939, the Baltic Exchange, minutes. (Baltic Exchange Archives)

Guide to Documents in the Public Record Office. (HMSO, 1972)

International Agreement on Principles having reference to the Continuance of Co-ordinated Control of Merchant Shipping. Cmd 6556, 5 August 1944.

Memorandum on *Shipping Problems* by Sir Cyril Hurcomb, Director-General of the Ministry of Shipping, March 4, 1940. File CAB 97, Shipping Problems Sept 14/4. Meetings 1 to 5, Papers 1 to 10. (Public Record Office)

Mercantile Marine Dept, Board of Trade; Shipping Defence Advisory Committee papers T.02828, File M.5937/1939. *Consideration of Crown's prerogative to take control of the Mercantile Marine in an emergency.* (Public Record Office)

Prime Minister's Office Papers, PREMIER 1/429, 1940 Trade. (Public Record Office)

War Cabinet Memoranda WP(40)21–WP(40)70. Vol. V, page 231: *The extent to which Shipping considerations call for a review of our import programme.* Report by the Lord Privy Seal, February 23, 1941. (Public Record Office)

APPENDIX A

Chairmen of the Baltic Mercantile and Shipping Exchange

1900–1976

1900–1913	W. Bridges Webb
1913–1916	H. W. Barnett
1916–1919	F. N. Garrard
1919–1922	C. W. Howard
1922–1924	Newton Dunn
1924–1928	Sir Ernest W. Glover, Bt
1928–1931	John E. Parry
1931–1933	Sir F. Vernon Thomson, K.B.E.
1933–1935	Sir Herbert T. Robson, K.B.E.
1935–1937	Sir John Niven
1937–1939	Frank E. Fehr, C.B.E.
1939–1946	Sir Frank S. Alexander, Bt
1946–1948	Sir W. Norman Vernon, Bt
1948–1951	Sir Henry C. Brewer, M.B.E.
1951–1953	B. H. Perl, M.C.
1953–1955	Sir J. Gibson Graham, M.C.
1955–1957	R. Tadman
1957–1959	R. D. Hyde
1959–1961	F. P. Whithouse
1961–1963	Cyril W. Warwick
1963–1965	Sir Leslie W. Phillips, C.B.E.
1965–1967	The Lord Kilmarnock, M.B.E.
1967–1969	W. Amedée Fairclough
1969–1971	Brian F. Turner
1971–1973	A. H. D. Granger
1973–1975	M. T. Turnbull
1975–	B. H. F. Fehr

APPENDIX B

Secretaries of the Baltic Committee

1823–1903

William Wilson Junr	Hon. Secretary	1823–1828(?)
Benjamin Lancaster	Hon. Secretary	1828(?)–1856
George Goss	Hon. Secretary	1856–1858
William Oxley	Secretary	1858–1889
Frederick Curtis	Secretary	1889–1899
Charles Oxley	Secretary	1899–1903

Secretaries of the Baltic Mercantile and Shipping Exchange

1900–1976

James Arbuckle Findlay	1900–1932
Gilbert Findlay	1932–1954
J. E. Walker	1954–1968
D. J. Walker	1968–

APPENDIX C

Significant events leading to the formation of the Baltic Committee in 1823

1381 Richard II enacts that English merchants must only import and export in vessels of King's allegiance.

1404–8 Henry IV grants royal letters of privilege to the Baltic Adventurers.

1473 Baltic Adventurers collapse.

1488 Henry VII's Navigation Act.

1537 City of London rejects Sir Richard Gresham's proposal for a Bourse.

1542 Henry VIII's anti-speculation laws for corn dealers.

1545 Henry VIII establishes Navy Board for civil administration of navy.

1553 English merchants open up Russian White Sea trade. Muscovy Company starts to operate.

1555 Mary I gives charter to Muscovy Company (first English joint stock company for trade).

1558 Elizabeth I temporarily abolishes laws of 1381 and 1488 restricting merchants to English ships.
      Merchants outside Muscovy Company trade with Russians at Narva on Baltic Sea.
      Act for Maintenance of the Navy reimposes shipping restrictions of Act of 1488.

1561 RICHARD CLOUGH, AGENT OF SIR THOMAS GRESHAM, SUGGESTS BOURSE FOR LONDON.

1563 Sir Thomas Gresham submits plan for Bourse to City aldermen.

1566 June 7: Elizabeth I lays foundation stone of Bourse.

1571 ELIZABETH I OPENS BOURSE AND NAMES IT 'THE ROYAL EXCHANGE'.
      End of the Stillyard, headquarters of the Easterlings, the representatives of the Hanseatic League.

O

1585   Sack of Antwerp; gold and credit of Netherlands bankers comes to England; London becomes financial centre.

1586   Muscovy Company reconstructed as Russia Company.

1587   Climax of English penetration of the Baltic Sea.
        Dutch take over from Hanseatics as main competitors.

1588   Elizabeth I enacts no English goods to be laden in foreign ships.

1600   December 31: Elizabeth I gives charter to EAST INDIA COMPANY.

1603   VIRGINIA WINE HOUSE OPENS IN THREAD-NEEDLE STREET.

1605   Merchants attack privileges of Russia Company.

1615   Following complaints of high freights of English ships in Baltic trade, Privy Council brings merchants and shipowners together.

1625   The Jerusalem Tavern opens (?).

1650   Council of Trade established.

1651   CROMWELL'S COMMONWEALTH NAVIGATION ORDINANCE – 'the Maritime Charter of England'.

1652   Anglo-Dutch War renewed; Baltic Sea cut off; masts from America.
        LONDON'S FIRST COFFEE-HOUSE OPENS.

1660   Monarchy restored.
        CHARLES II CONFIRMS NAVIGATION ACT (in force for next 189 years).
        Navy Board reconstituted.

1666   ROYAL EXCHANGE and JERUSALEM COFFEE HOUSE DESTROYED IN GREAT FIRE OF LONDON.
        Royal Exchange transfers activities to Gresham House.

1668   Charles II forms Board of Trade.

1669   REBUILT ROYAL EXCHANGE (No 2) OPENED.

1673   Act for Regulation of Brokers.

1674   Charles II's short-lived proclamation against coffee-houses.

1688   Lloyd's Coffee-House opens in Tower Street.

1691   Lloyd's Coffee-House moves to Lombard Street.

1694   William Patterson, Gilbert Heathcote and others found the BANK OF ENGLAND.

1696   William III establishes permanent BOARD OF TRADE.

1697	Second Brokers Act.
	Stockbrokers withdraw from Royal Exchange, accused of loitering and gambling; move to Jonathan's Coffee-House in Exchange Alley.
1698	Russia Company's monopoly ends; trade with Russia thrown open.
	Old East India Company dissolved and re-formed.
1704	Queen Anne's Naval Stores Act requiring American colonies to supply naval stores; Government subsidize pitch and tar.
1707	Merchants petition against Brokers Act of 1697.
1708	United East India Company formed.
1711	Robert Harley, Earl of Oxford, forms South Sea Company.
1720	South Sea Bubble.
1744	VIRGINIA AND MARYLAND COFFEE-HOUSE RENAMED 'VIRGINIA AND BALTIC'.
1746	Corn Exchange of London ('Old Corn Exchange') formed.
1748	Fire starting in Exchange Alley destroys the Jerusalem, Garraway's, Jonathan's.
1769	James Watt patents first steam engine.
1772	United East India Company in financial difficulties ask for government loan.
1773	Society of East India Commanders formed.
	Parliamentary inquiry into East India Company.
	STOCK EXCHANGE founded; jobbers move from Jonathan's to Sweetings Alley.
1775	October: East India Company Commanders Society at Antwerp Tavern.
1776	American Declaration of Independence.
	Adam Smith's *Wealth of Nations* propounds doctrine of *laissez-faire*.
1780	East India Company Commanders Society move to the Jerusalem.
1784	East India Company put under Board of Control.
	Britain ceases to be a grain-exporting country.
1796	Harris & Dixon founded.
	New charter for United East India Company.
1798	Robert Fulton's steamboat.
1799	July: The Jerusalem's Register of Shipping starts.
1800	British Government reject Henry Bell's plans for steamboat.
1802	Stock Exchange move to Bartholomew Lane.

1804   Building of East India Docks.

1805   Opening of London Docks.

1806   Russia breaks with England; Napoleon's Berlin Decrees.

1807   Suspension of all shipping to continent.
Robert Fulton builds 160-ton *Clermont* steam paddle boat.
Commercial Dock Company founded.

1810   Baltic Dock Company formed.
Virginia and Baltic Coffee-House moves to Antwerp Tavern (?).

1811   Henry Bell builds *Comet*, Europe's first steam boat.
East Country Dock built for Baltic trade.

1813   Earliest record of London Average Market Letter Committee (tallow).
Harris & Dixon charter-party for tallow.

1820   John Hubbard & Co, Russia merchants, founded.

1821   Greeks rise against Turks; massacre at Chios; 20000 Greeks flee to London.
Steam engine put in iron ship for first time – *Aaron Manby*.

1822   Navigation Act modified to allow imports from Netherlands, Germany, Turkey and Russia; tallow and tobacco added to 'enumerated articles'.

1823   COMMITTEE OF BALTIC COFFEE-HOUSE FORMED AT 58 THREADNEEDLE STREET.

Significant events
from the
formation of the Baltic Committee on April 22, 1823
to
its last meeting on July 9, 1903

1823–30   Treaties of Reciprocity; first weakening of Protection.
Tallow from South America and Australia breaks speculation.

1837   Death of William IV; succession of Queen Victoria.
Baltic Committee make first revision of rules.

1838   Fire destroys second Royal Exchange.

1842   Prince Consort lays foundation stone of third Royal Exchange.

Edward Moxhay opens Hall of Commerce at 52 Thread-needle Street.

1845 Queen Victoria opens third Royal Exchange.

1846 Corn Laws repealed.

1847 J. L. Ricardo calls for Select Committee on Navigation Act.

1849 Navigation Act repealed.

1851 Julius Reuter sets up in London.

1854 War breaks out in the Crimea.

Plates of *Great Eastern* laid at Millwall.

Second revision of Baltic rules.

1856 End of Crimean War.

1857 May: BALTIC SUBSCRIBERS BUY LEASE OF SOUTH SEA HOUSE.

'THE BALTIC COMPANY LIMITED' FORMED BY THEM TO FINANCE PROJECT.

October 22: THE BALTIC COFFEE-HOUSE MOVES TO 58 THREADNEEDLE STREET (SOUTH SEA HOUSE).

November: New rules, new committee of thirty.

1858 Baltic Company buys freehold of South Sea House.

Death of Thomas Tooke.

1863 Linseed Association formed.

1866 Baltic Committee becomes tenants of Baltic Company at South Sea House.

Baltic Committee reorganized.

1869 Suez Canal opened.

1870 Post Office take over telegraph system from private companies.

1873 New rules for Baltic.

1878 London Corn Trade Association formed.

1881 Linseed Association becomes Incorporated Oil Seed Association.

1886 London Corn Trade Association incorporated.

1889 Death of William Oxley, secretary of Baltic Committee and company.

Frederick Curtis appointed secretary of committee and company.

The Garrard Plan for reform of the Baltic.

'The Jerusalem' reorganized; seeks new members.

1891   Shipping Exchange mooted.

1892   February: London Shipping Exchange registered.

     March: London Shipping Exchange opens at 19 Billiter Street.

     April: Jerusalem Shipping Exchange opens at 22 Billiter Street.

     September: London Shipping Exchange acquires Jerusalem.

     Two exchanges combine at 19, 20, 21 Billiter Street.

     James Arbuckle Findlay appointed secretary of the London Shipping Exchange.

1893   January: London Shipping Exchange formally opened by Lord Mayor of London.

1894   Drop in Baltic membership.

1897   Futures market in grain opens on floor of the Baltic.

1898   Invitation to Baltic Committee from London Shipping Exchange to join forces and build new exchange on Jeffrey's Square rejected.

1899   January 3: At meeting called to approve plan to move Baltic to Wesleyan Centenary Hall, members give Baltic Committee powers to act as they see fit.

     January 7: Septimus Glover, chairman of Baltic Committee, invites Baltic Company to bridge their difficulties.

     January 12: Frederick Curtis resigns.

     January 14: Offer of Christ's Hospital rejected.

     January 17: Baltic Committee reject Baltic Company's offer to renew lease of South Sea House.

     January 19: Proposal to move Baltic to Fenchurch Street.

     February 2: Ernest Forwood given firm offer of Jeffrey's Square site for fourteen days; invited Baltic Committee to rent proposed building on site; offer is refused pending completion of negotiations with James Dixon over Fenchurch Street site.

     February 16: Ernest Forwood and others acquire Jeffrey's Square site.

     February 28: Majority of Baltic members vote to move Baltic to Fenchurch Street.

     March 16: At second ballot majority of Baltic members vote to remain at South Sea House in belief that Baltic Company intended to rebuild.

March 18: Baltic Company announce they have no powers to rebuild.

March 26: Baltic Committee renew lease of South Sea House for one year only (to September 30, 1900).

June 6: Ernest Forwood and others form City of London Exchange Syndicate to acquire Jeffrey's Square site in St Mary Axe.

August 10: Baltic Company sell South Sea House to British Linen Bank.

September 14: Voluntary winding up of Baltic Company.

October: Boer War.

October 19: At AGM of Baltic members pass resolution approving removal to Jeffrey's Square.

November 30: London Shipping Exchange reject Exchange Syndicate's proposals for amalgamation.

December 21: Sub-committee of Baltic Committee authorized to draft agreement with Exchange Syndicate over Jeffrey's Square.

1900 January 14: Baltic Committee decide to call new exchange the Baltic Mercantile & Shipping Exchange.

January 16: Baltic Committee/Exchange Syndicate covenant.

Exchange Syndicate agree to form Baltic Exchange.

January 17: The Baltic Mercantile and Shipping Exchange Ltd incorporated; first meeting of directors.

February 2: Full board meet for first time.

February 13: Exchange Syndicate agree to buy London Shipping Exchange.

March 1: London Shipping Exchange becomes part of Baltic Exchange.

March 2: Exchange Syndicate hand over assets and goodwill of the Baltic and the London Shipping Exchange to the Baltic Mercantile and Shipping Exchange Ltd.

March 5: The Baltic Exchange issue prospectus: new building to be ready by January 15, 1902.

April 4: Purchase of Jeffrey's Square by Exchange Syndicate for £87693 completed.

The Baltic Exchange set up committee to manage the London Shipping Exchange in Billiter Street.

April 24: The Jerusalem Limited wound up voluntarily.

May: Exchange Syndicate go into voluntary liquidation.

June 12: First (statutory) General Meeting of B M & S E.

June 18: Baltic Committee arrange to move temporarily to new Great Eastern Hotel annexe on October 1.

September 30: LAST DAY AT SOUTH SEA HOUSE.

October 1: The Baltic opens at Great Eastern Hotel, Liverpool Street Station (Abercorn Rooms).

Auction of furniture and fittings at South Sea House.

October 3: Deeds of South Sea House handed over to British Linen Company by Baltic Company.

October 22: Voluntary liquidation of Baltic Company: shareholders paid £730 per £100 stock.

1901   January: Death of Queen Victoria; succession of Edward VII.

June 25: Foundation stone laid of new building in St Mary Axe.

1902   January 15: Promised opening date of new exchange not kept.

May 14: At AGM of BM & SE, no new opening date announced.

October 16: Last AGM of members of the 'old' Baltic.

1903   April 21: OPENING OF BALTIC MERCANTILE AND SHIPPING EXCHANGE AT ST MARY AXE.

July 9: LAST MEETING OF THE BALTIC COMMITTEE.

July 16: Assets of the Baltic Committee become property of the B M & S E.

Significant events
from the
opening of the Baltic Exchange
at St Mary Axe on April 21, 1903
to 1946

1905   Baltic and White Sea Conference.

1906   August: London Cattle Food Trade Association formed.

1907 Baltic Amateur Dramatic & Orchestral Society formed (later the Baltic Amateur Dramatic & Operatic Society).

1910 London Oil & Tallow Trades Association formed.

1911 Formation of committee which led to Institute of Shipbrokers.

1912 B M & S E Benevolent Society formed.

1913 Institute of Shipbrokers formed.
Death of William Bridges Webb; Henry Barnett becomes chairman.

1914–18 World War I.

1920 Institute of Chartered Shipbrokers incorporated.

1922 Membership of the Baltic 2771.

1925 Chartered Shipbrokers Protection & Indemnity Association formed.

1927 J. A. Findlay publishes his *Short History of The Baltic.*

1929 First air charter party.
Grain futures market at St Mary Axe (LCTA).

1930 Gilbert Findlay appointed assistant secretary.
World Economic Crisis.

1932 The Baltic Exchange Clerks Pension Fund opened.
James Findlay retires; Gilbert Findlay succeeds as secretary.

1933 La Plata Maize Futures Market opened (LCTA).

1935 Death of James Findlay.
British Shipping (Assistance) Act.
Tramp Shipping Administrative Committee formed.
London Grain Trade Clerks Association formed.

1936 Food (Defence Plans) Department of Board of Trade set up.
Membership of the Baltic 1893.

1937 Chartered Shipbrokers Protection Association incorporated.

1938 Meeting to discuss opening air freight market on Baltic.

1939 September 3: Outbreak of World War II.
Ministry of Food established; together with Cereals Control Board for importing grain.
Government invites aid of Baltic in setting up Ship Chartering Committees.
Ministry of Shipping established.

1940 January 4: Government abandon chartering committee scheme and decide to requisition shipping.
Ministry of Shipping set up City Central Chartering Office.

1941   May: Ministry of Shipping and Ministry of Transport merged as Ministry of War Transport.

1945   End of World War II.
          United Maritime Authority maintain co-ordinated control of merchant shipping of the Allies.
          Chartering pools formed.
          Baltic Exchange Chartering Committee formed.
          Membership of the Baltic 1287.

1946   Sir Norman Vernon takes over as chairman of the Baltic from Sir Frank Alexander.

1948   Baltic's Air Freight Advisory Committee formed.

1949   Airbrokers Association formed.

1952   First stage in government de-control of grain trade.

1953   HRH The Duke of Edinburgh becomes Honorary Member of Baltic.

1954   Futures Market resumed on Baltic – imported coarse grains.
          Gilbert Findlay retires; Jack Walker succeeds as Secretary.

1955   Sir Winston Churchill lays foundation stone of annexe.

1956   Annexe opened by Queen Elizabeth II.

1959   New coat of arms for Baltic Exchange.

1964   Futures Market in home-grown barley opened at Baltic.

1965   Futures Market extended to home grown wheat.

1968   Jack Walker retires as Secretary; is succeeded by Derek Walker.

1971   Grain & Feed Trade Association (GAFTA) formed.
          Federation of Oils, Seeds & Fats Association (FOSFA) formed.

1973   150th ANNIVERSARY OF THE FORMATION OF THE BALTIC COMMITTEE and the opening of a Subscription Room on May 1.

1974   Women admitted as members.

1976   Membership of the Baltic 2500 (730 companies).

APPENDIX D

1-2 TARRAGONA–MALAGA RANGE/ALEXANDRIA
Bagged Wheat Flour (stow abt 54/55′)
Any size 6000/10000 (try larger but max draft 29′)
15/30 May, $4.90 1/1 FIOS, 200 HD max 800/200 HD max
1000, Synacomex C/P 6¼%.

The interpretation of the above is:

A charterer requires a ship to load a cargo of Wheat Flour in bags (which according to his experience or information given to him by the shippers can be expected to stow at about 54/55 cu. ft per ton of cargo when loaded in the ship's hold), to be loaded at one or two ports in southern Spain, between the ports of Tarragona and Malaga beginning during the dates 15/30 May – known as laydays and cancelling dates respectively.

The quantity available for shipment is between 6000 tons and 10000 tons but provided the draft of the ship, when loaded, does not exceed 29 ft (salt water) it may be possible to increase the cargo over 10 000 tons.

The contract terms for loading the cargo are 200 tons per hatch, per day but with a maximum daily rate of loading not exceeding 800 tons, which means if the ship has five hatches, she cannot accept more than 800 tons' daily load, whilst for discharging the rate is 200 tons per hatch per day, consequently the discharge rate for the same ship could be 1000 tons. The document covering the contract of affreightment is a charter-party, the form to be used in this instance is known by the code name of SYNACOMEX. The charterers' ideas of the rate they expect to pay for this business is U.S. $4.90 per ton basis 1 port load and to 1 port of discharge and address commissions and brokerages amount to a total of 6¼ per cent of the freight.

An owner's broker coming into possession of the circular quotation will have derived the above information from the quotation and from this will check whether his vessel is in a suitable position to present within the required dates and if there is some doubt, he will check whether the dates he needs for the ship are acceptable to the charterers and then after making the necessary calculations the owner will, if interested, make a firm offer.

The calculations include the daily cost of operating the ship plus fuel costs and port expenses over the time required to load and discharge (at the rates mentioned above) plus the passage time, allowing for calls at other ports for fuel and weather delays etc. Also he must check what quantity of cargo he can stow into the available cubic capacity of the vessel. If the vessel has 500000 cu. ft bale capacity he can only expect to load between 9259 tons at 54 cu. ft and 9090 tons at 55 cu. ft, thus even if he has a dead-weight cargo capacity of 10000 tons, to load that quantity the cargo must not exceed 50 cu. ft per ton. On the other hand, a vessel with a capacity of 600000 cu. ft bale could load 10909 tons of cargo, but when bunkers and stores are added, he would have to ensure he could agree the maximum draft of 29 ft.

TIMECHARTER

Require Vessel: About 500/600000 bale
Good gear inc H/L 25T or more
Able 7500 tons on 24 ft
Trip delivery Norrkoping 16/23 August
Redelivery Tema-Douala Range
Duration about 55 days
Adapted Produce 2.5% total

Here a liner company require a ship to load on their regular berth which has a schedule from Norrkoping (in Sweden) to Tema-Douala Range in West Africa. The cargo in this instance will probably be general liner cargo which can be built up to a total between 500/600000 cu. ft bale and of the intended cargo, some 7500 tons is to be loaded or discharged at a port where there is a draft restriction of 24 ft, consequently the shipowners will be required to give guarantees that the ship can lift this prescribed quantity on that draft after allowing for any fuel and stores that will be required for the voyage. As some of the ports to be called at will not have cargo handling facilities, the ship will need to have derricks or cranes in good working order including at least one heavy lift capable of 25 tons or more. Being liner business the ship will be taken on a time-charter basis, which means the owners will receive a daily hire payment (paid either monthly or half monthly in advance) from the time the ship is 'delivered' to the time of 'redelivery' to owners. The schedule of this voyage is estimated at a duration of fifty-five days and the charter-party form is known by the code name of New York Produce Form and there is a commission of $2\frac{1}{2}$ per cent deductable from the payments. Under a time charter the port charges and fuel costs are paid by the charterer for the duration of the charter.

Index

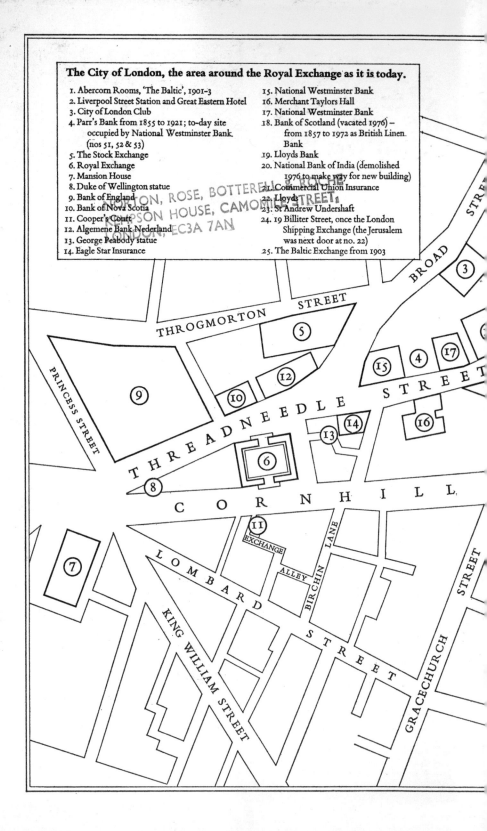

The City of London, the area around the Royal Exchange as it is today.

1. Abercorn Rooms, 'The Baltic', 1901–3
2. Liverpool Street Station and Great Eastern Hotel
3. City of London Club
4. Parr's Bank from 1855 to 1921; to-day site occupied by National Westminster Bank (nos 51, 52 & 53)
5. The Stock Exchange
6. Royal Exchange
7. Mansion House
8. Duke of Wellington statue
9. Bank of England
10. Bank of Nova Scotia
11. Cooper's Coutt
12. Algemene Bank Nederland
13. George Peabody statue
14. Eagle Star Insurance
15. National Westminster Bank
16. Merchant Taylors Hall
17. National Westminster Bank
18. Bank of Scotland (vacated 1976) – from 1857 to 1972 as British Linen Bank
19. Lloyds Bank
20. National Bank of India (demolished 1976 to make way for new building)
21. Commercial Union Insurance
22. Lloyds
23. St Andrew Undershaft
24. 19 Billiter Street, once the London Shipping Exchange (the Jerusalem was next door at no. 22)
25. The Baltic Exchange from 1903